ASSESSMENT OF BEHAVIORAL, SOCIAL, & EMOTIONAL PROBLEMS

ASSESSMENT OF BEHAVIORAL, SOCIAL, & EMOTIONAL PROBLEMS

DIRECT & OBJECTIVE METHODS FOR USE WITH CHILDREN AND ADOLESCENTS

Kenneth W. Merrell
Utah State University

Longman
New York & London

**Assessment of Behavioral, Social, and
Emotional Problems: Direct and Objective
Methods for Use with Children and
Adolescents**

Longman, 10 Bank Street, White Plains, N.Y. 10606

Associated companies:
Longman Group Ltd., London
Longman Cheshire Pty., Melbourne
Longman Paul Pty., Auckland
Copp Clark Pitman, Toronto

Acquisitions editor: Stuart Miller
Development editor: Virginia L. Blanford
Production editor: Linda S. Moser
Cover design: Inter Digital Design
Production supervisor: Richard Bretan

Library of Congress Cataloging-in-Publication Data
Merrell, Kenneth W.
    Assessment of behavioral, emotional, and social problems : direct
and objective methods for use with children and adolescents /
Kenneth W. Merrell.
        p.   cm.
    Includes bibliographical references and index.
    ISBN 0-8013-1107-1
    1. Behavorial assessment of children.   2. Behavioral assessment of
teenagers.   3. Psychodiagnostics.   4. Problem children—
    Psychological testing.   5. Problem youth—Psychological testing.
I. Title.
RJ503.5.M47   1993
618.92 ' 89075—dc20   93-19109
                                                                  CIP

1 2 3 4 5 6 7 8 9 10-MA-9796959493

Dedicated to my parents,
Robert Winston Merrell and Janett Rasband Merrell,
for their love, support, and encouragement

Contents

Preface

Behavioral, social, and emotional problems that are experienced and exhibited by children and adolescents can consist of a wide range of difficulties. These problems may be as diverse as anxiety, acting-out aggressive behavior, difficulties establishing or maintaining friendships, and severe depression coupled with social withdrawal. Professionals from a variety of education and human service disciplines who work with children and adolescents often find that evaluating these types of problems in their clients is central to their work. Some of the professional groups that may have particular or occasional interest in this type of assessment include psychologists, counselors, teachers, social workers, nurses, pediatricians, and psychiatrists.

Some types of assessment are specifically the "territory" of particular professional disciplines. For example, due to the intensive advanced training required for both administration and interpretation, psychologists have historically claimed the use of individually administered intelligence tests, while the use of certain sophisticated hearing tests is considered the realm of audiologists. This book has been carefully designed so that the types of assessment covered are generally methods that can be used by professionals across different disciplines. Although a few assessment instruments or specific techniques included (such as the MMPI tests) might be legitimately considered the realm of psychologists and although this book has been written from the standpoint of a psychologist (i.e., paying close attention to psychological theory and the psychometric adequacy of assessment methods), the majority of specific techniques within the five assessment domains (direct behavioral observation, behavior rating scales, interviewing techniques, sociometric methods, self-report tests) may be used by professionals from a variety of education and human service fields. Thus this book can be used by individuals from a variety of professional disciplines who are either studying behavioral/emotional assessment at the upper division or graduate preservice training level or who are currently working in their respective disciplines and need an up-to-date professional handbook on child and adolescent assessment.

As the subtitle of this book indicates, a unique feature is the focus on *direct* and *objective* methods of assessment. The distinction between direct and objective assessment methods and other types of assessment (presumably indirect and subjective methods) and the rationale for such a focus is discussed in detail in the first chapter. For purposes of this preface, it is sufficient to say that the direct and objective approach is emphasized due to the advantages it offers in terms of practical utility and technical adequacy. It is important to stress that other methods of assessing behavioral, social, and emotional problems (e.g., projective techniques and children's drawing tests) have their place and that in the right circumstances provide a valuable means of communication with or information about a given client. However, this book was not written to be all things to all professionals; rather it provides a clear focus on empirically sound assessment methods, useful in various types of decision making.

This book is essentially divided into three sections: Chapters 1 and 2 provide a foundation for the concept of direct and objective assessment of child and adolescent behavioral, social, and emotional problems, covering legal and ethical issues, social learning theory, assessment design, and classification or taxonomy issues within assessment. Chapters 3–7 provide separate detailed overviews of each of the five areas of direct and objective assessment: behavioral observation, behavior rating scales, interviewing techniques, sociometric approaches, and objective self-report tests. The final four chapters, 8–11, deal with application issues. Each of these four chapters details specific types of problems or areas to be assessed (externalizing problems, internalizing problems, social skills and peer relations, and severe behavioral, social, and emotional problems), showing how each of the five direct and objective assessment methods may be utilized within that particular realm.

Each of the two foundation chapters (1 and 2) and the five methods chapters (3–7) include a set of application problems at the end of the chapter. These application problems are designed to help readers integrate and solidify their understanding of particular concepts related to assessment of behavioral, social, and emotional problems. Chapters 8–11 each contain a case study relevant to the central topic of the chapter. The inclusion of application problems in chapters 1–7 and case studies in chapters 8–11 is warranted by the different types of material covered and the need to stress different types of operations. The case studies are based on actual data sets and "live" cases accrued from my own clinical work and from cases on which I have worked as a clinical supervisor of graduate students in professional psychology. All personally identifying details and other related characteristics of these cases have been modified in order to ensure absolute privacy and confidentiality for the clients and their families and to make the cases specifically relevant to the chapter in which they appear. These case studies are open-ended in that they provide a basic scenario and raw assessment data, and then the reader is asked to respond to various questions or tasks relating to the case. These cases are not designed to bring closure to the situation but to illustrate various issues and problems of assessment and then to assist the reader in integrating theory and practice.

Although I am the single author of this book, writing it has by no means been a "solo" effort. A number of persons have conducted varied and important work, resulting in a final product of which I am proud. I am grateful to the individuals who served as external reviewers at various stages of manuscript development:

Norman Abeles, Michigan State University

Douglas Cullinan, North Carolina State University

Susan Epps, University of Nebraska

William Evans, University of West Florida

Cathy Hall, East Carolina University

Randy Kamphaus, University of Georgia

Thomas Prout, Florida State University

Rick Short, American Psychological Association

Catherine Stanger, University of Vermont

Kevin Stark, University of Texas

Stephanie Stein, Central Washington University

Gary Stoner, University of Oregon

Their combined effort and professional insight resulted in significant improvements to every chapter, and they helped me to put together the final manuscript in a more cohesive and useful manner. Finally, I appreciate the efforts of the staff at Longman in carefully guiding this project: specifically, Ken Clinton, Stuart Miller, Virginia Blanford, Chris Konnari, Linda Moser, and Hillary Henderson. They all worked closely with me or provided other valuable assistance during the preparation of this book, making the result a product of their effort as well as mine.

In sum, this book alternately synthesizes and builds upon existing knowledge, while offering a focused and unique perspective. It is my hope that it will be both a step forward in the development of child and adolescent assessment as an empirically sound venture and a practical guidebook for professionals at both the preservice and inservice levels.

ASSESSMENT OF BEHAVIORAL, SOCIAL, & EMOTIONAL PROBLEMS

CHAPTER **1**

Conceptualizing and Assessing Behavioral, Social, and Emotional Problems

INTRODUCTION

This chapter introduces some important issues in behavioral-emotional assessment, provides a foundation for understanding the design and flow of subsequent chapters, and provides an overview of the current "state of the art"

1

in best assessment practices. The chapter begins with an orientation to the referral process and examines how this process should shape the approach to assessment. A discussion of the most pertinent legal and ethical issues in assessment follows, and specific recommendations for legal and ethical assessment practices are provided. Next, the chapter presents a discussion of how theory guides practice and provides a detailed outline of social cognitive theory, which is emphasized in this book. The last sections of the chapter map out direct and objective assessment and illustrate the preferred way for conducting assessments of behavioral, social, and emotional problems through the use of a multimethod, multisource, multisetting design. The chapter ends with a brief discussion of the criteria used for including specific assessment techniques and instruments in the book. This chapter is an introduction and guide to understanding the overall goals of the entire text.

UNDERSTANDING AND CLARIFYING ASSESSMENT REFERRALS

Any professional with experience in assessing children would agree that referrals for assessment come in many dimensions. Sometimes, the pervasive nature of the problems leading to the referral make the professional wonder why the referral didn't happen earlier. At other times, the character of the referral problems seems so benign that there is a question of whether a referral was needed in the first place. In order to conduct a sound assessment, the reasons for a referral and the circumstances leading up to it must first be carefully analyzed and explored. Practically every child at some time will exhibit behavioral, social, or emotional problems serious enough to cause parents or teachers some concern, but a relatively small percentage of these problems will ever result in a referral for assessment or treatment. What then are the factors that result in behavioral, social, or emotional problems being taken to the point of referral?

It is important to keep in mind that unlike adult mental-health clients, who are typically self-referred, children and adolescents are usually referred for assessment by someone else (such as a parent or teacher) and very often do not even recognize or admit that their perceived problems exist. Knoff (1986) suggests that referrals are often "the result of a perceived discrepancy between the referred child's behaviors, attitudes, or interpersonal interactions . . . and some more optimal level desired and defined by the referral source" (p. 4). The basis of these discrepancies is thought to stem from the different perspectives of the referral source's concept of what constitutes acceptable and unacceptable behavioral and emotional functioning.

Three specific perspectives that influence referral decisions have been postulated by Knoff (1986): the *sociocultural perspective,* the *community subgroup perspective,* and the *setting-specific perspective.* The sociocultural perspective involves the broad environment within a community and the generalized precepts about what constitutes acceptable and unacceptable ways of behaving that are pervasive at most levels within that given community or society. A child or adolescent who is referred because of a discrepancy related to this perspective would likely be exhibiting behaviors that are in opposition to overall societal standards. Community subgroup perspectives are shaped by smaller groups within a community—religious organizations, neighborhoods, and specific cultural or ethnic groups, for example. Referrals related to discrepancies in this perspective would likely involve behaviors or attitudes that are unacceptable within one subgroup but acceptable within another. For example, adolescents who listen to heavy metal or rap music and adopt attitudes based on these forms of music may cause considerable concern within some community subgroups but go almost unnoticed in other subgroups. The setting-specific perspective involves social-behavioral norms that are distinctive to individual settings, such as specific families and classrooms; in other words, what is tolerated as normal by given sets of parents or teachers may be totally unacceptable to others.

The essential point to consider in analyzing referrals from the standpoint of the perspective of the referral source is that the three perspectives are interdependent. One cannot focus singly on a given perspective without taking the others into account. A child who comes from a family background where there is open disrespect for general societal standards (such as obedience to law) may reject typically acceptable standards of behavior in the school or community while still maintaining solidarity with the standards set within his or her own family. On the other hand, a child whose family has recently immigrated from a distant part of the world might adopt values typical of his or her new majority culture, which may create dissension within the family but cause no trouble within the school or larger community. So it becomes the job of the clinician to examine carefully the reasons for referral and how these relate to the three perspectives. In some cases, referrals may need to be refused as improper, and in other cases, the referral will result in a complete assessment to determine the extent of behavioral, social, or emotional problems.

LEGAL AND ETHICAL ISSUES IN ASSESSING CHILDREN AND ADOLESCENTS

Although a truly comprehensive overview of the legal and ethical issues in assessment is beyond the scope of this book (see Bersoff, 1982a; DeMers, 1986, and Jacob & Hartshorne, 1991 for more complete treatments of the topic), it is useful to take a brief look at some of the issues that are particularly relevant for the assessment of behavioral, social, and emotional problems. By definition, legal issues involve aspects of assessment that are affected by either constitutional or statutory constraints. Ethical issues, on the other hand, do not always involve legal constraints but rather what is considered to be "right" professional practice, as dictated by the codes for ethical conduct developed by professional organizations such as the American Psychological Association (APA), National Association of School Psychologists (NASP), and American Counseling Association (ACA). Although it is sometimes possible to separate law from ethics, in reality, the two areas are intertwined. Legal constraints affecting assessment practices have often been developed from the professional practice codes, and these codes of ethics for professionals typically take into account important legal constraints affecting the profession.

The Basis for Legal Constraints on Assessment

According to DeMers (1986), there are two basic ways that testing and assessment practices can be affected by the law. The first means of jurisdiction involves constitutional protections to citizens. In this regard, the *equal protection* and *due process* clauses of the Fourteenth Amendment to the U.S. Constitution are the areas most likely to constrain assessment practices, particularly if the individual conducting the assessment is employed by the "state" (e.g., public school districts, hospitals, and clinics). The equal protection clause forbids the state to treat persons who are similarly situated in an unequal manner, unless there is a justifiable reason. Examples of assessment practices that would violate the equal protection clause would be any that result in members of a given minority group receiving inferior assessment, classification, or treatment services (e.g., the use of an assessment procedure that was systematically biased against a particular group). The due process clause was designed to prevent " . . . the government from denying life, liberty, or property without (*a*) a legitimate reason, and (*b*) providing some meaningful and impartial forum to prevent arbitrary deprivations of those protected interests" (DeMers, 1986, p. 37). Property and liberty interests have been defined quite broadly through a number of Supreme Court decisions—the concept of liberty is now thought to encompass rights to privacy, personal security, and reputation. In the assessment process, a number of activities could potentially infringe on liberty rights, including the actual conducting of the assessment and the writing and maintaining of confidential assessment reports.

The second way that assessment practices can be affected by law involves various statutory provisions that are invoked at the state and federal levels. These types of legal constraints typically do not directly involve constitutional provisions but consist of the passage of specific laws by legislative bodies. These laws are considered to be useful in governing professional practices. At the state level, laws for licensing or certifying psychologists and other service providers usually contain specific regulations pertaining to who can provide services, how privileged information and confidentiality must be handled, and to what extent clients must be informed of the procedures they may become involved in. Another example of state-level law that affects assessment practices is school law, which covers specific procedures and safeguards governing consent for assessment and release of assessment records. At the federal level, assessment practices in school settings are affected by the Individuals with Disabilities Education Act (IDEA)—formally referred to as P.L. 94-142, or the Education for All Handicapped Children Act (also known as the "Hatch" amendment of 1978)—and the Family Educational Rights and Privacy Act (FERPA) of 1974 (also referred to as the Buckley Amendment). Both of these laws contain provisions relating to parental access to student records and release of records to third parties. Additionally the IDEA contains provisions for selection of appropriate assessment instruments and procedures.

Specific Assessment Practices
Affected by Ethics and Law

To be more specific about how behavioral-emotional assessment practices can be affected by legal and ethical constraints, we can identify three distinctive areas that have been addressed. The first area involves *informed consent.* This area is broadly construed to mean that prior to any assessment services being conducted, clients (and/or the clients' parents, in the case of minors) must receive a sufficient explanation of the purpose and nature of the procedures to be done and the risks involved, if any, and that clients must give their express consent to participation. Informed consent regulations are a major feature of the due process stipulations in the Individuals with Disabilities Education Act (IDEA). Within the regulations of IDEA, there are three components: *knowledge* (parents are to be given complete explanation about the purposes and procedures of the assessment), *voluntariness* (consent is willfully granted and not obtained through coercion or misrepresentation), and *competence* (parents must be legally competent to give consent, which is usually assumed by school officials). Even when psychologists or other professionals are engaging in assessment activities outside the scope of the IDEA, there are similar ethical expectations for utilizing informed consent procedures, as indicated by principle 2 and principle 4 of the American Psychological Association's most recent code of ethical principles (APA, 1992), and section 3.5.4 of the National Association of School Psychologists' *Standards for the Provision of School Psychological Services* (NASP, 1984).

The second area that is addressed is the *validity of assessment procedures.* In this area, there is substantial agreement and overlap between the provisions of the IDEA, APA's principle 2, and NASP's standards 3.5 and 4.3. Some of the conditions stated in the public law and in the professional codes include (*a*) tests must be validated for the specific purposes for which they are being used, (*b*) tests must have adequate technical (psychometric) properties, (*c*) obsolete assessment results should not be used, and (*d*) assessment procedures must be administered only by persons with specific and adequate training. Although there have been many criticisms of the technical aspects of many behavioral-emotional assessment instruments, particularly those in the personality and projective technique realms (Bersoff, 1982b; Salvia & Ysseldyke, 1991), there have been few legal complaints stemming from the use of inadequate measures (DeMers, 1986). However, the potential for future litigation in this area appears to be great.

The third area involves the broad domain of the *right to privacy.* In this area, procedures and principles have not only been outlined by the IDEA and by APA and NASP standards but also by the Family Educational Rights and Privacy Act of 1974 (FERPA), the "Hatch" amendment of 1978, and numerous state statutes and court decisions inferred from the Fourteenth Amendment to the U.S. Constitution. Within the general area of right to privacy, the following are some of the key components relating to assessment practices: (*a*) Clients (and the parents of minor clients) are provided access to their records and assessment results, (*b*) assessment results are not released to third parties without the express consent of clients (or parents of minor clients), and (*c*) communications between professionals and clients are regarded as confidential unless clients have voluntarily waived their right to confidentiality or the information obtained in the professional relationship reveals a clear and imminent danger to the client or to other persons (the "duty to warn" principle). If the client is a minor, clinicians must be very careful about the way in which promises of confidentiality are stated. Given the legal status of children and adolescents, confidentiality of communication does not usually exist, in that parents have a right to be informed of whatever information is obtained (DeMers, 1986). There has been a long-standing concern among psychologists that using personality assessment instruments, and presumably other behavioral-emotional measures, may result in unjustifiable encroachment of privacy rights (Jacob & Hartshorne, 1991; Messick, 1965). Adhering to the three areas outlined in this section will reduce the likelihood of invading privacy rights within the context of behavioral-emotional assessment.

Some Concluding Comments on Legal and Ethical Issues

The type of assessment instruments that have most often been the targets of legal action are intellectual ability tests rather than behavioral-emotional tests (Bersoff, 1982b). There is a peculiar irony to this imbalance of legal action since tests of intellectual ability, as a whole, tend to have better psychometric properties and a more extensive research base than do most behavioral-emotional assessment instruments. When projective personality measures are included, the difference in psychometric quality becomes even more pronounced (Salvia & Ysseldyke, 1991). A possible reason for behavioral-emotional or personality measures not being legally targeted as extensively as intellectual tests has been articulated by DeMers (1986). He suggests that there is a limited legal basis for complaint against these types of measures because they have seldom been found to systematically discriminate against particular groups and are most often administered in the context of voluntary work by private citizens rather than as an action of the state.

A final interesting point in regard to legal and ethical issues is that they can change over time. The codes of ethical practice adopted by professional organizations tend to be influenced by changes in social thought, and statutory regulation at the state level tends to be influenced by changes in the ethical codes of professional organizations. For example, until the mid-1970s both the American Psychiatric Association and the American Psychological Association officially viewed homosexuality as a form of mental illness. Today, as attested to by many recent articles and letters to the editor in the *APA Monitor,* there is considerable controversy over whether it is ethical for therapists to work with clients who desire to change their sexual orientation. This shift in direction over a 20-year period has mirrored changing social attitudes toward homosexuality as an acceptable alternative lifestyle (Corey, Corey, & Callanan, 1988). In terms of behavioral-emotional assessment, it is not possible to predict how legal and ethical constraints will change over time, but it is likely, if not certain, that change will occur.

UNDERSTANDING THE ORIGINS OF BEHAVIORAL, SOCIAL, AND EMOTIONAL PROBLEMS

Think about this for a moment: Can a professional conduct reliable and valid assessments of youngsters with behavioral, social, and emotional problems without being firmly grounded in a theoretical orientation to how these problems develop, progress, and change? While one might administer some tests and possibly even interpret the results under this scenario, is this approach the most desirable? Probably it is not. Without a solid theoretical background and orientation, the assessor is relegated to the role of a technician or tester, and no matter how skilled, he or she may never integrate the assessment findings to the subject's past and future with an adequate degree of continuity or unity. Developing a solid theoretical understanding of the origins of behavioral, social, and emotional problems may have important implications when linking the assessment results to a workable intervention plan.

Without wishing to be dogmatic, this book was designed with a specific theoretical foundation in mind, namely social learning or social cognitive theory. Before delving into an exploration of social learning theory, this section will first provide a brief discussion of some traditional approaches to conceptualizing human behavior and then, in more detail, explore social cognitive theory and its related approach to explaining the influences on human behavior, namely triadic reciprocality.

To say that there is one traditional theory of human behavior, or even a small handful of such theories, in modern psychology is somewhat misleading. While psychodynamic theory and behaviorism were strong unitary forces in the early days of psychology, neither one of these schools of thought is currently a unitary force because as they have matured, both have to some extent split into factions or differing schools of thought with the same parentage.

In the modern world of behaviorism, there are divergent schools of thought that take significantly different approaches and yet still fall under the umbrella of behaviorism. The "true believers" in behaviorism are probably those who claim the strongest legacy from Skinner, Watson, and ultimately from Thorndike. This contingent of behaviorism is perhaps best exemplified by those active practitioners of applied behavior analysis, which can be traced directly to B. F. Skinner's brilliant and voluminous work, spanning the 50-year period from 1930 to 1990. To try to summarize applied behavior analysis or the work of Skinner in a few short sentences would be both simplistic and presumptuous, but there is an important point that can be made here. This school of thought within behaviorism contends that behavior is shaped by controlling and consequential forces within the environment and that such environmental control is the key to understanding, predicting, and changing behavior. On the other hand, a more recent school of thought within the behavioral world is made up of a diverse group of individuals with ideas for changing behavior that they call "cognitive behavioral therapy." This loose-knit faction does indeed claim some legacy from Skinner's work, as emitted behaviors, consequences, and the environment are important in their thinking. However the emphasis on internal cognitive processes and mediating events that characterize cognitive behavioral theories is a definite departure from the framework advocated by Skinner and his colleagues. In fact, shortly before his death in 1990, Skinner presented a keynote address at the annual meeting of the APA, in which he thoroughly lambasted "cognitive science," portraying it as a misguided attempt to explain human behavior through studying underlying mental processes and throwback to turn-of-the-century introspectionism.

This brief analysis of the evolution of modern behaviorism makes the point that the traditional theoretical schools of thought discussed in general psychology textbooks have evolved tremendously over the years, often branching into smaller groups that share common backgrounds. This same process is also true for other traditional theoretical schools of thought, such as psychodynamic theory, the neurobiological model, and the humanistic movement. The philosophical base of each of these schools has evolved tremendously over the years, and there are no longer just a few powerful theoretical schools with which a practitioner may be aligned. In fact, today's clinicians and researchers are much more likely to consider themselves "eclectic" in their theoretical approach to human behavior than to rigidly align themselves with a particular school of thought. These present circumstances have had a dual effect: On one hand, the decreasing amount of dogmatism has paved the way for acceptance of new and influential theories such as social cognitive theory, but on the other hand, the current generation of clinicians is perhaps less likely to pay a great deal of attention to theoretical orientation, which could lead to an unanchored approach to assessment and treatment.

Social Cognitive Theory: An Integrated Orientation

Social cognitive theory is a sophisticated, complex theory that takes into account not only the multiple causes of behavioral, social, and emotional problems but the reciprocal nature of the relationship between causes and effects. This theory is not overviewed in order to proselytize the nonbeliever; it is not a philosophy of life and does not necessarily carry any metaphysical implications. Although it is the bias of the author, social cognitive theory is proposed here as a solid foundation for assessment of children and adolescents because it takes into account many potential factors contributing to assessment problems, is flexible, and, in its fullest form, has strong implications for linking assessment data to intervention planning.

Components of Social Cognitive Theory.   Social cognitive theory and the related concepts of triadic reciprocality and observational learning are based on the work of Albert Bandura (1977, 1978, 1986). Most persons who have studied psychology and related fields at the graduate level are familiar with Bandura's famous work on social learning processes in aggression. These processes were demonstrated in the famous "Bobo Doll" experiments wherein the effects of models and perceived consequences were found to have a tremendous impact on both aggressive and prosocial behavior in school-age and preschool-age children. These particular demonstrations of social cognitive theory do not tell the full story, nor do they account for the entire complexity of the process. While it is impossible to completely account for social cognitive theory within a portion of one chapter (for a comprehensive account, see Bandura's 1986 book *Social Foundations of Thought and Action*), it is useful to at least detail its major components.

As stated by Bandura (1986), social cognitive theory holds that people "are neither driven by inner forces nor automatically shaped and controlled by external stimuli. Rather, human functioning is explained in terms of a model of triadic reciprocality in which behavior, cognitive and other personal factors, and environmental events all operate as determinants of each other'' (p. 18). The nature of persons is explained in terms of five basic human capabilities: *symbolizing capability, forethought capability, vicarious capability, self-regulatory capability,* and *self-reflective capability.*

Symbolizing capability involves the use of various symbols, including language, as a means of altering and adapting to different environments. The use of symbols allows communication with others, even at distant times and places. Forethought capability consists of the anticipation of likely consequences of behavior and is demonstrated by intentional and purposive actions that are future-oriented. Vicarious capability reflects the fact that not all learning results from direct experience but can occur through the observation of other persons' behaviors and of the consequences that follow them. Self-regulatory capability affects the development of a person's own internal standards and self-evaluative reactions to personal behavior, such as discrepancies between internal standards and actual behaviors which serve to govern future behavior. Self-reflective capability involves self-consciousness, or the uniquely human ability to think about and evaluate personal thought processes. Together these five fundamental human capabilities are the basis for our vast human potential, and they help explain the inner workings that result in behavioral output.

Triadic Reciprocality: Understanding the Determinants of Behavior. The social cognitive viewpoint supports a conception of the causes of human behavior due to *reciprocal determinism.* The idea behind reciprocal determinism is that the causes behind one's behavior become influenced and shaped by the behavior itself. Specifically the type of reciprocal determinism favored by social cognitive theory is known as *triadic reciprocality* (Bandura, 1977, 1978). This view contends that behavior, environmental influences, and various personal factors (such as cognition, temperament, biology) all work together in an interactive manner and have the effect of determining one another. Bandura's theory of triadic reciprocality is illustrated in Figure 1.1.

Triadic reciprocality in social cognitive theory can be exemplified in practical terms through an example of the interaction process between parents and a newborn child. For example, take a scenario where the infant happens to have a very "high-strung" or irritable temperament, which is present at birth and probably biological in nature. The infant's irritable temperament is an example of a personal factor. Since this particular infant tends to cry almost constantly,

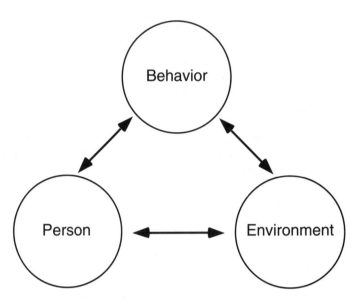

FIGURE 1.1   An outline of the theory of triadic
reciprocality

SOURCE: Adapted from A. Bandura, *Social Foundations of Thought
and Action* (Englewood Cliffs, NJ: Prentice-Hall, 1986).

is highly demanding, and sleeps only for short periods of time (behavioral factors), an environment is created where constant demands, noise, and limited opportunities for sleep interact with the personal factors of the parents to help shape their behavior and characteristics in the direction of being constantly tired, more irritable than normal, anxious, and perhaps mildly depressed. The behavior of the parents continues to shape the environment of the child, and the child's behavior continues to shape the environment of the parents, which in turn affects their personal characteristics. If the infant persists in being irritable and demanding and the parents tend to reinforce these demands with immediate attention, the child's irritable, demanding personal characteristics will probably become strengthened and persist. If the parents learn to deal with their child in a quiet and relaxed manner, the child's demanding irritability may be reduced, and the behavioral demands in the environment may change.

In expanding on Bandura's social cognitive triadic reciprocality model, Kauffman (1989) related it to what he terms an *interactional-transactional model* of influence. While triadic reciprocality and the interactional-transactional model are much too complex to do justice within a section of a chapter, they can be reduced to two points on family influences, which are highly salient for conducting assessments of behavioral, social, and emotional problems: "(1) children have effects on adults that are equal to adults' effects on children, and (2) family interactions are understandable only when reciprocal influences of parent and children on each other are taken into account" (Kauffman, 1989, p. 165). Patterson (1982) has also written extensively on these phenomena. His research group at the Oregon

Social Learning Center has conducted numerous investigations linking the development of child behavior, social, and emotional problems to coercive, reciprocal interactions within families. It takes only a small leap from these examples of parent-child interactions to understand that human behavior is shaped through complex, mutually influential interactions, whether in the home, school, workplace, or community.

In completing our discussion of triadic reciprocality, it is useful to understand that the three parts of the triad (personal, behavioral, and environmental factors) are thought to make different contributions at different points in time. As Bandura (1986) notes, "reciprocality does not mean symmetry in the strength of the bidirectional influences . . . (and) the triadic factors do not operate in the manner of a simultaneous holistic interaction" (pp. 24–25). In other words, there are times when an environmental factor may become the strongest influence in the reciprocal interaction, and at other times, personal factors may become preeminent. The important thing to keep in mind is that each factor will influence and shape the other two in some way.

Observational Learning: A Multiprocess Analysis.   To conclude our brief excursion into social cognitive theory, it is worthwhile to take a brief look at the process of *observational learning.* As outlined by Bandura (1977, 1986), observational learning is a model for understanding the learning process in a social context, fully compatible with social cognitive theory and triadic reciprocality. Individuals who have only a superficial knowledge of observational learning might consider it the equivalent of simple modeling or mimicking of behavior, but it is far more comprehensive than such comparisons would suggest. As Bandura (1986) stated, "most human behavior is learned by observation through modeling . . . (but) in skill acquisition, modeling is more accurately represented as rule learning rather than mimicry" (pp. 47–48).

What then are the elements that guide the process of rule learning? Bandura (1986) outlined five different types of *effects* that guide the process of modeling. *Observational learning effects* include new behaviors, cognitive skills, and standards of judgment that are acquired through directly observing others. These effects are thought to be stronger when the behavior observed is novel or unique. *Inhibitory and disinhibitory effects* determine how likely it is that a newly learned behavior will be demonstrated. It is more likely that a newly learned behavior will be performed if a person believes that a positive outcome will result and less likely if it is perceived that a negative outcome will result. A person's perception of what is likely or not likely to happen following a behavior will either inhibit or disinhibit him or her from performing the behavior. *Response facilitation effects* involve the actions of others that serve as social prompts for a person to engage in learned behaviors. Peer pressure or encouragement is an example of how a child is prompted to engage in certain social behaviors. *Environmental enhancement effects* encompass the physical circumstances of the observed environment that will result in a person performing a behavior in a certain way. For example, a child who has observed a playground fight between two other children in which one child "wins" by throwing a handful of dirt and gravel might engage in the same behavior if confronted with a conflict situation in the same spot. Finally *arousal effects* involve the level of emotional intensity or arousal that is elicited in observers. When emotional arousal is heightened, the form or intensity of ongoing behaviors can be altered; interactions that might normally result in a verbal argument might result in a fistfight in an environment of intense emotional arousal. In sum, these five modeling effects can serve to instruct, inhibit or disinhibit, facilitate, and enhance the behaviors engaged in, whether they are prosocial, neutral, or antisocial in nature.

Observational learning also involves four related cognitive processes that help determine how effectively we are able to learn through observation. According to Bandura (1986), these four processes work as follows:

1. *Attentional processes.* Learning will only occur through the observational process if adequate attention is focused on the event. It is interesting to note that humans do not give their attention equally to all stimuli; people are more focused and attentive if the behavior is novel or if they consider the model to have high status.
2. *Retention processes.* Retention processes involve the encoding of the event or behavior observed into memory. There is some evidence that two major memory systems are involved in retention processes: imaginal and verbal (Barnett & Zucker, 1990).
3. *Production processes.* This subprocess pertains to people's ability to actually perform the behaviors they have observed and retained. In this sense, motor abilities are often involved and may limit a person's ability to enact the behavior he or she has learned. While virtually all basketball aficionados would pay careful attention to and be able to retain a memory representation of one of Michael Jordan's trademark slam dunks, very few could actually produce the behavior.
4. *Motivational processes.* In social cognitive theory, there is a differentiation between learning and performance, as people tend not to enact everything they learn. Whether or not a person is motivated to enact a newly learned behavior depends mainly on the incentives involved. Incentives can be either internal or external, and they can be direct, vicarious, or self-produced.

In sum, while there are many competing theories on the development of human behavioral, social, and emotional problems, social cognitive theory has many advantages for conceptualizing and assessing child and adolescent behavioral and emotional problems, and it is emphasized in this text. Social cognitive theory and its related processes and components offer a highly sophisticated and relevant framework for conceptualizing the referral problems and treatment issues in assessing children and adolescents. Although it is not necessary to adopt social cognitive theory (or any other theoretical approach) in order to conduct technically adequate assessments, using it as a basis for understanding will provide a sound conceptualization of referral problems and a solid framework for dealing with the assessment-intervention process in a cohesive manner.

THE DIRECT AND OBJECTIVE
APPROACH TO ASSESSMENT

As the title of this book indicates, a conscious choice has been made to emphasize assessment approaches that are *direct* and *objective*. What exactly do direct and objective assessment methods consist of, and how are they different from nondirect and nonobjective methods?

The Basis of Direct and Objective Assessment

Direct approaches to assessment tend to de-emphasize mediating steps between obtaining and interpreting the assessment data. For an example of how a direct approach differs from a less direct approach, let's compare two techniques for assessing social status or peer relations. Sociometric assessment methods (e.g., use of peer nominations or peer ratings) are considered to be direct in this example. The obtained assessment data provide direct information about how a child or adolescent is perceived by their peers. The use of a human figure drawing test to provide information on social status or peer relations would be a less direct means. With this technique, the drawings are the obtained assessment data, but in order to convert the information into hypotheses about social functioning and peer relations, several intermediary steps are involved (e.g., measuring the size of the drawings, looking at the qualitative aspects of the drawings, looking at the placement of the different figures in relation to each other) before the issue is addressed.

Assessment methods that are objective in nature de-emphasize the need for making qualitative inferences in order to interpret the obtained data, whereas less objective methods require a greater degree of inference on the part of the examiner in order to make an interpretation. Using the example of sociometric assessment versus human figure drawings, one can again see the difference in the inference level required by the two methods. While some inference is needed in order to interpret the sociometric data and to link it with actual social status and peer relations, a much higher level of inference is needed to accomplish the same end with drawing tests. For example, one must assume that certain qualitative features of the drawings, such as their size or their placement on the paper, have some intrinsic meaning that will shed light on child or adolescent social functioning. In sum, direct and objective methods of assessment tend to allow for data gathering and interpretation with a minimal amount of intermediary steps and subjective inference.

Nomothetic versus Idiographic Assessment
and the Empirical Approach

To understand the emphasis on direct and objective assessment, it is necessary to overview some related assessment concepts: namely, the difference between *nomothetic* and *idiographic* assessment and the *empirical approach* to assessment. The division of assessment methods into a nomothetic-idiographic dichotomy dates to the early part of the twentieth century, and it has been the subject of considerable debate over the years. The issue became the point of much discussion in psychology with the publication of Paul Meehl's book *Clinical vs. Statistical Prediction* (1954). It this text, Meehl argued that clinical judgment was often a poor substitute for quantitative or actuarial prediction based on objective data. According to Barnett and Zucker (1990), nomothetic assessment focuses on actuarial and quantitative data, objective tests, and statistical prediction. Idiographic assessment, on the other hand, focuses more on individual and qualitative data, projective tests, and clinical judgment.

The empirical approach to assessment is more in line with nomothetic than idiographic assessment. The term *empirical* originates from the Greek word *empeiria,* which refers to *experience* (Achenbach & McConaughy, 1987). Empirical data is based on experience or observation, and it can be proven or disproven through direct experimentation or observation. In Achenbach and McConaughy's conceptualization of empirical assessment, this approach ". . . follows psychometric principles, including the use of standardized procedures, multiple aggregated items, normative-developmental reference groups, and the establishment of reliability and validity" (1987, p. 16). In essence, empirical assessment epitomizes many of the characteristics that are referred to under the title "direct and objective."

Why Emphasize Direct and Objective Assessment?

In this section, the terms direct and objective have been defined and discussed, the concept of nomothetic vs. idiographic assessment has been introduced, and empirically based assessment has been discussed. It is fair to say that the direct and objective approach to assessment favors nomothetic methods and is compatible with empirically based assessment, but what advantages are found in the direct and objective approach to justify its emphasis in this book?

Perhaps the greatest value of direct and objective approaches is their reduction of the amount of error that a clinician may bring into the assessment process. Particularly when used in an aggregated, multimethod manner, direct and objective approaches diminish the problem of bias, which may be introduced by overreliance on subjective clinical judgment or on a limited number of assessment techniques. Thus the use of direct and objective assessment methods allows the clinician to be more confident in the integrity of the assessment results and in any intervention recommendations stemming from them.

Another advantage of direct and objective approaches to assessment is that they put the clinician on more solid ground in terms of adherence to legal and ethical principles of assessment. The ethical standards of both the APA and NASP stress the need for assessment methods that are technically adequate and used only for the purposes for which they have been validated. These sentiments are echoed by the guidelines stated in IDEA and in the *Standards for Educational and Psychological Testing* (AERA, APA, & NCME, 1985). It is important not to overgeneralize on this point: Not all direct and objective approaches to assessment are technically sound and validated, and not all assessment methods that are less direct and objective fail to meet acceptable levels of measurement integrity. As a general rule, however, the more direct and objective an assessment method is, the more measurement integrity it is likely to have (Salvia & Ysseldyke, 1991; Worthen, Borg, & White, 1993).

To conclude, it is important to emphasize that although the focus of this book is on direct and objective methods of assessment, there is a place for clinical judgment and that the abandonment of all less direct and objective assessment methods is not being advocated. There are some projective assessment techniques that meet acceptable technical standards, and the use of subjective clinical techniques can sometimes provide useful and interesting assessment information within the context of a comprehensive assessment. It is also true that one cannot break down every method of assessment for behavioral, social, and emotional problems into empirical-direct and objective-nomothetic versus nondirect and subjective-idiographic categories. There are varying amounts of objectivity and directness in every possible assessment method.

DESIGNING A MULTIMETHOD, MULTISOURCE, MULTISETTING ASSESSMENT

Since about 1980, there have been significant advances in the research and technology base for conducting assessments with children and adolescents. One of the major developments has been the articulation of a model for a broad-based assessment design. The essential feature of this broad-based model is its use of various assessment methods with different informants or sources in several settings, thereby reducing the amount of error variance in the assessment and producing a comprehensive representation of the referred client's behavioral, social, and emotional functioning. This type of broad-based assessment design has been referred to by various names, including *multifactored assessment* (Barnett, 1983), *multisetting-multisource-multiinstrument assessment* (Martin, 1988; Martin, Hooper, & Snow, 1986), and *multiaxial empirically based assessment* (Achenbach & McConaughy, 1987). Although there are some differences in the way these different models have been articulated, the critical feature of obtaining assessment data through a number of different instruments, methods, sources, informants, and settings remains the same.

For this text, the term *multimethod, multisource, multisetting assessment* has been chosen to represent the features of the broad-based assessment that are most relevant to the topic. In Figure 1.2, a graphic representation of the model is displayed. For an example of how a multimethod, multisource, multisetting assessment would be conducted in actual practice, let's look at the hypothetical case of a child client who is referred to a clinic setting because of a variety of behavioral and emotional problems. In terms of method, it would be desirable to include behavioral observation, interviews, rating scales, and self-report instruments as part of the assessment from the outset, and within each method, a variety of instruments or specific techniques should be used whenever possible. In the event that the client was experiencing social adjustment problems and there

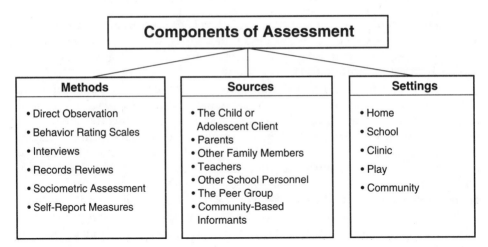

FIGURE 1.2 Potential components of a multimethod, multisource, multisetting assessment

was easy access to a social group (i.e., at school or in the playground) for assessment, it would be desirable under some circumstances to gather sociometric assessment data. In terms of sources, it would be necessary at a minimum to gather assessment data from both the client and his or her parent(s) and if possible, from other relevant informants who know the child well. These other sources of information might include school personnel, other family members, and community-based individuals such as clergy, youth group leaders, and so forth. In terms of setting, clinic, home, and school would be included in an optimum assessment and when feasible, community-based and play settings as well.

In reality, it is often difficult or impossible to include all of the relevant sources and settings, and it is sometimes a problem to include even more than a couple of methods. The main point is that as the assessment becomes more diverse and broad-based, an increasingly aggregated picture of the child's behavioral, social, and emotional functioning is obtained. Such an assessment design has the greatest possibility of reducing error variance and providing a comprehensive picture of the child (Achenbach & McConaughy, 1987; Martin, 1988; Martin, Hooper, & Snow, 1986; Merrell, Merz, Johnson, & Ring, 1992).

Some caution is warranted in considering the possibilities and advantages of an aggregated, multimethod, multisource, multisetting assessment. Though most current thinking suggests that such a design is indeed the best practice and most sophisticated way of implementing an assessment, there is some divergence of professional opinion. Some experts in child and adolescent psychopathology (e.g., Arkes, 1981; Loeber, Dishion, & Patterson, 1984; Reid, Baldwin, Patterson, & Dishion, 1988; Wiggins, 1981) have presented very persuasive arguments that in some cases aggregated, multiple-assessment data may actually *increase* error variance, due to covariation between different assessment sources and the inability of clinicians to effectively aggregate contradictory assessment data. A compelling and interesting argument, it is at least partially behind efforts to advocate the sequential or multiple-gating approaches to assessment, which are reviewed in chapter 2. Even some experts who advocate the aggregated, multiple-assessment model (e.g., Achenbach & Edelbrock, 1984) have acknowledged this possibility. So in light of these somewhat contradictory arguments, what is the best clinical practice? The position advocated throughout this book is that the informed and judicious use of an aggregated, multiple-assessment model is still the best practice for general referral and assessment cases. However, clinicians and researchers need to be informed of the potential liabilities of their assessment design. In the meantime, additional empirical evidence would be very helpful in articulating a state-of-the-art assessment model of the next century. Because most of the contradictory arguments on assessment design are theory-based but not yet empirically validated, being aware of both positions seems a prudent step at the present time.

CRITERIA FOR INCLUSION OF ASSESSMENT METHODS AND INSTRUMENTS

Throughout this book, five general assessment methods are emphasized: direct behavioral observation, interviewing techniques, behavior rating scales, socio-metric approaches, and self-report procedures. To varying degrees, each of these methods can be considered direct and objective, as the terms have been defined in this book. Given that there are many more specific procedures and instruments within each method than can be included in this book, the guidelines for including any one of them in this text follow three general sets of criteria, as follows:

1. Any procedure or instrument that is included must have met at least minimum standards for technical adequacy (i.e., have sufficient research behind it to demonstrate its psychometric properties and clinical utility).
2. Any procedure or instrument included must have a high degree of "usability" for the clinician. In other words, any particular technique or test requiring an extensive amount of specialized equipment or training that is overly burdensome for clinicians on a day-to-day basis have not been included, regardless of its technical properties.
3. In the case of standardized, norm-referenced instruments (such as behavior rating scales and self-report tests), these must (*a*) have reasonably large and representative normative populations and (*b*) be easily available (i.e., commercially published or easily accessible within the public domain) in order to be included in this text. Of course, this third criterion must be met in addition to the first two.

In some cases, the number of possible instruments or techniques that meet the inclusion criteria are well in excess of the capacity of this book. Thus, in some cases, instruments or specific approaches that are representative of their general domain are included as examples of what is available.

APPLICATION PROBLEMS—ETHICAL ISSUES IN ASSESSMENT

As we have seen in this chapter, the assessment of behavioral, social, and emotional problems in school and clinical settings sometimes presents the practitioner with a variety of legal and ethical dilemmas. Analyze the following examples of assessment scenarios by determining (*a*) whether the situation presents a potential ethical or legal problem, and if so, (*b*) what is the best professional solution to the problem.

1. Jason, a 15-year-old boy, is participating in a diagnostic interview with a psychologist at a community mental health center. He was referred to the center by his parents because of their concerns about possible depression. During the interview, Jason talks about being very jealous and angry at a former girlfriend who rejected him, and he seems almost obsessed with his anger toward her. At one point in the interview, Jason angrily states that "if she makes me look like a fool one more time, I'll kill her!"

2. A school counselor is assigned by the building principal and the district special education director to administer and interpret behavior rating scales and a self-report test for a student who has been referred for special education assessment due to behavioral and emotional problems. The school does not have access to a school psychologist. The counselor has not taken any coursework or received any supervision in this type of assessment. When the counselor discusses her concerns about lack of training or experience in this area with the administrators, they respond that she should "study the test manual and get up to speed on your own."

3. A Native American adolescent is referred for assessment due to concerns about possible psychotic symptoms (e.g., hearing voices, alternating between extremely withdrawn and highly agitated social behavior, hoarding objects). In addition to interviews with the subject and the subject's parents, the assessment battery includes two self-report tests and two behavior rating scales that do not include any Native Americans in the standardization sample.

4. A 14-year-old student who has been receiving special education services as "seriously emotionally disturbed" since grade 2 enters the main office of the school and, in a highly emotional and agitated state, demands to see her permanent behavioral file. This file includes several psychological, social work, and psychiatric reports, all of which contain some very sensitive information about the student and her family.

CHAPTER 2

Classification as Part of the Assessment Process

Chapter Outline

INTRODUCTION

When a practitioner conducts a formal assessment of children or adolescents and their environments to determine the nature and severity of behavioral, social, and emotional problems, one of the traditional primary purposes of the assessment is to determine an appropriate diagnosis or classification. The term *diagnosis* is historically linked with the medical model of psychological disorders, while the term *classification* is utilized more in education and by behaviorally oriented practitioners. Both terms imply a common element of categorizing and codifying an observable phenomenon based on an existing taxonomy or scheme. Without splitting hairs over conceptual or definitional differences between the two terms, both will be subsumed under the more generic term, *classification,* in this chapter.

There is some debate within the field as to how useful the process of classification is. The traditional view of classification is that the behavioral sciences, like the natural sciences, should develop and utilize classification taxonomies to create order, to provide a common ground for the use of different practitioners in describing problems, to help predict the future course of behavior, and ideally to prescribe a treatment scheme for the behavioral problem. Unfortunately, the state of the behavioral sciences is still far from meeting these goals for classification (Gresham & Gansle, 1992). The problems with traditional classification systems have led to great dissatisfaction by behaviorally oriented practitioners and researchers, as exemplified by Kauffman's (1989) statement that ". . . the usual psychiatric systems of classification have been quite unreliable . . . (and have) had little or no implications for treatment, particularly educational treatment" (p. 122).

This chapter deals with several important issues relating to the role of classification in assessment. First a rationale for conducting classification activities is proposed, which is followed by a discussion of differential diagnosis and classification error. The majority of the chapter is devoted to descriptions of current classification systems in behavioral and emotional assessment. Three major classification systems are overviewed, including the DSM system, special education classification, and the Behavioral Dimensions approach. Following the presentation of current classification systems is an overview of a promising new development in systematic assessment and selection for classification and treatment— multiple gating, a series of procedures and decision points. The chapter concludes with a brief discussion of some additional assessment-classification issues.

WHY CLASSIFY?

There is little doubt that current classification systems in psychology, psychiatry, and education are imperfect. Despite their present flawed state, there may be some wisdom in the thought that disregarding our current systems due to their imperfections may be throwing out the proverbial baby with the bath water. There are some solid pragmatic reasons why classification is often necessary and useful as part of the assessment process. The following are four reasons why doing a formal classification as part of an evaluation is often important:

1. Classification can provide some common ground of understanding for different professionals working with the same client.
2. Classification can provide access to services for clients.
3. Educational and health service institutions often require classification to remunerate the client or service provider for services.
4. In the absence of a totally reliable and valid classification taxonomy for behavioral and emotional problems, continuing to work with and refine present systems is a step in the direction of developing improved systems.

Although it is true that there are many problems with current classification systems and that they are often used and implemented cynically (one colleague half jokingly refers to the current psychiatric classification system as having a high degree of "Blue Cross and Medicaid validity"), abandoning the use of classification simply because the state of the art is currently poor is shortsighted at best and will lead to professional anarchy at worst. Therefore the purpose of this chapter is to orient the reader to the classification systems that are often used as part of the assessment process and to provide a rational argument for how current classification systems can be best utilized for assessment.

DIFFERENTIAL DIAGNOSIS AND CLASSIFICATION ERROR

The term *differential diagnosis* is often used in the psychiatric and psychological literature, but it is often not properly understood or utilized. The process of differentially diagnosing or classifying a behavioral, social, or emotional problem essentially involves two steps: (*a*) making a binary decision as to whether or not a problem is considered normal or abnormal in nature and (*b*) reaching a decision on how to specifically classify the problem (e.g., as a conduct disorder versus an oppositional-defiant disorder; a learning disability versus a serious emotional disturbance). This differential process is often difficult, and it is considered to be one of the most technically demanding aspects of the assessment process (Martin, 1988).

Given the imperfect nature of our current classification systems, it is inevitable that some error will be found in many differential diagnostic and classification decisions. Two types of error are of particular interest for clinicians making classification decisions. A *false-positive* error occurs when an individual is classified as having a particular disorder but in fact does not have it. A *false-negative* classification error occurs when an individual is classified as being "normal" or not having a specific disability or disorder when he or she in fact does have it.

Which type of error is worse? The answer to this question depends on what type of classification decision one is making and how high the stakes are. For example, when conducting initial screenings (e.g., to identify children who are in the early stages of developing behavioral, social, or emotional problems), the primary goal is to narrow down the number of *good suspects* and then look at that population in more detail. For a screening process, it would be preferable to make a false-positive error rather than a false-negative error because over-selection can be corrected at a later point, but underselection may mean that a child who is in need of help may go for a long period of time without receiving it. On the other hand, if you are making a decision as to whether an individual has a psychotic disorder, making a false-positive error sets up a potentially insidious situation in which the client is improperly labeled, has a good chance of being stigmatized for a long period of time, and may end up being the recipient of treatment that is not needed and that may have negative side effects (e.g., the prescription of antipsychotic medications).

In general, it is recommended that the higher the risks and consequences in a differential diagnosis and classification decision, the more conservative the approach to making the decision should be. In cases where there is potential for a great deal of adverse consequences, a clinician should go so far as to take a *disconfirmatory* approach, that is, approach the classification decision with the hypothesis that the disorder or disability under question is not present and reject that premise only when the evidence to the contrary clearly overwhelms the initial working hypothesis.

CURRENT CLASSIFICATION SYSTEMS

Three different classification systems for arranging behavioral, social, and emotional problems of childhood and adolescence are overviewed in this section. First the psychiatric-based DSM system, which is widely used by psychiatrists, by clinical psychologists, and in hospital-based day or residential treatment programs, will be overviewed. Then the classification categories and definitions based on special education law will be discussed. Finally a recent and promising approach to classification of behavioral, social, and emotional problems, namely the *Behavioral Dimensions* method, will be introduced.

The DSM System

Within the mental health professions in the United States, the most widely used system for classification of behavioral, social, and emotional problems is the psychiatric-based *Diagnostic and Statistical Manual for Mental Disorders* (DSM). The most current edition of this system is the revised third edition (American Psychiatric Association, 1987). At the time that the final version of this text was being edited (early 1993), a fourth edition of the DSM was also in the works. The DSM-IV is scheduled to be published and distributed in early 1994. More information on the DSM-IV is presented at the end of this section.

Assumptions and Structure of DSM.   The first edition of the DSM system was published in 1952, and like subsequent editions, it was based on a *medical model* of behavioral and emotional problems, one which views such disturbances as *mental diseases.* An underlying assumption of this model is that behavioral and emotional problems *reside within the individual,* although this assumption has been tempered to some extent by the influence of behavioral psychology, which provides an alternative framework for viewing such problems, namely as a product of eliciting and reinforcing stimuli within a person's environment.

The DSM-III-R uses a *multiaxial* approach to classification. That is, individuals are classified according to five different dimensions or axes, rather than as simply experiencing a given problem. The first two axes refer to types of psychological disorders. The other three axes refer to physical functioning, severity of psychosocial stressors, and level of adaptive functioning. Under axes I (clinical syndromes) and II (developmental and personality disorders) of the classification system, several of the disorders are relevant to children and adolescents, while other disorders are either specific to the developmental years or at least are considered to be first evident during childhood or adolescence. Table 2.1 provides a brief overview of the five axes of the DSM-III-R system, while Table 2.2 specifies the diagnostic categories that are usually considered to be first evident during infancy, childhood, or adolescence.

TABLE 2.1   An overview of the multiaxial structure of the DSM-III-R

Axis I	Clinical Syndromes Includes 16 general categories of disorders, with some categories having several subcategories
Axis II	Development Disorders and Personality Disorders Includes four different categories of developmental disorders and three different "clusters" of personality disorders
Axis III	Physical Disorders and Conditions The clinician notes any current physical problems that may be potentially relevant to the management of the case
Axis IV	Severity of Psychosocial Stressors Stressors are noted and coded on a 1 (none) to 6 (catastrophic) point scale
Axis V	Global Assessment of Functioning The individual's overall level of psychological, social, and adaptive functioning is rated and coded on a 1 (most severe) to 90 (most adaptive) rating system, with descriptive anchor points provided at 10-point intervals.

TABLE 2.2   DSM-III-R categories of disorders usually considered to be first evident in infancy, childhood, and adolescence

   I. DEVELOPMENT DISORDERS: Mental Retardation, Pervasive Developmental Disorders, Specific Developmental Disorders, Other Development Disorders
  II. DISRUPTIVE BEHAVIOR DISORDERS: Attention-Deficit Hyperactivity Disorder, Conduct Disorders, Oppositional Defiant Disorder
 III. ANXIETY DISORDERS OF CHILDHOOD AND ADOLESCENCE: Separation Anxiety Disorder, Avoidant Disorder, Overanxious Disorder
  IV. EATING DISORDERS: Anorexia Nervosa, Bulimia Nervosa, Pica, Rumination Disorder of Infancy, Eating Disorder Not Otherwise Specified
   V. GENDER IDENTITY DISORDERS: Gender Identity Disorder of Childhood, Transsexualism, Gender Identity Disorder of Adolescence or Adulthood—Nontranssexual Type, Gender Identity Disorder Not Otherwise Specified
  VI. DISORDERS: Tourette's Disorder, Chronic Motor or Vocal Tic Disorder, Transient Tic Disorder, Tic Disorder Not Otherwise Specified
 VII. ELIMINATION DISORDERS: Functional Encopresis, Functional Enuresis
VIII. SPEECH DISORDERS NOT CLASSIFIED ELSEWHERE: Cluttering, Stuttering
  IX. OTHER DISORDERS OF INFANCY, CHILDHOOD, OR ADOLESCENCE: Elective Mutism, Identity Disorder, Reactive Attachment Disorder of Infancy or Early Childhood, Stereotype/Habit Disorder, Undifferentiated Attention-Deficit Disorder

Using the DSM System in Assessment. As can be seen from a quick overview of Table 2.2, virtually any type of moderate to severe behavioral or emotional problem that might be experienced by a child or adolescent is potentially DSM-III-R diagnosable under one of the many categories available. The all-inclusive nature of the system is both an advantage and a problem. The advantage lies in a clinician being able to use the system to classify a broad range of problems, to share a common framework of understanding with other professionals, and to see possible implications for treatment (although many would argue this third point). The problem with such an all-inclusive system is that clinicians using it may end up making classification decisions (and potentially, intervention recommendations) that are outside their areas of professional expertise. For example, how many psychiatrists have sufficient training and experience with reading, writing, and arithmetic problems, which can be classified under the Developmental Disorders category? And how many psychologists or clinical social workers have any special training or expertise in diagnosing and treating speech and language problems? Thus the broad, all-inclusive nature of the DSM system, along with potential problems of unreliability between different raters (Achenbach & Edelbrock, 1983) does present some potential difficulties when using the system in assessment.

Another quandary that the DSM system poses for professionals conducting an assessment of behavioral, social, or emotional problems is that the specific criteria for each category of disorder are not tied to specific assessment techniques, nor are the classification categories clearly linked to common intervention techniques. Therefore the responsibility for selecting and using specific assessment techniques or instruments, and eventually developing an appropriate intervention plan, is fully on the shoulders of the clinician or team conducting the assessment. However the DSM does provide relatively objective criteria for clinicians to follow in making a classification decision.

Consider the diagnostic criteria for DSM-III-R code 313.81, Oppositional Defiant Disorder, a condition often seen in older children and adolescents who have been referred for psychological or other mental health services. The diagnostic criteria specify a clear time period (the condition must have lasted at least six months) and a list of behavioral manifestations (in which at least five of the nine specified must be present). The criteria also list conditions that would rule out a classification of Oppositional Defiant Disorder (presence of certain other DSM classifications), and three severity indicators (ranging from "mild" to "severe"). So the classification criteria do have at least the appearance of objectivity. Nevertheless by viewing the complete criteria for Oppositional Defiant Disorder shown in Table 2.3, it becomes clear that classification also involves a fair amount of subjectivity. For example, what does "often loses temper" mean—once a week, once a day, or several times a day? And does "often swears or uses obscene language" apply if an adolescent lets loose with a stream of expletives several times during an intense basketball game, or does it apply only if the youngster's language contains a constant barrage of "sewer talk"? Obviously the DSM system of classification, though it is widely used, has many potential pitfalls which clinicians need to be aware of, but, if used judiciously, it can help them achieve many of the goals and necessities of assessment.

TABLE 2.3   An example of criteria for a DSM-III-R diagnostic category: oppositional defiant disorder (313.81)

Note: Consider a criterion met only if the behavior is considerably more frequent than that of most people of the same age.

A. A disturbance of at least six months during which at least five of the following are present:

(1) often loses temper
(2) often argues with adults
(3) often actively defies or refuses adult requests or rules, e.g., refuses to do chores at home
(4) often deliberately does things that annoy other people, e.g., grabs other children's hats
(5) often blames others for his or her own mistakes
(6) is often touchy or easily annoyed
(7) is often angry or resentful
(8) is often spiteful or vindictive
(9) often swears or uses obscene language

Note: The above items are listed in descending order of discriminating power based on data from a national field trial of the DSM-III-R criteria for Disruptive Behavior Disorders.

B. Does not meet the criteria for Conduct Disorder, and does not occur exclusively during the course of a psychotic disorder, Dysthymia, or a Major Depressive Episode.

Criteria for Severity of Oppositional Defiant Disorder:

Mild: Few, if any, symptoms in excess of those required to make the diagnosis **and** only minimal or no impairment in school and social functioning.

Moderate: Symptoms or functional impairment intermediate between "mild" and "severe."

Severe: Many symptoms in excess of those required to make the diagnosis **and** significant and pervasive impairment in functioning at home and school and with other adults and peers.

From DSM-III-R to DSM-IV.   As already noted, at the time the final version of this text was being completed, a fourth edition of the DSM (DSM-IV) was under way. The fourth edition is reported to contain many minor modifications and changes, but it will retain the same general format as the current edition. Apparently, one of the primary purposes of the fourth edition is to develop more consistency with the World Health Organization's ICD-10 health classification system, which will be published in 1994 (Kendell, 1991). Spitzer (1991) reported that the threshold for adding new categories in the fourth revision of the DSM is higher than in previous revisions, which should result in a relatively conservative document that will depart from the DSM-III-R only when necessary to ensure consistency with the ICD-10 or to integrate new findings.

Earlier in this chapter, some of the problems of the current DSM relating to assessment and classification were discussed, and there has been no shortage of criticism of the DSM system, particularly when used with children and in school settings (e.g., Gresham & Gansle, 1992). However, there has been optimism that the changes in DSM-IV will result in a more reliable and valid classification system and will reduce or eliminate some of the problems associated with earlier versions of the manual. One of the aims of the current revision has been to provide substantial reliability and validity data for proposed revisions (Sartorius, 1988). The National Institute of Mental Health (NIMH) supported at least 11 reliability and validity studies for the DSM-IV, and similar studies have been conducted through other means. Widiger, Frances, Pincus, Davis, and First (1991) have noted that the major emphasis in this latest revision of the DSM has been to maximize the impact of the accumulating research and to document the rationale and empirical support for any changes that are made. Any substantial revision, addition, or deletion to the manual will have been preceded by a comprehensive literature review in which the reviewers are encouraged to follow standard meta-analytic procedures (Widiger, Frances, Pincus, & Davis, 1991). Thus the development of the DSM-IV appears to be positive step in improving the empirical integrity of the DSM classification system. If the procedures utilized to develop DSM-IV are indicative of a trend, the possibilities for the development of a scientifically sound taxonomy of human behavioral and emotional disorders appear to be improving, with the goal of a scientifically precise and reliable classification system within reach.

Classification under Special Education Law

While the DSM system is the most commonly used classification structure for behavioral, social, and emotional problems within the mental health professions, professional practice is governed also by an additional definition and classification structure within the public educational systems of the United States. In 1975, the U.S. Congress passed the Education for All Handicapped Children Act (also referred to as P.L. 94-142) as a result of "constitutionally based challenges to the exclusion of handicapped children" (Rothstein, 1990, p. xxiii). Now approaching the end of its second decade of existence, this federal law has had a profound impact on assessment and classification practices within school settings. This law, which is now referred to as the Individuals with Disabilities Education Act (IDEA), is designed to ensure a free and appropriate public education and related educational services to all children and youth with disabilities. As part of IDEA, classification criteria have been adopted, and specific guidelines for assessment have been enacted. It is beyond the scope of this book to provide a comprehensive understanding of IDEA, but it is important for both school-based and community-based practitioners to have a basic understanding of how IDEA impacts assessment and classification. Therefore this section will provide a basic outline of the assessment and classification procedures of IDEA, which are pertinent to assessing behavioral, social, and emotional problems. A specific emphasis is placed on the classification category Seriously Emotionally Disturbed, as it is obviously the most pertinent area.

General Assessment Guidelines in IDEA.   Before a student with a disability can receive special education services under the auspices of IDEA, he or she must first be identified as having a disability, and this process typically involves formal assessment practices. Within IDEA itself, and through a number of court decisions reached over the years, certain assessment requirements and safeguards have been put into place. Eight of the requirements and procedures most pertinent to our general topic are briefly listed as follows:

1. Parental consent must be obtained before the assessment is conducted.
2. When the school district requests that an evaluation be done, it is paid for at public expense.
3. Tests must be valid for the purpose they are being used.
4. No single evaluation procedure may be used as the sole criterion for classification or program eligibility.
5. The assessment procedures must be culturally and racially appropriate; children must be tested in their native languages or modes of communication when feasible.
6. The evaluation is conducted by a *multidisciplinary team* (MDT) or group of individuals, including at least one team member who is knowledgeable about the child's specific area of disability.
7. The student is assessed in all areas pertinent to the suspected disability.
8. The identified student's program must be reviewed annually, and the child must be reevaluated at least once every three years.

These eight examples from IDEA are deceptively simple and straightforward. It is easy to understand what the intent of the law is but often difficult to implement it. As an example, let's look at item 5. It is not uncommon for Anglo clinicians to conduct an assessment of Hispanic, Native American, or Asian-American children who have been raised in cultural conditions much different from those of the majority Anglo culture and for whom English is not a primary language. Given that few, if any, Anglo assessors have a proficient command of all the languages that might be needed to make this requirement, they may be inclined at first not to take cases like these. Yet there is a competing pressure which makes it difficult to refer such cases, particularly in isolated rural areas, where the assessment professional in question may be the only person available at the time with technical training in educational and psychological assessment. In a situation like this, the examiner is faced with a variety of ethical, technical, and legal dilemmas, the solution of which is often complex (for a good discussion of best practices in considering cultural factors, see Nuttall, DeLeon, & Valle, 1990).

Another good example of how these eight guidelines are easy to understand but complex to implement can be demonstrated by considering item 3—test procedures must be valid for the purpose they are being used. How many of the assessment instruments utilized by an examiner to determine whether a child is "seriously emotionally disturbed" have been validated for that purpose? Many, if not most, procedures typically used for this purpose are not adequately validated. For example, given the low level of reliability and validity of most projective techniques, it is doubtful that most, if any, would hold up under the scrutiny of a due-process hearing or court decision, particularly if they were used in isolation.

Item 6 should be of special interest to clinicians working in private practice or in some other nonschool mental health setting. The law is clear that the school MDT has the ultimate responsibility for conducting the evaluation and determining program eligibility; it is not appropriate for one person to make a unilateral decision, even though one person may have conducted a majority of the evaluation procedures. Many professionals working in community mental health centers or in private practices are unaware of this requirement, much to the consternation of school personnel when they receive a psychological report stating a child is eligible for special education services before the child has even been made a focus of concern by the MDT!

IDEA Definition of "Seriously Emotionally Disturbed."   In looking at all of IDEA's special education service categories, it is the category "seriously emotionally disturbed" (SED, as it is commonly described) which is most relevant to the practice of clinical assessment of behavioral, social, and emotional problems. Although such problems often occur concomitantly with other disability conditions (most notably, those in the category of mental retardation, which does include guidelines for adaptive behavior assessment), it is the SED category that most specifically addresses disturbances of behavior, social adjustment, and emotion.

Students who are classified as SED receive the same federal protections as students with other disability conditions (e.g., right to a free and appropriate public education and related services) and are potentially provided with a "cascade" of placement and service options, ranging from regular classroom placement with the assistance of a behavioral consultant to full-time placement in a residential treatment center. The specific type of placement and service a SED student receives depends on the nature and severity of the disability and what the student requires in order to benefit educationally.

In developing the rules and regulations for implementing the original Education of the Handicapped Act (section 121a.5), Congress adapted a proposed definition of "seriously emotionally disturbed" developed by Eli Bower (1969), based on his widely influential research with delinquent and disturbed youth in California. The definition in the federal law is as follows:

(i)   The term means a condition exhibiting one or more of the following characteristics over a long period of time and to a marked degree, which adversely affects educational performance:

  (A) An inability to learn which cannot be explained by intellectual, sensory, or health factors;
  (B) An inability to build or maintain satisfactory interpersonal relationships with peers and teachers;
  (C) Inappropriate types of behavior or feelings under normal circumstances;
  (D) A general, pervasive mood of unhappiness or depression, or,
  (E) A tendency to develop physical symptoms or fears associated with personal or school problems.

(ii) The term includes children who are schizophrenic or autistic. The term does not include children who are socially maladjusted, unless it is determined that they are also seriously emotionally disturbed.

(The preceding definition has since been revised to remove the term *autism*, which is now a separate diagnostic category.)

A careful reading of the federal SED definition shows that using these criteria to make a classification decision is a process, like using the DSM criteria, that is at least superficially objective but also involves a great deal of subjectivity. For example, what is a "long period of time"? Is six weeks too little time to be considered "a long period"? Is one year too much time? How about the statement "to a marked degree"? What kind of objective criteria can a clinician use to determine how marked the degree of a problem is? Obviously the federal definition of SED, like many of the DSM diagnostic criteria, does carry problems of interpretation and implementation and requires the clinician and members of the MDT to use a fair amount of professional judgment.

The SED vs. SM Issue.   One of the great controversies surrounding the federal definition of SED stems from a brief statement in part ii of the definition, namely that the category SED does not include children who are socially maladjusted unless it is determined that they are also seriously emotionally disturbed. What exactly does this statement mean, and what are its ramifications? Interestingly, while IDEA does include the term *socially maladjusted* within the definition of SED, no operational definition of the term is provided in the law. Traditionally the term social maladjustment has been used to indicate a pattern of behavioral problems that are thought to be willful, goal-oriented, and possibly reinforced by one's immediate social reference group—e.g., a gang member being encouraged by peers to attack a member of a rival gang. The volitional nature of the antisocial behavior is often linked with social maladjustment, as characterized by Kelly's (1989) statement: "The term socially maladjusted encompasses . . . most individuals described as 'conduct disordered' who demonstrate knowledge of appropriate family, social, and/or school rules and *choose* (emphasis added) not to conform to them" (p. 3). Social maladjustment also has been traditionally conceptualized as antisocial in nature, as typified by the type of behaviors exhibited in the DSM-III-R diagnostic categories Conduct Disorder and Antisocial Personality Disorder.

Because students identified as SED cannot easily be expelled from school and because considering students with severe behavioral problems as socially maladjusted provides a "loophole" for not providing special education services to them, there is a great deal of professional interest in this topic. While over half of the states have ignored or chosen not to deal with the social maladjustment issue in their definitions of SED (Mack, 1985), a number of states have set up or are actively pursuing procedures to disqualify children from special education services who are considered to be socially maladjusted. Although the federal SED definition provides no guidelines on how to identify social maladjustment, a number of professionals in education, psychology, and law have developed suggested classification procedures. A common approach, stemming from a legalistic interpretation of the DSM system, typified the opinions of attorney Jane Slenkovitch (1983), contends that a DSM-III-R diagnosis of Conduct Disorder should be equated with social maladjustment and could legitimately serve to disqualify students from being identified as SED. There have also been attempts to develop psychometric instruments that purportedly distinguish SED from social maladjustment (Kelly, 1986).

In view of the tremendous interest in this particular aspect of the SED definition (the third edition of the 1990 volume of *Behavioral Disorders* and the first edition of the 1992 volume of *School Psychology Review* are both specifically devoted to the issue), it is interesting to note that the term "socially maladjusted" was not a part of Bower's original definition and that, in fact, he is on record as being opposed to the inclusion of the term in the federal definition, as he considers it unworkable (Bower, 1982). There have been other compelling arguments for eliminating the social maladjustment clause from the federal SED definition (Council for Children with Behavioral Disorders, 1987; Nelson, Rutherford, Center, & Walker, 1987); however, there is no evidence that such a change is imminent. For now, professionals conducting school-related assessments of children and youth with behavioral, social, and emotional problems should be aware that there are no psychometrically valid and defensible assessment procedures that can be used to make this distinction. Clinicians and program administrators who are forced to deal with this issue must walk a perpetual fine line between empirically validated professional practices and the necessity of making pragmatic decisions based on policies and resource constraints. Of course, it should be recognized that the final addendum in the current federal definition does allow students who are considered to be socially maladjusted to receive special education services if *it is determined that they are also seriously emotionally disturbed.* Still the interpretation of this particular statement has been problematic, and the statement itself may be construed as circular logic. In commenting on this and related statements in the federal definition, Kaufman (1989) remarked that "the final addendum regarding social maladjustment is incomprehensible" (p. 25).

State Adaptations of the Federal Definition.   In practice, IDEA is carried out by each of the states, which are given a fair amount of leeway in adapting and implementing specific aspects of the rules and regulations. Not all states have adopted the term "seriously emotionally disturbed." Given that it tends to conjure up images of padded walls in psychiatric hospitals and highly disturbing behaviors, many individuals believe the term pejorative at best, and some states have adopted this part of IDEA using other terms. The state of Washington, for example, utilizes the term "Seriously Behaviorally Disabled," and the state of Utah refers to the category as "Behavior Disordered." Examples of other terms used by states and by local education agencies include "Emotionally Impaired," and "Behaviorally-Emotionally Handicapped." There is also some variation between states in the specific assessment procedures to be utilized in making a classification of SED. For example, several states require documentation of implementation of appropriate intervention plans prior to SED classification. Other states require specific assessment procedures, such as direct behavioral observation or rating scales, or an evaluation from a medical doctor prior to classification.

Regarding the differences among labels used to describe and implement SED from state to state, there is some evidence that "behaviorally disordered" is less stigmatizing and more accurate as a definitional term than "seriously emotionally disturbed" (Feldman, Kinnison, Jay, & Hearth, 1983; Walker, 1982). Also there seems to be a professional preference among special educators for the term "behavior disordered." Nevertheless, widely varying terms and practices continue to be the norm. The confused state of the field as to definitions and assessment criteria reflects the state of the field in general; there is no question that professions that provide psychological and educational services to children and youth with behavioral, social, and emotional problems are continually evolving and for good reason.

A Proposed New Definition.   Given that there is widespread dissatisfaction with both the title (seriously emotionally disturbed) and functional definition (the federal adaptation of Bower's definition) used to classify students with behavioral, social, and emotional problems under IDEA, it is not surprising that proposals for new terms and definitions have been developed. The most influential alternative definition proposed to date has been developed by the National Mental Health and Special Education Coalition, which comprises some 30 professional mental health and education associations. This coalition made modifications on the final definition from an earlier draft, proposed in 1991 by the Council for Children with Behavioral Disorders (CCBD). This proposed definition, which uses the term *emotional or behavioral disorder,* was detailed by Forness and Knitzer (1992) as follows:

(i) The term emotional or behavioral disorder (EBD) means a disability characterized by behavioral or emotional responses in school so different from appropriate age, cultural, or ethnic norms that they adversely affect educational performance. Educational performance includes academic, social, vocational, and personal skills. Such a disability

  (A) is more than a temporary, expected response to stressful events in the environment.
  (B) is consistently exhibited in two different settings, at least one of which is school-related; and
  (C) is unresponsive to direct intervention in general education or the child's condition is such that general interventions would be insufficient.

(ii) Emotional and behavioral disorders can coexist with other disabilities.
(iii) This category may include children or youth with schizophrenic disorders, affective disorders, anxiety disorders, or other sustained disturbances of conduct or adjustment when they adversely affect educational performance in accordance with section (i). (p. 13)

Groups within the National Mental Health and Special Education Coalition are actively lobbying to have this definition incorporated into IDEA to replace the current term and definition of seriously emotionally disturbed. Only time will tell whether this change indeed happens, but there does seem to be widespread support for it. In many respects, the proposed definition appears to be a definite improvement over the current definition. While still retaining the open features of a general definition, the new definition better operationalizes certain aspects of the definition (e.g., EBD can coexist with other disability conditions; problems must be exhibited in a school-related setting and at least one other setting). The term EBD itself has face validity of being more descriptive and less stigmatizing than SED. Moreover, the proposed new definition does not have the troublesome loophole permitting the exclusion of service to "socially maladjusted" children and youth.

At the time this book was in the final stages of preparation (early 1993), the U.S. Department of Education was actively studying the possibility of replacing the current regulatory definition of "children with serious emotional disturbance" with a definition very similar to the EBD definition. The Office of Special Education and Rehabilitation Services posted an invitation to comment on such a change in February 1993 (*Federal Register,* February 10, 1993), with the implicit assumption that comments would be taken into consideration and a recommendation made by late 1993 or early 1994. Interestingly the language of the revised regulatory definition has been modified only to a slight or moderate extent, but the title "seriously emotionally disturbed" has thus far remained.

Behavioral Dimensions: An Alternative Classification Paradigm

In addition to the DSM and special education classification systems, a third type of classification system has been making inroads in recent years. This method, referred to as the *Behavioral Dimensions* approach, shows considerable promise as an empirically sound way of taxonomizing behavioral, social, and emotional problems exhibited by children and youth. The paradigm utilized in the Behavioral Dimensions approach is rooted in empirical methods of measuring behavior and complex statistical procedures, which allow for the identification of *behavioral clusters,* that is, clusters of highly intercorrelated behaviors. The two most important statistical techniques in identifying intercorrelated behavioral syndromes are factor analysis and cluster analysis. The use of these techniques in the Behavioral Dimensions approach to classification became prominent between the late 1960s and early 1980s, mainly through the work of Thomas Achenbach and his colleagues (Achenbach, 1982; Achenbach & Edelbrock, 1981, 1983, 1984) and by Herbert Quay and his colleagues (Quay, 1975, 1977; Quay & Peterson, 1967, 1987). These researchers developed and refined Behavioral Dimensions approaches to classifying behavioral problems through the utilization of sophisticated rating scales with empirically derived factor structures.

Behavioral Dimensions and the Child Behavior Checklist System. Through the development of both parent and teacher rating forms of the *Child Behavior Checklist* (CBCL) (Achenbach, 1981; Achenbach & Edelbrock, 1984), Achenbach and his colleagues have utilized factor analytic studies to identify two general classification areas within the Behavioral Dimensions approach. The first general classification scheme is referred to as *broad-band syndromes,* indicating the existence of large general behavioral clusters accounting for many related behavioral problems. The two broad-band syndromes utilized in the CBCL system include *internalizing* behavioral problems, which relate to *overcontrolled* behavior, and *externalizing* behavioral problems, which relate to *undercontrolled* behavior. Examples of internalizing behavior problems include anxiety, depression, and social withdrawal. Examples of externalizing behavior problems include delinquent behavior, aggressive behavior, and hyperactivity. The second general classification scheme is referred to as *narrow-band syndromes*, which are smaller behavioral clusters indicating more specific types of behavioral, social, or emotional problems. The narrow-band problem syndromes utilized in the current CBCL system include Withdrawn, Somatic Complaints, Anxious/Depressed, Social Problems, Thought Problems, Attention Problems, Delinquent Behavior, and Aggressive Behavior.

The current CBCL system includes a variety of different rating and report forms, and these are discussed more specifically in chapter 4 of this book. Earlier versions of the instruments in the CBCL system utilized different narrow-band syndromes for different age and gender breakdowns, based on separate factor analytic studies, but the most current version, revised in 1991, utilizes the same "cross-informant" syndromes for each instrument regardless of gender and age range. The CBCL system is widely considered the most sophisticated series of behavior rating scales available (Martin, 1988), and they have become widely used by practitioners in both school and clinical settings, as well as by researchers. Table 2.4 shows the division of broad-band and narrow-band problem "cross-informant" syndromes utilized in the CBCL system.

Behavioral Dimensions and the Behavior Problem Checklist System. Another well-known dimensional approach to behavioral, social, and emotional problems of children and youth is based on the work of Quay, using his research with the Behavior Problem Checklist and other assessment methodologies (Quay, 1975, 1977; Quay & Peterson, 1967, 1987). The first widely circulated version

TABLE 2.4 Cross-informant syndrome categories utilized in the child behavior checklist system

Broad-Band Syndromes

Internalizing (overcontrolled)
Exernalizing (undercontrolled)

Narrow-Band Syndromes

Aggressive behavior
Anxious/depressed
Attention problems
Delinquent behavior
Social problems
Somatic complaints
Thought problems
Withdrawal

of the Behavior Problem Checklist (BPC) was developed during the 1960s (Quay & Peterson, 1967), and research associated with this instrument constituted one of the first large-scale efforts at developing a Behavioral Dimensions taxonomy. During several years of research with the BPC, four general patterns or dimensions of problem behavior were isolated. These four dimensions are listed as follows:

1. *Conduct Disorder:* Physical and verbal aggressiveness, defiant behavior, disruptiveness in classroom settings, and a pervasive attitude of irresponsibility and negativity
2. *Anxiety-Withdrawal:* Social withdrawal, shyness, oversensitivity, a general pattern of retreat from the environment
3. *Immaturity:* Passiveness, attentional problems, daydreaming, preoccupation, and delays in emotional development
4. *Socialized Aggression:* Gang activities, stealing in groups, truancy from school, and identification with antisocial/delinquent subculture

These four general areas have been consistently identified as separate dimensions through several years of research. An interesting difference between the BPC system and the CBCL system is that the former system has tended to focus more on overt conduct problems and less on the general class of internalizing problems than the latter. For example, the BPC contains fewer items measuring physical symptoms, sensory distortions, and the general area of social withdrawal than does the CBCL system.

In 1987, a revised version of the BPC was published (RBPC, Quay & Peterson, 1987), which included new factor analytic and discriminant validity studies and some additional items and rewording of original items. The overall dimensional structure of the RBPC is relatively similar to that of the BPC, with some exceptions. In addition to four major dimensions, two minor dimensions (consisting of fewer behavioral items) are included; these describe psychoticlike behaviors and unusually high rates of motor behavior. The six factors of the RBPC, along with examples of what behaviors are included in each dimension, are shown in Table 2.5.

TABLE 2.5 Summary of the six dimensions of the Revised Behavior Problem Checklist

Dimension	Behavioral Description
Conduct Disorder	Attention seeking, disruptive, annoying, bothersome, fights, temper tantrums
Socialized Aggression	Stealing in company of others, has delinquent friends, school truancy in groups, disrespect for rules and laws
Attention Problems/Immaturity	Attention and concentration problems, easily distracted, lethargic approach to tasks, doesn't think before acting
Anxiety/Withdrawal	Self-consciousness, easily embarrassed, overly sensitive, highly fearful and anxious, depressed mood state
Psychotic Behavior	Uses same forms of speech in a highly repetitive manner, has unusual "strange" ideas
Motor Excess	Is restless and has difficulty sitting still for even short periods of time, tense and unrelaxed

Behavioral Dimensions Approaches to Specific Classes of Behavior. The BPC/RBPC and CBCL systems conceptualize dimensions of behavior problems in a global sense by attempting to define and validate overall classes of behavioral, social, and emotional problems. However, some additional work by the researchers who developed these systems has demonstrated that a Behavioral Dimensions approach to smaller and more discrete classes of behavior is also possible. Using the specific class of delinquent behavior as an example, both research groups (Achenbach, 1982; Quay, 1975, 1986) have identified subtypes of delinquent behavior, using the same general Behavioral Dimensions methodology that has been overviewed.

Achenbach (1982) has identified three dimensions of subtypes of delinquent activity: (*a*) *socialized-subcultural* (low IQ and socioeconomic status, bad companions, gang activities, maintaining social status through illegal behavior), (*b*) *unsocialized-psychopathic* (aggressive, assaultive, irritable, defiant, insensitive, feeling persecuted), and (*c*) *neurotic-disturbed* (overly sensitive, shy, worried, unhappy). Likewise Quay's (1975) dimensional findings on delinquent behavior are extremely similar to those of Achenbach's, often using the same labels and terminology. One minor difference between the two dimensional approaches is that Quay has suggested the existence of a fourth category, namely, *inadequate-immature* (passivity, dependence, tendency toward daydreaming). Since both of these dimensional classification systems for delinquency subtypes are so similar, they are presented in a merged fashion by the four major categories in Table 2.6.

The purpose of presenting this overview of dimensional approaches to subtypes of delinquent behavior is not to provide information on assessing delinquency but to illustrate how the Behavioral Dimensions approach to classification extends not just the overall conceptualization of behavior into several broad classes but can be used within each dimensional class of behavior as well. One can assume that other general classes of behavioral, emotional, or social problems can be further developed into dimensional subtypes as well. These empirically derived findings are intriguing and suggest that the Behavioral Dimensions approach to classification may hold great promise in the future development of classification.

TABLE 2.6 An overview of dimensional subtypes of delinquent behavior: merging the findings of Achenbach (1982) and Quay (1975)

Dimensional Subtype	Behavioral Description
Socialized-Subcultural	Peer-oriented, group or gang activities, delinquent value orientation, lower in IQ and socioeconomic status, experiences less parental rejection than other subtypes
Unsocialized-Psychopathic	Unbridled aggression, assaultive, hostile, defiant, explosive, insensitive to feelings of others, impulsivity, thrill-seeking, responds poorly to praise or punishment, feels persecuted
Neurotic-Disturbed	Anxiety, guilt, overly sensitive, social withdrawal, worrying, unhappy
Inadequate-Immature	Highly dependent, passive, tendency toward day-dreaming

Some Comments on Using Behavioral Dimensions Systems.   One thing to keep in mind when looking at the examples of Behavioral Dimensions clusters overviewed here is that the names or titles of specific dimensions are developed somewhat subjectively by the researchers involved, and they can be misleading if taken too literally. When a researcher through factor analytic studies identifies the existence of specific behavioral clusters that factor together, the researcher develops a name for the factor based on the types of specific behaviors in the cluster. Sometimes the cluster can be labeled in a way that directly indicates what the specific behaviors are. For example, one might label a cluster of behaviors that includes "threatens others," "physically fights," "argues," and related behaviors as "aggressiveness," which seem to make good clinical sense. On the other hand, some clusters of behaviors may fit together well in a statistical sense, but coming up with an equally descriptive label for the cluster can be problematic. For example, one of the narrow-band clusters identified through the work of Achenbach and his colleagues has been labeled "Thought Problems." Intuitively, one might think at first glance that high scores on this cluster may indicate the presence of schizophrenia or other types of psychoses, but this is seldom the case. Some of the actual behaviors found in this cluster include "can't get his/her mind off certain things," "strange ideas," and "stares blankly." While these specific behaviors might be seen commonly in severely thought-disordered or psychotic individuals, they also can occur with frequency in individuals with lesser problems. Clinicians using assessment and classification systems based on Behavioral Dimensions need to look always at the specifically endorsed behaviors in a cluster, rather than strictly going by the label or name that a behavioral cluster has been given.

THE USE OF MULTIPLE GATING IN ASSESSMENT AND CLASSIFICATION

In chapter 1 of this book, a model for using multiple sources of assessment data, obtained from multiple sources and in multiple settings, was introduced as a "best practice" in assessing behavioral, social, and emotional problems. The advantages of this multiaxial model were presented, and there is little doubt that its use is preferable to single-source assessments from both a clinical and research standpoint. Yet, despite the obvious advantages it presents, there are some potential obstacles. One of the problems in conducting assessments using many sources and instruments is *behavioral covariation*. If many different sources of information are utilized in an assessment, a diverse, if not contradictory, portrait of a given child's behavioral, social, and emotional status may be portrayed. This may present a serious problem for data interpretation, as it is generally agreed that most clinicians are not very efficient or skilled at effectively aggregating the multiple-data sources and detecting covariation across the instruments (Achenbach & Edelbrock, 1984b; Reid, Patterson, Baldwin, & Dishion, 1988). Another problem that may become amplified with a multisource, multisetting, and multiinstrument assessment design is that detection of a class of target behavior or a specific syndrome with a very low base rate is difficult. If multiple-data sources are not used in a sequential and methodical fashion, the amount of error in classification may possibly be increased due to the behavioral covariation problem.

However, new developments in assessment technology are showing great promise in reducing the types of assessment problems just described. One of the most exciting and innovative developments in assessment and classification during the past decade has been the development and refinement of a model for sequentially obtaining multiple sources of behavioral, social, and emotional assessment data and then systematically using this information to make screening and classification decisions. This assessment model has come to be known as *multiple gating*. It is based on the sequential assessment strategy first introduced by Cronbach and Gleser (1965) for applications in personnel selection. Multiple gating in the assessment and classification of child and adolescent psychopathology was first formally articulated and presented by research scientists at the Oregon Social Learning Center (Loeber, Dishion, & Patterson, 1984; Reid et al., 1988).

The basis of multiple gating is that through a series of assessment and decision steps (gates), a large population is sequentially narrowed down to a small population of individuals who are highly likely to exhibit the behavioral syndromes in question across settings and over time. The first step or gate generally consists of screening a large population of interest, using time and cost-effective measures such as rating scales or teacher ranking procedures for the behavioral syndrome of interest (e.g., antisocial behavior, aggression, hyperactivity, internalizing problems). This screening data is used to narrow down the larger population to a more reasonable number by allowing only those whose scores rank at a specified level (e.g., over the 50th percentile) to pass through the first gate and onto the second. The initial criteria are established in a fairly liberal fashion, resulting in a number of false-positive errors (identification of individuals who do not exhibit the behavioral syndrome in question in a serious manner) but few or no false-negative errors (failure to identify individuals who should be identified). The next gate in the sequence might be additional low-cost data obtained across different situations, for example, by using more lengthy rating scales completed by persons who know the subject in different settings. Again a cutoff criterion is established to determine which individuals will pass through the second gate. Those who pass through the second gate (and their numbers should be fairly small at this point) are then assessed using more time-intensive procedures such as structured interviews with parents and behavioral observations at home and/or school. There are also established decision rules for passing through the final gate(s), and those who do pass through these are almost certainly considered to exhibit the behavioral syndrome of interest to a serious degree. These individuals are then referred for additional assessment, final classification, and potentially, for a program of intervention. The final classification does not necessarily have to be a DSM or special education category but could consist of any formal operational definition of specific problem areas of interest.

Two examples of published multiple-gating procedures are presented to illustrate the potential uses and steps involved. The first example is a community or clinic-based multiple-gating procedure developed at the Oregon Social Learning Center to identify youths at risk for delinquency. The second example is a school-based multiple-gating procedure to identify students with severe behavioral disorders.

A Community and Clinic-Based Multiple-Gating Procedure

A number of risk factors and behavioral variables have been found to correlate with juvenile delinquency. Loeber and Dishion (1983) ranked these etiological variable in terms of their predictive power and noted that the composite measures of parental family management techniques, early childhood conduct problems, poor academic performance, and parental criminality or antisocial behavior were the most powerful predictors. They then attempted to apply this predictive information to a sequential multiple-gating procedure, using data from 102 12- to 16-year-old boys (Loeber et al., 1984). The result was a three-stage screening procedure with a high correct classification rate and significantly less expensive than traditional methods of screening and assessment. This multiple-gating procedure is diagrammed in Figure 2.1.

Gate 1 in the procedure consisted of teacher ratings obtained for each boy in the study. These ratings were conducted using a brief 11-item scale that required the teachers to rate the boys on both academic competency and social-behavioral characteristics at school. Boys whose ratings were at the 47th percentile or higher ($N = 55$) were selected to be assessed at Gate 2. The second gate consisted of telephone interviews with the parents of the remaining 55 boys. There were at least five interviews with each family, in which questions regarding family organization, the whereabouts of the target child, and the occurrence of problem

FIGURE 2.1   Diagram of a clinic-based multiple-gating procedure used to identify youths at risk for delinquency

SOURCE: Adapted from R. Loeber, T. J. Dishion, and G. R. Patterson, "Multiple Gating: A Multistage Assessment Procedure for Identifying Youths at Risk for Delinquency," *Journal of Research in Crime and Delinquency* 21 (1984): 7–32.

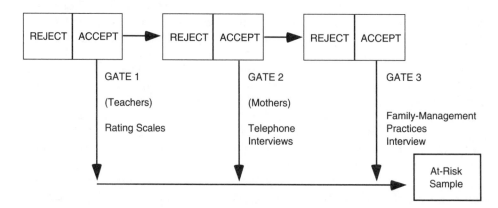

behaviors within a 24-hour period were asked. A risk score for this procedure was established, and boys scoring above the 47th percentile ($N = 30$) were moved on to the final gate. Gate 3 involved structured interviews with both the parents and target children. The content of the interviews was focused on family management procedures such as parental monitoring of child activities, parental discipline practices, and perceived disobedience of the target boys. Again a risk score for the procedure was developed, and boys whose scores were at the 47th percentile or higher ($N = 16$) were passed through this final gate. These subjects were found to have an extremely low false-positive error rate when follow-up data on involvement in delinquent activities by all subjects were pursued. The authors concluded that this study provided strong initial evidence for the use of multiple gating in classification, both from empirical and cost-effectiveness standpoints. Since the publication of the Loeber et al. (1984) study, researchers at the Oregon Social Learning Center have continued to refine the use of multiple-gating assessment in additional investigations. A revised multiple-gating model was presented by Reid et al. (1988).

The SSBD: A School-Based Multiple-Gating Procedure

Beginning the mid-1980s, attempts were made to utilize multiple gaiting in the development of reliable and cost-effective screening procedures to identify students with serious behavioral disorders in the school setting. The initial development of these procedures was based on methodology modeled after the findings of researchers at the Oregon Social Learning Center (Loeber et al., 1984; Reid et al., 1988). The rationale for the development of a school-based model was the desirability of identifying severe behavioral problems at early grade levels, thus being able to provide appropriate interventions in the incipient stages of developmental psychopathology rather than waiting until problems become extremely serious. The researchers involved in the early stages of this effort had noted that formal assessment and identification of students with severe behavioral disorders usually did not occur until the middle school years, but a review of these students' behavioral records often found strong evidence for the existence of severe problems as early as kindergarten or first grade (H. Severson, personal communication, August 18, 1992).

The result of these efforts was the development of a multiple-gating procedure that showed strong evidence of several forms of reliability and validity and was found to have high classification accuracy in screening students with severe behavioral problems (Todis, Severson, & Walker, 1990; Walker, Severson, Stiller, Williams, Haring, Shinn, & Todis, 1988; Walker, Severson, Todis, Block-Pedego, Williams, Haring, and Barckley, 1990). This multiple-gating system has since been revised and commercially published as the *Systematic Screening for Behavior Disorders* (SSBD) (Walker & Severson, 1992). The SSBD is a three-gate system that includes teacher screening (using a rank-ordering procedure) of students with internalizing and externalizing behavioral problems (gate 1), teacher ratings of critical behavioral problems (gate 2), and direct behavioral observation of students who have passed the first two processes (gate 3). The observational procedure used in gate 3 includes both academic behavior in the classroom and social behavior on the playground. The end result of the SSBD system is that students who are passed through all three gates become the focus of prereferral interventions and are potentially referred to child-study teams for formal assessment and special education classification. Figure 2.2 displays a diagram of the gates and procedures in the SSBD.

FIGURE 2.2   Diagram of the "gates" in the systematic screening for behavior disorders, a school-based multiple-gating procedure

SOURCE: Adapted from H. M. Walker and H. Severson, *Systematic Screening for Behavior Disorders* 2nd ed. (Longmont, CO: Sopris West, 1992).

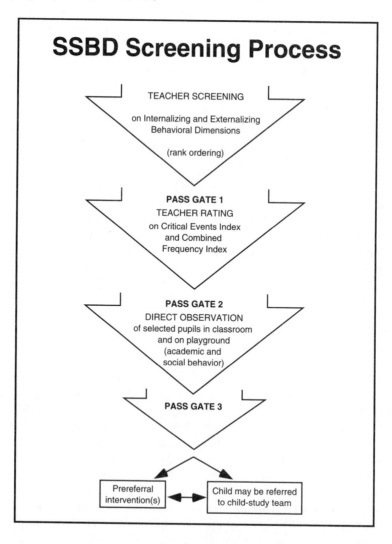

The complete SSBD package includes procedural, training, and technical manuals; normative data; recommendations for behavioral interventions; complete forms and protocols, and a videotape for training in the observational system. It is a unique and exemplary system, showing some of the best possibilities of how school-based assessment and subsequent special education classification of students with severe behavioral and emotional problems can be accomplished.

SOME CONCLUDING COMMENTS ON DIAGNOSIS AND CLASSIFICATION

Attempts have been made in this chapter to delineate suitable reasons for making diagnostic and classification decisions as part of the assessment process and to provide an overview of the three major systems of classification: the DSM, special-education service categories, and the emerging Behavioral Dimensions approach. The chapter concludes by posing the question: How do classification activities help link assessment of behavioral, social, and emotional problems to the process of intervention? While attempts have been made to impress the reader with the necessity and advantages of conducting classification activities during the assessment process, the answer to this question is not as hopeful as many would like. At the present time, the evidence supporting the *treatment validity* (usefulness in developing intervention or treatment plans) of current classification schemes is neither abundant nor compelling. While classification systems and activities may serve several appropriate purposes, taking a given classification category and automatically translating that into a set of interventions is seldom possible. Classifying human behavior is inherently more simple than changing it. Because of the wide degree of individuality and variation in the biology, behavior, and temperament that human beings exhibit, developing effective interventions for our behavioral, social, and emotional problems requires a tremendous understanding of the conditions under which those problems occur, as well as a great deal of clinical sensitivity on the part of the therapist. It will be an extraordinary challenge to the emerging generation of mental health professionals and educators to develop classification systems that not only reliably codify a wide array of problems but also provide information that will directly translate into valid treatment planning. On the other hand, the use of multiple-gating procedures shows tremendous promise in the development of systematic screening and assessment procedures which can be connected to various classification systems and subsequent programs of intervention.

APPLICATION PROBLEMS—ISSUES IN CLASSIFICATION

1. Define the term *differential diagnosis,* illustrating how it is utilized in the assessment and classification process.
2. Give examples of how *false-positive* and *false-negative* classification errors might occur in assessing behavioral, social, and emotional problems.

3. The DSM classification system has been widely criticized over the years, but it continues to be refined and is without question the preeminent classification system in the United States. List the major positive and useful aspects of the DSM which have helped expand its influence.

4. Compare and contrast the definition of *seriously emotionally disturbed* from the Individuals with Disabilities Education Act with the proposed definition of *emotional or behavioral disorder* from the National Mental Health and Special Education Coalition. What differing implications do each of these definitions have for assessing behavioral, social, and emotional problems?

5. What are the assumptions and procedures behind the *Behavioral Dimensions* approach to classification, and how do they differ from those of other classification methods?

6. Two different *multiple-gating* procedures for assessment and classification were described in this chapter. Identify the potential problems involved with instituting and utilizing a multiple-gating procedure, and determine what steps could be taken to reduce these problems.

CHAPTER **3**

Direct Behavioral Observation

Chapter Outline

Introduction

Behavioral Observation: Basic Principles and Concepts

General Methods of Behavioral Observation
   Naturalistic Observation
   Analogue Observation
   Self-Monitoring

Observational Coding Procedures
   Event Recording
   Interval Recording
   Time-Sampling Recording
   Duration and Latency Recording

A Review of Selected Observational Coding Systems
   School-Based Observation Systems
   Home-Based Observation Systems
   Clinic-Based Observation Systems

Issues in Behavioral Observation
   Defining the Observation Domain
   Observer Training and Reliability
   Use of Social Comparison Data
   The Problem of Reactivity
   Situational Specificity of Behavior
   Use of Inappropriate Recording Techniques

Direct Behavioral Observation and Decision Making

Application Problems—Selecting Appropriate Methods and Coding Procedures for Behavioral Observation

INTRODUCTION

This chapter provides a detailed introduction to the principles, specific uses, and problems of direct behavioral observation. This particular assessment technique is one of the "stock" tools of many clinicians and researchers who are involved in the assessment of behavioral, social, and emotional problems of children and adolescents, and it holds a prominent position as perhaps the most empirically sound of the direct measurement techniques.

The chapter begins with an overview of the basic principles and concepts of behavioral observation and then continues with a detailed look at both the general methods and typical coding procedures of behavioral observation. After the general foundations and methods of direct behavioral observation have been described, there is a review of six formal observational coding systems, which have been selected for inclusion based on their general-purpose design and their utility in conducting assessments in school, home, and clinic settings. An analysis of some of the major problems and issues in behavioral observation follows. Issues ranging from the problem of observer reactivity to situational specificity of behavior are covered, and specific suggestions for overcoming these problems and limitations of behavioral observation are provided. The chapter concludes with a discussion on how direct behavioral observation can be useful in making various decisions related to the assessment process.

BEHAVIORAL OBSERVATION: BASIC
PRINCIPLES AND CONCEPTS

Direct observation of behavior is a cornerstone of the assessment of behavioral, social, and emotional problems exhibited by children and adolescents. Whether the observation involves formal behavioral recording in naturalistic settings or whether it is done informally as part of other measurement strategies, behavioral observation is one of the most direct and objective assessment tools available. In direct behavioral observation, the observer(s) develop operational definitions of the targeted behaviors of interest, observe the subject(s), and record their behaviors systematically. Behavioral observation is one of the strongest nomothetic methods of assessment, and it has the advantage of being easily linked to the development of interventions.

The roots of behavioral observation are firmly grounded in behavioral psychology, as advocated by Watson, Skinner, and others. Researchers and clinicians who hold to behavioral psychology in its most radical forms contend that direct observation is the *only* empirically sound method of behavioral assessment. However since the 1970s, there have been increased efforts at integrating behaviorism and direct observation into broader models of conceptualizing human behavior. To that end, direct observation has been found very compatible with social learning theory (Patterson, 1969; Bandura, 1977, 1978), applied behavior analysis (Baer, 1982), and cognitive-behavior therapy (Meichenbaum & Cameron, 1982). Even an approach to treatment as different from behaviorism as Rogers's client-centered therapy (1951) relies on clinical observation by the therapist as an important part of understanding and treating the client, even though such observation is not as systematic as a good behaviorist would require.

Keller (1986) notes that the unifying factor of different behavioral approaches appears to be "their derivation from experimentally established procedures and principles" (p. 355). As such, most methods of behavioral observation, and specifically those methods and techniques covered in this chapter, have a strong emphasis on sound empirical methodology and a high degree of treatment validity. Alessi (1988) notes that one of the critical characteristics of observation methods for emotional and behavioral problems is that they permit a functional analysis of behavior and, as such, are intrinsically linked to valid interpretation of assessment data and development of systematic intervention plans.

GENERAL METHODS OF BEHAVIORAL OBSERVATION

Although there are a number of specific techniques and systems for use in observing behaviors, most can be included under the categories of naturalistic observation, analogue observation, and self-monitoring. This section illustrates the main characteristics and uses of each of these three general methods.

Naturalistic Observation

The most direct and desirable way to assess child and adolescent behavior in most cases is through naturalistic observation. The essential elements of naturalistic observation have been outlined by Jones, Reid, and Patterson (1979), and they include the observation and recording of behaviors at the time of occurrence in their natural setting, the use of trained objective observers, and a behavioral description system requiring only a minimal amount of inference by the observer-coders. Naturalistic observation differs from the other two general methods of observation in that a premium is put on obtaining observational data in typical day-to-day situations, with strong efforts to minimize any obtrusiveness or reactivity caused by the presence of an observer. Analogue or self-monitoring methods require more inference than naturalistic observation in determining whether or not observed behaviors are representative of what actually occurs in the subject's day-to-day environment.

What types of observational settings can be considered naturalistic? Perhaps more than any other setting, school-based assessments offer many opportunities for naturalistic observation. Whether the observation takes place in the classroom, on the playground during recess, in the cafeteria, or in the halls between classes, the school environment has great potential for unobtrusive data collection in situations encountered by children and adolescents on a regular basis. For younger children who are not yet in school, other possibilities for naturalistic observation include day care and play groups.

The home setting also offers opportunities for naturalistic observation but on a more limited basis. Observing a subject interact with his or her family in the home environment is potentially an excellent means of gathering data, but there are significant obstacles that must be overcome: the increased probability of obtrusiveness and reactivity and the physical circumstances of the home. Since most families are not used to having strangers enter their home and watch their ongoing activities, it is a given that they will behave differently under these conditions; most likely, they will make an effort to minimize the occurrence of any maladaptive or coercive behaviors by putting their "best foot forward." The design of most American houses and apartments and the lifestyles they shape also create considerable challenges for conducting observation. A typical middle-class home is sufficiently large and compartmentalized so that family members can distance themselves from one another (and from an observer) with relative ease by going into different parts of the home. Investigators at the Oregon Social Learning Center (OSLC) (e.g., Reid, Baldwin, Patterson, & Dishion, 1988) have worked extensively on the problems of conducting effective naturalistic observations in home settings and have developed methods of minimizing reactivity and physical barriers with their coding systems. A typical in-home observation by the OSLC team is structured so that family members agree to stay in a common area of the home and to do some activity together (other than watching television) during the observation period. In a sense, conducting a home observation in this manner is somewhat contrived and is akin to analogue observation, but it still allows for highly effective observation and coding of family interactions in the home setting (Patterson, Ray, Shaw, & Cobb, 1969).

Analogue Observation

Unlike naturalistic observation, which is designed to capture behavior as and where it normally occurs, analogue observation methods are designed to simulate conditions of the natural environment and to provide a highly structured and controlled setting where behaviors of concern are likely to be observed (Keller, 1986). The analogue observation might occur in a clinic or laboratory, but the specific environment developed for the observation will have been structured to simulate everyday situations in the natural environment. In many cases, the participants in analogue observation might be requested to role-play or engage in the observation activity in a specific way. Examples of situations that have been developed for analogue observation include parent-child interactions, family problem-solving approaches, and children's task orientation.

There is no question that analogue observation carries with it problems and obstacles. Compared to naturalistic observation, a greater deal of inference is required in drawing conclusions about behavior; many questions are likely to arise concerning the validity of the observational data. However analogue observation offers enough advantages that clinicians who conduct child and adolescent assessments would do well to become versed in its use. One of the chief advantages of the analogue method is that the observer can exert much greater control over the environment than with naturalistic observation, thus increasing the opportunities for eliciting important but low-frequency behaviors. For example, if one of the stated referral problems is noncompliance with teacher or parent directions, the observer can create a large number of analogue situations in which the subject must react to directions. A related advantage that the control aspect of analogue observation offers is that extraneous stimuli—those things that are inconsequential to or detract from the behavior in question—can be reduced or eliminated. Overall the analogue method offers many advantages and possibilities as long as the observer keeps its limitations in mind.

When conducting an analogue observation, it is important to structure the observational conditions so that they closely resemble those of the setting(s) in which the target problems are most likely to occur. By doing this, similarity in stimuli and responses between the two settings is maintained, and the observation is more likely to be conducive to the behavior in question. For example, if the assessment goal is to obtain observational data of interactions between a mother and child, it would be important to have them engage in activities they do at home, by having them role-play or work with materials they use at home. By carefully structuring the conditions of the analogue observation, the similarity to the natural environment can be increased, thereby enhancing the resulting validity and usefulness of the observation data.

Self-Monitoring

A third general method of observing is self-monitoring. The essential feature of self-monitoring is that the subject is trained in observing and recording his or her own behavior. The advantages of self-monitoring include its relatively low cost and efficiency, its utility in the measurement of covert or private events such as thoughts and subtle physiological changes, and its lack of intrusiveness (Keller, 1986). For example, it would be extremely difficult to conduct valid observations of mild seizures unless a subject was constantly hooked up to physiological measurement instruments, but the subject might be easily trained to record the occurrence of these events.

Of course, there are a number of drawbacks to self-monitoring, of which the reliability and validity of the self-monitored observations are major concerns (Nelson, 1977). It is difficult enough to train impartial observer-coders in the reliable use of observation technology, but when the observation is extended to include self-scrutiny by the subject (particularly with children), the implementation problems are likely to be increased. These potential reliability and validity problems can be decreased through specific procedures such as the following: (a) providing a sufficient amount of training to the subject, (b) using systematic and formal observation forms, (c) using self-monitoring procedures that require a minimum of time and energy by the subject, (d) conducting occasional reliability checks with the subject, and (e) reinforcing the subject for conducting accurate observations.

Self-monitoring tends to be used to a much greater extent in behavioral treatment programs than as part of a multimethod, multisource, multisetting assessment and, as such, is not addressed in any more detail in this book. For a more complete treatment of the use of self-monitoring procedures, consult Alberto and Troutman (1990) or the *Journal of Applied Behavior Analysis*. The former source is a textbook, which includes a number of school-based applications of self-monitoring in assessment and treatment, while the latter source is a scholarly journal, which has published a variety of articles about the many uses of self-monitoring.

OBSERVATIONAL CODING PROCEDURES

Behavioral observation data can be recorded or coded in a variety of ways. As many as six different observational coding procedures and useful combinations of procedures have been identified (Barton & Ascione, 1984), but in this chapter, the number of recording categories has been condensed into four general types of procedures.

Event Recording

Event recording is simply a measure or count of how many times specified target behavior(s) occur during the length of the observational period. Event recording is also known as *frequency recording.* Barton and Ascione (1984) suggested that this type of recording procedure is best suited for use with behaviors that meet three criteria. The first criterion is that the behaviors should have a clear beginning and end. For example, within the behavioral domains of physical aggression or asking for help, it is normally quite simple to determine starting and stopping points, but with behaviors such as making noise, this task becomes more difficult. The second criterion is that the behaviors should take approximately the same amount of time to complete every time they occur. If the observer is recording a class of behaviors that vary considerably in time from occurrence to occurrence, another recording technique, such as duration recording, should be used. Because event recording yields a simple tally of how many times the behavior(s) occurred, it is not useful for gauging aspects of behavior such as intensity or length. The third criterion is that the behavior should not occur so frequently that it becomes difficult to separate each occurrence. For example, if an observer was using event recording to measure self-stimulatory behavior (e.g., hair twirling, rocking, or lip rubbing) on the part of a child with severe disabilities, and these behaviors were occurring every few seconds, the event-recording procedure would become overly cumbersome. In such cases, the observer will have to make a decision whether the frequency of the behavior is so high that event recording will be difficult to implement.

Certain techniques can be used with event recording to maximize its usefulness as an observational recording procedure. One way the utility of event recording can be increased is to record events sequentially, that is, in the exact order in which they occur. By developing a sequential analysis of observed events, behaviors can be categorized according to antecedents and consequences, which may be helpful in fully understanding the behaviors and in developing intervention plans. A useful way of transcribing event recording into an analysis of behavioral antecedents and consequences is through the use of an A-B-C (antecedent-behavior-consequence) evaluation, which follows these steps: (*a*) Divide a sheet of paper into three columns, one each for antecedents, behaviors, and consequences; (*b*) list the specific behaviors that were recorded in the middle column (behaviors), and (*c*) note what events or behaviors preceded the recorded behaviors (antecedents) and what events or behaviors followed the recorded behaviors (consequences). Using this A-B-C procedure requires a bit more flexibility in the observation system because in some cases a targeted behavior that was recorded in the "B" column will also appear in the "A" column as an antecedent to another important behavior or event. However the payoff of using this technique comes in the form of an ecologically sensitive, observational recording system with strong implications for treatment. An example of using the A-B-C breakdown sheet with event recording is provided in Figure 3.1.

Another way that the use of event recording can be fine-tuned to yield more useful data is to report the events in different ways, depending on the length of the observation period. Barton and Ascione (1984) suggested three length-based ways of reporting data: (*a*) If each observation period is of the same length, report the actual frequency of each event; (*b*) if the observation periods differ to some extent, the data should be reported by rates of occurrence or by the number of responses divided by the time period in which the observations took place; and (*c*) behavioral events that are supposed to follow specific cues (such as compliance with directions from the teacher) should be reported as a percentage of opportunities in which the behavior occurred, as in three compliances for every five commands. Event recording in its most basic form is very easy, but by using some of these modifications, the observer will be able to make more insightful and useful observations.

Interval Recording

The essential characteristics of interval recording involve (*a*) selecting a time period for the length of the observation, (*b*) dividing the observational period into a number of equal intervals, and (*c*) recording whether or not the target behavior(s) occur during each interval. Interval recording is a good choice for observing behaviors that occur at a moderate but steady rate, but it is not as useful for behaviors that occur with relatively low frequency. Although it does not provide an exact count of behaviors, it is still a good choice for use with behaviors that occur on a very frequent basis. An example of a typical interval-based observation would be a 30-minute observation period divided into 90 equal intervals of 20 seconds each.

The use of interval recording requires the complete attention of the observer. It can be difficult to implement if the intervals are too short or the number of behaviors targeted for observation is too great. Normally the observational period will be less than one hour long, and the intervals will be no more than 30 seconds long (Cooper, 1981). The simplest form of interval recording involves using the procedure with one targeted behavior and recording a plus (+) or minus (−)

A-B-C Event-Recording Sheet		
ANTECEDENTS	BEHAVIORS	CONSEQUENCES
Teacher asks students to take out their workbooks	S does not take out workbook, talks to neighbor	Teacher reprimands S
Teacher reprimands S	S removes workbook from desk	Teacher focuses attention away from S
	S raises hand to ask question	Teacher works with another student
	S continues to raise hand to ask question	Teacher responds to S's question
Teacher responds to S's question	S puts head down on desktop	
S puts head down on desktop	S begins to tap leg against desk	Neighbor tells S to be quiet
Neighbor tells S to be quiet	S tells neighbor to shut up	Teacher warns S to get back to work
Teacher warns S to get back to work	S puts book in desk, places arms and head down on desktop	Teacher again tells S to get back to work
Teacher tells S to get back to work	S pounds hand on desk and swears at teacher	Teacher tells S to go to time-out chair
Teacher tells S to go to time-out chair	S kicks chair and goes to time-out chair	

FIGURE 3.1 An example of behavioral observation data using an event-recording procedure and the A-B-C technique

in boxes that have been drawn for each interval to indicate whether or not the target behavior occurred. If the intervals are short or if the number of behaviors targeted for observation are so numerous that it is difficult to make an accurate recording, brief recording intervals can be placed between each observation interval (Alberto & Troutman, 1990). For example, an observer might use

10-second intervals for the observation but use a 5-second scoring interval between each observation interval, thus allowing enough time to accurately record the behaviors and prepare for the next interval.

Interval recording can be divided into two general types: *whole-interval recording* and *partial-interval recording*. With whole-interval recording, the behavior being coded must be observed during the entire interval in order to be recorded. The whole-interval method is a good choice if the behaviors being coded are continuous (such as on-task behavior) and the intervals are short to medium in length (Shapiro & Skinner, 1990). With partial-interval recording, the observer codes the target behavior in question if it occurs at any time during the interval; once a specific behavior has been coded, it is no longer necessary to monitor that behavior until the next interval begins. The partial-interval method is a good choice for recording low-frequency behaviors (such as yelling), which are observed over fairly long intervals (Shapiro & Skinner, 1990). Both types of interval-recording procedures may result in error. Whole-interval recording tends to overestimate the frequency and underestimate the prevalence of behavior, while partial-interval recording tends to underestimate the frequency and overestimate the prevalence of behavior (Salvia & Hughes, 1990; Salvia & Ysseldyke, 1991). Which of these two methods of interval recording is the best? It depends on the behaviors being observed and the purposes for which the observation is being conducted.

Finally, to use interval recording effectively, special timing devices might be needed. If the observation intervals are long enough and if the number of targeted behaviors is limited, it is possible to use a digital or hand watch with second timers. However as the time intervals decrease or the number of behaviors targeted for observation increases, using a typical watch with a second timer becomes increasingly frustrating and the reliability and validity of the observation inevitably suffers as a result. Although they are difficult to find, special timing devices have been developed for interval recording. They use small battery-powered electronic timers that provide a cue (e.g., a beep or a tone) to the observer when the interval has elapsed. Some of these instruments are sophisticated enough to allow the observer to adjust the time intervals and to deliver the time cues through a small earplug, thus reducing the obtrusiveness of the observation. Obviously these types of instruments, like certain musical recordings advertised on late-night television, are not sold in any store. One must obtain them from specialized, psychological-testing equipment catalogues or have a local electronics technician specially design them.

Time-Sampling Recording

Time-sampling recording is similar to interval recording in that the observation period is divided into intervals of time. The essential difference between the two procedures is that with time sampling, behavior is observed only momentarily at the prespecified intervals. An additional difference between the two procedures is that in interval recording the observation intervals are generally divided into equal units, whereas in time sampling time intervals are divided randomly or in unequal units. As with interval recording, time sampling is most useful for observing behavior(s) that occur at a moderate but steady rate.

Time-sampling recording can be illustrated by using assessment of on-task academic behavior as an example. The observation might occur during a 20-minute period of academic instruction, which has been divided into 20 intervals of 1 minute each. As each minute ends, the observer records whether or not the subject was on task. In this example, the time units were divided into equal intervals, but these intervals do not need to be equal and could be generated randomly. If the time intervals used in time sampling are short or complex, the type of electronic timing devices mentioned in the preceding discussion of interval recording would be useful. Some innovative researchers and clinicians have even developed electronic timing devices that randomly generate audible tones at varying time intervals within a given range.

A major advantage of time-sampling recording is that it requires only one observation per interval and thus is less subject to the problems of getting "off track," which easily happens with interval recording. If the intervals are large enough, the time-sampling method may even free up the observer to engage in other activities. For example, a teacher could still direct an instructional activity while conducting an observation using time sampling, as along as the intervals are long enough and the recording simple. Interestingly the major advantage of time sampling is closely related to its largest drawback. Because time sampling only allows for the recording of behavior that occurs occasionally, an observer may end up not recording many important behaviors, and invalid conclusions may be reached. The longer the interval used with time sampling, the less accurate the data; as the interval increases, the sample of behavior decreases. Reaching an appropriate balance between the length of the interval needed and the necessity of freeing up the observer for other activities is the most reasonable way to use time sampling.

Duration and Latency Recording

Event recording, interval recording, and time-sampling recording all focus on obtaining exact or approximate counts of targeted behaviors that occur during a given time frame. Two additional techniques, duration and latency recording, differ from the first three in that their focus is primarily on the temporal aspects of the targeted behaviors rather than on how often the behaviors occur. Duration and latency recording are best used with behaviors that have a discrete beginning and end and that last for at least a few seconds each time they occur (Barton & Ascione, 1984).

In duration recording, the observer attempts to gauge the amount of time that a subject engages in a specific behavior. In other words, the most critical aspect of the observation is *how long the behavior lasts*. For school-based assessment, a good example of how duration recording might be used is the observation of out-of-seat behavior. If a student leaves the workspace during an instructional activity to wander around the classroom, it may be useful to understand how long the out-of-seat behavior lasts. There is a big difference between a student who gets out of his or her seat 3 times during a 30-minute observation but who is still academically engaged for most of the period and a student whose out-of-seat behavior occurs only once during the observation but who stays out-of-seat for most of the period. For clinic-based assessment, a good example of the use of duration recording is the observation of child temper tantrums. The parent of a six-year-old who engages in temper tantrums two to three times per week and whose tantrums last for 20 minutes or longer can provide the clinician with valuable information by measuring the length of the tantrums. A treatment that reduces the average number of tantrums from three per week to two per week might be less valuable than a treatment that does not change the average number of tantrums but reduces their duration to five minutes each.

In latency recording, the observer attempts to gauge the amount of time from the end of one behavior event to the beginning of the next. In other words, the most critical aspect of the observation is *how long it takes for the behavior to begin*. A typical example of how latency recording can be used is in the observation of a child referred for noncompliant behavior. In this case, it might be important to observe how long it takes from the parent or teacher request for action to the enactment of the behavior. Treatment progress could be gauged by seeing a consistent decrease in the amount of time between the request and the compliance.

A REVIEW OF SELECTED
OBSERVATIONAL CODING SYSTEMS

This section provides introductions and reviews of six different observational coding systems, which are relatively general in orientation. Observational coding systems useful for highly specific purposes, such as the measurement of hyperactivity or social withdrawal, will be reviewed in chapters 8–11 of this book. The six observational coding systems described here, which are summarized in Table 3.1, are divided into three types—school-based, home-based, and clinic-based—and have two representative coding systems selected for each category. With the exception of the Child Behavior Checklist-Direct Observation Form (Achenbach, 1986), these observation coding systems are not commercially published products. Most of these coding systems were reported in professional journals as one part of the research methodology employed in a study. Thus to obtain complete information on most of these observational systems, the reference cited with them must be located.

School-Based Observation Systems

Child Behavior Checklist-Direct Observation Form. The Direct Observation Form (DOF) was developed by Achenbach (1986) and his colleagues as the observational component of the multiaxial Child Behavior Checklist system for assessing child psychopathology. It was developed specifically for use in classrooms and in other group activities. The DOF, unlike most other observational coding systems, is at least partially based on rating-scale technology, as it includes 96 items rated on a 4-point scale following a 10-minute observation period. The rating-scale items are completed based only on what was observed during the observation period and not on a rater's general knowledge of a subject. In addition to the rating format, the DOF merges the use of event recording and time-sampling recording. The event-recording aspect of the DOF is included by having the observer write a narrative description of the child's behavior as it occurs during the observation period. The time-sampling aspect of the DOF is included by having the observer record whether or not the subject was on task at the end of each 1-minute interval.

Another characteristic of the DOF, which sets it apart from most other observational coding systems, is that it is a norm-referenced instrument—that is, a norm group of 287 children aged 5–14 is the basis for comparing individual observation scores. The norm group data was also used to develop a factor structure for the 96 rating items on the DOF, which, in addition to a total problems score, includes *internalizing* and *externalizing* scores consistent with the other measures in the CBCL system. Six additional narrow-band factor scores are also available through the use of an optional computer-scored profile.

The DOF, like the other components of the CBCL system, is a thoroughly researched instrument representing an empirically sound approach to assessment of behavior problems. It is easy to use and requires only a modest amount of training. The recommended observation and scoring procedure for the DOF allows for the obtaining of social comparison data with two observed control children on the checklist and on-task ratings. The psychometric properties of the DOF are good to excellent, with very acceptable levels of inter-rater reliability and discriminant validity (McConaughy, Achenbach, & Gent, 1988). The DOF is a good choice for group-based observations in which rather serious behavioral or emotional problems are likely to be observed in short time periods. However it is not particularly useful for observing children or adolescents in individual or solitary situations, nor is it a good choice for assessing low-frequency behaviors unlikely to occur within a 10-minute period.

Behavior Coding System.   Developed by Harris and Reid (1981), the Behavior Coding System (BCS) was designed to measure patterns of coercive behavior and aggression in classroom and playground settings. The BCS uses an interval-recording system with eight behavioral categories. The coding system of the BCS is easy enough so that paraprofessionals or trained undergraduate students can be effective observers. The reported psychometric properties of the BCS are quite good, with interobserver agreement at 93 percent in classroom settings and 86 percent in playground settings. Harris and Reid (1981) also reported satisfactory consistency in behavioral categories across different settings. The BCS was designed not only to provide a general observational measure of aggressive and coercive behaviors but also to provide data on the stability of these behaviors across different settings. As such, the BCS might be effective in determining whether aggressive behavior problems are setting-specific or whether they appear to generalize across settings.

Home-Based Observation Systems

Social Interaction Coding System.   Designed to assess family interaction behaviors along different dimensions and on general classifications, the Social Interaction Coding System (SICS) (Weinrott & Jones, 1984) provides an interesting and useful format for conducting home-based observations. The SICS uses a continuous-event recording procedure wherein 12 different behavioral categories are targeted. The methodology employed in field testing the SICS was somewhat unusual; the reliability of the coding system was studied using both *covert* and *overt* observation techniques. In both cases, the reliability of the SICS proved adequate to good, although it was somewhat higher for overt observations (.91) than for covert observations (.73).

Family Interaction Code.   Another observational recording system developed by Weinrott and Jones (1984) for home-based observation, and discussed in the same research report as the SICS, is the Family Interaction Code (FIC). Although the FIC was field-tested along the same dimensions as the SICS (overt vs. covert observations), its focus is somewhat different and its design and use varies considerably. The FIC uses a 6-second interval-recording system in which 29 different behavioral categories are targeted. As such, the complexity and difficulty of the FIC is great, and it should be used only by experienced, trained observers. The general area measured through the FIC is family interactions with a specific focus on aversive family behaviors. Like the SICS, the reliability level was somewhat higher on the FIC for overt (.87) rather than covert (.69) observations.

Clinic-Based Observation Systems

Child's Game/Parent's Game.   An innovative coding procedure useful for observing parent-child interactions in clinic settings is the system developed by Forehand and his colleagues (Forehand & McMahon, 1981; Forehand, Peed, Roberts, McMahon, Griest, & Humphreys, 1978). This coding system has not been formally named, but it is referred to herein as the Child's Game/Parent's Game due to the focus of tasks. The setting recommended for use of this observational coding system is a sound-wired clinic playroom that has a supply of toys and is equipped with a one-way window, allowing an observer to code parent-child interactions from an adjoining room. Alternatively, interactions could be videotaped and coded at a later time. Parent-child pairs are observed in two different situations of 5 or 10 minutes each. The first situation is referred to as the Child's Game, an unstructured or free-play setting where the child chooses the activity and rules. The second situation is the Parent's Game, in which the parent is instructed to choose an activity and rules. Therefore, the Parent's Game produces a situation in which the parent delivers commands to the child.

For both games, parent and child behaviors are coded using frequency counts at 30-second intervals. The only exception is inappropriate behavior, which is coded as occurring or not occurring during each interval. Six parent behavioral domains are coded, including rewards, attends, questions, commands, warnings, and time out. Three child behavioral domains are coded, including compliance, noncompliance, and inappropriate behavior. These codes are later summarized into rate per minute of various parent behaviors and percentages of child behaviors to various parent commands. An additional summary statistic includes the percentage of parental attention contingent on child compliance.

Several studies have demonstrated the Child's Game/Parent's Game coding system to have adequate technical properties, including an average interobserver agreement rate of 75 percent (Forehand & Peed, 1979), strong stability over time (Peed, Roberts, & Forehand, 1977), sensitivity to treatment effects (McMahon & Forehand, 1984), and discriminant validity for differentiation of clinic-referred and nonreferred children (Griest, Forehand, Wells, & McMahon, 1980). In sum, this clinic-based observational coding system is relatively easy to implement, requires a small amount of parent and child time, is unobtrusive, and appears to be a reliable and valid method of conducting behavioral assessment.

Teacher Behavior Code.   Unlike other observation systems reviewed in this chapter, the focus of the Teacher Behavior Code (TBC) is on the parent or caregiver rather than the child (Weitz, 1981). Specifically, the TBC was designed for assessing the amount of change in "teaching behavior" by parents who have participated in a parent-training program. Though developed specifically for use with parents of developmentally disabled children, there is no reason why the TBC cannot be used with parents of children with different types of problems. The TBC was selected for review in this chapter for a pragmatic reason; in clinical treatment of children with behavioral, social, or emotional problem, the parent is often the mediator or the initial target of treatment. As such, it is important

TABLE 3.1   Characteristics of selected general-purpose observational coding systems

Code Name	Setting	Measures	Uses
Child Behavior Checklist-Direct Observation Form	School	96-item rating scale, event recording, interval recording	Internalizing and externalizing behavior problems and on-task behavior
Behavior Coding System	School	8 categories, interval recording	Coercive and aggressive behavior
Social Interaction Scoring System	Home	12 categories, continuous event recording	General social-behavioral problems
Family Interaction Code	Home	29 categories, interval recording	Aversive family behavior
Child's Game/ Parent's Game	Clinic	7 parent behavior and 3 child behavior categories, coded in 30-second intervals	Child noncompliance, behavior problems during interactions with parent
Teacher Behavior Code	Clinic/Home	9 categories, interval-based "teaching trials"	Change in parent teaching behavior following training

to have a measurement technique that will assess parent responsiveness to consultation or parent training rather than focusing only on the resulting child behavior.

The TBC can be used in home as well as in clinic settings, and it includes nine targeted behavioral categories that are recorded using an interval measurement system during "teaching trials." The TBC can be used by trained graduate students, and perhaps even by trained paraprofessionals, as well as by experienced observers. The reported technical properties of the TBC are adequate to good, with an average interobserver agreement of 87 percent, and a range across categories from 69 percent to 98 percent. The TBC is a unique observation system worthy of consideration by clinicians and researchers who provide consultation or training to parents and who desire a formal system for assessing the level of change in parent behaviors.

ISSUES IN BEHAVIORAL OBSERVATION

Despite the strong empirical support and practical utility of using behavioral observation as a primary means of assessment, there are a number of potential limitations, problems, and cautions that should be kept in mind. Cone (1981) noted that the state of behavioral assessment methodology is still relatively primitive, and even the strongest proponents of observational assessment concede that the accuracy, validity, and reliability of behavioral observation data are often not adequately established (Merrell, 1989a). This concluding section addresses some of the potentially problematic issues surrounding the use of behavioral observation.

Defining the Observation Domain

One of the first tasks in developing an observational coding system or in using an existing system is defining what types of behaviors are important in the observation and then developing appropriate operational definitions for those behaviors. In defining behaviors to observe, the domain of behavior can be viewed as a continuum with broadly defined behaviors on one end and narrowly defined behaviors on the other end. Although defining each behavioral domain in a highly narrow manner may seem to make empirical sense, it may be impractical when actually conducting the observation. For example, if aggressive behavior is of particular importance in an observational assessment and the general category of aggressiveness is broken down into 15 different subcategories of behavior, the observational coding system will probably be cumbersome and of little use for all but the most esoteric scientific purposes.

On the other hand, defining a behavioral domain too broadly might increase the ease of coding for the observer but will tend to reduce the validity and reliability of the observational system (Epps, 1985). Using the general category of aggressive behavior, it is easy to see how two behaviors that are qualitatively different might be coded in the same way if the domain of aggressiveness is defined too broadly. Both arguing with and physically attacking another person are generally considered forms of aggression, but for most purposes, coding them as the same will not be particularly helpful, either for the assessment or for intervention planning.

In order to reduce the potential problems associated with defining the behavioral domain to be observed, care should be taken to ensure that the observational coding categories are defined neither too broadly nor too narrowly. The scope of the behavioral definition should be linked to the specific purposes of the observation, and treatment implications should be considered in creating the definitions if the purpose of the assessment is to evaluate a problem and develop an appropriate intervention. If the observational domain must be defined broadly, then the validity of the assessment can be increased by employing multiple measures. The use of multiple measures allows for the measurement of a broad range of behaviors while avoiding the practice of equating behaviors that are related but still qualitatively different (Kent & Foster, 1977).

Observer Training and Reliability

One of the universes of generalization in behavioral assessment referred to in Cone's Behavioral Assessment Grid (1978) is referred to as *scorer generalization.* What this term indicates is that behavioral assessment data may vary due to differences among persons who score or code the data. Therefore once the observational system has been developed or selected, it is imperative that those individuals who actually will be conducting the observations are properly trained. Failure to properly train observers in the use of specific coding systems and procedures will result in behavioral assessment data of questionable reliability and validity.

Once the observers are properly trained in the reliable use of an observational coding system, there is still potential for scorer generalization problems. It has been shown that over time observers tend to depart gradually from their original definitions when scoring or coding particular behaviors (Kent, O'Leary, Diament, & Deitz, 1974), a phenomenon referred to as *observer drift.* As with observers who are poorly trained, a substantial amount of observer drift will produce observational data of questionable utility. In order to reduce the tendency of different observers to drift from original definitions of behavior, retraining or reliability checks of observers can be conducted from time to time (Kazdin, 1981; Reid, 1982). Common procedures used in observer retraining include (*a*) periodic group meetings, (*b*) conducting observations on actual sets of events (using "live" or videotaped situations), (*c*) calculating the rate of interobserver agreement (agreements divided by agreements plus disagreements), (*d*) discussing points of disagreement and coming to common decision rules, and (*e*) practicing until an acceptable criterion of reliability is reached. A simple procedure for calculating interobserver agreement, expressed as a formula, is this:

$$\frac{\text{number of agreements}}{\text{number of agreements} + \text{number of disagreements}}$$

Although the problem of observer drift can be dealt with through the five steps noted, these are seldom possible for practitioners who work independently or without supervision. Clinicians who employ direct observation procedures under more solitary conditions can overcome this disadvantage in several ways. Enlisting the assistance of a colleague to act as a reliability check is one possibility. Other possibilities include doing an occasional self-check on observational reliability by videotaping observational situations and striving to keep aware of new information pertinent to the observational techniques being used.

Use of Social Comparison Data

During the observational process, the target of the assessment is generally a specific child or adolescent who has been referred for a variety of problems. So naturally, the observation should focus on that particular individual. However, if the observation does not also include the use of *social comparison data,* the results might lead to inappropriate conclusions about the nature and severity of the problems, and the validity of the observation might therefore be jeopardized. The use of social comparison data is important to determine whether the problem behaviors exhibited by a particular subject deviate significantly from those of peers in similar situations (Epps, 1985). In practice, obtaining social comparison data can be a relatively simple part of the observation. The observer might randomly pick two or three nonreferred subjects in the same setting and alternate the observation between the referred subject and the social comparison subjects on a rotating basis. The social comparison data obtained from rotating the alternate observation intervals may be considered to represent the behavior of a "typical" peer in a situation similar to that of the target subject.

Alessi and Kaye (1983) have suggested that obtaining observational social comparison data from the referred person's peer group may serve as a basis for identifying individuals whose behavioral problems are severe enough to warrant intervention. An important factor to keep in mind in obtaining social comparison data is the type of setting in which the behavior was observed. For example, if the assessment was conducted in a school setting in which the referred student was placed in both regular education and special-education classroom settings, it would be important to obtain social comparison data in both settings, as the behavioral norms in the two settings might vary considerably (Walker, 1983). Reaching an inappropriate conclusion on the basis of observational data without social comparison information can threaten the overall validity of the observational system.

The Problem of Reactivity

Anyone with experience in observing child and adolescent behavior in naturalistic settings can attest to the fact that the observer's presence can easily influence the behavior of the subjects, a problem referred to as *observer reactivity.* With uncanny perceptiveness, children seem to understand and react to the presence of a "stranger" in the observational setting, sometimes with amusing results. In my own experience conducting behavioral observations in classroom settings, the target subject on several occasions has walked directly over to me and said something to the effect of "you're hear to watch me, aren't you?" Other examples of children being aware of the presence of an observer are more subtle but equally illustrative of the reactivity problem. For example, it is not uncommon for a particular child who is not the target of the observation to spend a good deal of time during the observational period staring at the observer, asking questions like "what are you doing here?" and even showing off or trying to impress the observer. These examples all serve to illustrate the fact that obtrusiveness by the observer can cause a change in subject performance due simply to the presence of a new person in the environment (Kazdin, 1981).

In situations where there is a high degree of observer obtrusiveness, it is unwise to interpret the observational data without taking into account the possible reactivity effects. In cases where the presence of the observer has created significant reactivity, the data should be used with extreme caution, and attempts should be made to gather more valid observational data if possible. As with other threats to observational validity, the use of data obtained under conditions of significant observer reactivity may result in reaching unwarranted conclusions.

Fortunately a number of steps can be taken to reduce the potential effects of observer reactivity. One is to select observational settings where the presence of the observer does not create an unusual circumstance. For example, observations in playground settings can be done in such a way that the targeted subject(s) may not even be aware of the presence of the observer, while observations in the home setting are very likely to result in significant reactivity. In other words, the more private the observation setting the more likely observer reactivity will become a factor. In classroom observation situations, where the observation is usually considered to be naturalistic in character, the fact that subjects are being observed doing routine tasks is by itself a factor in reducing reactivity. Other common-sense measures employed to reduce the potential reactivity in classroom observations include these: (*a*) entering the classroom at the end of a recess or other activity period rather than during instructional time, (*b*) conducting the observation from an inconspicuous location such as the back of the room, (*c*) avoiding any unnecessary use of observational equipment that might attract the attention of the students, and (*d*) observing informally for a short period of time in order for students to adjust to the observer's presence before the formal observation is conducted (Merrell, 1989a).

Situational Specificity of Behavior

The concept of *situational specificity of behavior* is central to assessment from the behavioral perspective, and it has certain implications for conducting behavioral observations. Kazdin (1979, 1981, 1982) has written extensively on this topic and regards the essence of situational specificity as responses by subjects in a particular setting that may or may not reflect their performance in other settings; the ecological differences and stimulus control between settings may create very specific conditions for behavior. For example, a student might behave somewhat differently in two different classrooms. The classroom rules, teacher expectations and management style, composition of the students, and physical circumstances in the two classrooms may vary considerably, thus creating differences in the overall ecology of the classrooms that will elicit, shape, and maintain behaviors in a different manner.

The idea of situational specificity of behavior has been supported by findings from several research projects. Wahler (1975) found that child behavior tends to "cluster" between school and home settings. Even when deviant or antisocial behaviors are present in both the school and home setting, the specific types of deviant behavior tend to differ. Stokes, Baer, and Jackson (1974) found that subject responses tended to be specific to the presence of individual experimenters and observers. The important point to be drawn from both these studies is that changes in setting have been found to lead to different behavior patterns, indicating that generalization of behavior needs to be programmed into assessment and intervention strategies (Baer, Wolf, & Risley, 1968).

The problems of situational specificity occur during behavioral observation assessment under two conditions: (*a*) when generalized inferences are drawn based upon behaviors observed in specific settings, and (*b*) when the observer selects a setting for the observation that is inappropriate and does not adequately represent the behavioral tendencies found in other settings. Both of these problems can be minimized when observations occur in multiple settings and when caution is used in making behavioral inferences based upon observations in only one setting.

Use of Inappropriate Recording Techniques

Earlier in this chapter, four general observational coding procedures were discussed, namely event, interval, time-sampling, and duration or latency recording. Some authors (e.g., Barton & Ascione, 1984) have suggested that there are as many as six different categories of recording techniques. Whether or not one condenses or expands the categories of recording procedures, observational data can be recorded using at least four, and possibly more, procedures.

In addition to looking at specific recording procedures, behaviors can be categorized according to the dimensions under which they occur. These tend to correlate with specific recording techniques of choice. Alberto and Troutman (1990) identified six specific dimensions under which behaviors may occur, including these: (*a*) rate, (*b*) duration, (*c*) latency, (*d*) topography, (*e*) force, and (*f*) locus. The various dimensions under which behavior occurs may be expressed differently from these six categories, but the overall concept is still the same— behaviors occur under several dimensions. There is also a general similarity between systems for recording behavior and systems for explaining behavior, which leads to the conclusion that a specific category of behavior is probably best chronicled through the use of a related recording system.

A potential threat to the validity of an observation may occur when the observer chooses a system for recording the behavior not parallel with or appropriate to the behavior. For example, low-frequency but important behavioral occurrences are normally best recorded using event-recording techniques. Use

TABLE 3.2 Some potential threats to the validity of behavioral observations

Problem	Potential Consequences	Possible Solutions
Poorly Defined Observational Domains	Observational recording system is either too cumbersome or too vague	Carefully define and select behaviors to be observed based on assessment problems and intervention goals
Unreliability of Observers	Observers drift from original definitions; inter-rater reliability decreases	Provide high-quality initial training; conduct periodic reliability checks and retraining
Lack of Social Comparison Data	Interpretations of behavior are not based on a normative perspective; deviancy may be under- or overestimated	Include typical or randomly selected subjects in the same setting for behavioral comparison
Observer Reactivity	Subject behavior is influenced by the presence of the observer	Select and participate in observational settings in a discrete, unobtrusive manner
Situational Specificity of Behavior	Interpretations of observational data may not represent the larger picture	Conduct observations in multiple settings; don't overgeneralize from limited data
Inappropriate Recording Techniques	Behaviors are not adequately depicted; inappropriate conclusions are reached	Select recording systems carefully to match the behavioral domain

of interval or time-sampling techniques would probably result in these behaviors not even being recorded. The dimension under which the behavior occurs and the recording system must mesh to a reasonable degree, or inappropriate conclusions may be reached.

In sum, while there are several potential threats to the reliability and validity of systems for observing behavior directly, there are also a number of potential solutions. See Table 3.2. Becoming aware of what problems may be encountered as part of direct behavioral observation and then taking the appropriate preventative steps will greatly enhance the usefulness of the obtained behavioral assessment data.

DIRECT BEHAVIORAL OBSERVATION AND DECISION MAKING

The most important and powerful contribution that direct behavioral observation assessment methods can make to decision-making processes is in the arena of intervention and treatment-planning decisions. Behavioral observation has the capability of being the most direct and objective of any assessment method since fewer inferences and intervening steps are potentially needed in translating the observational data to intervention planning. Given that observational data may not only pinpoint specific problem behaviors but gauge the antecedent stimuli and controlling consequences of these behaviors, this assessment method can provide a great deal of information relevant to modifying the environment for the purpose of behavioral change.

In terms of screening and assessment decisions, direct behavioral observation is potentially useful but may be too costly (in terms of professional time) to implement effectively on a large scale. For example, observational data obtained during the course of a formal assessment may suggest that further types of assessment are warranted, but using direct observation during the initial stages of a large-scale screening typically would be unmanageable.

In making diagnosis or classification decisions, behavioral observations may provide extremely useful information, but they will probably be insufficient alone. Two problems are likely to emerge if observational data are used exclusively in making diagnostic decisions: (*a*) Child behavior tends to be variable across situations and time, possibly creating an incomplete observational picture of child behavior; (*b*) direct behavioral observation, to be used most effectively in making diagnostic decisions, needs to occur in several settings and over several time periods, possibly making it an expensive and difficult proposition.

For making placement decisions with children and adolescents, observational data are often necessary. In implementing the Individuals with Disabilities Education Act (IDEA), several states have required that direct behavioral observations be conducted prior to placing a student in a more restrictive educational setting. For making placement decisions involving psychiatric hospitalization or residential treatment, few (if any) credible institutions would consent to such placement without a staff member or associate first obtaining a direct assessment of the referred child's behavior through observation.

APPLICATION PROBLEMS—SELECTING APPROPRIATE METHODS AND CODING PROCEDURES FOR BEHAVIORAL OBSERVATION

Different types of problems often require different observational methods and coding procedures. For each behavioral scenario, do the following:

A. Select and specify one setting that would be appropriate for conducting a 20-minute observation.
B. Select what you consider the most appropriate observation method (naturalistic, analogue, or self-monitoring observation).
C. Select what you consider the most appropriate coding procedure (event, interval, time sampling, duration or latency recording).
D. Provide a rationale or justification for the methods and procedures you select.
E. List which behavior(s) you would specifically target for observation.

Scenarios

1. Observation of a primary-grade student referred because of frequent off-task behavior, difficult "staying put," and problems completing academic work.

2. Observation of a four-year-old child referred because of severe social withdrawal, significant interpersonal communication problems, and stereotypic self-stimulating behavior (rocking, twirling, and hand-flapping). The child attends a developmental preschool three hours per day.

3. Observation of an adolescent client referred because of self-reported depression. This client has made two suicide gestures or attempts in the past six months (cutting wrists, eating a bottle of aspirin).

4. Observation of a ninth-grade student referred due to severe acting-out and aggressive behavior at school, including attacking other students and throwing chairs or other objects. These types of behaviors are reported to occur an average of three to five times per week.

5. Observation of a fifth-grade student referred due to peer relationship problems, including teasing his/her classmates, difficulty making friends, and being rejected by other students.

Behavior Rating Scales

INTRODUCTION

During the past two decades, there has been an increasing amount of interest in using rating scales as a method of assessing behavioral, social, and emotional problems of children and youth. School and clinical psychologists frequently employ behavior rating scales either as a primary component of an assessment battery or as a key means of obtaining information on the child or adolescent client prior to the onset of treatment. At the same time that behavior rating scales have become more widely used, there have been numerous advances in research on rating-scale technology that have strengthened the desirability of using this form of assessment.

The purpose of this chapter is to acquaint the reader with the technology and use of ratings scales as a method for assessing behavioral, social, and emotional problems of children and adolescents. First a brief discussion on the nature and characteristics of rating scales is presented. Next sections on advantages and problems of rating scales and some of the measurement and technical issues involved in rating-scale technology will provide a broader understanding of some important measurement issues with this method. Following the foundation-laying first part of the chapter, overviews of three different general-purpose, problem-behavior rating scales are provided. Some "best practices" in using rating scales are then discussed, and the chapter ends with a discussion of the use of behavior ratings in making various decisions related to the assessment process.

CHARACTERISTICS AND NATURE OF BEHAVIOR RATING SCALES

Definitions and Foundations

Behavior rating scales provide a standardized format for the development of summative judgements about a child or adolescent's behavioral characteristics, supplied by an informant who knows the subject well. The informant is usually a parent or teacher, but other individuals who are familiar with the child or adolescent may also be a legitimate source for behavior rating-scale data as well. Examples of other persons with whom behavior rating scales could be used include work supervisors, classroom aides, temporary surrogate parents, and other persons giving direct care.

As an assessment methodology, behavior rating scales are less direct than either direct observation or structured behavioral interviewing (McMahon, 1984) in that they measure *perceptions* of specified behaviors rather than provide a firsthand measure of the existence of the behavior. However rating scales are an objective method, and they yield more reliable data than either unstructured clinical interviewing or projective techniques (Martin, Hooper, & Snow, 1986). As behavior rating scales became more widely used during the 1970s, they were typically viewed with suspicion and used as a "last resort" by behaviorally oriented clinicians (Cone & Hawkins, 1977), but as the research base and technological refinements of rating scales have become more advanced, there appears to be a broader acceptance of their use.

At this point, it is useful to differentiate the term *rating scale* from a relate term, *checklist*. A checklist format for identifying behavioral problems lists a number of behavioral descriptors, any or all of which the rater checks off when perceived in the subject. After the checklist is complete, the number of checked items can be summed. Hence checklists are considered to be *additive* in nature. Rating scales, on the other hand, not only allow the rater to indicate whether a specific symptom is present or absent but also provide a means of estimating *to what degree* the symptom is present. A common three-point rating system (and there are many variations of this) allows the rater to score a specific behavior descriptor from 0 to 2, with 0 indicating the symptom is "never" present, 1 indicating the symptom is "sometimes" present, and 2 indicating the symptom is "frequently" present. Because rating scales allow the rater to weight the specified symptoms differentially and each weighting corresponds with a specific numerical value and frequency or intensity description, rating scales are said to be *algebraic* in nature. Conners and Werry (1979) define rating scales as an ". . . algebraic summation, over variable periods of time and numbers of social situations, of many discrete observations . . . " (p. 341). In general, the algebraic format provided by rating scales is preferred to the additive format provided by checklists because the former allows for more precise measurement of behavioral frequency or intensity (Merrell, 1992). The difference between the additive nature of a checklist format and the algebraic character of a rating-scale format is illustrated by the sample items in Table 4.1.

Advantages of Using Behavior Rating Scales

The widespread popularity of behavior rating scales is not incidental for they offer many advantages to clinicians and researchers conducting assessments. The main advantages of behavior rating scales are summarized in the following six points:

1. When compared with direct behavioral observation, behavior rating scales are less expensive in terms of professional time and the amount of training required to utilize the assessment system (Merrell, 1992).

TABLE 4.1 An example of differences between checklist and rating-scale format and scoring

Behavioral Descriptor	Checklist Format		Rating-Scale Format		
1. Is noticeably sad or depressed	Y	N	0	1	2
2. Feels hopeless about his or her problems	Y	N	0	1	2
3. Wants to be left alone	Y	N	0	1	2
4. Has had a change in eating or sleeping habits	Y	N	0	1	2
5. Is irritable or disagreeable	Y	N	0	1	2
Total Values					

Key
Y = symptom is present
N = symptom is not present
0 = never occurs
1 = sometimes or to some degree occurs
2 = frequently or to a great degree occurs

2. Behavior rating scales are capable of providing data on low frequency but important behaviors that may not be seen in a limited number of direct observation sessions (Sattler, 1988). An example that illustrates this point is violent and assaultive behavior. In most cases, these types of behavior do not occur on a constant or consistent schedule, so they might be missed within the constraints of conducting two brief observations. Nonetheless it is extremely important to know about them.

3. As mentioned earlier in this chapter, behavior rating scales are an objective assessment method that provide more reliable data than unstructured interviews or projective techniques (Martin, Hooper, & Snow, 1986).

4. Behavior rating scales can be used to assess subjects who cannot readily provide information about themselves (Merrell, 1992). For example, consider the difficulty in obtaining valid assessment data on an adolescent who is in a lock-up unit in a psychiatric hospital or juvenile detention center and is unavailable or unwilling to be assessed through interviews and self-reports.

5. Rating scales capitalize on observations over a period of time in a child or adolescent's "natural" environment, that is, school or home settings (McMahon, 1984).

6. Rating scales capitalize on the judgments and observations of persons who are highly familiar with the child or adolescent's behavior, such as parents or teachers, and are thus considered to be "expert" informants (Martin, Hooper, & Snow, 1986).

Considering these advantages, it is easy to see why rating scales are widely used—they get at the "big picture" of the assessment problem in a short time, at moderate cost, and with a good deal of face and clinical validity.

Problems Associated with Using Behavior Rating Scales

Despite the salient advantages offered by rating scales, there are some disadvantages, as you might suspect. The most sophisticated rating scales available can help provide objective, reliable, and socially valid information on both broad and narrow dimensions of behavioral, social, and emotional problems, but the nature of rating-scale technology contains several potential flaws, which are important to understand. Before discussing problems associated with behavior rating scales, it is useful to remember that by their nature (i.e., they assess *perceptions* of problems), rating scales provide *idiographic* rather than *nomothetic* information. In other words, they provide a general idea, portrait, or conception of behavior but do not provide actual observational data.

Martin, Hooper, and Snow (1986) categorized the measurement problems of behavior rating scales in two classes: *bias of response* and *error variance*. Bias of response refers to the way informants completing the rating scales may create additional error by the way they use the scales. There are three specific types of response bias, including (*a*) *halo effects*—rating a subject in a positive manner because he or she possesses some other positive characteristic not pertinent to the rated item, (*b*) *leniency or severity*—the tendency of some raters to have an overly generous or overly critical response set when rating all subjects, and (*c*) *central tendency effects*—the proclivity of raters to select midpoint ratings and avoid end points of the scale such as "never" or "always."

Error variance is closely related to and often overlaps with response bias as a form of rating-scale measurement problem, but error variance provides a more general representation of the problems encountered with rating-scale assessment. According to Martin, Hooper, and Snow (1986), there are four different types of variance that may create error in the obtained results of a rating-scale assessment. These are outlined in Table 4.2 and are overviewed as follows. *Source variance* refers to the subjectivity of the rater and any of the idiosyncratic ways that he or she completes the rating scale. *Setting variance* occurs as a result of the situational specificity of behavior (Kazdin, 1979) in that humans tend to behave differently in different environments due to the varying eliciting and reinforcing properties present. *Temporal variance* refers to the tendency of behavior ratings to be only moderately consistent over time. This variance is partly due to changes in the observed behavior over time and also to changes in the rater's approach to the rating task over time. Finally, *instrument variance* means that different rating scales measure often related, but slightly differing, hypothetical constructs (e.g., aggressive behavior vs. delinquent behavior), and as a result, a severe problem-behavior score on one scale may be compared with only a moderate problem-behavior score on a different rating scale for the same person. Another problem of instrument variance arises because each rating scale utilizes different normative populations for scoring comparisons, and if the norm populations are not randomly selected and representative of the population as a whole, similar scores on two different rating scales may not mean the same thing.

While there are several types of problems inherent in using behavior rating scales, there are also effective ways of minimizing those problems. Notwithstanding the argument (considered in chapter 1) that in some cases it may actually

TABLE 4.2   Types of error variance found with behavior rating scales

Type of Error Variance	Examples
Source Variance	Various types of *response bias;* different raters may have different ways of responding to the rating format
Setting Variance	Related to *situational specificity* of behavior; eliciting and reinforcing variables present in one environment (e.g., classroom 1) may not be present in a closely related environment (e.g., classroom 2)
Temporal Variance	Behavior is likely to change over time, and an informant's approach to the rating-scale task may also change over time
Instrument Variance	Different rating scales may be measuring different hypothetical constructs; there is a range of continuity (from close to disparate) between constructs measured by different scales

increase error variance, the *aggregation principle* is particularly important in utilizing behavior rating scales, and we will consider this principle again in some detail in the "best practices" section of this chapter.

Measurement and Technical Issues

We have thus far reviewed some of the uses, advantages, and disadvantages of using behavior rating scales. This section will provide a brief overview of some of the measurement and technical issues affecting the psychometric properties of rating scales. One of the measurement characteristics of rating scales that can produce variation in the reliability and validity of a measure is the time element involved in making the rating. This is related to, but not the same as, the issue of temporal variance already discussed. According to Worthen, Borg, and White (1993), there is a tendency for recent events and behavior to be given disproportionate weight when a rater completes a rating scale. It is easier to remember behavioral, social, and emotional characteristics during the previous two-week period than during the previous two-month period. Rating scales differ as to the time period on which the ratings are supposed to be based. For example, the Child Behavior Checklist specifies that the rater should complete the rating items based on the observation of the child over the previous six-month period. The Walker-McConnell Scale of Social Competence and School Adjustment (Walker & McConnell, 1988), on the other hand, is an example of a rating scale that does not specify a precise time period for the observations, although the test manual does specify that at least two months of the new school year should have elapsed before a teacher completes the scale on any student. A related measurement issue raised by Worthen, Borg, and White (1993) is that raters remember unusual behavior more easily than ordinary behavior. Thus typical undramatic behaviors may be assigned less weight during a rating than novel, unusual, or highly distinctive behaviors.

Another measurement and technical variable that can affect the psychometric properties of rating scales is the construction of the actual rating format. The two most common rating formats for behavior rating scales are three-point and five-point scales. Typically each numerical value in the rating format is keyed or anchored to a descriptor (e.g., 0 = never, 1 = sometimes, 2 = frequently). As a rule, more accurate ratings are obtained when there is a tangible and understandable definition for each quality level. In terms of deciding how many rating points or levels of rating are appropriate in constructing a rating scale, Worthen, Borg, and White (1993) suggest that a common error in scale construction is using too many levels; the higher the level of inference needed to make the rating, the more difficult it is to reliably discriminate among the rating levels. Therefore another good rule of thumb for scale developers is to use the fewest rating levels needed to make the rating discrimination and, for scale consumers, to avoid rating scales that include a high number of inference points. It is also important to carefully review the descriptors or anchor points in a rating format to ensure that they are clear and meaningful before adopting a new behavior rating scale.

A final technical characteristic of behavior rating scales is the directions for using them. Some scales provide highly detailed instructions for completing them, such as who should use the rating scale, the time period involved, how to approach and interpret the items, and so forth. Other scales may provide a minimum of directions or clarifications. It is recommended that users of behavior rating scales select instruments that provide clear and tangible directions for conducting the rating, as well as decision rules for interpreting blurred distinctions (Gronlund & Linn, 1990). In sum, the characteristics of rating-scale technology that make behavior rating scales appealing may also negatively impact the consistency and utility of the measure. As with any type of measurement and evaluation system, consumers of behavior rating scales are advised to evaluate a potential instrument based on these important technical characteristics.

AN OVERVIEW OF SOME GENERAL-PURPOSE BEHAVIOR RATING SCALES

Now that the technical foundation for understanding the technology, uses, and problems of rating scales has been covered, we will take an in-depth look at three selected behavior rating scales or rating-scale systems that are frequently employed as assessment tools in school and clinical settings. The three instruments that have been selected for overview are the Child Behavior Checklist, the Revised Behavior Problem Checklist, and the Conners Rating Scales. Besides the fact that these three rating scales are frequently used and widely available, they have been selected for inclusion because they are general-purpose instruments. That is, they provide measures of a variety of behavioral, social, and emotional problems, including a range of internalizing and externalizing symptoms. Another reason these three scales or systems have been singled out as examples is that they can be completed by either parents or teachers, and therefore they are useful in a variety of assessment and treatment settings. A number of other behavior rating scales have been developed for more specific purposes such as assessing social skills, hyperactivity, depression, anxiety, antisocial behavior, and school-based behaviors. These could be referred to as specific-purpose instruments, and many of them will be overviewed in chapters 7–11 when assessment of specific problems is discussed.

The Child Behavior Checklist System

One of the most sophisticated and well-researched, broad-spectrum behavior rating scales is the Child Behavior Checklist (CBCL) system. I have referred to the CBCL as a system because it incorporates two separate rating scales for school-age children: the Child Behavior Checklist (Achenbach, 1991a) and a version of the instrument developed for use by teachers called the Teacher's Report Form (TRF) (Achenbach, 1991b). The CBCL system also includes a direct-observation form and a self-report form, which are discussed in other chapters, and a version of the CBCL for use with preschool-age children.

Description.   Both the parent and teacher versions of the CBCL include 120 problem behavior items that are rated on a 0 = not true, 1 = somewhat or sometimes true, 2 = very true or often true format. The 120 items on the two checklists have a high degree of continuity, although some of the items on the TRF have been modified or changed to make them more directly applicable for use in schools settings. The original CBCL provided norms on children between ages 4 and 16, but the scoring profile, norms, and manual were revised in 1991 to include an upward extension through age 18 (Achenbach, 1991a) and a separate instrument for two- and three-year-old subjects. Whereas the original TRF provided a behavioral profile based on norms from ages 6–16, the scoring profile, norms, and manual were revised in 1991 so that it can now be used with ages 5–18 (Achenbach, 1991b).

In addition to the problem-behavior rating scales on the CBCL and TRF, both instruments contain sections wherein the informant provides information on the adaptive behavioral competencies of the subject. On the CBCL, this division is referred to as the *social competence* section, and it allows for ratings pertinent to the child's preferred activities, social interaction patterns, and school competence. On the TRF, this section is referred to as the *adaptive functioning* section and is a measure of adaptive school-related skills.

Scoring System and Scale Structure.   Raw scores for both the CBCL and TRF are converted to broad-band and narrow-band scores based on a *T*-score system (a normalized distribution with a mean of approximately 50 and a standard deviation of 10). Both rating scales can be hand-scored using the test manuals and appropriate versions of the Child Behavior Profile, which includes scoring keys for the internalizing/externalizing total scores, the various subscale scores, and a graph to plot the scores. The hand-scoring process with both the CBCL and TRF is quite tedious, taking at least 15 minutes for an experienced scorer and even longer for a scorer who is not familiar with the system. However available scoring templates make this job quicker and easier, and computer scoring programs are also available (IBM and Apple II compatible, with MacIntosh compatibility possible through MAC and MS DOS conversion software), making scoring and profile plotting easier still.

For both instruments, three different broad-band problem-behavior scores are obtained. The first two are referred to as *internalizing* and *externalizing* scores and are based on the Behavioral Dimensions breakdown of overcontrolled and undercontrolled behavior overviewed in chapter 2. The third broad-band score is a total problems score, which is based on a raw-to-*T*-score conversion of the total ratings of the 120 problem-behavior items. The total problems score is more than a combination of the *internalizing* and *externalizing* scores; there are several rating items on each instrument that do not fit into either of the two broad-band categories but are included in the total score. The CBCL and TRF also provide *T*-score conversions of the data from the social competence and adaptive functioning portions of the instruments, which were previously discussed.

In terms of narrow-band or subscale scores, the 1991 versions of the CBCL and TRF score profiles provide a score breakdown into eight common subscale or syndrome scores, which are empirically derived configurations of items. These eight cross-informant syndromes include *aggressive behavior, anxious/depressed, attention problems, delinquent behavior, social problems, somatic complaints, thought problems,* and *withdrawn.* These eight syndromes are listed in Table 4.3, with examples of specific items from them.

The 1991 versions of the CBCL and TRF behavior profiles allow for the plotting of subscale scores in a manner that departs from previous versions. The eight cross-informant syndromes are scored from all instruments, for all age levels, and for both sexes. At least in the clinical and practical sense, this system of constant subscale configuration is a definite improvement over previous versions of the score profiles. Until 1991, the names of and items in the CBCL and TRF subscales varied depending on age levels and gender, and they were not constant between the instruments. This inconsistency made for some confusion in comparing scores obtained over a several-year period and between teachers and parents, and it also made it difficult to compare score profiles obtained on children of different genders or age levels. The latest versions of the CBCL and TRF behavior profiles are still based on different norms for males and females and by age group, and on all instruments, the names of the narrow-band syndromes are constant.

Development and Standardization. The instruments in the CBC system were developed based on an extension and revision of Achenbach's Behavior Problem Checklist (1966), generated from a survey of the literature and case histories of over 1,000 psychiatric patients. In the construction of the CBCL, Achenbach (1978) and Achenbach and Edelbrock (1979) used data from clinic-referred samples from a large number of eastern U.S. community mental health centers, and they analyzed the data using principal component analyses based on various gender and age configurations. This initial wave of analysis led to the development of the original narrow-band syndrome configurations used in the

TABLE 4.3 Subscale structure of the Child Behavior Checklist with sample items

Name of Syndrome	Sample Items
Aggressive Behavior	Argues a lot; cruelty, bullying, or meanness to others; gets in many fights
Anxious/Depressed	Unhappy, sad, or depressed; cries a lot; talks about killing self
Attention Problems	Impulsive or acts without thinking; can't concentrate, can't pay attention for long
Delinquent Behavior	Hangs around with children who get into trouble; runs away from home; lying or cheating
Social Problems	Doesn't get along with other children; not liked by other children
Somatic Complaints	Feels dizzy; overtired; physical problems without known medical cause (list of 8 problems)
Thought Problems	Hears sounds or voices that aren't there; confused or seems to be in a fog; sees things that aren't there
Withdrawn	Likes to be alone; isolates, doesn't get involved with others

CBCL. The 1991 versions of the CBCL and TRF include large new nationwide normative samples.

The origins of the TRF were rooted in the CBCL. The construction of items for the TRF was modeled after, revised from, and in many cases directly adapted from the CBCL. Correlations between the two instruments reported in the original TRF manual were statistically significant at the $p. < .001$ level, yet modest, ranging from .26 to .45 on the three broad-band scores. These modest correlations show that even with similar rating items the differences in behavioral ecology between school and home settings, as well as the differing normative perspectives of parents and teachers, can be significant.

The original normative sample for the CBCL was obtained from 1,442 "normal" children, randomly selected from homes in the Washington, D.C., northern Virginia, and Maryland region. As was stated previously, the new normative data have been extended to the 18-year-old range, whereas the previous age range only went to 16. The original normative data were analyzed for the effects of race, gender, and social class. There were no overall gender effects on total problems, and once the effects of social class were factored in, there were minimal to no effects based on racial group. Social class differences were found: Individuals from low socioeconomic status backgrounds obtained lower social competence scores and higher problem behavior scores as a group. However, income accounts for a small percentage of the variance and does not require use of separate norms.

The original TRF normative data also followed the process of obtaining data from a clinic-referred sample for development of the factor structure and a "normal" sample for use in developing appropriate score norms. A total of 1,700 cases from 29 community mental health centers in the eastern, southern, and midwestern United States was included in the clinic sample. The normative sample included a total of 1,100 cases rated by 665 teachers who randomly selected one boy and one girl from their classes. The teacher ratings were obtained from public and private schools in Nebraska, Tennessee, and Pennsylvania. The large 1991 TRF norm sample is considered more nationally representative than the previous TRF norms.

Psychometric Properties.   The psychometric properties of both the CBCL and TRF, as reported in the scale manuals, range from adequate to excellent. In terms of test-retest reliability, the majority of the obtained reliabilities for the CBCL, taken at one-week intervals, are in the .80 to mid .90 range, and they are still quite good at 3-, 6-, and 18-month intervals (.47 to .76 mean reliabilities at 18 months). On the TRF, the median test-retest reliability at 7-day intervals was .90 and at 15-day intervals was .84. The median TRF test-retest correlation at two months was .74 and at four months was .68. These data suggest that ratings from the CBCL system can be quite stable over short to moderately long periods of time.

Inter-rater reliabilities (between fathers and mothers) on the CBCL were calculated, with the median correlation across scales being .66. On the TRF, inter-rater reliabilities (between teachers and teacher aides) on combined age samples ranged from .42 to .72. While lower than the test-retest reliabilities, the inter-rater agreement is still adequate. On a related note, a highly influential study by Achenbach, McConaughy, and Howell (1987) looks at cross-informant correlations in ratings of child/adolescent behavioral and emotional problems, and it discusses in detail the problem of situational specificity in interpreting rating-scale data.

Various forms of test validity on the CBCL and TRF have been inferred through a number of different studies. Strong discriminant construct validity evidence is reported for each instrument, since they have been found to sort between clinic and normal samples with a high degree of accuracy. The concurrent validity for both scales was demonstrated by finding moderately high and statistically significant correlations between their scales and other rating scales, such as the Revised Behavior Problem Checklist (.92 correlation on total scores), the Conners Parent Rating Scale (.91 correlation on total scores) and the Conners Teacher Rating Scale (.85 correlation on total scores). Several other validity analyses are presented in the CBCL and TRF manuals, showing strong evidence that these instruments are valid for the purposes for which they are intended.

Clinical Utility and Concluding Comments.   These two rating scales in the Child Behavior Checklist system appear to have a great deal of clinical utility in that they provide both general and specific information on the nature and extent of a subject's rated behavioral, social , and emotional problems. Many reviewers (e.g., Christenson, 1990; Elliot & Busse, 1990) agree that the CBCL system is a highly useful clinical tool for assessing child psychopathology. Martin (1988) refers to these instruments as the most sophisticated behavioral rating system available.

One of the advantages of the TRF and CBCL is also a potential weakness. Many of the behavioral symptoms on the checklists are rather clinical in nature (e.g., hearing voices, bowel and bladder problems, handling one's genitals in public) and certainly have a great deal of relevance in assessing childhood psychopathology. On the other hand, many of the more severe, low-rate behavioral descriptions on the scales are not usually seen in most public school settings, and some teachers and parents find them irrelevant, if not offensive, for the specific children or adolescents they are rating. Therefore while the Child Behavior Checklist system is perhaps the best rating scale currently available for assessing severe symptoms of childhood psychopathology, as a rating scale for garden-variety behavioral problems in home and school settings, it may not always be the best choice.

The Revised Behavior Problem Checklist

The Revised Behavior Problem Checklist (Quay & Peterson, 1987), like Achenbach's Child Behavior Checklist System, is a well researched, widely used, and highly respected behavior rating scale. The RBPC is a revision of the Behavior Problem Checklist (Quay & Peterson, 1967), which was one of the first child-behavior rating scales to gain wide acceptance by clinicians and researchers in the United States. The original version was a 55-item scale based on empirical behavioral data, which included five subscales. The revision process included increasing the number and length of items in the scale, improving the quality of item descriptions, changing from a checklist format to a rating-scale format, and developing a new standardization group and a new factor or subscale structure.

Description.   The RBPC includes 89 problem-behavior items rated according to a three-point scale (0 = no problem, 1 = mild problem, and 2 = severe problem). The scale can be completed by anyone familiar with the child's behavior, either parents or teachers. It is designed to be used with children and adolescents from ages 5 through 16. Completion of the RBPC typically takes between 5 and 10 minutes. The scale includes six empirically derived factor or subscale scores.

Score System and Scale Structure.   Raw scores for the six RBPC factor scores (*conduct disorder, socialized aggression, attention problems-immaturity, anxiety-withdrawal, psychotic behavior,* and *motor excess*) are obtained through the use of a set of scoring keys, which are straightforward and easy to use. The six factor raw scores are then converted to *T*-scores using the conversion tables for different sets of normative groups provided in the scale manual. There is no configuration for converting the total raw score to a *T*-score; only the six subscale scores are typically used. The RBPC subscale structure with sample items is presented in Table 4.4. The factor structure was developed by comparing factor analyses of the instrument obtained on four separate sets of data on children and adolescents with behavioral, emotional, and learning problems. The number of subjects in the four factor analytic samples ranged from 114 to 276. The factor loading data presented in the RBPC manual indicate that the six subscale factor structure is sound, even across different populations of children and adolescents.

Development and Standardization.   The technique used by Quay and Peterson (1987) in the development of normative data for the RBPC was to provide descriptive statistics (*n*'s, means, standard deviations, and score ranges) for several different specific populations, as well as raw-to-*T*-score conversion charts based on grade-level ranges and gender groups. The specific populations

TABLE 4.4   Subscale structure of the Revised Behavior Problem Checklist with sample items

Name of Scale	Sample Items
Conduct Disorder	Fights; brags and boasts; teases others
Socialized Aggression	Stays out late at night; cheats; belongs to a gang
Attention Problems-Immaturity	Has trouble following directions; irresponsible, undependable; inattentive to what others say
Anxiety-Withdrawal	Feels inferior; shy, bashful; lacks self-confidence
Psychotic Behavior	Expresses strange, farfetched ideas; repetitive speech, incoherent speech
Motor Excess	Squirms, fidgets; restless, unable to sit still; tense, unable to relax

available for comparison include gifted fourth-grade students, middle–elementary-age students from a university laboratory school, rural middle school students, children in public school classrooms for seriously emotionally disturbed students, students from a special school for children with behavior disorders, learning disabled students, students from the general population rated by mothers, outpatient clinical cases rated by parents, inpatient psychiatric cases rated by staff, and institutionalized juvenile delinquents. The raw score-to-*T*-score conversion tables are based on teacher ratings of a sample of 869 cases of public school children in South Carolina, New Jersey, and Iowa.

Psychometric Properties.   The technical data presented in the RBPC manual and in subsequent published studies indicate that the instrument has adequate to excellent psychometric properties. Several types of reliability data on the RBPC are known. Internal consistency coefficients from six different samples range from .70 to .95 for the six scales. Inter-rater reliability coefficients from a small number of teachers range from .52 to .85 for the six scales, whereas agreement between mothers and fathers of 70 children ranges from .55 to .93. Test-retest stability of the RBPC was determined by obtaining teacher ratings of 149 elementary-age children at two-month intervals, with the resulting coefficients ranging from .49 to .93.

Validity of the RBPC has been inferred through research presented in the test manual and through several subsequent studies. The main validity evidence presented in the manual relates to the ability of the instrument to differentiate between groups of children with behavioral, social, and emotional problems and normal comparison groups. No convergent validity evidence relating to correlations between the RBPC and other rating scales is presented in the manual, but several studies published since 1987 have attested to convergent validity with other instruments (e.g., Cohen, 1988). The original version of the instrument was highly researched and shown to have strong discriminant validity in sorting populations of normal from populations of delinquent and disturbed children. The current version of the instrument has also been shown to differentiate "deviant" from normal children through both discriminant function analyses and tests of significance for group means (Aman & Werry, 1984). Comparisons between RBPC scores and direct observational data presented in the scale manual indicate that the conduct disorder scale correlates highly with playground observations of aggressive behavior (.60). Various scales of the RBPC have been found to correlate highly with peer nomination data for aggression, withdrawal, and likability. Hagborg (1990) found four of the six RBPC scales to be significantly correlated with sociometric ratings of peer acceptance.

Clinical Utility and Concluding Comments.   The RBPC is a well-respected instrument with strong psychometric properties and a notable history of research that has validated it for many purposes. At its face value, the instrument appears to be more relevant for the assessment of conduct disorders and general antisocial behavior than for assessment of a broad range of internalizing problems. Although many of the problems included in the internalizing dimension are represented in the RBPC items, they are not as numerous or as prevalent in the factor structure as the problem items included in the externalizing dimension. Therefore if the major focus of concern in conducting an assessment is on problems relating to social withdrawal, depression, and somatic complaints, it is recommended that specific rating scales for these problems be included in the assessment battery.

The RBPC descriptive statistics for specific populations are informative and quite useful for comparison purposes. The raw-to-T-score conversion tables are based on a limited number of cases with unknown ethnic and cultural backgrounds and are not representative of the geographic breakdown of the U.S. population. Therefore some caution should be used in making inferences based on the T-score conversions from the normative group.

The Conners Rating Scale System

The Conners rating scales (Conners, 1990) are referred to as a system because they form a set of four different behavior rating scales (two parent rating scales and two teacher rating scales) that share many common items and are conceptually similar. These scales vary in length from 28 to 93 items. Different versions have been in use since the 1960s (Conners, 1969), and their use has been widely reported in the research literature over the years. The scales have also found a fair amount of use by clinicians. Though a broad range of behavioral, social, and emotional problem descriptions are included in the scales, they have been used primarily as a measure for assessing hyperactivity (Martin, 1988). It was not until 1990 that these scales became commercially available and a manual was published integrating the description, use, and scoring of the four scales into one source.

Description. The Conners system includes 39-item (CTRS-39) and 28-item (CTRS-28) rating scales for use by teachers and 48-item (CPRS-48) and 93-item (CPRS-93) rating scales for use by parents. Since the CTRS-39 and CTRS-48 have been the most widely used versions of the scales and much more is known about their psychometric properties, these two will be discussed in some detail in this chapter. The CTRS-28 and CPRS-93 will not be specifically discussed any further, although much of the information presented on the first two scales is also relevant to these two. The Conners scales all use a common four-point rating scale, in which 0 = not at all, 1 = just a little, 2 = pretty much, and 3 = very much. Although both scales have been used with a number of different age groups, the age range in the manual norms for the CTRS-39, is 3–14, while the CPRS-48 range is 3–17.

The CTRS-39 includes six subscales, while the CPRS-48 includes five. Additionally, both scales (as well as the other two rating scales in the Conners system) include a *hyperactivity index,* which is a group of 10 items technically not a part of the factor structure of the scales but which includes items taken from various subscales for the purpose of researching the effects of stimulant medication on child behaviors.

Score System and Scale Structure. Raw scores are converted to subscale scores using the *T*-score method for all scales in the Conners system. Total scores are typically not obtained and used with the Conners scales, and they are not part of the published scoring systems, although some investigators and clinicians have utilized a total score in interpreting scores. The six basic subscales of the CTRS-39 include *hyperactivity, conduct problems, emotional-indulgent, anxious-passive, asocial,* and *daydream-attention problems.* The five basic subscales on the CPRS-48 include *conduct problem, learning problems, psychosomatic, impulsive-hyperactive,* and *anxiety.* The scale structure of the CTRS-39 with sample items is presented as an example in Table 4.5. The *hyperactivity index* that is common to each of the scales in the Conners system is not presented in this chapter but will be discussed in detail in chapter 8.

The rating scales in the Conners system are easily scored and converted to standardized subscale scores based on gender and age-level breakdowns, using an innovative "quickscore" format on NCR-type forms that requires a minimum of time and reduces the chance of scoring errors. Microcomputer on-line administration and scoring programs for the Conners scales are also available from the publisher. The computer programs provide not only administration and scoring possibilities but also the generation of brief interpretive paragraphs related to individual score configurations and levels.

While the subscale structures of the two rating scales illustrated in this chapter are the configurations presented in the 1990 system manual, the items in each factor and the number of factors in each instrument have varied somewhat in the research reported throughout the years. In fact, Martin (1988) stated that it was a common practice for investigators using the Conners scales to independently develop their own factor structure and report it in their research reports. For example, Cohen and Hynd (1986) identified a factor structure for the CTRS-39

TABLE 4.5 Scale structure of the 39-item version of the Conners Teacher Rating Scales with sample items

Name of Scale	Sample Items
A. Hyperactivity	Constantly fidgeting; hums and makes other odd noises; quarrelsome
B. Conduct Problems	Acts "smart"; destructive; steals; temper outbursts, explosive and unpredictable behavior
C. Emotional-Indulgent	Temper outbursts, overly sensitive; demands must be met immediately, easily frustrated
D. Anxious-Passive	Appears to be easily led; appears to lack leadership; submissive
E. Asocial	Isolates him/herself from other children; appears to be unaccepted by group
F. Daydream-Attention Problem	Fails to finish things she or he starts, short attention span; daydreams
I. Hyperactivity Index	Cries often and easily; disturbs other children; mood changes quickly and drastically

as used with special education students that varied somewhat from the most commonly used subscale structure. In general, the factor structures for the Conners scales presented in the 1990 manual are the structures most commonly reported and widely used in the research literature. Now that an integrated manual with set scoring systems for the scales is available, the use of a number of different factor configurations for the scales is likely to diminish. These standardized changes incorporated into the 1990 manual are a major improvement over what was previously available.

Development and Standardization.   The development of the first version of the Conners rating scales commenced during the 1960s by clinicians at Johns Hopkins University Hospital in Baltimore. These clinicians, who were implementing and researching psychopharmacological and psychotherapeutic interventions with children, developed a set of rating-scale items that were used informally and qualitatively to obtain further information from teachers. In discussing how the scales progressed from this earlier informal prototype to the standardized versions now in use, Conners (1990) noted that ". . . when I compared data from normal children and clinical cases, it was clear that they differed on several different dimensions, not just in the number of total symptoms. Factor analysis confirmed that existence of stable clusters of items, . . . having much more clinical interest than a simple catalogue of problems" (p. vi). Research on this first standard version of the scales was published by Conners in 1969, and this version is essentially the same as the present version of the CTRS-39. The 28-item version of the teacher rating scale was later developed as shorter form with slightly different content and properties. The first version of the parent rating scale was the 93-item version, with the 48-item version developed later "after a careful consideration of accumulated psychometric evidence of the original version." The 48-item version was thought to "represent a more abstract, and consequently abbreviated, formulation of child problem behaviors" (Conners, 1990, p. 1).

One of the drawbacks of the normative standardization data for the scales in the Conners system is that these instruments were not originally developed with the idea of creating widely available, norm-referenced instruments from random, stratified populations. As such, comparative normative data and factor structures were devised later in the development process, sometimes after several iterations of the original instrument. Therefore in reading reviews of the Conners scales and in studying the integrated 1990 manual, one finds a number of different studies using diverse research methodologies, which sometimes report slightly different results.

The factor structure and normative data reported in the 1990 manual for the CTRS-39 are based on an extremely large, stratified, random sample (9,583 Canadian school children) obtained by Trites, Blouin, and Laprade (1982). Factor analytic data and gender- and age-based score norms for the CPRS-48 were developed by Goyette, Conners, and Ulrich (1978), and they included 570 children aged 3 through 71. This normative population was obtained from the Pittsburgh, Pennsylvania area, using a stratified sampling procedure.

Psychometric Properties.   Test-retest reliability for the scales of the CTRS-39 has been reported to range from .72 to .91 at one-month intervals (Conners, 1969) and from .33 to .55 at one-year intervals (Glow, Glow, & Rump, 1982). No test-retest data on the CPRS-48 had been reported at the time of publication of the 1990 manual. Several studies of inter-rater agreement on the CTRS-39 scales have reported reliabilities ranging from a low of .39 (on the *inattentive-passive* scale) to as high as .94 (on the *hyperactivity index*). Agreement between parents on the CPRS-48 was reported in the Goyette et al. (1978) study, with obtained reliability coefficients ranging from .46 to .57 with a mean correlation of .51.

Evidence for several forms of validity for the various Conners scales has been presented in a large number of published research reports. For example, several studies have documented the validity of the Conners scales in differentiating between distinct diagnostic groups, including hyperactive and normal children (King & Young, 1982), learning disabled and regular education students (Merrell, 1990), boys referred to juvenile court and a normal control group (Berg, Butler, Hullin, Smith, & Tyler, 1978), and behavior disordered and nonspecial education students (Margalit, 1983). In terms of predictive validity, the CTRS-39 has been found to be highly predictive of hyperactivity at age 10, based on behavior ratings obtained at age 7 (Gillberg & Gillberg, 1983). Finally, the convergent validity of various versions of the Conners scales has been demonstrated through several studies that found significant correlations between them and other instruments, such as the Child Behavior Checklist (Edelbrock, Greenbaum, & Conover, 1985), the Behavior and Temperament Survey (Sandoval, 1981), the Behavior Problem Checklist (Campbell & Steinert, 1978), the School Behavior Survey, and the School Social Behavior Scales (Merrell, 1993). Note that the majority of the validity studies cited involved the use of the CTRS-39 and that less is known about the properties of the CPRS-48.

Clinical Utility and Concluding Comments.   In sum, the CTRS-39, CPRS-48, and the other two rating scales in the Conners system have been widely utilized in clinical practice and tested in various ways in a significant number of published studies. There is no question that the CTRS-39 is the version of the Conners scales for which the most empirical data are available; less has been demonstrated about the CPRS-48 and the other two Conners scales. However there is a good deal of overlap between the different scales in the Conners system, which should lend a substantial degree of "face validity" to the versions of the scales not extensively researched. The size of the CPRS-48 norm population is relatively small, and the geographic and racial composition of the norm sample is so limited that the generalizability of norm-based scores should be questioned. Clinicians using the CPRS-48 for assessment of children or youth should be aware of these limitations, and they should also become familiar with the properties of the other Conners scales so they can make proper interpretations.

The 1990 publication of an integrated manual and standard scoring systems for the Conners scales has filled a very large void in the understanding and use of these instruments and may result in their increased clinical use. Since the CTRS-39 and CPRS-48 are relatively brief instruments (having half as many or fewer items than the other scales reviewed in this chapter), they are excellent choices for conducting initial screenings, but it is important to supplement them with other evaluation methods in conducting comprehensive clinical assessments.

BEST PRACTICES IN USING
BEHAVIOR RATING SCALES

This chapter has provided an overview of the uses, advantages, and limitations of behavior rating scales, as well as a survey of three widely used, commercially published, general-purpose rating scales or rating-scale systems. To effectively use behavior rating scales requires more than just a cursory understanding of their characteristics. Thus three "best-practice" suggestions for using rating scales in an effective and useful manner are offered.

The first suggestion is to *use rating scales routinely for early screening.* Effective screening practices involve systematically picking out with a high degree of accuracy children in the early stages of developing behavioral, social, or emotional problems. The identified subjects are then evaluated more carefully to determine whether their social-behavioral problems warrant special program eligibility and intervention services. The purpose of screening for social-behavioral problems is usually for *secondary prevention,* that is, the prevention of the existing problem from becoming worse (Kauffman, 1989). Screening for early intervention is one of the best uses of behavior rating scales, as they cover a wide variety of important behaviors and take very little time to administer and score. For general screening purposes, my recommendation is to include students whose rating-scale scores are one or more standard deviations above instrument normative means in terms of problem-behavior excesses. This practice will narrow down the screening pool to approximately 16 percent of the overall population, and this selected group can then be evaluated more comprehensively.

The second suggestion offered is to *use the aggregation principle.* This principle involves obtaining ratings from a variety of sources, each of which may present a slightly differing picture. When using rating scales for purposes other than routine screening, obtaining aggregated rating-scale data is recommended in order to reduce bias of response and variance problems in the assessment. In practice, using aggregated measures means obtaining rating evaluations from different raters in different settings and using more than one type of rating scale to accomplish this (Martin, Hooper, & Snow, 1986).

A final suggestion is to *use behavior rating scales to assess progress during and after interventions.* It has been demonstrated that continuous assessment and monitoring of student progress following the initial assessment and intervention are very important in successful implementation of behavioral interventions (Kerr & Nelson, 1989). Progress toward behavioral intervention goals can be easily assessed on a weekly or bi-weekly schedule using appropriate rating scales. Though rating scales may not be the best measurement choice for daily assessment data, there are a number of other simple ways of assessing progress daily, such as using performance records or brief observational data.

Additional assessment following the intervention can also be a useful process. The main reason for follow-up assessment is to determine how well the intervention effects have been maintained over time (e.g., after 3 months) and how well the behavioral changes have generalized to other settings (e.g., the home setting and other classrooms). In actual practice, a follow-up assessment might involve having teacher(s) and parent(s) complete behavior rating scales on a child after a specified time period following the student's participation in a social skills training program. The data obtained from this follow-up assessment can be used to determine whether or not follow-up interventions seem appropriate, and the information may be useful in developing future intervention programs if it is determined that social-behavioral gains are not being maintained over time or generalized across specific settings.

BEHAVIOR RATING SCALES AND DECISION MAKING

Given the various characteristics, advantages, and problems associated with behavior rating scales, how are they best used in making decisions? Perhaps their most natural use is in decision making associated with screening and additional assessment. Rating scales are an excellent choice for use in either individual- or large-group screening, as they tend to be quick and easy to administer, and if the screening criteria are set low enough, they will yield very few false-negative errors. For making decisions regarding the need for additional assessment, behavior rating scales can identify specific dimensions or behavioral clusters that may need to be investigated in more detail. The multiple-gating systems described in chapter 2 utilize rating scales as one of the important first steps in narrowing down a large population to a smaller population of potentially at-risk individuals before additional assessment methods are utilized.

Although behavior rating scales should never be used alone for making classification or placement decisions, they can provide some potentially useful information in this regard. Given the development of the Behavioral Dimensions approach to classification and the fairly recent application of sophisticated, multivariate statistical techniques to rating scales, they are capable of isolating specific dimensions of problem behaviors useful in making classification decisions, particularly if used across raters and settings. Several state education agencies have recommended or required that local education agency personnel utilize behavior rating scales in systematic or prescribed ways in the identification of students for special education services under certain classification categories.

For making intervention or treatment planning decisions, behavior rating scales are less useful in identifying specific target behaviors and potential reinforcers than direct observation or behavioral interviewing. However, rating scales can be used to identify specific cluster areas of behavioral deficits or excesses that may require intervention. As was stated earlier, another potential use of rating scales in the intervention process is the assessment of progress or behavioral change during or after the intervention.

APPLICATION PROBLEMS—UNDERSTANDING
AND USING BEHAVIOR RATING SCALES

1. From both conceptual and practical standpoints, describe the major differences between behavior rating scales and behavior checklists. Related to this first point, what is considered to be the major advantage of using rating scales instead of checklists?

2. For each of the four types of *error variance* described in this chapter, describe at least one practical way to implement the assessment in order to minimize or overcome potential error.

3. Consider the not-too-unusual case of a clinician asking a parent and two different teachers to rate a referred child using the same behavior rating scale and then, upon scoring the instruments, finding that the scores obtained from the three sources are considerably different. Suggest some potentially effective ways of interpreting and then following up on data of this kind.

4. One of the cautions in using behavior rating scales is that the subscales of various instruments are usually named or labeled by the test developer in a somewhat arbitrary fashion, and too literal interpretation of the names of subscales can lead the clinician into errors of judgment. To get an idea of how the subscale-naming process works, select one behavior rating scale that you occasionally use or have access to, analyze the specific items in each subscale, and then use your "clinical judgment" to give the subscale an alternative label or name.

CHAPTER 5

Interviewing Techniques

INTRODUCTION

Whether meeting informally with the teacher of a referred student, conducting a problem identification interview with a parent, or undertaking a diagnostic interview with a child or adolescent, interviewing is one of the most widely used assessment methods. As we shall see, the popularity of the interview is no fluke; as an assessment method, it offers many advantages to the clinician. This chapter provides a broad overview of the topic of interviewing children and adolescents, as well as specific recommended procedures and techniques for conducting high-quality interviews.

The chapter begins with a discussion of the role of the interview as an assessment method, including sections on developmental issues in interviewing, factors that affect overall interview quality, and selection of specific interview methods for specific purposes. The majority of the chapter is devoted to discussions of three types of interviews: the traditional or unstructured interview, behavioral interviewing, and structured or semistructured diagnostic interviews. The chapter concludes with a brief discussion of how interviews can be used in decision-making processes.

THE ROLE OF THE INTERVIEW IN ASSESSING CHILDREN AND ADOLESCENTS

There is no question that the use of interviewing as an assessment method holds a place of prominence in psychology, psychiatry, social work, and counseling. Among clinicians who have a psychodynamic orientation or who are strongly influenced by specific schools of humanistic psychology, the interview has a particularly exalted position (Martin, 1988). This venerated attitude toward the interview process has been perpetuated in popular media and thus has strongly shaped the beliefs of the lay population, sometimes to the point of nearly mystifying what is actually accomplished during the course of interviews. Most psychologists and psychiatrists have experienced the public mystification of the interview process and the supposed diagnostic powers possessed by clinicians, even when conducting such mundane business as standing in line at the supermarket, getting their hair cut, or having major appliances serviced. When queried by strangers as to what their occupation is, the answer frequently draws responses such as "Are you analyzing me now?" or "Oh no, you'll figure out what my problems are by talking to me!" Of course, an honest reply to such questions usually would be disappointing to both the professionals and those inquiring about their skills, since both would like to believe that the clinicians' prowess in interpersonal communications results in more "clinical insight" than is usually the case.

If the process of interviewing is not always a mystical conduit to the secrets of the human soul, then what is it? Essentially interviewing is structured communication, mainly verbal, but nonverbal as well. Martin (1988) notes that an interview resembles a conversation but differs from day-to-day conversation in that it (*a*) is purposeful, (*b*) is usually "controlled" by the interviewer through the initiating of interchanges and the posing of questions, and (c) has unity, progression, and thematic continuity.

Interviews come in several forms, ranging from unstructured stream-of-consciousness interchanges to formalized and highly structured interview schedules for use in exploring very specific problems. Although the purposes, underlying theories, and level of structure among different types of interviews vary considerably, all forms of client interviewing share some common ground and have specific advantages when compared with other assessment methods. Perhaps the most salient advantage of interviewing is the flexibility it provides the clinician. Throughout the course of an interview, the clinician has the opportunity to shorten or lengthen, to change directions when needed, and to focus on whichever specific aspects of the client's thought, behavior, or emotion emerge as most important at the time. Another advantage of interviewing is that it provides the clinician with the opportunity to observe the client directly under structured conditions. Client characteristics such as social skills, verbal ability, insight, defensiveness, and willingness to cooperate can all be assessed to a degree throughout the course of an interview. When interviewing children, the observational advantage of the interview process is particularly important, as their limited experiences and unsophisticated verbal mediation skills make it difficult for them to express their concerns, needs, and problems directly. In cases where the client is not available or otherwise incapable of providing high-quality information in an interview context (a typical concern with young children), interviews can be conducted with individuals who know them well, such as parents or teachers. Finally the process of interviewing can be an important bridge in the therapeutic process; through the establishment of rapport with the client during assessment interviews, a level of trust and comfort can be obtained that is critical to the implementation of an intervention plan.

Of course, like other methods of assessment, interviewing does have its flaws. Perhaps the most easily criticized feature of interviewing is that the flexible, nonstandardized nature of many interviews (which is also considered an advantage) can lead easily to unreliability or inconsistency, both over time and between different interviewers. This drawback can be effectively addressed through the use of more structured interview formats, which will be covered in this chapter. Another potential problem is that interviewing requires a great deal of training and experience to do well, particularly when less structured interview formats are used.

Understanding Developmental Issues That Affect Children's Responses

Stated simply, interviewing children or adolescents is a much different endeavor than interviewing adults. Although the basic tasks of interviewing children and adults have some superficial similarity, a qualitatively different approach is needed in order to obtain a useful and informative verbal report. As children develop and change in terms of their physical, cognitive, social, and emotional functioning, their ability to respond to the tasks required of them in an interview format likewise changes. In order to conduct interviews with children and adolescents most effectively, interviewers must have a knowledge of the basic aspects of these developmental issues. This section will provide a general understanding of some basic developmental issues that may affect the interview process. For a more complete discussion of developmentally sensitive interviewing, consult the book chapters by Bierman (1983) and Hughes and Baker (1990) that are specifically devoted to this topic.

Preschool and Primary-Age Children.   Young children tend to be particularly difficult to interview, and they pose what is perhaps the greatest challenge to the interviewer. As Bierman (1983) noted:

> Young children are able to describe their thoughts and feelings, but they require specialized interview techniques to do so. Moreover, characteristics of conceptual organization and information processing associated with cognitive and linguistic development result in a phenomenological world for the young child that is qualitatively different from the adult's world. Clinicians who are unfamiliar with the thought processes associated with various developmental levels are likely to find children's reasoning extremely difficult to follow or comprehend. To conduct effective child interviews, clinicians must acquire an understanding of the characteristics of developing social-cognitive processes, and they must make some major adjustments in their interviewing techniques and strategies. (pp. 218–219)

In Piagetian terms, children between the ages of about two and seven are in what is term the *preoperational* stage of cognitive development, characterized by the child's representing things with words and images and lacking logical reasoning abilities (Piaget, 1983). Children in this age range can be confused easily by distinctions between reality and appearance, find it easier to follow positive instructions ("hold the blocks carefully") rather than negative ones ("don't drop the blocks"), and tend to be *egocentric,* that is, they have difficulty in taking or understanding the viewpoint or experience of another person. Children in this developmental stage tend to have difficulty in recalling specific information accurately because they usually have not developed memory retrieval strategies (McNamee, 1989). Preoperational children tend to focus on just one feature of a problem, neglecting other important aspects, a tendency referred to as *centration.* They often exhibit difficulty in understanding that actions can be reversed. To young children, behavioral actions are considered to be right or wrong depending on what consequences they bring ("stealing is wrong because you get put into jail"). Kohlberg (1969) referred to this type of moral reasoning as at a *preconventional level.* In terms of emotional development, younger children may experience a wide range of emotions and affect but typically can describe these experiences only along a limited number of dimensions (i.e., happy or sad, good or bad, mean or nice).

Interestingly, recent evidence has put into question some of the absolutist aspects of developmental stage theories with young children. Hughes and Baker (1990) reviewed several studies from the 1970s and 1980s, demonstrating that the apparent cognitive limitations of young children are often artifacts of the way they are questioned or the way tasks are presented to them. It is now thought that young children are capable of producing higher-quality self-report information than was previously believed. The chances of obtaining high-quality interview information from young children are increased if the children are comfortable in the interview situation and are questioned by an interviewer who understands their cognitive development and appropriately modifies interview tasks for them (Gelman & Baillargeon, 1983). In terms of specific techniques for increasing the quality of the interview with young children, Hughes and Baker (1990) recommend that interviewers (*a*) use a combination of open-ended and direct questions, (*b*) not attempt to assume too much control over the conversation, (*c*) gain familiarity with children's experience and use this understanding in developing questions, (*d*) reduce the complexity of interview stimulus to the greatest extent possible, and (*e*) reduce the complexity of children's responses by allowing them at times to communicate with props or manipulatives.

Elementary-Age Children.   As children move from the preschool and primary years into the elementary years, their capabilities for verbal communication tend to increase dramatically. Thus while conducting an effective interview with elementary-age children can still be a challenging endeavor that requires special understanding and methodology, the probability of obtaining high-quality interview information is increased.

In developmental terms, elementary-age children are what Piaget (1983) referred to as in the *concrete operations* stage of cognitive development, which extends from roughly 7 to 11 years. Children at this developmental stage are able to use simple logic but generally can perform mental operations only on images of tangible objects and actual events. During the concrete operations stage, many principles are mastered that were elusive to children in the preoperational stage, including *reversibility, decentration,* and *conservation* (understanding that a change in appearance does not always change a quantity). Concrete operational children learn to develop simple hierarchical classification abilities but still do not have the ability to use formal logic or abstract reasoning. Elementary-age children are learning to function socially beyond the family in a broader social realm. Eriksen (1963) referred to this developmental stage as *industry versus inferiority.* If elementary-age children master these new social challenges, they will develop a strong sense of self-competence but may be plagued by feelings of low self-esteem if they do not. Most elementary-age children make moral decisions in a more complex way than they did during their preschool and primary years. Kohlberg (1969) suggests that most children in this age range reach what he referred to as *conventional morality,* wherein rules and social conventions are viewed as absolute guidelines for judging actions.

Aside from simply understanding the developmental aspects associated with the elementary years, effective interviewing of elementary-age children can be greatly facilitated by the interviewer's use of specific methods and approaches. Establishment of adequate rapport and familiarity with the child prior to the actual assessment has been found to be a critical variable in influencing the amount and quality of responses (Fuchs & Fuchs, 1986). Although elementary-age children generally have developed a reasonable mastery of language, the interviewer should avoid the use of abstract or symbolic questions, which will probably confuse the child. Hughes and Baker (1990) suggest that interviews with elementary-age children may be enhanced by (a) relying on familiar settings and activities during the interview, (b) allowing children to use manipulatives and drawings during the interview, (c) avoiding constant eye contact (which elementary-age children are typically not used to), and (d) providing contextual cues (such as pictures, colors, and examples) along with requests for language interaction.

Adolescents.   By the time of adolescence, children around 12 to 14 years of age are usually capable of participating in an interactive interview situation to a much greater extent than younger children, and in many ways, the interview task is similar to that of interviewing an adult. However clinicians who assume that interviewing an adolescent is the same as interviewing an adult risk reaching invalid conclusions or obtaining low-quality information, due to their lack of sensitivity to the unique developmental aspects of adolescence.

In Piagetian terms, most individuals move toward the *formal operations* stage of cognitive development at about age 12 (Piaget, 1983). This stage is characterized by the ability to use formal logic and to apply mental operations to abstract as well as concrete objects. Adolescents tend to become more systematic in their problem-solving efforts rather than using quick, trial-and-error methods of attacking problems. Keep in mind that some individuals (i.e., those with impaired cognitive functioning or developmental disabilities) do not reach this stage of cognitive functioning; there is no guarantee that because a subject is 17 years old that he or she will be able to think abstractly and logically, and clinicians should screen the subject's academic/intellectual history prior to conducting an interview.

During adolescence, some persons reach what Kohlberg (1969) referred to as *postconventional moral reasoning,* a stage at which actions are judged based on individual principles of conscience rather than on their consequences or social conventions. Thus some adolescents (particularly older adolescents) may make decisions about right or wrong behavior based on abstract internalized ideals rather than on conventional guidelines, such as school or family rules, or fear of consequences. Although there is not a great deal of empirical data on how many adolescents make decisions in postconventional terms, it can be generalized that this stage is more likely to be reached toward the end of adolescence and that many individuals do not reach this stage of moral reasoning at all.

One of the features of adolescent development, at least in Western industrialized cultures, is the emotional "Sturm und Drang"(storm and stress) that tend to go along with identity formation and striving for independence. During this stage, which Eriksen (1963) characterized as the *identity versus confusion* crisis, individuals tend to have a wider variation of emotional intensity than they will have as adults—the well-known, almost bipolar proclivity of adolescents to vacillate between extreme emotional highs and lows. Although some researchers have contended that the notion of storm and stress in adolescence has been oversold, clinicians who work with troubled adolescents should expect that their clients may experience a great deal of emotional intensity and lability.

Conducting interviews with adolescent clients can be a very rewarding experience and one that is less constrained or frustrating than interviewing young children. Nevertheless, clinicians must keep the unique developmental aspects of adolescence in mind in order to elicit useful interview information and to make sound inferences. While adolescents may be very adultlike in their approach to the interview and most may actually enjoy the attention, it is extremely important to consider the intensity and variability of adolescent emotionality. Since it is normal for adolescents to experience more extremes in their social-emotional functioning than most adults, inferences must be conservative. Any diagnosis of severe affective or behavioral problems should be tempered by the understanding of normal adolescent development, and adult standards of behavior and emotionality should not be applied exclusively. Making decisions on an adolescent's social and emotional behavior in the same manner as with adults may lead to faulty conclusions. Archer (1987) demonstrated that about 25 percent of adolescent subjects will provide MMPI results suggestive of psychotic behavior when their profiles are strictly interpreted according to adult norms.

Factors That Affect the Quality of the Interview

Knowledge of child development and methods of making interviews developmentally appropriate do not by themselves result in effective and useful interviews with children or adolescents. There are a number of other factors, aside from developmental issues and interview format, that contribute to the overall quality of the interview.

The Interpersonal Context.   Whether the interview is with a child, parent, or teacher, the interpersonal relationship established prior to and during the course of the interview may significantly affect the extent and quality of client self-report data. One of the key tenets of Rogerian *person-centered therapy* is that the development of a positive relationship between the interviewer and the client is critical to both the quality of client self-disclosure and the effectiveness of therapy. Three core relationship conditions are considered essential: (*a*) *empathy,* or accurate understanding of the client's concerns; (*b*) *respect,* or positive regard for the client; and (*c*) *genuineness,* which can be described as congruence between the interviewer's verbal and nonverbal messages to the client (Rogers, Gendlin, Kiesler, & Truax, 1967). Although these interpersonal considerations were first described and used within the context of person-centered therapy, they obviously have value for other forms of interviewing and therapy as well.

Cormier and Cormier (1985) further elaborated on the relationship-building aspects of the interview and suggested that *expertness, attractiveness,* and *trustworthiness* are additional characteristics that enhance the interpersonal context of communication. Expertness is related to the client's perception of how competent the interviewer is, with an emphasis on characteristics of interviewer competence that are *immediately evident* to the client. Attractiveness goes far beyond the client's perception of the interviewer's physical characteristics and includes such attributes as friendliness, likability, and similarity to the client. Trustworthiness includes such variables as the interviewer's reputation for honesty, the congruence of nonverbal behaviors, and the amount of accuracy, openness, and confidentiality evident during the interview process. Clinicians who successfully incorporate these interpersonal characteristics and behaviors into their interviewing methods will likely increase the value of their interviews with clients.

The Cultural Context.   Given that the cultural and ethnic composition of the United States is becoming increasingly diverse, clinicians also need to be aware of cultural factors that may affect the overall quality of interviews. In discussing information about differences between cultural or ethnic groups, it is important to keep in mind that most of the available information is based on generalizations from studies of groups. There will always be individuals who do not fit the typical group characteristics; therefore caution is essential to avoid stereotypical overgeneralizations of group differences.

Two of the dimensions of the interview interaction that may have immediate cultural importance are the degree of eye contact and the amount of physical distance between the interviewer and the client. Sue and Sue (1990) noted that white U.S. Americans make eye contact with the person they are listening to about 80 percent of the time, but they tend to avoid eye contact about 50 percent of the time when they are speaking to others. This is in contrast to the eye-contact patterns of many African Americans, who tend to make greater eye contact when speaking and less frequent eye contact when listening. On the other hand, Native Americans are more likely to have indirect eye contact when speaking or listening, while Asian Americans and Hispanics are more likely to avoid eye contact altogether when speaking to persons they perceive as having high status. In terms of comfortable physical proximity or distance between persons, Sue and Sue (1990) noted cultural differences. For Latin Americans, Africans, African Americans, Indonesians, South Americans, Arabs, and French, a much closer physical proximity between communicators is comfortable than would be for most white Americans. Some of the culturally based aspects of interpersonal communication styles among U.S. cultural groups are reflected in the information presented in Table 5.1.

The Behavioral Context.   Some specific interviewer behaviors are likely to enhance or detract from the amount and quality of interview information obtained from a client. Whether the interview will be in a structured or unstructured format, there is some evidence that by preparing the client and instructing him or her in desirable ways of responding, the interviewer will increase the amount of self-disclosure by the client (Gross, 1984). For example, beginning the interview with the parent of a referred child, the clinician might say something like, "When you tell me about problems you are having with Sarah, I would like you to be very specific; for example, tell me exactly what she does that you see as a problem, how it affects you, and what you generally do about it."

TABLE 5.1 Generalized communication style differences among major cultural groups in the U.S.: Overt activity dimension, nonverbal and verbal communication

Native Americans	Asian Americans and Hispanics	Whites	African Americans
1. Speak softly/slower	1. Speak softly	1. Speak loud/fast to control	1. Speak with affect
2. Indirect gaze when listening or speaking	2. Avoidance of eye contact when listening or speaking to high-status persons	2. Greater eye contact when listening	2. Direct eye contact (prolonged) when speaking but less when listening
3. Interject less, seldom offer encouraging communication	3. Similar rules	3. Heads nods, nonverbal markers	3. Interrupt (turn taking) when possible
4. Delayed auditory (silence)	4. Mild delay	4. Quick response	4. Quicker response
5. Manner of expression: low key, indirect	5. Low key, indirect	5. Objective, task-oriented	5. Affective, emotional, interpersonal

SOURCE: Adapted from *Counseling the Culturally Different* (2nd ed.), by D. W. Sue and D. Sue copyright © 1990, John Wiley & Sons, Inc. Reprinted by Permission of John Wiley & Sons, Inc.

Another interviewer behavior that may increase the quality of the interview is the use of reinforcement. With both children and adults, the selective use of praise or appreciative statements has the effect of increasing both the amount and quality of subsequent self-disclosure (Gross, 1984). For instance, a clinician who is interviewing a boy about how the divorce of his parents has affected him might say something like:

> Scott, you really did a good job of telling me what it was like for you when your mom and dad split up. I know that was a very hard thing for you to talk about, but you were able to tell how you feel about it in a very clear way. The more you can tell me about how you feel and what has happened to you, the better I can understand you and help you.

Other forms of reinforcement may also be effective with younger children. Edible primary reinforcers such as raisins, nuts, or small pieces of candy are one possibility, although they should be used with caution to avoid both satiation effects and the interview revolving solely around them. As an alterative to edible reinforcers, stickers are often popular with children as are tokens that can be exchanged for small rewards following the interview.

Finally the type of questioning used is another important interviewer behavior. The use of closed questions (those that can be answered with one-word responses) should be avoided except in cases where very specific information is needed. A barrage of closed questions from an interviewer may leave clients feeling as though they are being interrogated. With adults, adolescents, and older children, the use of open-ended questions (e.g., "What do you like to do with your friends?") is generally preferred. With very young children, it is generally most useful to use a combination of open and closed questions (Hughes & Baker, 1990).

Selecting an Appropriate Interview Method

In this chapter, interviewing methods used for assessing behavioral, social, and emotional problems of children and adolescents are divided into three categories: traditional interviewing techniques, behavioral interviews, and structured or semistructured interviews. It is certainly possible to divide or categorize interview methods into more classifications than these, but this three-part division provides a useful grouping into general methods that typically are used in school or clinic-based assessments.

The choice of a particular interview method will depend on several key factors, such as (a) the theoretical orientation of the clinician, (b) the level of training and experience the clinician has in conducting interviews, and (c) the overall goals and specific objectives for conducting the interview. The clinician's theoretical orientation will influence the choice of interview methods in that personal beliefs and biases may limit the level of comfort he or she has in using different methods. For instance, a clinician who has a very strong behavioral orientation may not be comfortable using a traditional, open-ended interview format, perceiving that the type of information obtained will be of little use in identifying key elements and sequences of problem behaviors and in developing an intervention. On the other hand, a psychodynamic or humanistic-oriented clinician may experience some of the highly structured, diagnostic interview schedules as restricting and confining.

The clinician's level of training and experience may affect their choice of methods as well. Being able to conduct a traditional, open-ended interview effectively without a great deal of preimposed structure requires a significant amount of clinical judgment, which is only gained through experience. Conducting an effective behavioral interview requires a solid grounding in behavioral psychology if the results are to be used in identifying the factors that elicit and maintain problem behaviors and in the subsequent development of an intervention plan. Some of the available structured and semistructured interview schedules require a high degree of very specific training in that particular system, while others can be used easily and effectively by paraprofessionals and lay persons with a minimum amount of training.

In addition to the clinician's theoretical orientation and level of training, the choice of interview techniques will be shaped also by the specific purposes for conducting the interview. Traditional interview formats are considered useful when there is a premium on obtaining historical information and in establishing rapport with the client in the context of a less formal, client-focused interview. Behavioral methods of interviewing are considered useful particularly when the preeminent goal is the development of an immediate intervention by means of which the critical behavioral variables can be identified and modified. If diagnostic or classification purposes are of paramount importance, many of the semi-structured or structured interview schedules are considered good choices, particularly if the purpose is a psychiatric diagnosis via the DSM system.

TRADITIONAL INTERVIEWING TECHNIQUES

What is referred to in this chapter as *traditional interviewing* is not really a specific format or type of interview. Rather the term represents a broad construct, that is, interviews that are relatively open ended, less structured, and highly adaptable to the situation. Traditional interviewing techniques can include a wide range of specific types of interviews—psychodynamic, case history, nondirective, and so on. Within our discussion of traditional interview techniques, two areas are covered that are germane to virtually any type of interview: obtaining background information from parents and teachers and methods of developing the interview with child or adolescent clients.

Obtaining Relevant Background Information from Parents and Teachers

Aside from identifying specific problems and developing intervention plans, which are covered in the behavioral interviewing section of this chapter, one of the main purposes for interviewing the parent(s) or teacher(s) of a referred child is to obtain a report of relevant background information. Why obtain background information? While one could make an argument for using only information that is current and directly linked to the presenting problem, this approach is short-sighted. By carefully reviewing important historical information, clues sometimes are provided to both the causes of and potential solutions to child behavioral or emotional problems. An example from my own clinical experience illustrates this point. When interviewing the mother of a child who was having difficulty with both sleeping and bedwetting, I discovered that the child was taking a prescription medication for a seemingly unrelated health problem. Upon consulting the *Physicians Desk Reference,* I discovered that bedwetting and sleep disturbances were possible side effects of the medication being taken. A quick phone call to the pediatrician (who was not aware of the bedwetting and insomnia the child was experiencing) resulted in a modification of the prescription and an elimination of those symptoms. Another benefit of interviewing parents or teachers is the opportunity to build trust and rapport with them, which is a crucial ingredient when it is time to implement interventions.

What type of background information should be obtained? The answer to this question will depend to some extent on the nature of the presenting problems, but there are some standard areas that typically are explored in the process. Table 5.2 includes five general areas of inquiry, each with some specific recommended areas of questioning. The general areas include medical history, developmental history, social-emotional functioning, educational progress, and community involvement. Of course, this format is not all inclusive; other general areas and specific questions can be identified as the need arises. The five general areas of inquiry presented here are not equally applicable to all adults whom you might interview. For example, specific medical and developmental history may not be known to a foster caregiver or a teacher. Likewise when interviewing a teacher, the focus on educational background and performance of necessity will be the major area of discussion.

Developing the Interview with Children and Adolescents

Interviewing a child or adolescent client provides the opportunity for two important elements of the assessment: directly observing their behavior under controlled conditions and obtaining their own report as to their concerns, problems, and goals. The interview also provides an opportunity to develop rapport with the child or adolescent client, which will prove especially important if the interviewer will be functioning also as a therapist following the completion of the assessment.

Areas to Target for Observation. Although the specific aspects of client behavior most important for the interviewer to observe depend to a great extent upon the purpose of the interview and the nature of the presenting problems, there are four general areas that are almost always useful to target. These include physical characteristics, overt behavioral characteristics, social-emotional

TABLE 5.2   Recommended questioning areas for obtaining background information

Medical History

Problems during pregnancy and delivery

Postnatal complications

Serious illnesses/high fevers or convulsions

Serious injuries or accidents

Serious illnesses in family history

Allergies or dietary problems

Current health problems or medications

Vision and hearing

Developmental History

Ages for reaching developmental milestones—crawling, talking, walking, toilet training, etc.

Developmental delays (communication, motor, cognitive, social)

Development in comparison with siblings or peers

Social-Emotional Functioning

Temperament as an infant/toddler

Quality of attachment to caregiver(s) as infant/toddler

Quality of relationships with parents

Quality of relationships with siblings and peers

Discipline methods: what works best, who does she or he mind best

Behavioral problems at home or in community

Number and quality of friendships with peers

Any traumatic/disturbing experiences

Any responsibilities or chores

Who provides afterschool care

Educational Progress

Initial adjustment to school

Academic Progress: delayed, average, high achieving

School grades

Any school attendance problems

Behavioral problems at school

Quality of peer relations at school

Favorite subjects, classes, or teachers

Extracurricular activities

Community Involvement

Membership in any organizations or clubs (scouts, YMCA, etc.)

Organized team sports

Part-time job (for adolescents)

Church attendance/religious background

Relationships with extended family

functioning, and cognitive functioning. Table 5.3 includes a more complete breakdown of child characteristics to observe within each of these four areas. Of course, in some cases, the clinician will need to add to or subtract from this list, depending on the specifics of the interview. Many clinicians who routinely conduct interviews as part of a broader assessment find it useful to make notes of the important characteristics observed during the interview, so these can be detailed in the report at a later time.

Areas of Questioning to Target.   As we have already discussed, the traditional child interview is amenable to some very specific types of interviews, ranging from psychodynamic to basic rapport building. We have also discussed the use

TABLE 5.3 Important child characteristics to observe during interviews

Physical Characteristics

Unusual or inappropriate attire
Height and weight in comparison to same-age peers
Obvious physical problems
Direct signs of possible illness
Motor coordination

Overt Behavioral Characteristics

Activity level
Attention Span
Interaction with environment
Distractibility
Impulsivity

Social-Emotional Functioning

Range and appropriateness of affect
Mood state during interview
Reaction to praise
Reaction to frustration
Apparent social skills
Obvious anxiety or nervousness
Ease of separation from caregiver (for young children)

Cognitive Functioning

Communication skills
Overall intellectual competence
Level of insight
Logic of reasoning
Temporal and spatial orientation
Level of organization in activities
Inferred planning ability

TABLE 5.4 General areas of questioning for child/adolescent interviews

Intrapersonal Functioning

  Eating and sleeping habits

  Feelings/attributions about self

  Peculiar or bizarre experiences (e.g., hearing or seeing things)

  Emotional status (depressed, anxious, guilty, angry, etc.)

  Clarity of thought/orientation to time and space

  Insight into own thoughts and concerns

  Defensiveness/blaming

  Understanding of reason for interview

Family Relationships

  Quality of relationships with parents

  Quality of relationships with siblings

  Family routines, responsibilities, chores

  Involvement with extended family members

  Level of perceived support from family

  Perceived conflicts within family

Peer Relationships

  Number of close friends

  Preferred activities with friends

  Perceived conflicts with peers

  Social skills for initiating friendships

  Reports of peer rejection and loneliness

School Adjustment

  Current grade, teacher, school subjects

  General feelings about school

  Previous and current academic performance

  Favorite or preferred subjects or teachers

  Difficult or disliked subjects or teachers

  Involvement in extracurricular activities

  School attendance patterns

  Perceived conflicts or unfairness at school

Community Involvement

  Involvement in clubs or organizations

  Participation in community activities

  Church attendance/activities

  Level of mobility within community

  Part-time jobs (for adolescents)

  Relationships with other individuals in the community

of questioning strategies (e.g., open versus closed questions) and developmental considerations when conducting interviews with child or adolescent clients.

While traditional interview techniques for specific purposes and problems and with specific ages of clients vary to some extent, there are still some commonalities and some general areas of questioning. Table 5.4 (see p. 99) lists five general areas usually important to target when interviewing children or adolescents. These five areas include intrapersonal functioning, family relationships, peer relationships, school adjustment, and community involvement. Within each of these, specific areas for recommended questioning are provided, which can be increased or decreased, depending on the interview situation. When conducting traditional open-ended interviews, many clinicians find it useful to develop the interview and take notes according to a breakdown such as that shown in Table 5.4. Such a breakdown allows for a degree of structure and a logical progression in the interview, while still leaving it flexible and open ended.

THE BEHAVIORAL INTERVIEW

Essential Elements of Behavioral Interviewing

Behavioral interviewing differs from traditional interview methods in both the level of structure imposed by the interviewer and the purposes for conducting the interview. The roots of behavioral interviewing are found in behavioral psychology, discussed in chapters 1 and 3. As Gross (1984) notes, "the primary objective of behavioral assessment is to obtain descriptive information about problem behavior and the conditions maintaining it" (p. 62). The behavioral interview then is viewed as a specific type of behavioral assessment with the same objectives as other behaviorally oriented assessment methods. The clinician who conducts a behavioral interview is interested in pinpointing the problem behaviors and identifying variables that may have controlling or maintaining effects on those behaviors. As such, the behavioral interview requires a relatively high degree of structure by the interviewer in order for the primary goals to be met.

Several models of behavioral interviewing have been proposed, and each model has a different level of emphasis on such variables as cognitive competencies of the subject, organismic factors, analysis of the environment, and historical information. What the different models of behavioral interviewing have in common is their emphasis on description and clarification of problem behaviors and identification of antecedent stimuli and consequences of these behaviors. Haynes and Wilson (1979) have identified the essential elements of the behavioral interview as an organized interaction between the subject or a mediator and the behavioral interviewer for eight specific purposes, ranging from gathering information about client concerns to communicating specifically about the procedures and goals of the assessment and any subsequent intervention. The eight specific purposes of behavioral interviewing outlined by Haynes and Wilson are illustrated in Table 5.5.

TABLE 5.5   Specific purposes of behavioral interviewing

1. Gather information about client concerns and goals
2. Identify factors that elicit and/or maintain problem behaviors
3. Obtain relevant historical information
4. Identify potential reinforcers
5. Assess the mediation potential of the client
6. Educate the client
7. Obtain informed consent from the client
8. Communicate about the goals and procedures of assessment and intervention

SOURCE: Adapted from S. N. Haynes and C. C. Wilson, *Behavioral Assessment* (San Francisco: Jossey-Bass, 1979).

As a specific interview technique, the behavioral method offers several advantages over other forms of assessment, including other interview techniques. Behavioral interviewing has been touted as the most economical method of obtaining behavioral information (Wahler & Cormier, 1970), especially in comparison to direct observation. Given that interviews can be conducted with an informant who is familiar with the target subject, behavioral interviewing offers flexibility in the event that the subject is not directly available to observe or interview or is not capable of providing detailed interview information. Another advantage is that when conducted with the client, behavioral interviewing allows the clinician to directly observe various social behaviors and communication skills of the client, which may be useful in developing intervention strategies. Additionally, conducting a comprehensive behavioral interview with a *mediator* (i.e., parent or teacher) allows the clinician to assess how receptive he or she might be to the implementing of an intervention and to which specific types of interventions the mediator would be amenable (Gresham & Davis, 1988). Finally in comparison with such behavioral assessment techniques as direct observation and rating scales, interviewing is flexible enough to allow the clinician to expand or narrow the scope of the assessment, depending on what areas emerge as specific problems.

Implementing the Behavioral Interview with Parents and Teachers

When the client is a child or adolescent, it is almost always necessary and desirable to interview the parent(s), a teacher, or both as part of the initial assessment of the problem. Interviewing the parent(s) or teacher of the referred child or adolescent can be an extremely important part of the assessment for several reasons: (*a*) They are a potentially rich source of behavioral data due to their daily observations of the child's behavior in naturalistic settings, (*b*) they may be able to provide information on the child's behavior not available to the interviewer through other methods of assessment, and (*c*) they will often function as mediators in the intervention process, so it is critical to obtain their report and assess their ability to implement an intervention. Although conducting behavioral interviews of parents and teachers has been treated as separate topics, the processes involved have much in common and will be dealt with together in this chapter.

Conceptualizing the behavioral interview process as part of an overall behavioral consultation model for working with parents and teachers, Gresham and Davis (1988) identified three different types of behavioral interviews: (*a*) the problem identification interview, (*b*) the problem analysis interview, and (*c*) the problem evaluation interview. Since the problem evaluation interview is designed for implementation following an intervention, it is beyond the scope of this assessment text. This chapter will deal only with the first two types of behavioral interviews. Although it is possible to treat problem identification and problem analysis together, for purposes of conceptual clarity, they are overviewed individually.

The Problem Identification Interview. Identification of the problem is considered the most important phase in the consultation process because it defines what will be focused on and how the problem will be envisioned (Gresham & Davis, 1988). In the beginning of a problem identification interview, a clinician typically will start by obtaining demographic information and asking general questions about the child (''What concerns do you have about your child?'') but will soon begin to probe more specifically and in more depth (''How often does this student engage in aggressive behavior?''). The main idea is for the interviewer to assess the variety of problems reported, identify the problems of most concern, and then obtain very specific behavioral information relating to those problems.

Gresham and Davis (1988) have identified six major objectives for the problem identification interview, as follows:

1. Specification of the problem to be solved in consultation.
2. Elicitation of an objective description of the target behavior.
3. Identification of environmental conditions surrounding the target behavior.
4. Estimation of the frequency, intensity, and duration of the problem behavior.
5. Agreement on the type of data-collection procedures that will be used and who will collect the data.
6. Setting a date for the next interview, which will be the problem analysis interview.

In addition to identifying and gathering specific information on the problem behavior exhibited by the child or adolescent, Gross (1984) suggests obtaining information on their behavioral assets. By specifically asking the parent(s) or teacher what behavior is desired in place of the problem behavior, the interviewer can then work on assessing whether or not the child or adolescent has that behavior within their repertoire. Another example of gathering information on behavioral assets involves focusing the interview on what the child or adolescent finds particularly enjoyable or rewarding. This information could be used later in developing a menu of potential reinforcers.

The Problem Analysis Interview.   Problem analysis will ideally occur after a problem identification interview, which sets the stage for an appropriate plan for obtaining baseline data. Gresham and Davis (1988) have identified four objectives for the problem analysis interview, as follows:

1. Validation or confirmation of the problem through an examination of the baseline data. If the problem is confirmed, then this step would also include determining any discrepancies between the child's existing performance and what is desired.
2. Analysis of conditions surrounding the behavior. In other words, what are the antecedents, sequences, and consequences that affect the behavior?
3. Design of an intervention plan to alter the identified problem behavior. This objective includes developing both general approaches and precise plans for how the interventions will be implemented.
4. Setting a date for the problem evaluation interview, assuming that an appropriate intervention plan has been developed and agreed upon.

Admittedly it is often difficult to divide the problem identification and problem analysis aspects of the behavioral interview into two separate interview sessions, with the parent or teacher agreeing to gather appropriate baseline data in between the sessions. In typical school or clinic-based practice, there are often strong time pressures and needs to develop interventions immediately that make it necessary to combine both aspects of the behavioral interview in one extended session. However by doing this, there is no opportunity for the gathering of baseline data, and the clinician will need to rely on the verbal report of the client and rating-scale data and then work on gathering progress data as the intervention is implemented and modified. The following interchange of dialogue between a therapist and the parent of a six-year-old boy illustrates how the elements of a problem identification interview and a problem analysis interview can be merged into one session:

THERAPIST: You've told me about several problems that are happening with Jason. Which behavior do you see as being the biggest problem?

PARENT: That would have to be the temper tantrums.

THERAPIST: Tell me, very specifically, what Jason does when he is having a tantrum.

PARENT: It usually starts out with screaming and yelling, kind of mixed with crying. He'll call me names, make threats, and if it is a really bad one, he'll sometimes kick the walls, push over furniture and lamps, and even try to kick me or hit me.

THERAPIST: What kinds of things are usually going on just before Jason starts behaving like this?

PARENT: It's usually when he wants something that I won't let him have or do, or when he has gotten into an argument with his older brother.

THERAPIST: And where does it usually happen?

PARENT: Always at home. Usually inside the house. And now that I think about it, most of the time, it happens in the evenings.

THERAPIST: How long do these tantrums last?

PARENT: Oh, maybe 10 or 20 minutes. A really bad one might go on for almost an hour.

THERAPIST: Tell me what kinds of things you do, both just before the tantrums happen, and then during or after them, as a way to get them stopped.

PARENT: It seems like when the arguments start before the tantrums, I am usually tired or in a bad mood, and I yell at him or come down with some big unreasonable order. Once it gets started, it all depends on the situation and how I am feeling—it seems like if I'm worn out and irritated, I yell back at him, and sometimes I even try to hold him or give him a spank. If I'm not so out of sorts, I might try and send him to his room, or just sit down calmly and try to listen to him.

THERAPIST: And what seems to work best?

PARENT: Well, when I've thought about it, the thing that works best is to not let the argument get so bad, like try and distract him by getting him to do something else or to sit down calmly and listen to him. But I usually only do that when I'm not tired or irritated. Once it gets going, I know that the worst thing I can do is to get into it with him, but sometimes I don't care. It seems like moving him into his room for a few minutes until he settles down works better than that.

This example was taken from a recording of a 50-minute intake interview with a parent. Obviously, much more ground was covered during the interview, but the dialogue shows how a therapist can ask specific questions to pinpoint the greatest problem and determine its intensity, duration, and locus, and environmental variables that might be eliciting or maintaining it.

Implementing the Behavioral Interview with Children and Adolescents

Because behavioral interviewing techniques are strongly associated with the behavioral consultation model of problem identification and treatment, there is a definite emphasis on conducting the interview with parents and teachers, who will ultimately serve as mediators in the intervention process. However, in many cases, the referred child or adolescent can also become an important participant in the behavioral interview process. As a general rule, the younger the client is, the more difficult it is to obtain useful behavioral data from him or her in an interview, and the more important other behavioral assessment sources will be (e.g., parent interviews, direct observations, rating scales). Although interviews with young children can lead to the establishment of rapport and to the clinician's being able to observe their social behavior directly, Gross (1984) suggests that interviews with children under six years of age typically provide little in the way of content information.

As children become older and more sophisticated in their verbal mediation skills, the likelihood increases that they will be able to provide valuable descriptive information in the behavioral interview process. When conducting a behavioral interview with a child client, it is important to carefully move from a general to a more specific level of questioning. The interview might start out with some general questions about why the client thinks she is being interviewed, giving her an opportunity to talk about her interests but ultimately leading to specific probes of suspected problem behavior (e.g., "Tell me what usually happens before you get into fights"). As is true in the case of interviewing parents or teachers, it is important to ask questions pertaining to the child or adolescent client's behavioral assets. Obtaining a client's perspective on what positive and appropriate behaviors she can marshall, as well as what her strongest likes and dislikes are, can be important information for constructing an intervention plan. The following example illustrates some of the elements of conducting a behavioral interview directly with the child client. In this case, the client is an 11-year-old girl who has been referred for peer-relationship problems, and the clinician is a school psychologist, conducting a formal assessment:

PSYCHOLOGIST: Stacy, tell me what happens when you get into fights with the other girls you told me you had problems with.

STACY: Well, on Friday I got into a bad fight with Monica and Janeece. It was during recess, and I knew they were talking about me behind my back. I walked up to them and told them to shut their damn mouths.

PSYCHOLOGIST: You said you knew they were talking about you. How did you know that?

STACY: I could see them talking, while they were walking away from me, and they were looking at me.

PSYCHOLOGIST: So you figured they were talking about you, even though you couldn't hear what they were saying. What happened next?

STACY: Well, Janeece told me to shut up, so I said, "Why don't you make me?" She called me a bitch, so I pushed her away, then Monica hit me and we really starting going at it. The playground monitor sent me to the principal's office, and I told her that I wasn't the one who started it, but she never believed me.

PSYCHOLOGIST: Do these kind of fights usually happen during recess?

STACY: Mostly. But sometimes during lunch and one or two times while I was waiting for the bus.

PSYCHOLOGIST: But not during class?

STACY: Not usually, 'cause the teachers won't let me sit by kids who bother me all the time, and my homeroom teacher has my desk away from them altogether. Also, the teacher is usually there to stop it right away.

Like the previous example, this excerpt is a small part of a longer interview, but it illustrates how a clinician can ask specific questions regarding the circumstances and location of specific problem areas.

An additional consideration in involving the child or adolescent client in a behaviorally oriented interview is that it may be useful to conduct a brief joint interview with the adult and child. Particularly in the case of clinic-based assessments of child behavior problems, observing the parent and child together can provide the clinician with a rich source of direct observation data. Being able to observe the extent and quality of parent-child interactions and how they react to each other in both positive and negative situations affords the opportunity for a valuable merging of behavioral interviewing and direct behavioral observation.

STRUCTURED AND SEMISTRUCTURED INTERVIEWS

Although child interviewing techniques have historically been rather informal, there have been a number of efforts since the 1970s to develop highly structured and standardized interview schedules for use with children and adolescents. Most of these structured or semistructured interview schedules have been designed for use in psychiatric settings, but they may have a degree of usefulness in other settings as well. Three interview schedules representative of what is available will be reviewed in some detail, and some comments on additional interview schedules will follow these three reviews.

Schedule for Affective Disorders and Schizophrenia, School-age Children

Also referred to as the Kiddie-SADS or K-SADS, the Schedule for Affective Disorders and Schizophrenia for School-age Children (Puig-Antich & Chambers, 1978) is a semistructured, diagnostic interview for children and adolescents in the 6- to 17-year-old range. It was developed as a downward extension of the Schedule for Affective Disorders and Schizophrenia (Endicott & Spitzer, 1978). Although its title implies that it is for the purpose of assessing affective and psychotic disorders, the K-SADS is a broadly based interview useful for eliciting information on a wide range of emotional and behavior problems and then classifying these problems according to DSM diagnostic criteria.

Two versions of the K-SADS are available. The Present Episode version (K-SADS-P) is designed for use in assessing current or present (within the past year) episodes of psychopathology. The Epidemiologic version (K-SADS-E) is designed for use in assessing psychopathology that has occurred over the course of the subject's entire life. Hughes and Baker (1990) have noted that when the K-SADS is used to diagnose disorders that require detailed historical information, both versions of the schedule should be utilized and that when administering the K-SADS-E, the interviewer should be particularly careful to ensure that the child or adolescent subject is appropriately oriented to time. This review will focus on elements of the K-SADS common to both versions.

The K-SADS should be used only by experienced interviewers who have received specific training since the format is fairly complex and requires a degree of sophisticated judgment. Both versions of the K-SADS include a parent interview first and then follow with an interview of the child or adolescent. Each interview takes approximately one hour (or longer), so the interviewer must plan on two to three hours for the entire interview process. The interviews include a combination of unstructured or open-ended questions and questions regarding highly specific symptoms, which are scored on a rating scale. The K-SADS allows for skipping certain areas of questioning not relevant to the particular client. In addition to providing specific open-ended and structured interview questions, the K-SADS has a format for rating the overall behavioral characteristics and performance of the subject.

Data reported by Chambers et al. (1985) indicate that the K-SADS-P has moderate test-retest reliability with both parents and children over a 72-hour period (average = .54 across symptom categories) and adequate inter-rater reliability (.86 for parent interviews and .89 for child interviews) across symptom categories. A study of the validity of the K-SADS-E by Orvaschel, Puig-Antich, Chambers, Tabrizi, and Johnson (1982) compared K-SADS-E diagnoses of 17 subjects who were previously diagnosed using an earlier version of the K-SADS and found that 16 of the 17 subjects received the same diagnosis. Although the empirical data on the K-SADS interview schedules are limited, they suggest adequate psychometric properties. The K-SADS may be a good choice in some situations where DSM diagnostic criteria are very important, and these interviews appear to be most widely used at child and adolescent inpatient psychiatric facilities.

Diagnostic Interview for Children and Adolescents-Revised

The Diagnostic Interview for Children and Adolescents-Revised (DICA-R) (Reich & Welner, 1989) is a highly structured interview schedule for children aged 6 to 17. The DICA-R is a revision of the original DICA, developed by Herjanic and her colleagues (Herjanic & Reich, 1982) in the Division of Child Psychiatry at Washington University. The original DICA was patterned after the adult Diagnostic Interview Schedule (DIS) (Robins, Helzer, Croughan, & Radcliff, 1981).

The DICA-R includes three closely related interview schedules, designed for use with children 6 to 12 years of age, adolescents 13 to 17 years of age, and parents of children aged 6 to 17, respectively. The three versions are essentially similar, the only notable differences being changes in item wording to make them more appropriate to the specific age group of the child and adolescent clients or for use by parents in evaluating their children on specific symptoms. In terms of differences between the DICA-R and the original DICA, Hughes and Baker (1990) noted that the items on the DICA-R were modified in order to "produce a more conversational style between the examiner and respondent" (p. 70).

Administration of the DICA-R takes approximately one hour. The instrument contains 267 items that are coded in a structured manner (i.e., "yes," "no," "sometimes," and "rarely"). The DICA-R is structured so that the interview begins with a brief demographic session that includes both the parent(s) and child, after which it is recommended that separate interviewers concurrently meet with the parent(s) and child for the completion of separate interview forms. The interviews conclude with an assessment of psychosocial stressors, an observational checklist, and a clinical impressions section completed by the examiner. The interview data are scored according to specific criteria included in the interview booklet, and the obtained scores are used to diagnose DSM-III-R axis I disorders. Although the DICA-R can be administered by interviewers who are only minimally trained, training of interviewers can increase the reliability and validity of the data (Reich & Welner, 1989).

Studies published on the original DICA have indicated relatively high percentages of inter-rater agreement (85 percent to 89 percent) on child symptoms (Herjanic & Reich, 1982) and within-interviewer agreement (80 percent to 95 percent) on child symptoms at 2 to 3 month intervals (Herjanic, Herjanic, Brown, & Wheatt, 1975). The rate of agreement on symptoms between children and parents has also been explored (Herjanic & Reich, 1982), with the results showing rates of agreement ranging from very modest to quite strong, depending on the particular diagnostic category and number of subjects. Herjanic and Campbell (1977) reported data on the DICA that show it can differentiate from a moderate to a strong degree between children referred to psychiatric and pediatric clinics. At the present time, there are no published reports attesting to the validity and reliability of the DICA-R, but it can be assumed that the technical properties of the revised interview are similar to those of the original DICA. Edelbrock and Costello (1988) noted that although the DICA has several strong features, further validation is needed before it can be recommended strongly for use as a clinical research tool.

Child Assessment Schedule

The Child Assessment Schedule (CAS) is a semistructured interview schedule designed for use with children aged 7 to 16 (Hodges, Kline, Stern, Cytryn, & McKnew, 1982; Hodges, 1987). Although most of the research on the CAS has been on its direct use with children, a modified version for use with parents is also available. Like most of the other interview schedules reviewed in this section, the CAS is useful for making DSM diagnostic classification decisions, as many of the items are similar to the diagnostic criteria found in DSM childhood disorders.

The CAS is utilized in evaluating the child or adolescent client's functioning in several areas, and scores are yielded in 11 different content areas (school, friends, activities and hobbies, family, fears, worries and anxieties, self-image, mood and behavior, physical complaints, acting out, and reality testing). CAS includes 75 questions that are coded "yes," "no," "ambiguous," "no response," or "not applicable." The CAS takes approximately 45–60 minutes to administer, including a 53-item observational rating completed by the examiner following the interview. The developers of the CAS recommend that interviewers with clinical training be used in administering the interview schedule, but satisfactory results have also been obtained by interviewers without formal clinical training (Hodges, McKnew, Burbach, & Roebuck, 1987).

Published studies relating to the stability of the CAS have demonstrated moderate to high inter-rater reliability (90 percent and above) on CAS total scores (Hodges et al., 1982; Turner, Beidel, & Costello, 1987), and adequate test-retest reliability through showing statistically significant correlations on diagnostic classifications and instrument scores (Hodges, Cools, & McKnew, 1989). Concurrent validity of the CAS has been demonstrated through finding significant relationships with self-report measures of anxiety and depression (Hodges et al., 1982). Discriminant validity of the CAS has been demonstrated by showing that the instrument differentiated between groups of normal, behaviorally disturbed, and psychosomatic children (Hodges, Kline, Barbero, & Flanery, 1985; Hodges, Kline, Barbero, & Woodruff, 1985). There is probably a greater amount and variety of published reliability and validity research on the CAS than on any other structured or semistructured interview schedule currently available.

Concluding Comments on Formal Interview Schedules

In Table 5.6, some of the major characteristics of the three reviewed interview schedules are overviewed for comparison purposes. As was stated earlier, these three interview schedules do not represent the entire domain of semistructured and highly structured interview schedules available for use with children and adolescents. The National Institute of Mental Health Diagnostic Interview Schedule for Children (DISC) (Fisher, Wicks, Shaffer, Piacentini, & Lapkin, 1992) is another widely used structured interview for use in assessing child and adolescent behavioral-emotional problems. The DISC is examined in some detail in chapter 8. Other structured interview schedules reported in the child psychiatry and psychology literature include the Interview Schedule for Children (ISC) (Kovacs, 1982), and the Mental Health Assessment Form (MHAF) (Kestenbaum & Bird, 1978). The three interview schedules reviewed in this chapter were featured due to factors such as availability, amount and quality of psychometric data, ease of use, and general purpose design. A new instrument, the *Semistructured Clinical Interview for Children* (SCIC) has recently been released by the University Associates in Psychiatry group at the University of Vermont (McConaughy & Achenbach, 1990), and it appears to have a great deal of promise as a clinical tool. SCIC is designed for use with 6- to 11-year-old children, and it takes 60 to 90 minutes to administer. However, the SCIC is still considered to be a provisional instrument, as extensive training materials or published research studies are not yet available.

The development of formal structured and semistructured interview schedules is important in the area of child and adolescent assessment. For the most part, they represent high-quality attempts to integrate a stronger empirical base into the process of clinical interviewing. At the present time, most of the formal interview schedules have a decidedly psychiatric bent, in that they are utilized specifically for generating DSM diagnoses and have been developed and validated primarily in psychiatric settings. It remains to be seen how useful these efforts will be in general school and clinic-based assessment, but there is cause for optimism that appropriate applications in these areas will be found.

TABLE 5.6 An overview of three selected semistructured and structured interview schedules for use with children and adolescents

Name	Format	Purpose	Level of Structure	Time Required	Comments
Schedule for Affective and Schizophrenic Disorders for School-age Children (K-SADS)	Combination of open-ended and structured questions; interviews for both parent and child subject	Diagnosis of major child disorders according to DSM criteria	Semistructured	2–3 hours for complete interviews with parent and child	Life-time and present episode versions available; requires extensive training
Diagnostic Interview for Children and Adolescents, Revised (DICA-R)	267 highly structured items that are systematically coded; interviews begin with a joint demographic interview with both subject and parent	Diagnosis of major child disorders according to DSM axis I categories	Highly structured	About 1 hour	Parent, adolescent, and child versions available; requires some training; still lacking in reported validity data
Child Assessment Schedule (CAS)	75 items coded according to 5 different criteria; child and parent versions are available	Evaluation of various aspects of child functioning; DSM diagnoses	Semistructured	45 minutes to 1 hour	Can be administered by interviewers with limited experience and training; relatively large amount of reliability and validity training

INTERVIEWS AND DECISION MAKING

How useful are interviews when it comes to decision making? They can range from moderately useful to extremely useful, depending on the specific decision-making process. For making additional assessment decisions, interviewing can provide excellent information regarding specific additional areas that need to be assessed. During the process of interviewing, additional information may surface that will persuade the interviewer of the necessity for observation or other objective assessment in specific areas. Interview information can be important for diagnosis and classification decisions, though it should seldom be used alone. For special education classification, it is essential that decisions not be made based on a single assessment method. For making DSM diagnostic decisions, the interview will normally serve as an adjunct to additional assessment methods, though in some cases DSM diagnoses can be made based on interview data alone, particularly through the use of structured or semistructured diagnostic interviews. In making placement decisions, interview data can provide necessary clues and be used to support inferences drawn from additional information sources but are seldom sufficient to be used by themselves. One of the best uses of information obtained through interviews is for intervention or treatment decisions. If the interviews were carefully structured to identify specific problems and the environmental conditions eliciting and maintaining those problems (e.g., behavioral interviewing), there may be obvious implications for developing an intervention plan.

APPLICATION PROBLEMS—DEVELOPMENTALLY SENSITIVE INTERVIEWING

The major assumption behind "developmentally sensitive" interviewing is that a child or adolescent's ability to understand an interview question and respond to it in an informative way is to a great extent a function of his or her particular level of cognitive, social, and emotional development. Using the information in the section of this chapter titled "Understanding Developmental Issues That Affect Children's Responses" as a general guide, write developmentally appropriate interview questions and statements that might be used with typical children at three different levels (preschool–early childhood, elementary–middle childhood, secondary–adolescence) in order to obtain useful information in the following areas:

1. Discussion with the interviewee to make sure he or she understands the purpose of the interview.
2. Confrontation of the interviewee regarding information he or she has given which is obviously not true.
3. Pursuit of a strong suspicion that the interviewee has been sexually abused.
4. A follow-up query with an interviewee who has said he or she intends to harm someone with whom he or she is very angry.
5. A follow-up question with an interviewee who has said he or she intends to break a rule or law, which could lead to negative consequences.
6. Discussion with an interviewee regarding his or her perceptions of a parent, i.e., how much affection he or she feels for the parent, how strongly attached, and so forth.

CHAPTER **6**

Sociometric Assessment Methods

INTRODUCTION

This chapter deals with the sociometric assessment of children and adolescents. Sociometric assessment includes a variety of procedures designed to measure such related constructs as social status, popularity, peer acceptance or rejection, and reputation. Although sociometric assessment is not new, as it has been utilized in educational-clinical practice and research on a fairly wide basis since the 1930s, a number of important research efforts in this area have occurred since the 1960s. These studies (e.g., Cowen, Pederson, Babigan, Izzo, & Trost, 1973; Dodge, Coie,

& Brakke, 1982; Roff, 1961) have emphasized the importance of social functioning in childhood and thus have underscored the importance of clinicians who work with children having a knowledge of sociometric assessment methods.

The chapter begins with a discussion of the conceptual and historical foundations of sociometric assessment, along with some information on what is known about the validity of sociometry for various clinical and research purposes. The largest section of the chapter is devoted to detailed overviews of four general types of sociometric methods: peer nominations, peer ratings, sociometric rankings, and alternative sociometric procedures. Both general and specific aspects of assessment using these four approaches are discussed, and numerous examples are presented. Following the overview of specific sociometric assessment techniques, some of the ethical and pragmatic issues that have surfaced in recent years regarding sociometric assessment are presented. Surprisingly, many of the common concerns about the use of sociometrics are not supported by the research, and there is some evidence to the contrary. The chapter ends with a discussion on how sociometric assessment can be used most effectively in making various types of clinical and educational decisions.

SOCIOMETRIC ASSESSMENT: ITS IMPORTANCE, HISTORY, AND EMPIRICAL BASE

The basis of sociometric assessment procedures is directly gathering information from within a peer group (usually in a classroom setting) concerning the social dynamics of that group. The key ingredient of sociometric assessment is that data on various aspects of the social status of persons within a peer group *is obtained directly from the members,* rather than from observations or ratings by impartial outside evaluators. These procedures allow the assessor to tap directly into the ongoing social dynamics of a group, an obvious advantage since there are many aspects of social relationships within a group that are not easily discernable to the casual observer (Worthen, Borg, & White, 1993).

Sociometric assessment provides an avenue for measuring constructs such as level of popularity, acceptance or rejection status, and attribution of specific positive and negative characteristics such as leadership ability, athletic or academic prowess, aggressiveness, and social awkwardness. Unlike many other assessment methods, sociometric procedures typically are not norm referenced, standardized, or commercially published. Instead, they tend to consist of different variations of a few relatively simple methods originally developed for use by researchers but fully capable of being translated into school or clinical practice.

Why Study Social Status?

In 1917, a prominent educator by the name of C. R. Beery published a series of books titled *Practical Child Training.* In this series, Beery offered some practical advice to mothers who had children with few friends and difficulties in approaching peers. Beery suggested that mothers could help these children by facilitating opportunities for peer interaction such as picnics that would include their children's classmates. Beery noted that these types of activities would help children to "have a royal good time" and further suggested that if a child shows fear in approaching other children, the mother should "not scold or make any scene, but simply appear to pay no attention to him" (Asher & Parker, 1989, p. 5). This anecdote goes a long way toward showing that the quality of children's social interaction has been of academic and practical importance for many years.

As we shall see, the study of social status is indeed important, as peer relationship problems during childhood may have a large, negative, and lasting impact on later adjustment in life. But how extensive are peer relationship problems during childhood? Based on research by Hymel and Asher (1977) wherein typical elementary school children were asked to nominate their three best friends, Asher (1990) provides a conservative estimate that about 10 percent of all children experience significant peer relationship difficulties. This estimate is based on Asher and Hymel's (1977) finding that about 10 percent of the children in the study were not named as anybody's best friend. Asher (1990) notes that if the criterion of reciprocal friendship nominations is used, the estimated percentage of children with peer relationship problems is substantially higher. Thus we can make a conservative estimate that at least 10 percent of all school-age children experience problems in developing friendships and in gaining social acceptance. Given the poor long-term prognosis that may follow these children, this figure is alarming.

The study and assessment of children's social status is also important because of the positive developmental purposes that children's friendships serve. Fine (1981) noted that children's friendships make a significant contribution to the development of their overall interactional competence. In other words, through the processes that friendship building requires and refines, children learn not only to interact effectively with their friends but also to develop social-interactional skills that generalize to many other situations and persons as well. Fine (1981) specifically identified three functions of preadolescent friendships that contribute to general interactional competence:

> First, friendships provide a staging area for behavior. Friendships are situated in social environments that have implications for the acquisition of interactional competencies. Second, friendships are cultural institutions, and as such they provide didactic training. Third, friendships provide a context for the growth of the child's social self, a context within which he or she can learn the appropriate self-image to project in social situations. (p. 49)

Understanding some of the positive developmental dynamics of children's friendships makes clearer why peer relationship problems in childhood can be so detrimental. The development of positive peer relationships via friendship making is a critical aspect of a youngster's overall cognitive and social development.

Historical Development of Sociometric Assessment

The use of sociometric assessment procedures dates back to the 1930s with the first clinical and research uses of these techniques being conducted by educators and sociologists. One of the first published works on sociometry was Moreno's influential book *Who Shall Survive?* (1934). The earliest attempts to use sociometric assessments were experimental and novel, but by the late 1930s and early 1940s, reports of the systematic use of sociometry began appearing in scholarly journals. The journal *Sociometry* began to be published in the 1930s, and it included a mix of articles showing applications of sociometric techniques in both educational practice and sociological research. Several research reports using sociometric assessment were published in the *Journal of Educational Psychology* in the early 1940s, such as articles by Bonney (1943) and Young and Cooper (1944).

By the 1950s, the state of sociometric assessment had advanced considerably, and a number of books were published on the topic (e.g., Cunnignham, 1951; Laughlin, 1954; Taba, Brady, Robinson, & Vickery, 1951). During this period and through the early to mid-1960s, sociometric procedures were commonly used as a means of measuring social adjustment in public school settings. Starting in about the mid-1960s, the use of sociometrics as a typical school-based assessment procedure appeared to decline. Possible reasons for the declining clinical or practical use of sociometrics may include the advancement of other forms of assessment (specifically behavior rating scales and objective self-report measures) and public and professional concerns that sociometric assessment may have some negative effects on some children. Interestingly, although concerns do exist about the possible negative affects of sociometric assessment, these concerns have not been substantiated through research. More on the ethical-professional concerns associated with sociometric assessment will be discussed later in this chapter.

Although sociometric techniques still are widely used by researchers in the fields of child development, education, sociology, and psychology, they appear to be used less as a standard method for assessing social adjustment problems in schools than they were two to three decades ago. In fact, surveys of school psychologists during the 1980s (Goh & Fuller, 1983) and 1990s (Hutton, Dubes, & Muir, 1992) indicate that sociometric procedures were so seldom used by practitioners that they did not appear on tables of survey results. Whether there will be increased use of sociometric assessment in the future is unknown, but it is doubtful that sociometry will regain the level of popularity it had during the 1940s and 1950s because of the advent and refinement of so many other competing assessment procedures that were not available at that time.

Validity of Sociometric Assessment

Dimensions of Social Status.   Early researchers in the use of sociometrics tended to view social status in a fairly unidimensional manner (Landau & Milich, 1990). However, more recent efforts in this area have led investigators to conclude that the construct of social status is both complex and multidimensional. Coie,

Dodge, and Coppotelli (1982) used peer preference questions in a sociometric technique with a large number ($N = 537$) of elementary and middle school age children. They analyzed the obtained data to develop five social status groups: *popular, rejected, average, neglected,* and *controversial.* An analysis of the characteristics of the students indicated that, while there was some overlap between categories, each category had some distinct features. Popular children were those who were rated by peers as being cooperative, having leadership ability, and engaging in very little disruptive behavior. Rejected children were rated as frequently fighting, disruptive, uncooperative and lacking leadership traits. Neglected children were those who were largely ignored by other children and were seen as being socially unresponsive. The fourth nonaverage group, controversial children, tended to exhibit features of both the popular and rejected groups, being considered disruptive and starting fights, but were also perceived as being assertive leaders. This widely cited conceptualization of social status ratings shows how complex social dynamics within peer groups can be, and suggests that sociometric procedures can indeed provide complex and useful social assessment data. Table 6.1 presents the four nonaverage groups from the Coie et al. (1982) study, with a listing of the social-behavioral characteristics found to be pertinent for each group.

Technical Adequacy of Sociometric Procedures.   The technical and psychometric aspects of various sociometric procedures have been researched in several studies, and they have generally shown favorable evidence of technical soundness. Temporal stability of sociometric assessments has been shown to be relatively high at both short- and long-term stability periods (Hartup, 1983; Roff, et al., 1972). Landau and Milich (1990) reviewed several studies of inter-rater correspondence in sociometric procedures and noted that moderate to high levels of correspondence between raters have generally been found. However, there is one interesting finding in this regard—a gender difference on social

TABLE 6.1   Descriptions of four nonaverage child and adolescent social status groups

Group	Sociometric Findings and Social-Behavioral Characteristics
Popular	Receive the most positive and fewest negative nominations; described by peers in prosocial terms and perceived as leaders
Rejected	Receive the most negative nominations; described by peers as being disruptive and likely to fight; perceived as having poor leadership skills and being uncooperative
Neglected	Receive few positive or negative peer nominations; described by peers as being shy and unassertive; perceived as having poor social skills
Controversial	Have characteristics similar to both popular and rejected groups; described by peers as being active and assertive leaders but also perceived as being disruptive, demanding, and frequently not liked

SOURCE: Based on research by J. D. Coie, K. A. Dodge, and H. Coppetelli, "Dimensions and Types of Social Status: A Cross-Age Perspective," *Developmental Psychology* 18, 1982: 557–570.

convergence in ratings wherein both boys and girls tend to attribute more positive attributes to members of their own sex and more negative attributes to members of the opposite sex.

Predictive Validity of Sociometric Assessment.   The predictive validity of sociometric assessment procedures has been established through several widely cited studies. Cowen et al. (1973) used the Class Play peer assessment procedure in a longitudinal study of 537 children who were tested in three different cohorts in either the first or third grade. The children who were nominated more frequently for negative roles in the Class Play assessment were more likely to receive psychiatric services as adults, based on their names appearing on registers of psychiatric services.

Roff et al. (1961) conducted a prospective study of 164 boys who were referred to child guidance clinics and who later served in one of the branches of the U.S. military. Based on a review of the subjects' case histories as children and their adult service records, those who were reported to have poor peer adjustment were significantly more likely to receive bad conduct discharges from the military than the children who were reported to have good peer relations. Interestingly, approximately half of the subjects in this study ultimately received bad conduct discharges. Another widely cited study by Roff and his colleagues (Roff & Sells, 1968; Roff et al., 1972) used a longitudinal design in studying various social-behavioral characteristics of approximately 40,000 children who were enrolled in grades 3 through 6 in public schools in Minnesota and Texas. The sociometric assessment data for this study included peer nominations and teacher ratings. When records of delinquency were evaluated four years following the completion of the sociometric assessments, it was found that low-rated children were significantly more likely to appear on juvenile delinquency rosters.

Sociometric status has also been shown to be a significant factor in school dropout patterns. Ullman (1957) studied peer and teacher sociometric ratings of students in 11 ninth-grade classes and found that positive sociometric ratings were predictive of being named on honor rolls at graduation, while negative sociometric ratings were predictive of the students' dropping out of school prior to graduation.

In sum, while sociometric assessment procedures tend not to be standardized or commercially published like many other forms of assessment, they have nonetheless been demonstrated to have favorable technical properties and should be viewed as a potentially useful method of assessing peer relations and social status.

AN OVERVIEW OF SPECIFIC SOCIOMETRIC ASSESSMENT PROCEDURES

Since most sociometric assessment procedures are nonstandardized and have a considerable amount of overlap with one another, it is difficult to divide them into distinct categories. However there are distinctive similarities and differences among different methods that make a general categorization possible. This section provides an overview of some commonly used sociometric procedures based on a division into four categories: (*a*) peer nomination procedures, (*b*) peer rating procedures, (*c*) sociometric ranking procedures, and (*d*) alternative sociometric procedures. In some cases, these categories involve general descriptions common to many methods within the category. In other cases, the categorical description is unique to a specific procedure.

Peer Nomination Procedures

The oldest and most widely used sociometric approach and the basis for most other types of sociometric measures is the nomination method, originally introduced by Moreno (1934). The basis of the peer nomination technique is that students are asked to nominate or name classmates whom they prefer according to specific positive criteria. This approach typically involves the student's naming one or more classmates with whom they would most like to study, play during free time, work on a class project, or be with in some other positive way. For children with sufficient reading and writing ability, peer nomination procedures can be administered by either an item-by-peer matrix or a questionnaire wherein they fill in names of classmates on blank lines following questions.

The item-by-peer matrix consists of having the names of all children in the class across the top of the page, and the social interaction items listed vertically on the left side of the page. The students are instructed to put an ''x'' under the name(s) of the students to whom they think each item applies (e.g., ''Which student would you most like to have as your best friend?''). Use of a questionnaire format accomplishes essentially the same thing (e.g., ''Write the names of three students in your class whom you would like most to have as your best friends'' followed by three numbered blank lines). Scoring of peer nominations is typically done by totalling the number of nominations that each child receives. Worthen, Borg, and White (1993) suggest that the results of positive peer nomination procedures can be classified and interpreted according to a frequently used set of criteria. *Stars* are individuals who are frequently chosen. *Isolates* are individuals who are never chosen in the process. *Neglectees* are those who receive only a few nominations. The results can also be plotted on a *sociogram,* which shows the patterns of choice for each student and helps in identifying not only frequently and never nominated students but also cliques or small groups as well. A *mutual choice* occurs when an individual is chosen by the same student whom they selected. A *cross-sex choice* occurs when a boy chooses a girl or a girl chooses a boy. A *clique* is identified as a small group of students who choose each other and make few or no choices outside of that group. *Cleavage* is identified when two or more groups within a class or social unit never choose someone from other group(s). Using these scoring and classification criteria, one can easily see how a procedure as deceptively simple as the peer nomination method can yield information that is both striking and complex. Figure 6.1 presents an example of an anonymous item-by-peer matrix that could be used in a peer nomination assessment in a classroom setting. It includes both positive and negative items. Figure 6.2 presents an example of a sociogram based on a positive nomination procedure used with 15 elementary-age boys who were asked to select two boys with whom they would most like to be friends.

PLEASE LIST THE NAME OF YOUR TEACHER _____

WHAT GRADE ARE YOU IN? _____

I AM A (circle one): BOY / GIRL

DIRECTIONS: We are interested in finding out how well children are able to notice the behavior of other children. Please help us by answering some questions about the other children in your class. Follow along as the questions are read out loud, and try to answer each question the best you can. For each question, you will be asked to pick one student that you think the question is most like, and then put an X in the box under their name for that question. Remember that there are no right or wrong answers, and the way you answer these questions will not affect your grade. Your classmates and your teacher will not know how you answered the questions. If you don't understand what to do or need help, please raise your hand.

Who would you most like to be best friends with?									
Who is angry or mad a lot?									
Who would you like to invite over to your home?									
Who gets in fights?									
Who gets along well with the teacher?									
Who is in trouble a lot?									

FIGURE 6.1 An example of an item-by-peer matrix for a peer nomination procedure that includes both positive and negative items. This matrix is for an anonymous assessment where the identity of the rater will not be known.

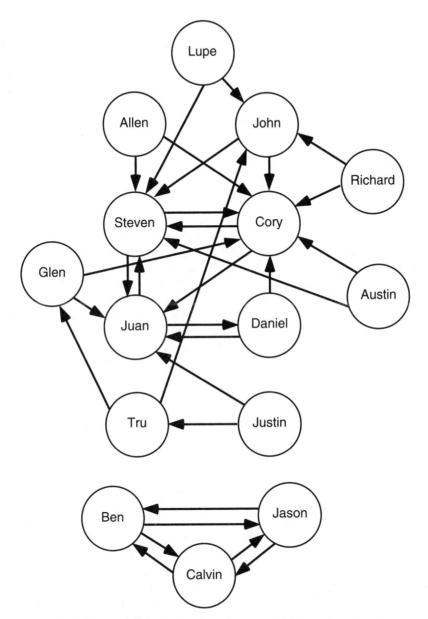

FIGURE 6.2 An example of a sociogram plotted for a group of
15 elementary-age boys who were asked to select the two boys
in the classroom with whom they would most like to be friends.

Although the peer nomination technique has most often involved the use
of positive items indicative of high social status, many practitioners and
researchers have used variations of this method by employing negative
nominations, using items created to identify students who are socially rejected
by peers (e.g., ''Who would you least like to play with?'' or ''Who would you

never want to be friends with?''). Negative nominations are scored and interpreted in a variety of ways, including finding specific patterns of social rejection within a group and identifying rejected students who receive a large number of negative nominations. When used in conjunction with positive nominations, negative nominations can provide more detailed information about the subtle dynamics of social status within a group, as exemplified by Coie and others' division of social status (1982) into five different groups.

Peer Rating Procedures

The use of peer ratings, also referred to as the *roster rating method,* constitutes a form of sociometric assessment conceptually and psychometrically quite different from peer nominations. In the peer rating procedure, the children within a group are asked to respond to a sociometric question *for each child in the group.* A typical procedure for implementing the peer rating method involves providing each member of a group with a roster that has the names of all other group members and a list of sociometric questions and then rating each member of the group on each question, using a 5-point scale (Connolly, 1983). For younger children, a variation of the 5-point scale is often used, consisting of a series of 3 or 5 faces, ranging from frowning to smiling, anchored to different scale values. Using this method, the children are asked to circle one of the faces in lieu of a numerical rating (Asher, Singleton, Tinsely, & Hymel, 1979). A sample peer rating assessment form is displayed in Figure 6.3. This particular example shows a peer rating-scale format that might be used with children in grades 3–6.

Psychometrically and statistically, peer rating methods are considerably different than peer nomination methods. Each child's score is based on an average of all the ratings he or she receives. Since each child is rated by all classmates, a broader picture of each one's social status is obtained. Compared with peer nomination methods, ratings are more stable within a group and are less affected by the size of the group (Connolly, 1983). With younger children, the increase in score stability using rating methods is particularly noticeable (Asher et al., 1979). Another interesting measurement characteristic of peer ratings is that they tend to provide distributions that are less skewed than those provided by some other forms of sociometric assessment (Hops & Lewin, 1984).

In addition to having measurement qualities different from peer nomination procedures, peer rating methods are conceptually different as well, and they can measure a somewhat different construct. Peer ratings are thought to produce a measure of average *likability,* whereas peer nominations are thought to produce a measure of *popularity.* Although likability and popularity have some obvious similarities, there are some subtle yet important differences between these constructs. For example, using the peer rating method, a child might receive scores indicating an average amount of likability, yet it is possible that the same child might not receive any positive nominations. In this case, if the sociometric interpretation were based on the peer nomination data alone, the child might be considered erroneously to be socially isolated or neglected. There is a relatively large degree of measurement overlap between these procedures. Oden and Asher

Peer Rating Form

Please List the Name of Your Teacher: _____

What Grade Are You In? _____

I AM A (circle one):   BOY   /   GIRL

DIRECTIONS: We are interested in finding out how much the students in your class would like to work with each other or play with each other. For each student on this list, circle one of the numbers to show how much you would like to play with them and circle one of the numbers to show how much you would like to work with them. This is what the numbers mean:

1 = NOT AT ALL (I definitely would not like to work or play with this person.)
2 = NOT VERY MUCH (I don't think I would want to work or play with this person.)
3 = DON'T CARE (It really wouldn't matter to me if I played with this person or not.)
4 = SORT OF (I think I would like to work or play with this person.)
5 = VERY MUCH (I definitely would like to work or play with this person.)

Since your name is not on this form, your teacher and the other students in the class will not know how you answered. There are no right or wrong answers, and the way you fill out this form will not affect your grade. If you have any questions or if you need help, raise your hand.

NAME	WORK WITH?					PLAY WITH?				
1. _____	1	2	3	4	5	1	2	3	4	5
2. _____	1	2	3	4	5	1	2	3	4	5
3. _____	1	2	3	4	5	1	2	3	4	5
4. _____	1	2	3	4	5	1	2	3	4	5
5. _____	1	2	3	4	5	1	2	3	4	5
6. _____	1	2	3	4	5	1	2	3	4	5
7. _____	1	2	3	4	5	1	2	3	4	5
8. _____	1	2	3	4	5	1	2	3	4	5
9. _____	1	2	3	4	5	1	2	3	4	5
10. _____	1	2	3	4	5	1	2	3	4	5

FIGURE 6.3 A sample peer rating assessment form. This particular form utilizes a 5-point scale, is anonymous, and would be most useful with children in grades 3–6.

(1977) reported a correlation of .63 between the two measures. Yet in another study (Asher & Hymel, 1981) of 23 children who received no positive nominations, 11 of them received high positive ratings from their peers.

By combining the nomination and rating procedures in a sociometric assessment, the obtained sociometric data may differentiate popular/likeable and unpopular/unlikeable children more powerfully than single-source data would (Asher & Renshaw, 1981). Another advantage of using peer rating procedures is that they can provide information regarding both positive and negative social status without the use of negative questions. This can be done by wording questions positively or neutrally and then simply looking at the distribution of scores. This advantage may be particularly important when attempting to obtain consent from parents or program administrators who are uncomfortable with the use of negative nomination methods.

Sociometric Ranking Procedures

Unlike the peer nomination and peer rating procedures just overviewed, socio-metric ranking procedures are designed to provide information on child social status and peer relations through data contributed by adults rather than peers. In most instances of sociometric ranking procedures reported in the literature, the informant is a teacher and the peer group consists of same-grade classmates. However it would also be possible to implement sociometric ranking procedures in nonschool settings, such as group homes, residential or day treatment programs, and perhaps in clinic-based therapy groups.

Because the object of sociometric assessment is to obtain information on status and relations within a peer group, what advantage is there in going outside of the peer group to an adult informant to collect this data? Connolly (1983) noted that when using the peer group as a source of information, one must assume that children are capable of making accurate social distinctions, and with normal children of elementary age or older, this assumption appears to be valid. However with younger children and perhaps with older children who have moderate to severe cognitive impairment, the completion of sociometric tasks may be difficult and may result in lower reliability. Another reason for employing teachers as sociometric informants is that they tend to be expert objective observers of child behavior and thus understand the social dynamics within their classroom. Additionally, educators are understandably often hesitant to commit blocks of academic time for nonacademic student tasks, and they might be more willing to provide sociometric ranking data themselves rather than have their students spend instructional time on it.

There are two general ways that sociometric ranking can be completed by classroom teachers. The first method involves the teacher rank-ordering every student in the classroom according to some sociometric criteria, such as popularity with classmates and positive interactions with peers. Previous studies employing this type of ranking procedure have shown that the obtained data tend to be highly reliable and may correlate better with independent ratings and observations of child social behavior than do peer nominations or ratings (Connolly & Doyle, 1981; Greenwood, Walker, Todd, & Hops, 1979). Note that when the object of interest is negative social interactions or peer rejection, teacher rankings have been found to correlate with independent ratings and observations of child behavior to a lower degree than negative peer nominations (Landau & Milich, cited in Connolly, 1983).

A related method for obtaining teacher sociometric rankings involves first determining which students in a classroom fit a given social-behavioral description and then rank-ordering those students according to how strongly they fit those criteria. When this method of ranking is used, not all students in a classroom are ranked but only those found to meet given criteria. An example of this method of selective rank-ordering is found in stage 1 of Walker and Severson's *Systematic Screening for Behavior Disorders* (SSBD, 1992), a multiple-gating screening and assessment procedure that was overviewed in chapter 2. This rank-ordering procedure involves teachers' selecting 10 students in their classrooms whose behaviors most closely match an objective description of internalizing behavior problems and then rank-ordering those students according to the severity of their symptoms. Examples from the description of internalizing problems include not talking with other children; being shy, timid, or unassertive; not participating in games and activities; and being unresponsive to social initiations by others. Following the rank-ordering along the internalizing dimension, a separate rank-ordering procedure is conducted in a similar manner for students who exhibit externalizing social-behavioral problems. Examples from the description of externalizing problems include arguing, forcing the submission of others, disturbing others, and stealing. The instructions for rank-ordering students with internalizing behavior problems are presented in Figure 6.4. Research data reported in the SSBD technical manual indicate that the stage 1 rank-ordering procedures have adequate to strong inter-rater agreement between teachers and classroom aides (.89 to .94 for the externalizing dimension and .82 to .90 for the internalizing dimension) and good test-retest reliability at 10- to 30-day intervals (.81 to .88 for the externalizing dimension and .74 to .79 for the internalizing dimension). Additionally the stage 1 ranking procedures of the SSBD have been found to have a strong degree of sensitivity in discriminating students with behavioral disorders from peers with normal levels of problem behaviors.

Alternative Sociometric Procedures

In addition to peer nominations, peer ratings, and sociometric rankings, other sociometric procedures have been developed that have some similarities with one or more of these categories but which are in many ways unique. Three of these alternative sociometric assessment procedures are reviewed in this section: picture sociometrics, the Class Play, and "guess who" techniques.

Picture Sociometrics.   Picture sociometric procedures involve presenting to each child in a classroom an arbitrary assortment of photographs of every other child in the class and then asking the child to answer a series of questions by pointing to or selecting a photograph of a peer. This is an adaptation of other peer nomination methods that is useful for work with preliterate subjects. Landau and Milich (1990) state that it is the preferred method for

Rank-Ordering on Internalizing Dimension

Internalizing refers to all behavior problems that are directed inwardly (i.e., away from the external social environment) and that represent problems with self. Internalizing behavior problems are often self-imposed and frequently involve behavioral deficits and patterns of social avoidance. *Non-examples* of internalizing behavior problems would be all forms of social behavior that demonstrate social involvement with peers and that facilitate normal or expected social development.

Examples include:

- having low or restricted activity levels,
- not talking with other children,
- being shy, timid, and/or unassertive,
- avoiding or withdrawing from social situations,
- preferring to play or spend time alone,
- acting in a fearful manner,
- not participating in games and activities,
- being unresponsive to social initiations by others, and
- not standing up for one's self.

Non-Examples include:

- initiating social interactions with peers,
- having conversations,
- playing with others, having normal rates or levels of social contact with peers,
- displaying positive social behavior toward others,
- participating in games and activities,
- resolving peer conflicts in an appropriate manner, and
- joining in with others.

Column One
List Internalizers

Student Name
(Most Exemplifying Internalizing Behavior)

Column Two
Rank-Order Internalizers

	Student Name
1 (Most)	
2	
3	
4	
5 (Internalizing)	
6	
7	
8	
9 (Least)	
10	

Instructions:

1. First, review the definition of internalizing behavior and then list all students in your class.

2. Next, in Column One above, enter the names of the ten students whose characteristic behavior patterns most closely match the internalizing behavioral definition.

3. Finally, in Column Two, rank-order the students listed in Column One according to the degree or extent to which each exhibits internalizing behavior. The student who exhibits internalizing behavior to the greatest degree is ranked first and so on until all ten students are rank-ordered.

FIGURE 6.4 Instructions for rank-ordering students with internalizing social-behavioral problems from stage 1 of the *Systematic Screening for Behavior Disorders.* A rank-ordering procedure for externalizing problems is also included in stage 1.

SOURCE: From the *Systematic Screening for Behavior Disorders,* by H. M. Walker and H. Severson. Copyright, 1992, Sopris West Publishing. Reprinted by permission of the publisher.

preschool through second-grade subjects. Examples of questions that have been used in this technique include "Who do you like to play with the most?" "Who is your best friend?" and "Who is the best student in your class?" As with most other sociometric techniques, specific items can be developed based on the clinical or research questions, and these items can be produced to indicate either social acceptance or social rejection.

The original picture sociometric technique and minor variations of it are scored based on totalling the number of times each child was nominated by classmates in answer to questions indicating positive social status. Using this scoring scheme, rejected or neglected children would have significantly lower scores than accepted children with higher social status. Of course, variations in scoring procedure would be needed if there were any significant deviations in administration method from the original study by McCandless and Marshall (1957). For example, questions that reflect both positive (e.g., "Who do you most like to do schoolwork with?") and negative (e.g., "Who are you afraid to be around on the playground?") social status could be mixed and the scoring system divided into positive and negative status categories.

The use of picture sociometrics was first reported by McCandless and Marshall (1957) and has been used in a number of other published studies. The psychometric properties of picture sociometric techniques have been shown to be quite good, with relatively high inter-rater reliability, very high short-term test-retest reliability, and adequate long-term test-retest reliability (See Landau & Milich, 1990). Validity of the picture sociometric method has been demonstrated by producing significant discriminations between groups of aggressive, aggressive-withdrawn, and normal boys (Milich & Landau, 1984). Interestingly this technique has been shown to produce more effective discriminations of social status than information provided by teachers, particularly when negative ratings or nominations are involved.

The Class Play. The Class Play procedure was first utilized and described by Bower (1969), and it has been further revised by Masten, Morrison, and Pelligrini (1985). It has been used in several large-scale investigations, including the classic 11–13-year follow-up study of elementary-age children by Cowen and his colleagues (Cowen et al., 1973). The basis of this procedure is that children are asked to assign their peers to various roles (usually both positive and negative roles) in an imaginary play. The original Class Play described by Bower (1969) included both positive (e.g., "someone who will wait their turn") and negative (e.g., "someone who is too bossy") roles, but it had a scoring procedure wherein only a single score (negative peer reputation) was derived. It was done by calculating the number of negative roles given to a child and dividing that by the total number of roles given to the child. Large percentages indicate a high degree of peer rejection, while low percentages indicate higher social status. As with most sociometric approaches, the specification of roles in the Class Play procedure (as well as the method of scoring) can be manipulated by clinicians or researchers to suit their goals. Also the scoring system advocated by Bower (1969) has been criticized for being on empirically shaky ground (Landau & Milich, 1990), which may warrant some caution.

The use of Class Play procedures in sociometric assessment is attractive for two reasons other than their measurement capabilities. One advantage is that children (particularly younger children) appear to enjoy casting their peers into various play roles. The second advantage is that teachers and administrators seem to view this procedure more positively than some other sociometric methods, and thus it is more likely to be supported and approved than some other approaches. Masten et al. (1985) suggest that because of the diversity of roles needed in a play, this procedure will reduce the probability of disapproving labels on children with high negative scores by other children in the rating/casting process.

"Guess Who" Measures.   The "guess who" technique is a sociometric approach wherein brief descriptions are provided to students, and they are asked to write down the names of a few other students (usually three or fewer) who they think best fit the descriptions. For example, students might be asked to respond to descriptions such as "Guess who is often in trouble," "Guess who does the best job on schoolwork," "Guess who no one knows very well," or "Guess who is often angry at other children." The descriptions can be provided to the students either verbally or in writing. The content of the "guess who" items can be made up by teachers, clinicians, or researchers based on the specific characteristics they are interested in identifying. Scoring of these measures is done by making simple frequency counts of each question/description. More elaborate scoring methods are also possible, such as grouping descriptions into categories of similar content (e.g., antisocial behaviors, helping characteristics, peer popularity, etc.) and obtaining frequency counts within each broader category.

An example of a "guess who" measure used with a large number of students and carefully investigated is the Revised PRIME Guess Who Measure, developed for use in Project PRIME, a large-scale investigation of students with disabilities who had been integrated in regular education classrooms for part of their instructional day (Kauffman, Semmell, & Agard, 1974). The original instrument consisted of 29 questions/descriptions and was administered to over 13,000 students in grades 3–5. Factor analytic procedures conducted on the instrument divided the items into four major factors, labeled "disruptive," "bright," "dull," and "well behaved." A revised scale including 20 items (the 5 items contributing the most to each factor) was developed by Veldman and Sheffield (1979), who reported reliability coefficients ranging from .56 to .77 for each factor score. They also developed a satisfactory concurrent validity procedure for the instrument by correlating the instrument items with teacher ratings along similar dimensions.

In sum, the "guess who" technique is flexible and easy to administer and score, and it has been used in a large number of studies and projects and found to have satisfactory technical properties.

ETHICAL CONCERNS IN USING
SOCIOMETRIC PROCEDURES

The sociometric assessment approaches overviewed in this chapter, as well as other types of sociometric measures, have a great deal of appeal to clinicians and researchers, and they have a long history of use in psychology, sociology, and education. However these approaches are not without controversy. Many sociometric methods involve negative ranking or nomination procedures, that is, having children single out peers based on negative characteristics. Largely because of the use of these negative nomination procedures, parents, and sometimes teachers and administrators, may be hesitant or alarmed at the possibility of their children participating in sociometric assessments for fear of their child or other children being singled out by peers and further ostracized because of it. There seems to be a common concern that children will compare their responses after the assessment to find out which children were singled out for negative nominations, and this process will end up in increased isolation or social exile for the children who were commonly perceived in negative terms. The author is personally familiar with two separate research projects that had to undergo major methodological modifications because of threats by parents and some educators to "shut the study down" because of the use of negative peer ranking or nomination procedures.

It is important to recognize that none of the concerns about negative effects from sociometric assessment ever have been demonstrated through research. Landau and Milich (1990) noted that several large-scale longitudinal investigations with at-risk children have been conducted using sociometric procedures (e.g., Pekarik, Prinz, Liebert, & Weintraub, 1976; Serbin, Lyons, Marchessault, Schwartzman, & Ledingham, 1987) with no reports of negative consequences to the participants. An ambitious and intriguing investigation by Hayvren and Hymel (1984) found that there were no observable negative consequences within peer groups immediately following the use of sociometric assessment procedures. However this study was conducted with a population of preschool-age children, and it is unclear whether the same results would generalize to elementary- or secondary-age children. At the present time, there is no empirical evidence that negative nomination or rating procedures are harmful to individuals who participate in them; however there is a lack of evidence on the effects of sociometric assessment in general. Clinicians or researchers considering the use of sociometrics would do well to interpret the available evidence as indicating "we don't know" rather than "we know it's not harmful."

Whether or not concerns about the effects of sociometric assessment are well founded, clinicians and researchers utilizing sociometric approaches are advised to choose the most appropriate method for their purposes, communicate closely and carefully with their constituent groups, and educate those involved on the purposes and procedures involved. Landau and Milich (1990) suggest that the use of positive nomination procedures or peer ratings instead of negative nomination procedures may be necessary when working with systems or individuals who are suspicious of the use of sociometrics. In the meantime, additional research on any peer effects of sociometric measurement involving negative ranking or nomination would be extremely useful.

SOCIOMETRIC APPROACHES
AND DECISION MAKING

Perhaps the best use of sociometric assessment is in making decisions about screening and assessment. As a screening tool, various sociometric approaches can quickly identify individuals who might be at heightened risk for developing social-behavioral problems. As part of a comprehensive assessment system, sociometric methods can help to confirm or disconfirm hypotheses about peer relationship problems or other social risk factors developed through the use of other assessment methods.

Sociometric assessment may have some use as a means of identifying individuals who might benefit from special social skills interventions, but if used for this purpose, it would be important to augment the sociometric approaches with other objective assessment methods. It would also be important to word the sociometric assessment questions or instructions very carefully in order to match the type of intervention that is intended. For example, if a school counselor or psychologist was attempting to identify potential participants for an anger control group, a peer nomination question such as ''List five students who easily lose their temper'' might be useful in conjunction with other selection data. For making specific intervention decisions, it is difficult to see how sociometric data would be very useful, but they certainly could be used to make the general types of decisions illustrated in the anger control group example.

An intriguing potential use of sociometric assessment data is for grouping students in classroom settings for maximum cooperation and appropriate modeling. For example, a student who lacks social skills and comes out as socially neglected in a sociometric assessment might be paired strategically with another student with strong social competence who is identified in the sociometric assessment as being well liked and accepting. Such a pairing might result in the socially neglected student being exposed to a positive social model and a potential source of social support. Likewise a teacher who is assigned a group of students that he or she does not know well might use a sociometric assessment to ensure that seat assignments and work-group pairings include an appropriate mix of students and that students at heightened risk for engaging in negative social behavior (e.g., rejected and controversial students) are not clustered together.

For making diagnosis/classification or placement decisions, sociometric assessment procedures appear to be less useful. These types of decisions tend to require objective information on whether an individual meets specific criteria. The only possible use of sociometrics in this regard would be as a means of confirming or disconfirming other data used in determining whether or not the criteria have been met.

In sum, sociometric assessment, like other forms of assessment used to gauge emotional and behavioral problems, is more relevant for certain types of decision-making processes. The decision-making process that appears to be most relevant to sociometric assessment is screening and assessment. Sociometric assessment may also have some relevance, when used in conjunction with other forms of assessment, for making general decisions about interventions for peer relationship problems.

APPLICATION PROBLEMS—UNDERSTANDING SOCIOMETRIC ASSESSMENT METHODS

Formal sociometric approaches to assessment of behavioral, social, and emotional problems are infrequently stressed or modeled in preservice and graduate-level assessment courses. As a consequence, many practioners are not fully aware of the uses and advantages of sociometric assessment. The following questions are designed to help you integrate and synthesize some of the main points on sociometrics that were discussed in this chapter.

1. List two advantages of obtaining peer-referenced sociometric assessment data rather than relying solely on teacher ratings or observations of social interaction patterns.

2. Briefly describe some of the evidence attesting to the predictive validity of sociometric assessment.

3. Compare and contrast peer ranking and peer rating procedures. Under what circumstances might each procedure be best utilized?

4. Describe two different ways of employing positive nomination procedures. Under what circumstances might each procedure be best utilized?

5. List and describe three possible ways of implementing sociometric assessment procedures with children who cannot yet read or write.

6. Develop a list of five different "guess who" questions that you might utilize to help select the three students in a third-grade classroom who are most likely to benefit from participation in a social skills training group wherein friendship making and peer interaction skills will be stressed.

7. The use of negative peer nomination procedures has generated a great deal of controversy. Regarding this issue, respond to the following questions: (*a*) What are some of the possible negative outcomes of using negative nomination procedures? (*b*) What evidence exists attesting to the negative effects of these procedures? (*c*) What are some potential alternatives to negative nominations that will provide the same type of data but be less socially intrusive?

Objective Self-Report Tests

INTRODUCTION

This chapter deals with the development and use of a broad category of assessment instruments referred to as *objective self-report tests*. This is an assessment category inextricably linked to the field of personality assessment. Some assessment texts define self-report assessment separately from personality assessment, while other texts include additional categories of assessment methods in this vein. For this book, it was decided to refer to this general category of assessment instruments as objective self-report tests because this terminology is descriptive of the type of activity the assessment involves and because many (if not most) of the self-report tests reviewed in this and later chapters are not designed to measure the broad construct of "personality" but to assess very specific aspects of social and emotional behavior based on the subject's own perceptions of them.

Even with this relatively broad and functional way of defining objective self-report assessment, the fact that it is so strongly linked to personality assessment may be troublesome, if not distasteful, to behaviorally oriented practitioners or researchers. This skeptical view is alluded to by Salvia and Ysseldyke (1991) who begin their chapter on personality assessment as follows:

> Personality development is a nebulous concept, ill-defined and subjectively measured. In fact, you could probably debate long and hard about the meaning of adequate personality development. Personality is never assessed. Rather, we observe and/or measure behaviors and infer a thing called personality. (p. 324)

In the introductory chapter of this book, the terms *direct* and *objective* were highlighted as an important part of what is covered in the text. For various reasons, the broad category of projective personality assessment methods was excluded from the book, though it is the author's opinion that these methods do have their place in assessment. Therefore, this chapter lays the groundwork for understanding *objective* self-report assessment, an important field within psychology.

The chapter begins with a broad examination of the important foundations of objective self-report assessment, including historical and psychometric considerations. A good portion of the chapter is then dedicated to evaluative reviews of four different objective instruments for the assessment of children and adolescents. These four instruments differ from the types of objective self-report measures reviewed in chapters 8–11, as these tests are omnibus or general-purpose assessment instruments for measuring personal adjustment and psychopathology. The types of objective self-report instruments discussed in the remaining chapters are for the most part instruments developed for assessing very specific constructs, such as depression, anxiety, social competence, and self-concept. The chapter ends with a discussion on how data from objective self-report tests can be used in making important decisions related to the assessment process.

FOUNDATIONS AND METHODS OF OBJECTIVE SELF-REPORT TESTS

To truly appreciate the best uses of objective self-report tests in the assessment of behavioral, social, and emotional problems, it is first necessary to lay a foundation for understanding. This section will present both a historic and psychometric overview of the basis of objective self-report testing. First a brief historical account of the personality testing movement is presented, followed by some basic definitions and discussion of objective measurement. Then information specific to methods of objective test construction and some of the measurement problems associated with this form of assessment are presented.

Historical Foundations of Personality Testing

As was noted in the introduction to this chapter, objective self-report assessment is closely linked to, if not an integral part of, the field of personality assessment. As noted by McReynolds (1986), interest in the assessment of personality may actually be older than psychology. The first formal efforts connected to assessing the personality structure were found in free association techniques, such as those developed by Freud and Jung in their psychoanalytic work, and Kraepelin's use (1892) of the technique in studying physiological effects of hunger, fatigue, and drugs (cited in Anastasi, 1988). As advances in the study of personality continued in the early 1900s, more of a distinction was made between projective methods (such as the Rorschach test, apperception tests, and drawing tests) and objective methods of personality assessment, the latter being the focus of the remainder of this historical overview.

Anastasi (1988) notes that the prototype of the modern personality/self-report inventory was the Personal Data Sheet, developed by Woodworth during World War I as a test to screen out men with serious emotional problems from military service. By the late 1920s and early 1930s, a number of objective personality questionnaires, surveys, and inventories had been developed for research and clinical purposes. Many of these early efforts did not meet the current criteria for objective self-report measures, but they were objective in the sense that they incorporated methods distinctly different from associative and projective techniques. By the late 1930s and early 1940s, advances in personality theory, psychometric theory, and statistical analysis set the stage for major advances in objective personality assessment. In the first edition of his highly influential book, *Essentials of Psychological Testing,* Cronbach (1949) noted that the Berneuter's Personality Inventory published in the 1930s, an instrument based on four personality traits, was widely used in clinical and other applied settings. This assessment instrument became the prototype for a number of later objective measures. The most notable of these later measures was the Minnesota Multiphasic Personality Inventory (MMPI), published in 1943. The MMPI was the first instrument to use the sophisticated *empirical criterion keying* method of construction, a technique on which many current tests are based.

During the 1950s, 1960s, and 1970s there were many challenges to the validity of traditional personality assessment. Some of these challenges arose from the increasing influence of behaviorism in graduate psychology training, a school of thought often seen as highly dogmatic and parochial in those days. The growth of humanistic psychology in the 1950s and 1960s also posed some challenges to traditional personality assessment, as many humanistic practitioners considered personality assessment to be impersonal and invasive. Some of the challenges to personality assessment during these three decades also arose from the fact that many of the commonly used assessment instruments had very poor psychometric and other technical qualities and limited evidence of validity. In the past two decades, the field of personality assessment has undergone many changes, but it has not disappeared as some predicted. In fact, there has been an increase in interest in personality assessment since the 1970s (Knoff, 1986). Barnett and Zucker (1990) noted that there are now at least six professional organizations and at least five scholarly journals specifically devoted to the assessment of personality. Some of the reasons for the apparent revitalization of interest in personality assessment include (*a*) increasing eclecticism among practitioners and researchers, (*b*) a decline in dogmatism and parochialism is specific schools or fields of psychology, and (*c*) the development and refinement of sophisticated mathematical models and statistical techniques for studying personality and developing objective self-report instruments.

Psychometric Foundations of Objective Test Construction

In the subtitle of this book the terms *direct* and *objective* are emphasized as characteristics of the types of assessment methods recommended to measure behavioral, social, and emotional problems of children and adolescents. In chapter 1, these two terms were discussed in general, and several subsequent chapters have discussed the concept of direct assessment as applied to specific assessment modalities, but up to this point the concept of objective assessment has not been addressed in detail. Since the focus of this chapter is objective self-report tests, what exactly is meant by "objective?"

Martin (1988) proposed four essential characteristics or criteria that must be present for an assessment instrument to be considered an objective test, as follows:

1. There must be individual differences in the responses of persons to the test stimuli, and these differences must be sufficiently consistent over time, across test items, and in different assessment situations.
2. The measurement must involve the comparison of one person's responses to those of other individuals, and the items must be presented to different persons in a consistent manner.
3. The assessment device must include normative data so that individual scores can be assigned a place on a scale for purposes of comparison against a larger group of persons.
4. The test responses must be shown to be related to other meaningful behavior. In other words, the measurement must be shown to be useful in predicting behavior. This criterion is referred to as the *validity requirement.*

Therefore, an objective self-report test is one in which subjects respond to various items or questions about their own social-emotional behavior in a standardized manner, their responses are compared to those of a normative group, and evidence is provided as to the psychometric properties (reliability and validity) of the measure. Martin's four criteria (1988) and the subsequent summation of these key points show that the other assessment methods discussed in previous chapters (observation, rating scales, interviewing, and sociometric measures) cannot be considered *objective* self-report measures, though they sometimes meet one, two, or even three of the four essential characteristics. To these four characteristics, it is useful to add a brief definition of how self-report responses are scored using objective procedures: Each possible response on an item is associated with a predetermined score, and therefore there is no room for inference or individual judgment in the scoring process.

With regard to the first essential criterion of objective measurement (consistent measurement of individual differences), self-report or personality measures tend to have lower levels of reliability than tests that measure various forms of cognitive functioning, such as intelligence and achievement tests (Worthen, Borg, & White, 1993). Part of the difficulty in obtaining high reliability coefficients on personality or behavioral measures is that social-emotional behavior in humans tends to be less stable or predictable than human cognitive functioning (Brown, 1983). A second possible reason for psychometric problems on self-report tests, noted by Brown, is that these tests have all too often been accepted uncritically or used for purposes for which they were not intended. Given that the psychometric measurement of social and emotional behavior is a newer phenomenon than the measurement of human cognitive functioning, it is likely to take some time before the necessary level of measurement sophistication is reached. Given the differences in predictability between social-emotional and cognitive functioning in humans, the psychometric gap between the two areas may be reduced but perhaps never closed.

Three Approaches to Developing Objective Tests

Experts in the field of personality assessment agree that the number of approaches to constructing objective self-report tests is quite small, with most experts listing only three categories of test construction methods (Martin, 1988). In this regard, the only significant variable is the name assigned to each category or type of approach. For a further analysis of the basic types of test construction categories and names, consult the works of Anastasi (1988), Lanyon and Goldstein (1984), and Goldberg (1974). For purposes of this book, the names assigned to the three basic categories of objective test construction include the *rational-theoretical* approach, the *factor analytic* approach, and the *empirical criterion keying* approach. These are discussed as follows.

Rational-Theoretical Approach. The rational-theoretical approach to developing objective self-report tests involves the assumption by the test developer that a given set of personality traits and behavioral correlates can be measured by developing a set of items or scales that logically appear to fit within the definitions of those traits and behaviors. If the test developers simply use their own ideas about what constitutes appropriate items or scales, the test is said to be *intuitively* developed. If test developers use the judgments of experts in developing and selecting items, the process is called a *content validation* method.

The development process is said to be *theory based* if the construction of items or scales is done according to a recognized theory of personality or personal social-emotional functioning.

The rational-theoretical approach can be illustrated using the development of an objective test for measuring depression. A test developer might generate a list of items that he or she believes represents the construct of depression (intuitive), ask a group of mental health professionals to evaluate or generate possible items thought to measure depression (content validation), or develop potential items based on how closely these concur with an accepted theory of depression (theory based). In reality, these rational-theoretical test construction methods are often used in conjunction with one another. In many cases, an objective measure is initially developed using rational-theoretical methods, and then it is subjected to other forms of developmental validation.

The main advantages of the rational-theoretical approach is that if the item and scale development proceeds thoughtfully, the end result is a group of items or scales that have strong face validity and appear to be psychologically meaningful and theoretically unified. The main disadvantage of this approach is that regardless of how much face validity the instrument may appear to have, the resulting items or scales may not necessarily have acceptable psychometric properties or be able to differentiate between normal and abnormal behavior.

Factor Analytic Approach.   This approach to objective test construction relies on a sophisticated group of statistical procedures (called *factor analysis* or *principle components analysis*) to sort and arrange individual test items into mathematically related groups, or factors. Presumably, the arrangement of test items into statistically related groups allows for more precise measurement and interpretation of various personality or behavioral constructs. Normally the test developer also utilizes a rational-theoretical approach in developing the test items prior to subjecting them to factor analysis and subsequent interpretation.

Chapter 4 of this book provided several examples of how factor analytic procedures were used in the development of some of the most commonly used behavior rating scales and how the obtained factor solutions are commonly interpreted. The same general procedures and practices are also true of factor analytic approaches to the development of objective self-report measures. An example of a well-known objective personality test for adults that employs factor analytic procedures is Cattell's 16PF Questionnaire (Cattell, Eber, & Tatsuoka, 1970). Additionally virtually all individually administered tests of cognitive ability (such as the Wechsler and Stanford-Binet scales, the Woodcock-Johnson Psycho-educational Battery, and the Kauffman Assessment Batteries) rely on factor analytic procedures to group subtests into interpretable factors or area scores.

The major advantage of the factor analytic approach is its production of mathematically precise groups of items, bringing a high degree of scientific precision to self-report measurement of behavioral, social, and emotional characteristics. This mathematical sophistication can also be a disadvantage. Even among psychologists who have received graduate training in measurement and psychometrics, very few have the skills to understand the nuances of factor analysis and to make consistently good decisions on factor analytic test data produced by computer programs. Factor analysis is difficult to understand and even more difficult to implement adequately in the development of a clinical test. If the test items themselves are poorly constructed, the mathematical sophistication offered by factor analysis will be of little use and may only confuse matters. It is not unusual to find test items in the same factor that do not appear to have a great deal of clinical similarity based on their face validity. Thus, factor analysis cannot enhance a test that was poorly constructed in the first place. As the saying goes, "garbage in, garbage out."

Empirical Criterion Keying Approach.   Anastasi (1988) has referred to the third objective test construction method as *empirical criterion keying.* This term refers to the development of scoring keys in terms of some external criterion. The way the procedure is actually implemented typically involves administering a large number of test items to two groups of persons who are known to differ in some psychologically meaningful way (e.g., those who are clinically depressed and those who are not, or delinquent and nondelinquent groups). After the pool of items is administered, it is analyzed to determine which items reliably discriminate or differentiate between the two groups. The discriminating items are then considered to be a scale that is used in predicting or classifying membership in the particular groups. Of course, the pool of items initially administered to the two groups is not just random descriptions of behavior; the items typically are developed carefully and selected using rational-theoretical construction methods.

The actual steps in the empirical criterion keying approach are more complex than this brief description might indicate. Readers who are interested in learning more about the specific steps in empirical criterion keying are referred to more thorough descriptions in other assessment texts. Martin's treatment (1988) of the subject is particularly detailed and illuminating. Some of the most widely used objective self-report measures are based on the empirical criterion keying approach. The three instruments that will be reviewed in detail in this chapter are all based to some extent on the use of empirical criterion keying.

The major strength of the empirical criterion keying approach is its reliance on the empirical properties of particular test items or scales rather than on the presumed clinical expertise of the test developer or the actual behavior of the person who takes the test. With this approach, the clinical implications of the actual contents of items are less important than the fact that the items are known to meaningfully "sort" between different groups of persons. For example, if the item "I do not sleep well at night" is found to differentiate between persons who are highly anxious and those who are not, we do not actually know whether the anxious individuals have trouble sleeping. The important consideration is that they *report* not sleeping well, and this discriminates them from nonanxious persons. Of course, the empirical criterion keying approach also has a number of drawbacks. Martin (1988) reports that the scales of many tests constructed in this fashion do not have high internal consistency. Another problem is the precision with which different diagnostic groups used to develop scales were selected in the first place. For example, if the tests or other selection procedures used to identify depressed and nondepressed persons are unreliable or only reliable within specific geographical and cultural boundaries, then the utility of an empirical criterion keying scale that will differentiate these groups is suspect.

Response Bias and Error Variance

While each of the three major forms of objective test construction has some advantages and disadvantages, trying to determine which is the "best" method is not a fruitful endeavor. In fact, some empirical attempts to answer this question (Burisch, 1984; Hase & Goldberg, 1967) have concluded that the psychometric properties and validity evidence of individual tests are more important markers of their usefulness than the method employed in their construction. Regardless of the approach or method to test construction, objective self-report measures are invariably subject to some degree of *response bias* on the part of the examinee, a phenomenon that leads to *error variance.*

Error variance is defined by Martin (1988) as "variation of responses that is uncorrelated with the trait being assessed and with any nontest behavior of interest" (p. 60). This problem is created by the response bias of the examinee, which can be defined as either conscious or unconscious attempts to respond to items in particular directions or to create a specific type of impression. Whether response bias is either deliberate or unconscious on the part of the examinee, it can increase error in the assessment.

Response bias can take several forms. One of the most well-researched forms is *acquiescence,* a tendency of some test takers to answer true/false or yes/no items in one direction consistently (Anastasi, 1988). Acquiescence is a particular problem when test items are ambiguous or unclear. A common method of attempting to control for acquiescence involves developing items and scales that have equal numbers of true/false or yes/no responses keyed into specific scales. Another well-known type of response bias is the *social desirability response set.* This term refers to the conscious or unconscious tendency of most test takers to endorse items in a socially desirable direction. For example, virtually all test takers faced with the statement "boys and girls should both be treated equally and fairly by teachers" would answer "true," regardless of their personal awareness or convictions regarding sexism, gender roles, and public policy. It is interesting that both well-adjusted and poorly adjusted persons tend to respond to items in the socially desirable direction, and their responses are usually indicative of their true behavior or feelings (Martin, 1988). Therefore, it is difficult to gauge how much, if any, error variance is created through this response set. Another form of response bias is *faking,* which involves deliberate attempts by test takers to manipulate or distort their responses to test items in order to create a particular impression. Faking usually takes the direction of manipulation to create a favorable or positive impression (e.g., a test taker applying for a job or a person accused of a crime undergoing pretrial assessment), but it can also involve deliberate distortion by the examinee to create a negative impression or exaggerate their psychopathology (e.g., a "cry for help" or malingering). Several objective self-reports incorporate sophisticated methods for detecting faking. The most notable example is the MMPI with its L, F, and K validity scales, which are designed to detect falsification, random answering, and defensiveness. Another type of response bias is *deviation,* or the tendency to answer test items in unusual or unconventional ways. The deviation hypothesis was proposed by Berg (1967), who argued that deviation in test responses is content free and can be found on either verbal or nonverbal tasks. Little is known about deviation as a form of response bias, and it is unclear how it may contribute to error variance in objective self-report testing.

It has thus far been demonstrated that several forms of response bias exist in testing and that they may contribute to the error variance found in a given assessment situation. Test construction methods can include efforts to reduce or control response bias, but what is the probable overall effect of response bias? While response bias in objective self-report assessment continues to be a problem, Anastasi (1988) contends that some aspects of it may be "a tempest in a teapot" (p. 554). Perhaps the best solution to reducing error variance caused by response bias is to make systematic efforts to detect response styles and response sets and then evaluate an examinee's responses to individual test items in terms of his or her motivations, cognitive ability, and social-emotional status.

SELECTED GENERAL-PURPOSE SELF-REPORT TESTS FOR CHILDREN AND ADOLESCENTS

Chapters 8–10 of this book contain reviews and comments on objective self-report tests for children and adolescents that are designed for assessing specific types of behavioral and emotional problems. Several psychometrically sound and clinically useful self-report instruments for children and adolescents have been developed for assessing specific theoretical constructs and types of problems, such as depression, anxiety, social competence, and self-concept. When it comes to general, rather than specific, measures of personal and social adjustment, few instruments have been developed specifically for use with adolescents, and even fewer have been developed for use with children. Of those that are available, many do not meet the types of technical or clinical standards that would make them suitable for inclusion in this book. For example, the only general-purpose objective measure for younger children included in this chapter is the Personality Inventory for Children (PIC), which is not actually a self-report measure. None of the general-purpose objective self-report tests designed specifically for children under the age of 11 was considered to have strong enough technical properties to warrant inclusion.

This section includes overviews and comments on four instruments. The Personality Inventory for Children is intended for use with both children and adolescents. The Youth-Self Report is designed primarily for use with adolescents, though its norms extend down to age 11. The Millon Multiaxal Adolescent Personality Inventory is intended for use specifically with adolescents. The Minnesota Multiphasic Personality Inventory, intended primarily for use with adults, has a long history of use with adolescents, and an adolescent-specific version of the instrument has recently been introduced.

Personality Inventory for Children

Description of the PIC.   The Personality Inventory for Children (Wirt, Lachar, Klinedinst, & Seat, 1990) is an objective instrument providing descriptive assessments of the behavior, affect, and cognitive status of children and adolescents between the ages of 3 and 16. The test includes up to 420 items that are responded to as either "true" or "false" by the subject's parent or parent surrogate. These inventory items are composed of objective descriptions of child behavioral and emotional characteristics, as well as parent and family characteristics (e.g., "Little things upset my child," "I am afraid my child might be going insane," and "There is a lot of swearing at our house"). All 420 items of the PIC can be used, or it can be administered in two shortened versions—131 items (Part I) or 280 items (Part II). The 420-item version of the PIC includes 4 factor scales, 4 validity and screening scales, and 12 clinical scales. These scales are listed by area in Table 7.1. As noted in the table, the 131-item, shortened version only includes the four factor scales and one validity scale, while the 280-item, shortened version includes all scales, but the clinical and four of the five validity scales are in shortened versions.

The PIC can be administered either in a traditional booklet format or with the use of a microcomputer program that both administers and scores items. The test can also be scored with hand-scoring keys or by using scannable answer sheets, scored by mailing them to the test publisher. Raw scores are converted to scale scores using a *T*-score system with a mean of 50 and standard deviation of 10. Four separate sets of scoring norms are used for the PIC, based on gender and age (3–5 and 6–16) breakdowns.

Development and Construction of the PIC.   The PIC is technically not a child or adolescent self-report instrument, as it is completed by a parent or parent surrogate. However it traditionally has been classified with personality tests rather than behavior rating scales due to differences in rating format, scale construction methods, and underlying theory. As Lachar (1990) states,

> Although it may superficially resemble other behavior rating scales, the PIC is unique in that its interpretation and clinical use are based on empirically replicated correlates—correlations between specific scale elevations and independent measures of child status such as ratings by teachers, parents, and clinicians—and actuarial rules for the interpretation of specific scale elevations. (p. 1)

Seven of the PIC scales (defensiveness, adjustment, achievement, intellectual screening, delinquency, psychosis, and hyperactivity) were constructed using empirical criterion keying methods, and the remaining PIC scales were constructed using "rational" construction methods. The empirically constructed scales were based on methods developed by Darlington and Bishop (1966), which are thoroughly described in the PIC manual. The rationally constructed scales were

TABLE 7.1 Scales of the Personality Inventory for Children (PIC)

Factor Scales

I: Undisciplined/Poor Self-Control

II: Social Incompetence

III: Internalization/Somatic Symptoms

IV: Cognitive Development

Validity and Screening Scales

Lie (L)

Frequency (F)

Defensiveness (DEF)

Adjustment (ADJ)

Clinical Scales

Achievement (ACH)

Intellectual Screening (IS)

Developmental (DVL)

Somatic Concern (SOM)

Depression (D)

Family Relations (FAM)

Delinquency (DLQ)

Withdrawal (WDL)

Anxiety (ANX)

Psychosis (PSY)

Hyperactivity (HPR)

Social Skills (SSK)

Note: This table lists the scales that are included in the 420-item version of the PIC. For the two possible abbreviated versions of the PIC, the scales differ somewhat. The Part I version (items 1–131) of the PIC includes only the four factor scales and the lie (L) validity and screening scale. The Part II version (items 1–280) includes all of the scales from the complete version, but some are in shortened form. All of the clinical scales and all of the validity and screening scales except for L from the Part II version are identified with an -S after the scale abbreviation to note that they are shortened versions.

developed by having "expert" judges nominate items and then empirically testing them with clinical samples.

Although the PIC has been through three different revisions, the basic structure of the instrument remains the same, and the normative data for score conversions are still based on the original sample. The norms were gathered between 1958 and 1962 on a sample of 2,390 public school children, primarily from the Minneapolis area. Additional items and scales were developed during the 1970s. The first PIC manual was published in 1977 and contained summarizations of the research conducted on the instrument in the intervening years in addition to various statistical, technical, and clinical information. An interpretive guide for the PIC was published in 1979 which included information on actuarial interpretation of the scales, obtained through an additional sample of 431 subjects. In 1984, two updated manuals for the PIC were published, and the instrument was referred to as the "revised format" edition. The 1984 PIC revision retained the 600 items of the previous version, but the order of some of them was changed so that the first 420 items were considered the standard items and the remaining 180 items optional or experimental items. The first 420 items were organized so that any or all of three levels of "clinical specificity" could be assessed, with Part I (items 1–131) including the four broad-band factor scores and the lie scale, Part II (items 1–280) including all of Part I plus shortened versions of the remaining validity and clinical scales, and Part III (all 420 items) including complete versions of all factor, validity, and clinical scales. In 1990, the PIC and test manual were again revised. This revision dropped the experimental scales, retaining only the 420 items comprising Parts 1–3. The 1990 revision also involved an updating of the PIC manual to include additional research findings and discussions of the PIC versions published since 1984.

Technical Characteristics of the PIC.   The reliability data in the current PIC manual are essentially the same as those published for previous versions. Test-retest reliabilities for the PIC scales have been reported to range from .46 to .94 in three different studies, with average scale reliabilities ranging from .71 to .89. Internal consistency reliabilities have been reported to range from .57 to .86 with a mean of .74. Mother-father inter-rater reliability figures have also been reported, ranging from .21 to .79 with mean reliabilities of .64 and .66 in two different studies. The PIC manual also documents a large number of validity studies with the majority of studies documenting concurrent, discriminant, factorial, and convergent forms of validity. These studies, too numerous to review here, have generally provided solid support for various clinical and research uses of the PIC.

Overall Evaluation of the PIC.   The PIC has a number of strengths. It has a long history of clinical and research use. The technical properties and potential clinical uses of the PIC have been documented in a respectable number of studies published in scholarly journals and in the various versions of the test manual. Although there are some unanswered questions, the technical properties of the PIC have proven generally to be adequate to good. The PIC is relatively easy to administer and straightforward to score. The test manual is comprehensive and well written, and it provides useful guidelines for clinical use. Because the PIC is completed by a parent informant but constructed more like a traditional personality inventory than a behavior rating scale, the PIC provides an interesting alternative to the use of rating scales and probably measures somewhat different constructs.

In spite of the strengths of the PIC and its significant contribution to the field of child assessment, it still has a number of significant problems that have not been corrected. Perhaps the most disturbing problem is that the normative data provided for the most recent version are still from the original 1958–1962 sample. Commenting on this problem in a review of the PIC from the *Tenth Mental Measurements Yearbook*, Knoff (1989) stated that

> While the original norms were a monumental achievement for their time, they are now unacceptable for clinical use. They are dated, geographically localized, their stratification was weak and now is passe, and the social and societal perceptions of normality and abnormality on which they are based certainly differ from the early 1960s. (p. 627)

Knoff further suggested that the "norms should be considered untested and experimental" (p. 628), and he made a strong call for a new PIC standardization. It is indeed unfortunate that the need for restandardization was not addressed in the 1990 revision. The same problems mentioned by Knoff (1989) are still a concern and may even be amplified by the passage of years. An additional problem with the PIC normative data is that they are based only on the responses of the mothers of the assessed children. Given the moderate inter-rater reliability between mothers and fathers on this instrument, there is reason for concern that completion of the PIC by anyone but the mother of the subject may yield data difficult to interpret and of unknown normative value.

In addition to the major concerns over the PIC norms, the instrument has other potential problems. Even with the standard change of the complete instrument from 600 to 420 items, completing the PIC is still a formidable task, and this onerous length will discourage the use of multiple informants. Although the PIC is reasonably straightforward to administer and score, interpretation is difficult due to the number of scales and the subtle nuances of interpretation for each. The use of a true-false format rather than a standard 3- or 5-point response scale may oversimplify the intensity of observed problems. Finally the division of age ranges on the PIC norms into 3–5 and 6–16 ranges may reduce the clinical utility and discriminant power of the instrument. It is difficult to imagine that constructs such as anxiety, social skills, and delinquency are very similar for subjects at the extreme ends of the older age breakdown.

In sum, the PIC is a significant, complex, and unique assessment instrument for measuring behavioral and emotional problems. The PIC has many positive characteristics but continues to be plagued by a number of potential problems. The archaic and restricted norms are perhaps the chief obstacle, and Knoff's statement, "without a restandardization, the PIC's clinical utility will continue to be questioned, and the field will lose a tool of great importance" (1989, p. 628), is perhaps even more salient now than when it was written.

Youth Self-Report (YSR)

Description of the YSR.   The Youth Self-Report (Achenbach, 1991c) is the self-report component of the multiaxial Child Behavior Checklist system. Although the YSR can be used alone, it is intended for use as a "cross-informant" assessment instrument in conjunction with the CBCL and TRF, and it was designed and normed for use by subjects between 11 and 18 years of age. To complete the YSR requires about a fifth-grade reading level. The first section includes seven adaptive competency items wherein subjects provide information about their interests, hobbies, peer and family relationships, and school performance. These first seven items yield several competence scale scores. The remaining 119 items are descriptive statements rated by the subject using a three-point scale ("not true" to "very true"). Of these 119 items, 103 are statements about various problem behaviors, while 16 reflect socially desirable items endorsed by most subjects. The socially desirable items are not scored but were placed in the checklist to provide a balance to the problem items and to help detect indiscriminate responding. The 103 problem items are scored along two broad-band scales (internalizing and externalizing), eight narrow-band syndromes, and a total problem score. The narrow-band, cross-informant syndrome scores are the same as those used on the CBCL (see Table 4.3). All raw scores are converted to *T*-scores in the scoring process, and the YSR can be scored either by hand or with a computer scoring system. The scoring system provides separate scores for boys and girls.

Technical Characteristics of the YSR.   The standardization sample for previous versions of the YSR was criticized as being too small and restricted (Elliott & Buse, 1990). However the latest version of the YSR scoring profile and manual is based on a large norm sample ($N = 1,315$) that is nationally representative with respect to socioeconomic status, race, and urbanism.

Data reported in the YSR manual are indicative of acceptable levels of test-retest reliability at one-week intervals (median $r = .81$; range of broad-band and total score reliabilities $= .83$ to $.87$), although the range for narrow-band and competence scores is somewhat large ($.39$ to $.83$). Evidence of validity of the YSR presented in the manual includes sufficient factorial validity data and correlational data among the YSR, CBCL, and TRF (which are in the $.40$ range). Several independent studies using the YSR were published in the late 1980s and early 1990s showing moderate correlations with social competence instruments (Gresham & Elliot, 1990), strong correlations between the YSR internalizing scale and a self-report measure of depression (Hepperlin, Stewart, & Rey, 1990), and significant relationships between DSM-III diagnoses of conduct disorders and the YSR delinquency scale (Weinstein, Noam, Grimes, & Stone, 1990). However some studies have produced findings that question the validity of the YSR for specific purposes. For example, the YSR was found to have only limited usefulness in screening for childhood psychopathology in a community screening procedure (Bird, Gould, Rubio-Stipec, & Staghezza, 1991), and it was found to have poor discriminant validity and elevated rater variance in a study of 108 adolescent girls hospitalized due to various emotional and behavioral problems (Thurber & Snow, 1990).

Overall Evaluation of the YSR.   In spite of some apparent problems, the YSR has the potential for being a very useful self-report assessment instrument when used with other forms of assessment. One of the major problems may be that the instrument does not have any validity scales to detect the presence of deviant response sets or manipulation on the part of the child or adolescent client. Thus it may be possible for a subject to deliberately provide questionable self-report data on the YSR without this problem being detected. However the YSR has a number of strengths and features that warrant its use, including an easy-to-use response format, a well-written manual with a great deal of technical information, and the empirical and logical connection between the YSR and the other components of the CBCL multiaxial assessment system.

Millon Multiaxal Adolescent Personality Inventory (MAPI)

Description of the MAPI.   The Millon Multiaxal Adolescent Personality Inventory (Millon, Green, & Meagher, 1982) is a 150-item, true-false test format for use with 13–19-year-old subjects. The test was designed to assess and predict a wide range of psychological characteristics typical of adolescents and to be used by psychologists, counselors, and social workers. The MAPI includes a total of 20 subscales located along three basic dimensions, including *personality style, expressed concerns,* and *behavioral correlates.* The eight subscales that comprise the *personality style* dimension are based on Millon's theory (1969, 1981) of personality, which suggests that personality styles consist of combinations of reactive and proactive behavior patterns (e.g., passive detached, active detached). The *expressed concern* dimension also includes eight subscales, and it appears to measure various developmental concerns of adolescents. The *behavioral correlates* dimension consists of empirically derived scales developed to discriminate between the probability of membership in various troubled groups. The three dimensions of the MAPI with the corresponding subscales are shown in Table 7.2. The MAPI also includes three validity measures: (*a*) a reliability index based on responses to three items that directly inquire about how honestly or attentively the subject is completing the test, (*b*) a validity index based on three nonsensical items that are designed to detect random responding, and (*c*) an adjustment score that alters the scores on either the *expressed concern* or *personality style* dimensions. Raw scores are converted to base rate (cutoff) scores, rather than standard scores, due to the test authors' theory that the dimensional scores are not normally distributed.

The test protocol is completed on a National Computer Systems (NCS) response form, and all scoring and interpretation are done through NCS computerized scoring procedures. Hand-scoring keys are not available at the present time. Prepaid, mail-in scoring sheets are available from NCS in both clinical and

TABLE 7.2 Dimensions and scales of the Millon Multiaxal Adolescent Personality Inventory (MAPI)

Personality Styles
Introversive
Inhibited
Cooperative
Sociable
Confident
Forceful
Respectful
Sensitive

Expressed Concerns
Self-Concept
Personal Esteem
Body Comfort
Sexual Acceptance
Peer Security
Social Tolerance
Family Rapport
Academic Confidence

Behavioral Correlates
Impulse Control
Societal Conformity
Scholastic Achievement
Attendance Consistency

guidance forms. The guidance form is designed for use in adolescent counseling, while the clinical form provides more detailed interpretative information for clinicians. In addition to mail-in scoring, the MAPI can be scored and interpretive reports generated on-site, using special NCS software or by uploading and downloading software via a modem. Regardless of the method of scoring and report generation, the MAPI is very expensive to use. When purchased in small quantities, test scoring and clinical interpretive reports cost $20.85 each, while scoring and guidance interpretive reports cost $9.95 each. These prices are based on information from the 1992–1993 NCS catalogue.

Technical Characteristics of the MAPI.   The test manual for the MAPI is well written and comprehensive. Normative data for the MAPI were obtained from a sample of over 2,000 subjects. The manual includes both test-retest and internal consistency reliability data; subtest reliabilities range from .45 to .84 with most in the low .60s to upper .70s. Concurrent validity data between the MAPI and other personality tests (i.e., the California Psychological Inventory, 16PF test, and Edwards Personal Preference Schedule) suggest adequate to strong relationships between particular MAPI subscales and various subscales for the other tests. The test manual also includes factor analytic data via an intercorrelation matrix of the test's subscales. Although the test manual is generally thorough and well written, there are two problems that may emerge when using it. The first problem is that adequate interpretation of the various subscales is not easy and may require a solid background in both psychometrics and personality theory. The second potential problem is that Millon's personality theory (which the *personality style* dimension is based on) is not clearly laid out and is difficult to understand fully.

Overall Evaluation of the MAPI.   The MAPI has many strong points and can be recommended for use as a self-report instrument for research or clinical work with adolescents. The test takes approximately 20 minutes to complete, is written at about a sixth-grade reading level, and uses language that most adolescents should be able to relate to and understand. The development and publication of the MAPI was an important development in the area of adolescent personality assessment, as it was designed specifically for use with adolescents rather than as a downward extension of an adult test. Also the test meets technical adequacy standards much better than the few other adolescent-specific personality tests.

Although the MAPI can be recommended for use and has many strengths, it also has a number of weaknesses and drawbacks. One of the chief (and perhaps most annoying) complaints about the MAPI is that it can be scored only by National Computer Systems. The lack of hand-scoring keys not only has inhibited further research and probably more widespread use of the test but it puts the clinician in the position of having to place absolute trust in the quality of the NCS computer-generated report. The sole reliance on the MAPI report is a problem in that the interpretations are based primarily on deductive inference and not so much on actuarial prediction and empirical evidence. Although the MAPI manual does provide some sophisticated evidence for the technical properties of the test, it is still lacking in several regards. What would be most useful is evidence of the discriminant validity of the test for groups and individuals known to meet specific diagnostic or classification criteria. There is also concern that the empirical evidence for many of the MAPI subscales is weak (Lanyon, 1984). While the MAPI seems to have great potential, one reviewer commented that its ". . . commercial production has preceded adequate empirical evaluation" (Widiger, 1985, p. 981). The shortage of empirical evidence on the MAPI is strangely ironic in that the test publisher's decision not to allow on-site hand scoring has probably been the single greatest obstacle to the flow of additional research support for the test.

MMPI and MMPI-A

The Minnesota Multiphasic Personality Inventory (MMPI) has for many years been the most widely used objective measure of adult personality and psychopathology in the world. Its clinical applications, research uses, and psychometric properties have been the subject of thousands of published research studies and dozens of widely read professional books. Brown (1983) reported that the *Ninth Mental Measurements Yearbook* contained over 5,000 references to the MMPI, an astounding number. Indeed, the MMPI is firmly established in the pantheon of psychological assessment. Given that entire volumes have been devoted to the description, development, uses, and properties of the MMPI, this section will not attempt to replicate the immense body of literature currently available. Instead, it will briefly focus on uses of the MMPI and the newly developed adolescent version of the instrument as they apply to the assessment of adolescent clients. Readers who desire more complete information on the MMPI are referred to the many volumes devoted specifically to the instrument, especially the excellent books by Archer (1987), Butcher (1990), Graham (1987, 1990), and Greene (1980, 1991).

Development of Different Versions of the MMPI.   The original MMPI was first published in 1943 as a paper-and-pencil test for use in diagnostic personality assessment with adults. The authors of the MMPI utilized the empirical criterion keying method in developing the various validity and clinical scales, a new technique at that time. As time went on, the MMPI with its 566 true/false statements became very widely used and, as previously mentioned, has been the subject of scores of research reports and books. The basic validity and clinical scales of the MMPI are presented in Table 7.3. In addition to these basic scales, numerous additional scales have been developed for the MMPI, ranging from highly experimental to widely used and researched. Perhaps the most commonly used of these additional scales are the 21 supplementary scales and the 28 Harris-Lingoes subscales.

TABLE 7.3 Basic validity and clinical scales of the MMPI

Scale Number	Original Scale Name
Validity Scales	
L	Lie
F	Infrequency
K	Defensiveness
?	Cannot Say
Clinical Scales	
1	Hypochondriasis
2	Depression
3	Hysteria
4	Psychopathic Deviate
5	Masculinity-Femininity
6	Paranoia
7	Psychasthenia
8	Schizophrenia
9	Hypomania
0	Social Introversion

By the late 1970s it became apparent that in spite of the tremendous body of validation literature on the MMPI, the test was badly in need of a revision and restandardization. There were two main concerns that drove the need for revision and restandardization. First the original 1943 MMPI normative group, though exemplary for its time, did not meet modern standards for test development. The original normative group consisted of 724 persons who were visiting friends or relatives at the University of Minnesota Hospitals, and this group was very racially, socioeconomically, culturally, and geographically homogeneous. The second major concern involved problems with the MMPI item content. Some of the language and many of the references in the 566 statements had become obsolete and archaic, many of the original items used sexist language, and a number of items were considered objectionable for reasons such as focusing on bowel and bladder functions, Christian religious beliefs, and sexual behavior. There was also a lack of items in areas considered important in modern personality assessment, such as suicide attempts, alcohol and other drug use, and treatment-related behaviors. The MMPI revision process was conducted during the 1980s, and the revised and restandardized instrument (MMPI-2) was published in 1989. While retaining the same basic validity and clinical scale configurations as the MMPI, the MMPI-2 included a large representative normative sample, as well as numerous changes in item wording and content.

The MMPI-2 was never intended to be used with adolescent clients. During the same general time period that the MMPI-2 project was conducted, separate adolescent norms were gathered using the experimental restandardization booklet, and additional research and development efforts continued on the uses of the MMPI with adolescents for some time. In late 1992, three years after the publication of the MMPI-2, the Minnesota Multiphasic Personality Inventory-Adolescent (MMPI-A) was published, the first version of the MMPI designed specifically for use with adolescents. The MMPI-A will be described later in this chapter.

Using the MMPI with Adolescents.   Although the original MMPI was designed to be used with adults, it has a long history of clinical and research applications with adolescents. The MMPI was administered to large groups of adolescents in Minnesota as early as 1947 (Hathaway & Monachesi, 1963), and a large number of research studies were published in the 1960s, 1970s, and 1980s detailing specific empirical findings and clinical applications of the instrument with adolescent populations (e.g., Archer & Gordon, 1988; Ball, 1962; Baughman & Dahlstrom, 1968; Ehrenworth & Archer, 1985; Marks, Seeman, & Haller, 1974; Rutter, Graham, Chadwick, & Yule, 1976). Most comprehensive books on the MMPI include sections on its applications with adolescent populations (e.g., Graham, 1987, 1990; Greene, 1991), and several chapters in edited works on the MMPI have detailed the uses of the instrument with adolescents (e.g., Reilley, 1988; Williams, 1985). Perhaps the most comprehensive treatment of the use of the MMPI with adolescents has been Archer's excellent book, *Using the MMPI with Adolescents* (1987). In addition to the numerous research reports and books that have dealt with the MMPI and adolescents, a number of test publishing and scoring companies offer products such as special adolescent MMPI profile forms and interpretative score reports. In sum, though the MMPI is intended primarily for use with adults, it has been used and investigated with adolescent populations more than any other objective self-report instrument developed specifically for use with adolescents.

Although the use of the MMPI with adolescents has a strong historical and empirical basis, there are numerous problems that may be encountered along the way. As Archer (1987) noted, the MMPI is at the same time the most widely used and widely abused personality inventory for adolescents.

Perhaps the key to understanding and preventing the misuse of the MMPI with adolescent clients is to develop a strong understanding of normal adolescent development. Archer (1987) stated that there are three essential developmental factors that must be considered when the MMPI is administered to adolescents, as follows:

1. *Cognitive changes.* Piaget observed that most children move from the concrete operations stage of cognitive development to the formal operations stage between the ages of 11 and 13. The emergence of formal operational thinking allows for abstract reasoning, formal logic, and advanced symbolism. Many of the items on the MMPI may be answered differently by individuals simply based on their level of cognitive development. Two examples of such MMPI items are "My father was a good man," and "I loved my father." If an adolescent client completing the MMPI is still in the concrete operations stage, they are likely to interpret the past-tense meanings of the words "was" and "loved" on a very concrete level, perhaps not knowing how to answer the items if his or her father is still alive.

2. *Physical and sexual maturation.* Adolescence is a time of great physical change, and it is not unusual for the adolescent years to include gains in height and body weight of 25 percent and 100 percent, respectively. Some of the questions on the MMPI must be considered within this context of rapid physical change. For example, the item "I am neither losing or gaining weight," when endorsed negatively, appears on the MMPI depression scale. Yet it would be expected that an adolescent would answer "false" to this item because of the weight gains that typically occur. A related area is sexual maturation. As children reach puberty and enter into adolescence, they are likely to be preoccupied with their sexual maturation, and they may not be entirely comfortable with it. Thus typical adolescent responses to MMPI items dealing with sexuality may be different in character from those of typical adults.

3. *Emotional and social changes.* In Western culture, adolescence is often accompanied by a period of increasing independence from the family, increased attention to the peer group, and great emotional lability. Eriksen (1963) referred to this social-emotional transition as an identity versus role confusion crisis; the adolescent typically begins to deal with internal questions such as "Who am I?" and

"What do I want out of life?" This period is often seen as a time of great emotional turmoil, and it has been well established that adolescents have a greater degree of emotional reactivity and intensity than do adults. Thus MMPI items that refer to conflict with family (e.g., "No one seems to understand me" and "My relatives are all in sympathy") or emotional intensity (e.g., "At times I feel like smashing things" and "Often I can't understand why I have been so cross or grouchy") may be answered differently by typical adolescents than typical adults, simply as a function of normal developmental changes.

The three developmental areas of adolescence noted by Archer (1987) provide some clear examples of why clinicians should exercise caution in administering the MMPI to young clients. Additionally Reilley (1988) suggested that because adolescence often involves extreme sensitivity to what others think, conflicts with authority, and unresolved self-concept issues, young subjects may approach the test-taking task in a defensive or uncooperative manner. Using these potential issues as examples, it is easy to see the possibility of a young client faking good or faking bad on the MMPI to either present themselves in a particular manner or to obstruct the validity of the testing altogether. Therefore clinicians who use the MMPI with adolescent clients must be constantly aware of the potential effects of normal adolescent development on MMPI responses, and they should remain vigilant for threats to test validity.

Given the numerous challenges faced in administering the MMPI to adolescent subjects and then appropriately interpreting their MMPI profiles, how should one go about this process? The first step is deciding whether it is appropriate to administer the MMPI to an adolescent client. Given Archer's comments (1987) on developmental cognitive changes during adolescence, one should attempt to discern whether the adolescent client is still cognitively functioning on a concrete level. This decision can usually be made by reviewing current school records or by directly interviewing the client. Archer (1988) suggested that the MMPI should never be administered to a subject who has an IQ below 70, and for adolescents, this criterion appears to be almost too liberal. The reading level of the subject should also be taken into account. Graham (1990) estimated that effective completion of the MMPI-2 requires about an eight-grade reading level. It can be assumed that the original MMPI items require a similar level of reading competence, if not slightly higher due to some of the dated language. Therefore if an adolescent subject cannot read at about an eighth-grade level, the MMPI normally should not be administered to them. The reading level of the client can be estimated by reviewing recent academic testing records or administering brief formal or informal reading screens to the client prior to the MMPI administration. Archer (1988) suggested that having the client read a few of the MMPI items and the directions out loud is an easy way to determine if the reading level is high enough to take the test.

Once the decision has been made to administer the MMPI to an adolescent client, examiners should make themselves available to answer questions that may arise during the testing and should provide clear directions to subjects. Archer (1988) suggested that the adolescent client simply be told that the MMPI is a widely used test with many questions and that the examiner give these instructions, "I'd like you to take a test which will tell us a little bit about you and how we can help you."

In terms of interpreting the adolescent profile, a number of procedures have been researched and suggested, but perhaps the most advisable procedures are the following four steps recommended by Archer (1987):

1. Examine the completed protocol for unanswered items and unusual response sets in order to determine if it is a valid profile.
2. Sum the raw score values for each scale using standard scoring procedures.
3. Convert the raw score totals to *T*-scores by using supplementary adolescent norm tables found in books by Archer (1987), Graham (1990), and others. Make sure that the conversion table is age and gender appropriate. The supplementary adolescent norms do not include K-corrections.
4. If scores are plotted on adult profile sheets, *do not use K-correction procedures or T-score conversions based on adult norms.* Special adolescent MMPI plotting sheets have been developed and are available through various assessment materials catalogues.

Given that the use of adolescent norms without K-corrections will result in lower *T*-scores and thus increase the possibility of false-negative error, Archer (1987) suggested that 65 be considered a critical *T*-score value (the lower limit of the abnormal range on a given scale) rather than the traditional value of 70, if his recommended adolescent scoring procedure is followed. To conduct a comprehensive interpretation of the obtained MMPI scale scores, the use of MMPI code-type comparisons rather than simple evaluations of individual MMPI scale score levels is recommended. MMPI interpretation based on code types is beyond the scope of this chapter, and the reader is referred to books dealing with this method in depth such as those by Archer (1987), Butcher (1990), Graham (1987, 1990), and Green (1980, 1991).

Introduction to the MMPI-A.   In late 1992, National Computer Systems and the University of Minnesota released the long-awaited adolescent version of the MMPI, the MMPI-A. Although the original MMPI had been used for many years with adolescents, the MMPI-A was the first version of the test designed specifically for this age group.

The MMPI-A contains 478 true/false items, a reduction of nearly 100 from the MMPI and MMPI-2. The items in the MMPI-A are based on the original MMPI but with items, scales, and norms specific to the adolescent population. The new items cover areas considered critical in adolescent assessment such as alcohol and other drug use, school adjustment problems, family conflict, and maladaptive eating behavior. As in the case of the MMPI-2 revision, several of the items of the MMPI-A that were retained from the original MMPI were reworded to make them more applicable and contemporary. The MMPI-A was designed specifically for use with ages 14–8, and the new norms reflect this age group composition. These adolescent norms are based on a nationwide sample of 805 14–18-year-old subjects representative of this age group in the United States. Additionally

TABLE 7.4   Basic and content scales of the MMPI-A

Scale Abbreviation	Scale Name
Basic Validity Scales	
VRIN	Variable Response Inconsistency
TRIN	True Response Inconsistency
F1	Infrequency 1
F2	Infrequency 2
F	Infrequency
L	Lie
K	Defensiveness
Basic Clinical Scales	
Hs	Hypochondriasis
D	Depression
Hy	Conversion Hysteria
Pd	Psychopathic Deviate
Mf	Masculinity-Femininity
Pa	Paranoia
Pt	Psychasthenia
Sc	Schizophrenia
Ma	Hypomania
Si	Social Introversion
Content Scales	
A-anx	Anxiety
A-obs	Obsessiveness
A-dep	Depression
A-hea	Health Concerns
A-aln	Alienation
A-biz	Bizarre Mentation
A-ang	Anger
A-cyn	Cynicism
A-con	Conduct Problems
A-lse	Low Self-Esteem
A-las	Low Aspirations
A-sod	Social Discomfort
A-fam	Family Problems
A-sch	School Problems
A-trt	Negative Treatment Indicators

a "clinical" sample of 420 boys and 293 girls ages 14–18 was recruited from clinical treatment facilities in Minnesota. As with the MMPI and MMPI-2, the adolescent version includes separate norms for males and females.

Many of the features of the original MMPI were retained in the MMPI-A, such as the L and K validity indicators, slightly revised versions of the F validity scale, and the basic clinical scales. However a number of significant changes in scale structure are found in the MMPI-A, including some new validity scales and 15 new "content" scales highly specific to adolescent concerns and problems. In addition to the basic validity-clinical scales and the content scales, the MMPI-A includes 9 supplementary scales and 27 Harris-Lingoes subscales that are quite similar to those developed for the MMPI and MMPI-2. The basic and content scale breakdown of the MMPI-A is shown in Table 7.4 (see p. 155). Like the MMPI and MMPI-2, the MMPI-A can be hand-scored using answer keys or may be scored on-site or by prepaid mailers with computer software from NCS that also generates interpretive reports. An interesting and useful change in the MMPI-A from the MMPI is that uniform *T*-scores across eight of the clinical scales (the exceptions being Mf and Si) and the content scales are provided for percentile-ranking equivalency.

At the time this chapter was being written (late 1992), the MMPI-A had been introduced only recently. Thus the amount of published research on the MMPI-A other than what appears in the test manual was limited in comparison to what will likely become available in the next few years. Despite this issue of timing, several publications have already been appeared on the MMPI-A (Ben-Porath & Butcher, 1989; Williams & Butcher, 1989a, 1989b; Williams, Butcher, Ben-Porath, & Graham, 1992). Robert Archer (1992) has produced an excellent follow-up to his 1987 book on using the MMPI with adolescents, specifically oriented to the MMPI-A. At this point, the psychometric properties of the MMPI-A appear to be commensurate with those of other MMPI versions, based on information provided in the test manual. Based on its heritage from the MMPI, the MMPI-A should become an excellent and widely used tool for assessing adolescents. The MMPI-A is a much needed major development in the assessment of adolescent personality and psychopathology, and it promises to become a significant instrument, eventually replacing the MMPI as the most widely used instrument of this type with adolescents.

OBJECTIVE SELF-REPORT TESTS
AND DECISION MAKING

Like each of the other forms of assessment covered in this book, objective self-report tests can be very useful for screening purposes and for making decisions about additional forms of assessment that may be warranted. Not only can the administration of objective self-report tests provide "red flags" that may be indicative of general social or emotional distress, but in some cases, they can isolate specific areas of concern where additional assessment is needed. For example, each of the three general-purpose tests reviewed in this chapter provides specific information that can be used to generate hypotheses about additional assessment of depression, low self-esteem, anxiety, conduct problems, and even psychotic behavior.

Like most other forms of assessment, objective self-report tests should never be used by themselves to make diagnosis or classification and placement decisions. These types of decisions require a broad, multifactored assessment design wherein specific aspects of the decision process are weighed against specific pieces of evidence obtained through a carefully planned and implemented assessment process.

In terms of intervention or treatment planning decisions, objective self-report tests are used normally in conjunction with other forms of assessment data to generate broad hypotheses about what to do, but they seldom provide sufficient evidence by themselves to warrant the design and implementation of intervention plans. The possible exception to this rule may be the use of the MMPI and MMPI-A. Because of the vast history of research and clinical use of the MMPI, a great deal is understood about using actuarial assessment data from this instrument in developing treatment plans, and the MMPI-A promises eventually to yield the same type of extensive database. Butcher (1979, 1990) and others have written extensively on the actuarial application of MMPI data to treatment planning, and there is currently a great deal of interest in expanding and refining work in this area.

APPLICATION PROBLEMS—UNDERSTANDING OBJECTIVE SELF-REPORT ASSESSMENT

The training focus for objective self-report assessment is often weighted toward specific instruments, while the underlying ideas and assumptions regarding this form of assessment are often paid little attention. These questions are designed to help develop understanding of the principles underlying objective self-report assessment.

1. Three major methods of objective test construction were highlighted in this chapter: the *rational-theoretical, factor analytic,* and *empirical criterion keying* approaches. Briefly describe the main aspects of each approach.

2. What are the advantages and disadvantages of each of the three major methods of objective test construction? Is there a single "best" approach?

3. The focus in this book is on direct and objective assessment methods, and this particular chapter stresses the use of objective approaches to self-report assessment. Are there times when nonobjective approaches to self-report assessment are desirable? If so, describe some scenarios and circumstances when nonobjective assessment would be valuable.

4. Robert Archer has described three types of adolescent developmental changes that may affect responses and interpretation on objective self-report tests. List each of these three areas of developmental change, and also provide a general example of how objective assessment may be affected by each change.

5. In this chapter, three broad-purpose self-report tests (the YSR, MAPI, and MMPI/MMPI-A) were reviewed and discussed. Describe one scenario for each of these three tests when it would be the self-report instrument of choice within an assessment battery, explaining why each test would be preferred in the given situation.

CHAPTER 8

Externalizing Disorders: Assessment of Disruptive and Antisocial Behavioral Problems

Chapter Outline

Introduction

An Overview of Externalizing Problems
  Undersocialized Aggressive Conduct Disorder
  Socialized Aggressive Conduct Disorder
  Attention-Deficit Hyperactivity Disorder

Prevalence, Etiology, and Prognosis of Externalizing Disorders

Methods of Assessing Externalizing Problems
  Direct Behavioral Observation
  Interviewing Techniques
  Behavior Rating Scales
  Sociometric Approaches
  Assessment with Self-Reports

Linking Assessment to Intervention

Case Study

INTRODUCTION

The domain of externalizing problems and disorders represents a particularly troubling area for parents and teachers. By their nature, externalizing behavior problems are difficult to overlook since they are usually annoying and disruptive and often create problems for other individuals in the same environments as the children or adolescents who exhibit these problems. Fortunately externalizing problems and disorders can be effectively assessed using direct and objective methods, and some of the these methods may be extremely helpful in developing solid intervention plans.

This chapter begins with an overview of externalizing problems, including a detailed look at the three most prevalent types of disorders within the externalizing domain: undersocialized aggressive conduct disorder, socialized aggressive conduct disorder, and attention-deficit hyperactivity disorder. Following this introduction to the externalizing domain, the prevalence, etiology, and prognosis indicators associated with the three major types of disorders are covered. The bulk of the chapter is devoted to discussions of the five methods of direct and objective assessment featured in this book and how they may be best utilized in evaluating the externalizing problems. This chapter concludes with a brief discussion on how well our five general methods of assessment are linked to developing interventions for the treatment of externalizing disorders and problems.

AN OVERVIEW OF EXTERNALIZING PROBLEMS

Experts in the field of child psychopathology generally agree that the behavioral dimension of *externalizing* disorders includes a broad array of aggressive symptomology and hyperactivity (Cicchetti & Toth, 1991). Other terms that have been used to identify this behavioral dimension include *undercontrolled* and *outer-directed* behavior. Regardless of the terms used by researchers to classify this broad behavioral dimension, the essential characteristics are the same: aggressive, acting-out, disruptive, defiant, oppositional, and hyperactive behaviors. A child or adolescent who exhibits externalizing problems will not necessarily demonstrate all of these types of behaviors, but the congruence or relatedness among such symptoms has been well established.

The area of externalizing behavior problems has received significantly more attention than internalizing problems in the research literature, perhaps due to the debate over the reliability and long-term implications of internalizing disorders (Cicchetti & Toth, 1991). A number of empirical studies have provided solid support for the construct of an externalizing dimension of behavior problems (e.g., Achenbach, 1985; Ackerson, 1942; Coie, Belding, & Underwood, 1988; Robins, 1966; Sroufe & Rutter, 1984). In addition to the types of externalizing symptoms noted at the beginning of this section, most of these sources identified another commonality of externalizing disorders, namely peer rejection stemming from aggressive behavior.

Quay (1986a) reviewed over 60 studies that applied multivariate statistical approaches to the classification of child psychopathology. These studies commonly identified eight different narrow-band dimensions of symptoms with each area of symptomology consisting of core behaviors and characteristics replicated at least several times. Under the broad-band domain referred to as *externalizing,* Quay isolated three narrow-band dimensions of disorders, including undersocialized aggressive conduct disorder, socialized aggressive conduct disorder, and attention-deficit hyperactivity disorder. Our discussion of externalizing disorders follows this three-part categorization, and Tables 8.1 and 8.2 provide examples of specific behaviors that fit within these domains.

Undersocialized Aggressive Conduct Disorder

The narrow-band externalizing dimension that Quay (1986a) has referred to as undersocialized aggressive conduct disorder includes a cluster of behaviors that involve aggression, violation of rules, temper tantrums and irritability, attention seeking and impertinence, and a variety of other negative and oppositional behavioral characteristics. Quay (1986a) notes that this particular domain has emerged in multivariate classification studies "almost without exception" (p. 11), indicating that it is a relatively stable confluence of associated behaviors. In addition to a pattern of aggressive, disruptive, and noncompliant behaviors, the undersocialized aggressive conduct syndrome includes two other noteworthy features. The first is that hyperactive and restless *behaviors* (but usually not full-blown attention-deficit hyperactivity disorder) often occur concomitantly with this syndrome, suggesting an element of motor overactivity within the domain but not necessarily attentional problems. The second noteworthy feature is that "stealing has not been found at all central to this dimension" (Quay, 1986a, p. 11). Instead, stealing behaviors are more central to socialized aggressive conduct disorder, which will be discussed in the next part of this section.

Interestingly the diagnostic criteria for *conduct disorder* in DSM-III-R do not fit fully within the multivariate framework identified through empirical studies. Instead, the DSM-III-R conduct disorder criteria are rather omnibus in nature, requiring that a minimum of 3 out of 11 listed characteristics be present within a six-month period. These 11 behavioral characteristics range from stealing without confrontation of the victim to being physically cruel to other people. The current DSM system includes three *types* of conduct disorders within this omnibus framework, including *group type* (the problem behaviors occur primarily as a group activity), *solitary type* (the problem behavior is initiated by an individual rather than in a group context), and *undifferentiated type* (a mixture of the first two types). Note that the previous version of DSM (the unrevised third edition) had a different breakdown of conduct disorders, including socialized and undersocialized types with and without aggressive features.

Socialized Aggressive Conduct Disorder

The second type of conduct disorder identified in Quay's analysis (1986a) of multivariate classification studies is referred to as *socialized aggressive conduct disorder*. This cluster of behavior is seen less frequently than undersocialized aggressive conduct disorder, but it still has received strong empirical support (Loeber & Schmaling, 1985). The principal features of this narrow-band dimension include involvement *with peers* in illegal or norm-violating behaviors. Some of the specific characteristic behaviors of socialized aggressive conduct disorder include having "bad" companions, truancy from school and home, stealing (both at and away from home), lying, and gang activity.

TABLE 8.1   Major behavioral characteristics of two types of conduct disorders identified through multivariate statistical techniques

Undersocialized Aggressive Conduct Disorder	Socialized Aggressive Conduct Disorder
Assaultive behavior (fights, hits)	"Bad" companions
Disobedient and defiant	Truancy from home and school
Temper tantrums	Gang membership
Destructive behavior	Stealing with others
Impertinent or "sassy"	Steals at home
Uncooperative	Lies and cheats
Attention seeking	Stays out late at night
Domineering/threatening behavior	Loyalty to delinquent friends
Demanding/disruptive behavior	
Loud and boisterous	
Irritable and explosive	
Negativity and refusal	
Restlessness	
Dishonest and undependable	
Hyperactive	

SOURCE: Adapted from H. C. Quay, "Conduct Disorders," in H. C. Quay and J. S. Werry (eds.), *Psychopathological Disorders of Childhood,* 3rd ed. (New York: Wiley, 1986).

Again the essential feature of the behavior problems in this disorder is that they occur as a way of maintaining social acceptance within a deviant or antisocial peer group. Given that these conduct problems frequently violate the rights of other persons and defy social institutions, they often result in delinquent behavior and involvement with juvenile justice systems. The onset of socialized aggressive conduct disorders typically occurs at a later developmental stage than undersocialized aggressive conduct disorders, usually in late childhood or early adolescence (Quay, 1986a). Another interesting feature of socialized conduct disorder is that it is much more likely to occur with males and is often accompanied by deficits or lack of development in moral reasoning (Smetana, 1990).

Attention-Deficit Hyperactivity Disorder

The third narrow-band dimension of externalizing behavior problems identified by Quay (1986a) is referred to as attention-deficit hyperactivity disorder. This disorder is characterized by notable problems in maintaining concentration and attention, and it often includes associated behavior features such as impulsivity, clumsiness, and passivity. Note that overt motor overactivity (what we commonly think of as hyperactivity) is not always a feature of this disorder. In fact, behaviors that are characteristic of *underactivity* are often prominent features. Essentially attention-deficit hyperactivity disorder is a diverse group of behaviors and characteristics, and there are extremes in how the level of motoric activity is manifested in individual cases. Some children who exhibit this disorder are constantly "on the move," fidgety and restless, and they may be at heightened risk for developing other conduct problems. On the other hand, the disorder may be exhibited in children who are more withdrawn and passive and who seldom engage in aggressive or antisocial behaviors. As such, this particular disorder does not fit into the broad band of externalizing problems as neatly as unsocialized and socialized aggressive conduct disorders. However attention-deficit hyperactivity disorder has been lumped in more often with the externalizing than with the internalizing broad-band dimension, based on both statistical and clinical evidence. In fact, one of the principal problems in classification of the behavioral symptoms of attention-deficit hyperactivity disorder has been distinguishing them from conduct disorders, due to the existence of so many overlapping behaviors (Campbell & Werry, 1986). There is strong evidence that active and aggressive behavior usually coexist at a very early developmental stage (Campbell, 1991).

The third edition of the DSM categorized this behavioral dimension as *attention deficit disorder with hyperactivity* or *attention deficit disorder without hyperactivity,* though an "undifferentiated" third category of attention deficit disorder was possible. With the DSM-III-R, the name for this category of disorders was changed to *attention-deficit hyperactivity disorder* (ADHD), which was consistent with the Quay's label (1986a) if not with the actual behaviors. The DSM-III-R criteria for ADHD require the presence of 8 of 14 symptoms, ranging from fidgeting to thrill-seeking behavior. This most recent version of ADHD does not differentiate between cases where overt motor activity is present or not present. As is true of the other externalizing disorders, ADHD occurs at a significantly higher rate among males than females.

TABLE 8.2 Major behavioral characteristics of attention-deficit hyperactivity disorder identified through multivariate statistical techniques

Poor concentration, short attention span, distractibility

Daydreaming

Poor coordination and clumsiness

Stares into space; preoccupied

Passivity and lack of initiative

Fidgeting and restless behavior

Fails to complete tasks

Lazy or sluggish behavior

Impulsivity

Lack of interest and general boredom

Hyperactivity motor behaviors

Drowsiness

SOURCE: Adapted from H. C. Quay, "Conduct Disorders," in H. C. Quay and J. S. Werry (eds.), *Psychopathological Disorders of Childhood,* 3rd ed. (New York: Wiley, 1986).

PREVALENCE, ETIOLOGY, AND PROGNOSIS OF EXTERNALIZING DISORDERS

Prevalence estimates for externalizing disorders vary depending on definitional criteria, specific populations studied, and assessment methodology. However there is a general consensus that externalizing problems tend to be quite common, and a surprisingly high percentage of children and adolescents are thought to exhibit externalizing symptoms. The DSM-III-R states that for the younger-than-18 age group, conduct disorder occurs in about 9 percent of males and 2 percent of females. Martin and Hoffman (1990) cited conservative prevalence studies which placed the range for conduct disorders from about 4 percent to 8 percent in the entire school-age population, with males outnumbering females at a 3-to-1 ratio on average.

Attention-deficit hyperactivity disorder (ADHD) is thought to occur somewhat less frequently in children and adolescents than conduct disorders. DSM-III-R estimates suggest that about 3 percent of children exhibit ADHD, and the disorder is 6 to 9 times more common in males than females. Barkley (1990) cites several studies that placed prevalence estimates of ADHD in the 3 percent to 5 percent range. In sorting out these different prevalence estimates for externalizing problems, two findings are consistent: (*a*) Externalizing disorders are more common in the school-age population than internalizing disorders, and (*b*) externalizing disorders are much more likely to be exhibited by boys than girls.

An interesting finding that has emerged in the literature on externalizing disorders in children is that there is often a comorbid pattern with respect to ADHD and conduct disorders (Hinshaw, 1987; Loney & Milich, 1982; Paternite & Loney, 1980). While the existence of one of these disorders does not necessarily indicate the presence of the other, they have been linked through theory and research for quite some time. Two decades ago, Safer and Allen (1976) reported that 75 percent of children with symptoms of ADHD also have symptoms of conduct disorders. Loeber (1985) posited an interesting speculation on the link between the two disorders, suggesting that ADHD symptoms (and particularly hyperactive behavior) may be a necessary precursor for the development of severe forms of conduct disorder in many children. Whatever the relationship between ADHD and conduct disorders, it is clear that both types of externalizing disorders share common ground and that children who exhibit one set of problems are probably at risk for developing symptoms of the other set.

The etiology or origin of externalizing disorders has been the focus of much speculation and a good deal of research. The major models for explaining causation have been social learning, biochemical/neurological, and familial/genetic approaches, or variants thereof. With respect to attention-deficit hyperactivity disorder, Campbell and Werry (1986) note that although there has been a tremendous amount of speculation on a biological basis for the disorder, "specific conclusions remain elusive" (p. 116). If there is a biological basis for ADHD as Deutsch and Kinsbourne (1990) contend, it may be obscured due to its heterogeneous nature. With respect to conduct disorders, there is increasing speculation of a biologically based etiology (Werry, 1986), but again specific conclusions are difficult at this point. Despite the increasing attention placed on a potential biochemical or neurological basis for conduct disorders, the social learning model offers a more clearcut model of etiology at the present time. For example, Patterson's research group at the Oregon Social Learning Center has conducted a number of studies demonstrating that such factors as harsh and inconsistent discipline practices, lax parental monitoring, and exposure to adult models of antisocial behavior are all powerful predictors of the development of aggressive and antisocial behavior in children (e.g., Patterson, 1976, 1982, 1984; Patterson & Bank, 1986; Patterson & Dishion, 1985). Both ADHD and conduct disorders may have a familial/genetic connection, as they have been shown to run in families to some extent (Deutsch & Kinsbourne, 1990; Plomin, Nitz, & Rowe, 1990). However even with the inclusion of some well-designed twin and adoption studies, ferreting out the specific contributions of social learning and genetics has been problematic (Deutsch & Kinsbourne, 1990; Hetherington & Martin, 1986; Werry, 1986). Perhaps the most useful method of approaching the etiology of conduct disorders for assessment purposes is to integrate the various findings and speculations into a reciprocal determinism model consistent with Bandura's social cognitive theory (1986). It is likely that behavioral, environmental, and personal factors all contribute to the development of externalizing disorders and that they work together in an interactive fashion.

There is more evidence on the developmental patterns and long-term implications of externalizing disorders than for internalizing disorders (Cicchetti & Toth, 1991). The general developmental course of ADHD appears to include several components: onset in infancy or early childhood, continuation during childhood and adolescence with concomitant academic, behavioral, and social problems, and marginal adjustment to the disorder during adulthood (Campbell & Werry, 1986). Longitudinal studies of ADHD (e.g., Weiss, 1983; Weiss, Hechtman, Perlman, Hopkins, & Wener, 1979) have suggested that while individuals with ADHD may exhibit less impulsivity, restlessness, and antisocial behavior as adults than they did as adolescents, they are more likely to be "underemployed" than individuals without ADHD. These same studies have indicated that ADHD by itself is not necessarily predictive of severe psychopathology later in life. However if ADHD during childhood is accompanied by other externalizing disorders, familial discord, and low levels of intelligence and academic achievement, the long-term prognosis is poorer, and there is a greater likelihood of criminal behavior and psychiatric problems (Barkley, 1990).

With respect to conduct disorders, the developmental course and long-term prognosis seem to be related to the amount and intensity of aggressive behavior. Quay (1986b) has suggested that aggression is more likely to be a major characteristic of unsocialized rather than socialized conduct disorders and that the best prognosis for long-term adjustment is likely with individuals who have socialized aggressive conduct disorder in conjunction with high intelligence and good social skills. Previous research on aggressive behavior has resulted in findings that indicate reasonably strong stability over time. The likelihood that children's aggressive behavior will persist into adulthood increases with age. In other words, there is a modest probability that very young children (e.g., preschoolers) who exhibit persistent patterns of aggressive behavior will also exhibit aggressive behaviors as adults, but if these children are still exhibiting the same pattern of behavior by age 10 or 12, the probability of aggressive behavior as adults increases significantly. This pattern of continuity was demonstrated in a classic review of the literature from 1935 to 1978 by Olweus (1979), who found that stability of aggressive behavior was almost as strong over 10-year periods (.60) as that of intelligence (.70). Quay (1986b) suggested that the pattern of persistence of aggressive behavior is stronger for males than for females. Interestingly whether or not aggressive and antisocial conduct results in involvement with the justice system (i.e., reported delinquent and criminal behavior) seems to be strongly related to whether or not the child or adolescent has a parent who was convicted of a crime before he or she reached the age of 10 (Farrington, 1978). To sum up our discussion on the long-term implications of conduct disorders, it is important to emphasize two important findings: (*a*) Present aggressive behavior is the most important variable in the prediction of future aggressive and antisocial behavior (Quay, 1986b), and (*b*) although almost all adults with antisocial aggressive behavior exhibited these same patterns as children, most antisocial children do not become antisocial adults (Martin & Hoffman, 1990; Robins, 1974).

METHODS OF ASSESSING EXTERNALIZING PROBLEMS

Each of our five direct and objective assessment methods can be used in measuring externalizing disorders and problems. In terms of the state of the art and the utility of each method for day-to-day assessment of externalizing problems, direct observation and rating scales have received more attention in the literature. In terms of interview techniques, the behavioral interview with parents or teachers offers a great deal in the assessment of externalizing problems, and the structured interview schedules developed over the past two decades also have shown some promise. Sociometric and objective self-report assessments also have been used in evaluating externalizing problems, but they appear to be more limited in scope and utility than the other three methods. Each of the five methods will be discussed in this section of the chapter.

Direct Behavioral Observation

There is widespread professional agreement that direct behavioral observation is one of the most useful procedures for assessing externalizing behavior disorders (Alessi, 1988; Reid, Baldwin, Patterson, & Dishion, 1988). McMahon and Forehand (1988) have suggested that behavioral observation is ". . . the most reliable and valid assessment procedure for obtaining a functional analysis of conduct disorders in children" (p. 138). There are two major reasons why direct behavioral observation is the preferred method for assessing externalizing problems. The first reason has to do with the nature of externalizing disorders. Unlike internalizing disorders, which often involve highly subjective perceptions of internal states, externalizing disorders tend to be characterized by overt behavior patterns that are easy to observe, such as excessive motor activity, physical aggression, and verbal intimidation and opposition. Therefore, behavioral observation is a highly objective assessment method that easily measures externalizing target behaviors. The second reason for the preference for direct observation in assessing externalizing disorders has to do with behavior-environment interactions and the need to identify aspects of the environment that may be modified usefully in a treatment plan. Like internalizing problems, externalizing behavior problems do not occur in a vacuum; they are elicited and maintained in a very complex interaction between the person, the behavior, and the environment, as illustrated in Bandura's notion of reciprocal determinism (1977, 1978, 1986). However unlike internalizing problems, the interactive relationships in externalizing behavior problems are easier to observe directly. Therefore specific interactions and environmental variables that may play a role in the development of interventions are relatively easy for a skilled observer to identify.

Chapter 3 of this book includes a detailed discussion of general observation methods and coding procedures, including examples of systems useful in clinic, home, and school settings. In this chapter, we will not repeat this information but will focus on one example of a direct observation system that has been successfully employed in the assessment of externalizing disorders in clinic settings. Although home-based and school-based observation systems for externalizing problems have been successfully demonstrated (refer to chapter 3 for examples), our focus in this section will be on a clinic-based example, as this is a setting that can be easily utilized by the majority of clinicians on a day-to-day basis.

Although mental health, medical, or school psychology clinics usually are not considered to be naturalistic settings for conducting observations, these clinic environments can serve as very effective atmospheres for observing externalizing behavior problems (Hughes & Haynes, 1978). Clinic observations usually are analogous in nature, meaning that conditions can be created which simulate the home setting. The major advantages of clinic-based observation are that it is more efficient, cost-effective, and less obtrusive than home-based observations (McMahon & Forehand, 1988).

An excellent example of a clinic-based observation system is Eyberg and Robinson's Dyadic Parent-Child Interaction Coding System (DPICS) (1983), a coding procedure that has proven a highly reliable and valid method for the assessment of externalizing problem behaviors of children. What makes the DPICS particularly interesting is that it goes beyond simply focusing on child behavior problems and assesses those behaviors in the context of parental interactions in the parent-child dyad. The DPICS requires observation of the parent-child dyad in three different situations in the clinic: a free-play situation (child-directed interaction), a situation in which the parent guides the child's activity (parent-directed interaction), and a situation referred to as clean-up, in which the parent attempts to get the child to clean up the toys in a playroom. The observations occur for 5 minutes in each of the three settings, using a continuous frequency recording system for a total of 15 minutes of direct behavioral observation. Parent behaviors are coded along 12 different domains, including direct and indirect statements, descriptive and reflective statements, description and reflective questions, acknowledgement, irrelevant verbalization, unlabeled and labeled praise, positive and negative physical interactions, and critical statements. Child behaviors are coded along seven different domains, including cry, yell, whine, smart talk, destructive, physical negative, and change activity. The authors of the DPICS (Robinson & Eyberg, 1981) have also developed composite behavioral coding variables (total praise, total deviant, total commands, command ratio, no opportunity ratio, compliance ratio, and noncompliance ratio), which consist of specific combinations of individual coding domains.

Results of several studies have shown the DPICS to have solid psychometric properties. The inter-rater reliability of the DPICS has been found to range from .65 to 1.00 (Aragona & Eyberg, 1981; Eyberg & Matarazzo, 1980), with mean reliability coefficients of .91 and .92 for parent and child behaviors in the standardization study (Robinson & Eyberg, 1981). Although the DPICS has been utilized primarily in clinic-based observations, one investigation (Zangwill & Kniskern, 1982) found overall cross-setting interobserver agreement of .68 and .69 between home and clinic observations.

In terms of validity evidence, Robinson and Eyberg (1981) demonstrated that the DPICS can discriminate accurately groups of children with conduct disorders from their siblings and from normal children and that it has a high correct classification rate for each of these child groups and their families. Other studies have shown the DPICS to be sensitive to treatment effects (Eyberg & Matarazzo, 1980; Webster-Stratton, 1984). Also DPICS appears to be relatively easy to implement with trained observers, and it provides assessment data not only descriptive of problems but useful in building treatment plans as well.

The DPICS is just one example of a clinic-based coding procedure that has proven useful in assessing externalizing problems. A number of other clinic-based, empirically validated systems for assessing externalizing disorders have been reported in the literature. Of course, one of the main advantages of behavioral observation is that the methodology is flexible and easily tailored to the specific assessment problem in question. Well-researched observational coding systems offer certain advantages, but clinicians and researchers who understand the dynamics of observational assessment are able to develop systems uniquely suitable for the settings in which they are working. If the referred child/adolescent client is reported to exhibit serious behavioral problems at school as well as at home, it may be necessary also to observe directly in the classroom, using an observation system similar to the school-based examples looked at in chapter 3. As McMahon and Forehand (1988) have suggested, the therapist usually does not have the option of observing teacher-child interactions in the clinic, and as a result, naturalistic observation in the classroom may be warranted. Of course, if the problem behavior is related to a school-based referral, direct observation in the classroom should be a high priority, if not an essential part of the assessment.

Interviewing Techniques

Of the interviewing techniques discussed in chapter 5, the behavioral interview appears to be the most effective approach for assessing externalizing disorders. Although traditional (i.e., unstructured) interviewing techniques may be useful in getting a general appraisal of the cognitive and affective status of the client or informant, they are not as likely to result in a clear picture of the specific problems that are occurring. Given that child and adolescent conduct problems tend to be conceptualized in terms of interaction with others (McMahon & Forehand, 1988), the behavioral interview should include input from parents and from teachers if the conduct problems are present in the school setting. The characteristics of the three types of externalizing disorders discussed in this chapter are likely to make conducting an effective interview directly with the child or adolescent client very difficult. For both socialized and unsocialized aggressive conduct disorders, characteristic problems such as lying, defiance of authority, and oppositional behavior may result in the child/adolescent client providing information that is suspect. On the other hand, children or adolescents with attention-deficit hyperactivity disorder may not show such overt defiance in the interview, but they may still provide poor quality data due to their difficulties in concentrating and being aware of the subtle aspects of their own behavior. Thus behavioral interviews with parents and/or teachers will be an important first step in the assessment of externalizing disorders.

Whether the externalizing problems in question involve conduct disorders, attention-deficit hyperactivity disorder, or some combination thereof, the effectiveness of the behavioral interview will be greatly enhanced by the specificity of questions. For assessing ADHD, DuPaul (1992) suggests a semistructured behavioral interview format in which teachers and/or parents are asked questions pertaining to the presence or absence and intensity of symptoms from the DSM-III-R criteria. Forehand and McMahon (1981) have described the use of the Problem Guidesheet, a semistructured format for conducting behavioral interviews to assess child conduct problems. This interview format, shown in Figure 8.1, assists the clinician in structuring questions so that specific information on the frequency, duration, and parent or child responses to the problem behaviors can be obtained. The Problem Guidesheet also provides a format for asking questions about problem behaviors in specific settings and at specific times (e.g., at mealtime, in public places, etc.). The Problem Guidesheet is not intended to be a standardized interview instrument but simply a format to help clinicians structure behavioral interviews so that useful information about conduct problems can be obtained.

In terms of using standardized structured and semistructured interview schedules to assess externalizing problems, the three instruments overviewed in chapter 5 (K-SADS, DICA-R, and CAS) may be of some use. These instruments were all designed to assess a broad range of child disorders along the lines of DSM criteria and thus are not specifically designed for assessing externalizing problems. However, conduct disorder and attention-deficit hyperactivity disorder are both in the DSM-III-R section for disruptive behavior disorders, and thus various characteristics of these disorders are covered within the K-SADS, DICA-R, and CAS.

The National Institute of Mental Health Diagnostic Interview Schedule for Children (DISC) (Fisher, Wicks, Shaffer, Piacentini, & Lapkin, 1992) is an additional structured interview schedule highly relevant for assessing externalizing problems. The DISC is an interview schedule for use with children aged 9–17 and their parents. This interview schedule was originally designed as a screening instrument

Name of Child:			Interviewer:		
Name of Interviewee(s):			Date of Interview:		
Setting/ Time	**Description**	**Frequency**	**Duration**	**Parent Response**	**Child Response**
At bedtime					
At mealtime					
At bath time					
With parent on the phone					
With vistors at home					
When visiting others					
Travel in the car					
In public places					
At school					
With siblings					
With peers					
With other parent/ relative					
Disciplinary procedures					
Other:					

FIGURE 8.1 An adaptation of Forehand and McMahon's Problem Guidesheet (1981), a format for conducting behavioral interviews to assess child conduct problems

SOURCE: From *Helping the Noncompliant Child: A Clinician's to Parent Training*, by R. L. Forehand and R. J. McMahon. Copyright, 1981, the Guilford Press. Reprinted by permission of the publisher.

for research purposes, but its clinical uses are currently being refined and investigated. The DISC provides scores in 27 symptom areas outlined according to DSM classification criteria. The child version of the DISC has 264 items and requires from 40–60 minutes to administer, while the parent version includes 302 items and takes 60–70 minutes to administer. Both versions are highly structured and include specific codes for each item. The DISC requires very little training to administer and score, although interpretation is a somewhat more difficult task. Edelbrock and Costello (1988) reviewed several studies indicating that the DISC has very strong inter-rater reliability, fair to adequate test-retest reliability, and modest agreement between parent and child forms. The DISC has also been shown to have strong concurrent validity with the DICA-R and weaker but still significant concurrent validity with the parent version of the Child Behavior Checklist (Costello, Edelbrock, Dulcan, & Kalas, 1984). For the most current edition (version 2.3) of the DISC (Fisher et al., 1992), a comprehensive user's manual and an IBM-compatible DSM-III-R computer diagnostic program are available. Additionally the current research group developing the DISC for the National Institute of Mental Health periodically offers training seminars in the use of the DISC at two separate locations (Columbia University in New York City and Emory University in Atlanta). If an easy-to-use and highly structured interview schedule is needed for assessing externalizing problems, the DISC appears to be a good choice.

Behavior Rating Scales

Behavior rating scales are potentially one of the most useful parts of the assessment design when attempting to measure externalizing behavior problems. Since externalizing behavior is usually directly observable, an informant who knows the child or adolescent client may be in a position to provide a comprehensive rating of a wide variety of problem behaviors. Like direct observation, rating scales can provide relatively objective measurement, yet they take much less time to utilize. As a method of initial screening of problem behaviors and subsequent hypothesis generation, behavior rating scales may be one of the best choices. Theoretically though, there are some important differences between even the best rating scales and direct observation, and these differences usually indicate the need for using both types of measures. Rating scales usually provide a *retrospective* method of assessment, in that a parent or teacher rates child or adolescent problem behaviors according to their observations and perceptions over a past time period, say the preceding six months. On the other hand, direct observation provides a format for measuring behaviors *as they occur* over a limited time period. Thus rating scales will seldom provide information on environmental variables relating to problem behaviors, while direct observation over short time periods is likely to miss low-frequency but important behaviors. The multimethod, multisource, multisetting assessment model described in chapter 1 provides a format for overcoming the limitations of individual assessment sources while utilizing their strengths.

For most purposes, the three broad-purpose problem behavior rating scales or systems illustrated in chapter 4 (Child Behavior Checklist System, Revised Behavior Problem Checklist, and Conners Rating System) will be good choices for assessing externalizing behavior problems. These rating scales all have a number of items and scales specific to the externalizing domain, while allowing for an assessment of internalizing problems at the same time. In our previous discussion of the Conners Rating Scales, a 10-item hyperactivity index that is common to all four versions of the scales was mentioned. As you might remember, these 10 items do not constitute a separate factor but are comprised of common items from various other subscales that have been demonstrated to be most sensitive to behavioral change from pharmacological treatment in studies of children with attention-deficit hyperactivity disorder (Conners, 1990). Because these 10 items are of specific interest in this chapter, they are presented in Table 8.3. The School Social Behavior Scales, discussed in chapter 10, may also prove useful in assessing externalizing problems, as scale B of this instrument (antisocial behavior) provides a specific format for measuring aggressive, disruptive, and antisocial behavior in conjunction with a rating of social skills from scale A.

There may be times when it is useful to assess externalizing problems using rating scales designed to measure specific components of the externalizing domain. Thus this section will include brief overviews of some "narrow-purpose" rating scales. These include the Eyberg Child Behavior Inventory, a measure for assessing conduct problems, the Home and School Situations Questionnaires, which are related measures for assessing the situational aspects of externalizing behavior problems, and the Attention Deficit Disorders Evaluation Scales, a relatively new set of instruments designed specifically for assessing the behavioral symptoms of ADHD.

Eyberg Child Behavior Inventory (ECBI).   The Eyberg Child Behavior Inventory (Eyberg, 1980) is a 36-item scale designed to obtain parent ratings of externalizing conduct problems in children aged 2–16. The 36 items are rated using a 7-point scale which assesses frequency of occurrence as well as a yes/no problem identification checklist. The original ECBI normative data were divided

TABLE 8.3 Descriptors from the 10-item hyperactivity index of the Conners Rating Scales

Constantly fidgeting
Demands must be met immediately; easily frustrated
Restless or overactive
Excitable, impulsive
Inattentive, easily distracted
Fails to finish things she or he starts; short attention span
Cries often and easily
Disturbs other children
Mood changes quickly and drastically
Temper outbursts, explosive and unpredictable behavior

into 2–12 and 13–16 age groups. Since the original publication of ECBI norms, new standardization data have been published for large samples of children and adolescents (Burns, Patterson, & Nussbaum, 1991). The ECBI was originally considered to be a unidimensional scale primarily measuring overt conduct problems. However a more recent analysis (Burns & Patterson, 1991) has suggested that the ECBI in fact may be a multidimensional scale with three factors isolated that approximate the DSM-III-R diagnostic categories of conduct disorder, oppositional-defiant disorder, and attention-deficit hyperactivity disorder.

Several published research reports have demonstrated that the ECBI has a strong internal consistency and adequate test-retest reliability (e.g., Eyberg & Robinson, 1983; Robinson, Eyberg, & Ross, 1980), but no evidence of inter-rater reliability has been presented. Evidence for validity of the ECBI has come from studies showing that it differentiates between groups of conduct problem, clinic control, and normal children (Eyberg & Robinson, 1983), is sensitive to treatment effects (Eyberg & Robinson, 1982), and correlates significantly with the broad-band scales of the Child Behavior Checklist, especially the externalizing dimension (Boggs, Eyberg, & Reynolds, 1990).

The ECBI is easy to administer and score, and it appears to be a useful instrument in assessment batteries where measuring externalizing disorders is the primary or only concern. The ECBI has not been commercially published, and clinicians or researchers will need to obtain copies of the various published research articles in order to utilize it.

Home and School Situations Questionnaires. The Home Situations Questionnaire (HSQ) and School Situations Questionnaire (SSQ) are a set of related behavior rating scales introduced by Barkley (1981) in his book on the diagnosis and treatment of hyperactivity in children. These scales are different in nature from most problem-behavior rating instruments in that they help to assess the *settings* in which children exhibit problem behaviors. Thus the HSQ and SSQ are designed to measure both *behaviors* and *environments.* These instruments were developed from a parent interview format for obtaining information on problem behaviors often exhibited by hyperactive children (Barkley, 1981, 1988). The HSQ asks parents about 16 situations in the home and in public where their children's problem behaviors are exhibited (e.g., mealtimes, getting dressed in the mornings, when child is asked to do a chore, etc.). Parents first respond in a yes/no fashion to whether each item constitutes a specific problem, and then they rate the severity of each situation using a 1 (mild) to 9 (severe) rating scale. The SSQ is similar in format to the HSQ but specifies 12 situations specific to school settings (e.g., in the hallways, during small group work, etc.). Both instruments yield two scores: the total number of problem settings (from the yes/no checklist) and a mean severity rating (the average score of the 1–9 ratings).

Studies published by Barkley and his colleagues have provided normative data for the HSQ and SSQ and demonstrated that these instruments have adequate psychometric properties, treatment sensitivity, and discriminant validity in differentiating children with attention-deficit hyperactivity disorder from other children (Barkley & Edelbrock, 1987; Barkley, Karlsson, Pollard, & Murphy, 1985;

Befera & Barkley, 1985; Pollard, Ward, & Barkley, 1983). More recent research efforts have included examinations of the factor structures of both scales (Breen & Altepeter, 1991) and provided additional normative data and verification of psychometric properties (Altepeter & Breen, 1989). While the HSQ and SSQ are much briefer and more specific than the broad-purpose rating scales we looked at in chapter 4, they are innovative, unique, and potentially very useful for assessing externalizing behavior problems. They appear to have a great degree of clinical and research utility in assessing situational factors for treatment planning and evaluation, particularly surrounding behaviors often seen in children with attention-deficit hyperactivity disorder.

Attention Deficit Disorders Evaluation Scales.   A relatively recent addition to the pool of available rating scales for assessing externalizing problems is the Attention Deficit Disorders Evaluation Scales (ADDES), a set of instruments designed specifically for measuring the behavioral characteristics of attention-deficit hyperactivity disorder in children and adolescents age 4 through 20 and for making program planning and intervention decisions (McCarney, 1989a; 1989b). Two versions of the ADDES are available: a 46-item home version designed to be completed by parents and a 60-item school version designed to be completed by teachers and other school-based professionals. Items on the ADDES are descriptions of a variety of impulsive, hyperactive, inattentive behaviors. These items are rated on a rather unique five-point scale where each rating point is anchored to a specific time range in which the behaviors may occur (0 = "does not engage in the behavior," 1 = "one to several times per month," 2 = "one to several times per week," 3 = "one to several times per day," and 4 = "one to several times per hour"). The items are divided into three subscales constructed using rational-theoretical methods: inattentive, impulsive, and hyperactive. Raw scores are converted to standard scores for the subscales and to a percentile score for the total score, and these scores are keyed to three different diagnostic levels (normal score, some problems, serious problems), based on standard deviation units from the normative population.

   Technical manuals for the home and school versions of the ADDES provide a variety of information on the technical properties of each instrument. Both versions of the ADDES were normed on very large nationwide population samples (N = 1,754 for the home version, N = 4,876 for the school version). The stability of the ADDES across time, settings, and raters appears to be very good. Test-retest reliability at 30-day intervals is in the low .90 range for the total scores and from .89 to .97 for the subscales. Mean inter-rater reliabilities of the ADDES are also very high with an average r of .85 between pairs of teachers on the school version and .82 between parents on the home version. Internal consistency coefficients are in the .90 range for the scales of each version of the ADDES. Although the subscale structure of the ADDES was developed using rational-theoretical methods, the data were subjected to factor analysis procedures, which provide some limited support for the existing scale structure and reveal that the ADDES is a factorially complex instrument. Diagnostic validity data gathered during the standardization of the ADDES show that each version of the instrument can discriminate between groups of children who have been diagnosed as having

ADHD and randomly selected comparison subjects. Moderate to very strong correlations between the ADDES and two instruments from the Conners Rating Scale System (CTRS-39 and CPRS-48) provide some evidence of the convergent validity of the instruments.

The main caution in recommending the ADDES for clinical use is that the amount of validity evidence available to date is relatively scarce; the ADDES technical manuals provide only a few empirical studies, and no additional published studies on properties of the ADDES were found in a computer search of the literature between 1989 and 1992. Although the existing evidence is supportive, additional encouraging validity evidence would increase the confidence with which these instruments could be used. Specifically comparisons of ADDES ratings and direct behavioral observations, concurrent validity studies with additional rating scales, and additional evidence supporting the diagnostic integrity of the three subscales would be useful. In spite of this caution, the ADDES appears to be a very useful instrument for assessing characteristic symptoms of ADHD and thus can be strongly recommended as a research tool and tentatively recommended as a clinical tool.

Sociometric Approaches

In chapter 6, the methods and rationale of sociometric assessment were examined, including four different general procedures: (a) peer nomination, (b) peer rating, (c) sociometric ranking, and (d) alternative procedures such as picture sociometrics, the Class Play, and "guess who" measures. If properly applied, any one of these sociometric procedures are potentially an excellent choice for screening and assessment of externalizing disorders.

The utility of sociometrics for assessing externalizing problems depends on two variables: (a) the specific design of the sociometric question or task, and (b) the purposes for which the sociometric assessment will be used. To be most effective in assessing conduct disorders or attention-deficit hyperactivity disorder, the sociometric tasks will need to be structured carefully so that the peer or teacher informants will make selections based on externalizing characteristics. For instance, negative ranking or rating procedures where participants are asked to list or rate peers who "fight a lot" is likely to be more effective in externalizing assessment than procedures where participants are asked to list or rate peers who "don't get along with other students." The latter example obviously could have a great deal of correlation with internalizing problems as well. Sociometric assessment of externalizing problems is generally a more useful procedure for screening purposes than for individual assessment. It is true that conducting a sociometric procedure as part of an individual assessment in the classroom of a referred student might provide some useful data on that student, but the amount of time and intrusiveness involved rarely would be warranted.

Since chapter 6 provides an overview of the specifics of conducting sociometric assessments, this information will not be repeated here. However some examples of studies employing sociometric procedures to assess externalizing characteristics and outcomes will be useful. In their review of studies documenting the predictive validity of sociometrics, McConnell and Odom (1986) cited several investigations where sociometric procedures were employed in the assessment of externalizing problems. One of the most extensive and frequently cited studies is Roff, Sells, and Golden's longitudinal investigation (1972) of peer and teacher ratings of 40,000 children. One of the interesting findings of this classic study was that children rated least liked by their peers were significantly more likely to appear on registers of juvenile delinquents than children who were rated most liked by peers. Other longitudinal studies have found that peer ratings or nominations of classmates as mean, noisy, or quiet (Victor & Halverson, 1976) and troublesome or dishonest (West & Farrington, 1973) were significantly related to conduct problems and juvenile delinquency at a later age. Roff (1961) conducted a prospective study of 164 male children who were referred to child guidance clinics and later served in the military, and he found that children whose records indicated poor peer adjustment were significantly more likely later to receive bad conduct discharges from military service than those with good peer relations. Other studies documenting the utility of sociometric procedures in assessing externalizing problems could be cited, but these four classic studies provide sufficiently strong evidence. In sum, sociometric procedures have been demonstrated to be effective in the assessment of a variety of externalizing conduct problems and are particularly useful for screening and research purposes.

Assessment with Self-Reports

In chapter 9, the use of objective self-report tests is presented as the method of choice for assessing internalizing disorders. However a much different picture of the utility of this assessment method emerges when applied to the measurement of externalizing behavior disorders. There are three measurement problems that emerge in using self-report tests for assessing conduct disorders and attention-deficit hyperactivity disorder. First externalizing problems usually are best assessed through direct measurement and unbiased reporting by objective observers (McMahon & Forehand, 1988). Second children and adolescents with externalizing disorders are often not reliable reporters of their own behavior (Barkley, 1988). Third the very nature of most objective self-report tests requires that a fair amount of inference be used in applying the results to actual behaviors exhibited, particularly with conduct problems. Thus while objective self-report tests often are very useful in the assessment of internalizing problems, they are probably the least effective and most indirect method of assessing externalizing behavioral problems.

In spite of the apparent limitations of using objective self-report tests in assessing externalizing problems, there are time when it is desirable to include a suitable self-report instrument in an assessment battery. For instance, a clinician may want to gather systematic data on a child or adolescent client's perceptions of his or her behavior or to compare the client's personality profile to that of a normative or clinical group. Fortunately, there are a few standardized self-report instruments that potentially are an acceptable or valuable addition to the multimethod, multisource, multisetting assessment design for measuring externalizing disorders.

The three self-report instruments examined in chapter 7 (Youth Self-Report, Millon Multiaxal Adolescent Personality Inventory, Minnesota Multiphasic Personality Inventory-Adolescent) may all be useful to a modest extent in assessing externalizing problems and their correlates. Each of these instruments includes subscales associated with externalizing and antisocial behavior problems, such as the psychopathic deviate and conduct problems scales of the MMPI-A, the impulse control and societal conformity scales of the MAPI, and the aggressive behavior, attention problems, and delinquent behavior scales of the YSR. The MAPI and MMPI-A are described best as measures of personality that may be useful in predicting psychopathology, while the YSR requires subjects actually to rate their own levels of specified problem behaviors. It is important to understand that these and other self-report instruments do not directly assess externalizing behaviors but measure patterns of responding that are *associated with* these problems. For example, a number of investigations have shown that the MMPI two-point code type of 4-8 or 8-4 (psychopathic deviate-schizophrenia) is a common pattern of individuals who have been incarcerated for severe antisocial acting-out behavior. In fact, this MMPI two-point code type is the most common code type of male rapists (Graham, 1990). Yet the MMPI does not actually assess antisocial and violent behavior; the vast amount of research on the instrument has merely identified response patterns that are correlated with these behaviors based on group research.

Jesness Inventory of Adolescent Personality (JIAP).   In addition to the three self-report instruments previously examined, the Jesness Inventory of Adolescent Personality (Jesness, 1988) is a self-report test worth discussing in this chapter. This test is one of the few, if not the only, widely used self-report test specifically developed for assessing externalizing conduct disorders. The JIAP is a 155-item true/false questionnaire designed to measure attitudes and personality characteristics associated with antisocial and delinquent behavior. This test was developed during the early 1960s, based on outcome research with delinquent youths in California (Jesness, 1962, 1963, 1965). The 155 items yield *T*-scores on 11 different scales. Three of the scales (social maladjustment, values orientation, immaturity) were developed using methods similar to the empirical criterion keying approach used on the MMPI clinical scales. Seven of the scales (autism, alienation, manifest aggression, withdrawal, social anxiety, repression, denial) were developed using cluster analysis, a statistical procedure for identifying clusters of similar items, which Jesness chose to employ rather than factor analysis. The remaining scale (asocial index) includes items from all the scales that were combined by using a discriminant function analysis procedure in order to develop a single measure discriminating between delinquent and nondelinquent populations. As with all arbitrarily named test scales, the scales on the Jesness Inventory may not necessarily measure what literal interpretations of the scale names might suggest. For example, the autism scale is not designed to measure autism, but it includes items whose central theme is distortion of reality or superficial self-enhancement. The asocial index is described by Jesness (1988) as a measure identifying general tendencies to behave in ways that transgress social rules.

Normative data for the JIAP are based on samples of 970 delinquent and 1,075 nondelinquent males ages 8–18 and 450 delinquent and 811 nondelinquent females ages 12–19. The normative data were gathered during the initial development of the JIAP in California during the early 1960s. Reliability of the JIAP has been criticized as insufficient (Shark & Handel, 1977), but it is close to the same general range as the MMPI clinical scales, with split-half coefficients ranging from .62 to .88 and test-retest coefficients ranging from .40 to .79. The JIAP scales showing the most stability include values orientation, manifest anger, social maladjustment, alienation, and depression. A number of studies have demonstrated various forms of validity of the JIAP. Concurrent validity has been demonstrated through strong correlations between specific JIAP scales and various scales of the MMPI and California Psychological Inventory (CPI). The JIAP has been shown in several outcome studies to be sensitive to treatment changes with delinquent youths (e.g., Kahn & McFarland, 1973; Roberts, Schmitz, Pinto, & Cain, 1990; Shivrattan, 1988). Validity evidence found in the JIAP test manual indicates that the test has been effective in differentiating delinquent from nondelinquent youths, but the JIAP has been criticized for having a high false-positive error rate because of the relatively low base rate of serious delinquent behavior (Mooney, 1984).

The JIAP can be recommended as an objective self-report test for assessing conduct problems and delinquent attitudes, with some reservations and cautions. Some of the techniques employed to develop the JIAP scales are not in line with current thinking and technology applications for test development, and this is particularly true for the JIAP scales developed through cluster analysis. As a result, some of the JIAP scales have poor psychometric properties. The normative data were gathered over 30 years ago and are limited geographically. Because the JIAP was developed over three decades ago, some of the items may be dated and may not reflect the complexity of organized antisocial and delinquent behavior which has emerged in the United States since the 1980s (i.e., large-scale and highly organized gang activity). Multi-Health Systems, the current publisher of the JIAP, has announced that efforts are underway to revise and restandardize the test. It is hoped that these concerns will be addressed in the revision process.

In spite of the reservations and cautions concerning the JIAP, this test has withstood many of the criticisms directed at it, primarily because of the body of sophisticated research on it that has emerged over the years. As Mooney (1984) stated:

> . . . the research of the Jesness Inventory shows it is remarkably resilient to these potential "insults" to its functioning. A number of its scales, most notably social maladjustment, value orientation, and the asocial index, appear to tap into delinquent attitudes and degree of delinquent involvement . . . As a personality inventory relevant to delinquent attitudes and behavior, it appears to have no rivals. (p. 391)

In sum, if used with appropriate caution, the JIAP has the potential of being a very good addition to assessment designs aimed at evaluating externalizing conduct disorders, particularly socialized aggressive conduct disorder.

LINKING ASSESSMENT TO INTERVENTION

Each of the five general methods for assessing externalizing disorders that we have looked at in this chapter has its own advantages and limitations, and each is useful for different purposes and situations. However, when it comes to linking assessment data to interventions for externalizing problems, it is fairly clear that the five methods are not equal. Direct behavioral observation, particularly observation coding systems that take into account environmental variables and interactions between the subject and significant others, is the method of most use in developing intervention plans. Because a carefully designed and implemented observation system allows for direct measurement of environmental situations and interpersonal interactions that help to elicit and maintain problem behaviors, it will also help to generate hypotheses about methods for reducing problem behaviors and increasing desired behaviors. Behavioral interviewing with parents and teachers of the referred child/adolescent client is another assessment method that allows for collection of the same type of intervention-linked and functional assessment data, albeit in a less direct fashion. Behavior rating scales are typically less useful than direct observation or behavioral interviews in designing interventions for externalizing problems, but they may offer some help. If rating scales completed by different raters in different settings consistently portray certain behaviors or situations as significant problems, then the clinician will have some salient clues as to what specific behaviors or situations to focus on in the intervention plan. The developers of two of the rating scale systems reviewed in this chapter (Home/School Situations Questionnaires and Attention Deficit Disorders Evaluation Scales) have produced intervention manuals keyed to a great degree to the behavioral descriptions on these instruments, and these materials appear to be useful in designing intervention plans. Sociometric assessment of externalizing problems is perhaps best used as a descriptive method for screening or research and as such offers a much weaker link to intervention planning. Objective self-report tests also provide a most tenuous link to treatment planning for externalizing disorders, because they assess responding and personality patterns rather than actual behaviors. There have been some attempts to link MMPI profile types to treatment planning (e.g., Butcher, 1990), but these efforts cover only one specific self-report instrument, and they are in need of further empirical validation. In sum, externalizing disorders, by their very nature, are suited distinctly to the most direct methods of assessment, which in turn are capable of providing the most useful links to intervention planning.

CASE STUDY

Background Information

T.C., an eight-year-old boy in the second grade, was referred for assessment by the multidisciplinary child study team at his elementary school. The primary referral concerns focused on acting-out and aggressive behavior in the school setting. T.C.'s second grade teacher, who originally initiated the referral, noted that although T.C.'s performance is "average" on his academic work, he has difficulty completing assignments. His primary problems in the classroom are reported to involve intimidation of and physical aggression toward his classmates, as well as constant violations of classroom and school rules. T.C.'s teacher reports having documented a behavior management plan using rewards for nonaggressive and compliant behavior and time out from the classroom for aggressive-noncompliant behaviors but noted that "behavior management doesn't work with T.C."

T.C. lives with his parents and his three-year-old sister in the suburbs of a large metropolitan area. T.C.'s father is a long-haul truck driver and is often away from home for up to 10 days at a time. The father has had minimal contact with the school staff, but he was at T.C.'s last parent-teacher conference when the issue of the behavior problems was discussed at length and permission to conduct the assessment was processed. Mr. C. was willing to grant permission for the assessment but wrote on the form "I don't want my boy labeled or put on any drugs." Mr. C.'s opinion is that T.C.'s aggressive behaviors are "just like most boys'." Mrs. C. appears to be somewhat more concerned about T.C.'s behavior at home than is Mr. C.; she agreed that he is sometimes difficult to manage at home and that he occasionally "plays too rough with his sister and other kids in the neighborhood."

Assessment Data

The following behavioral, social, and emotional assessment data were gathered as part of this assessment:

Behavior Rating Scales. T.C. was rated by each of his parents using the Child Behavior Checklist and by his classroom teacher using the Teacher Report form of the Child Behavior Checklist. Additionally T.C.'s mother and teacher rated him using the Revised Behavior Problem Checklist. The obtained *T*-scores for these tests were as follows:

CBCL scores

Cross-Informant Syndromes and Broad-Band Areas	T.C.'s Teacher	T.C.'s Father	T.C.'s Mother
Aggressive Behavior	78	62	70
Anxious/Depressed	55	55	57
Attention Problems	72	70	72
Delinquent Behavior	72	63	68
Social Problems	70	60	62
Somatic Complaints	57	55	55
Thought Problems	55	55	58
Withdrawn	55	55	55
INTERNALIZING PROBLEMS	57	56	57
EXTERNALIZING PROBLEMS	74	64	69
TOTAL PROBLEMS	68	60	65

RBPCL scores

RBPCL Subscale	T.C.'s Teacher	T.C.'s Mother
Conduct Disorder	72	65
Socialized Aggression	70	62
Attention Problems-Immaturity	68	71
Anxiety-Withdrawal	46	52
Psychotic Behavior	68	62
Motor Excess	70	70

Behavior Observation Data. T.C. was observed during two 15-minute time periods by a special education resource teacher: once during a reading and spelling activity in the classroom and once during the recess playground period. The classroom observation was conducted utilizing a series of behavioral codes at 20-second intervals using the partial-interval method (45 intervals total). T.C was out of seat during 12 different intervals, more than three times as often as the social comparison students who were observed. He was coded as being off task during 17 intervals, more than twice as often as the social comparison students. He was also coded as engaging in physically negative behavior (pushing or kicking classmates near him) during 6 intervals, while the social comparison students did not receive this coding at all. The playground observation consisted of an event recording procedure with a checklist of observed problem behaviors completed at the end of the 15 minutes. T.C. was observed engaging in various forms of physically aggressive behavior eight times during the observation, and he was also observed being rejected by peers (who ran away from him) three times. The critical problem behaviors checked at the end of the observation included "physically aggressive," "threatens peers" "violates playground rules," and "peer problems." No social comparison data were collected during this observation.

Interview Data. Behavioral interviews were conducted by the school psychologist with T.C.'s teacher and with T.C.'s parents, using a problem identification interviewing model to pinpoint the most significant or bothersome problems. Stated briefly, the "most bothersome" problem behaviors identified during the interview included:

Teacher Behavioral Interview	Parent Behavioral Interview
Physically aggressive to classmates	Plays roughly with other children
Intimidates and bullies other children	Difficulty following directions
Frequently out of seat	"Doesn't think before he acts"
Frequently off task	
Difficulty completing assignments	

Questions to Consider

1. The assessment data presented here are preliminary screening data. What other information regarding T.C.'s social-emotional behavior would be useful, and what assessment tools would best provide this information?

2. Based on the Behavioral Dimensions approach to conduct problems and the three types of externalizing disorders identified in Tables 8.1 and 8.2, do T.C.'s behavioral characteristics fit any of these types? If so, which types are the most likely and why?

3. Are the assessment data congruent with the reasons for referral? Do these data suggest the presence of problems not noted in the reasons for referral and background information?

4. Compare the scores from the three CBCL profiles. What do the differences and similarities among these scores suggest about source and setting variance?

5. Compare the scores from the two RBPCL profiles. What do the differences and similarities between these scores suggest about source and setting variance?

6. Compare the scores from the CBCL and RBPCL profiles. What do the differences and similarities between the scores of these two rating scales suggest about instrument variance in this case?

7. Based only on the data presented in this case study, how severe do T.C.'s externalizing behavior problems appear to be?

CHAPTER 9

Internalizing Disorders: Assessment of Depression, Anxiety, and Related Problems

INTRODUCTION

With this chapter we move into the area of assessing internalizing problems of children and adolescents, of which depression, anxiety, social withdrawal, and diminished self-esteem are major characteristics. Internalizing problems represent an intriguing and problematic area because they can be difficult to detect, with the symptoms often mingled together. Some have even referred to internalizing problems in children as "secret" illnesses (Reynolds, 1992). This chapter explores the complexity and dimensions of internalizing problems and shows how various types of assessment strategies are utilized in the investigation and identification process.

The chapter begins with a theoretical discussion of the nature of internalizing problems, including overviews of each major area of internalizing symptomology. This introductory overview is followed by discussions of the implications of developing internalizing problems and how this broad band of symptoms is related to the self-concept. Following the general format of this book, the chapter will go on to provide detailed information on the direct and objective methods of assessing internalizing problems, including behavioral observation, rating scales, interview techniques, sociometric approaches, and self-report tests. A special assessment section is also provided for methods of measuring the self-concept. The chapter ends with a brief discussion of the challenges of linking assessment of internalizing problems to intervention.

AN OVERVIEW OF INTERNALIZING PROBLEMS

As reported in chapters 2 and 8, recent efforts at creating sophisticated and empirically sound taxonomies of child psychopathology (i.e., the Behavioral Dimensions approach) have tended to sort general types of behavioral and emotional problems into two broad dimensions. These two domains have been referred to by several different terms (e.g., inner-directed and outer-directed, undercontrolled and overcontrolled, self-related and other related), but the most commonly used terminology for categorizing the two broad classes of behavioral and emotional problems is *internalizing* and *externalizing* (Cicchetti & Toth, 1991).

The broad band of internalizing problems or disorders includes a seemingly wide variety of symptomology, such as the development of dysphoric mood states (depressive symptoms), social withdrawal, anxious and inhibited reactions, and the development of somatic problems. Yet while these different internalizing conditions may appear at least superficially to be distinct symptoms, there is strong historical evidence that they often exist together in a *comorbid* relationship (Ackerson, 1942; Fish & Shapiro, 1964). Currently there is a large and growing body of evidence that strongly indicates a great deal of behavioral covariation among the characteristics of mood disorders, anxiety disorders, and somatic complaints (e.g., Maser & Cloninger, 1990). Thus the chances are quite good that a child or adolescent who presents the obvious symptoms of depression may also experience anxiety, social inhibition and withdrawal, as well as physical concerns. Therefore, it is useful, if not necessary, to study the assessment of these types of problems within a common framework.

The DSM system includes a number of general diagnostic categories that fit within the internalizing domain, including anxiety disorders, mood disorders, and certain aspects of eating disorders, tic disorders, and somatoform disorders. In keeping with our previous discussions of the Behavioral Dimensions classification approach, specific areas of internalizing problems have been identified using multivariate statistical techniques. Quay (1986) has identified the two major dimensions that coincide with internalizing problems as *anxiety-withdrawal-dysphoria* and *schizoid-unresponsive*. These dimensions are quite similar to the divisions of internalizing problems that will be used in this chapter. The general behavioral characteristics of these two dimensions are illustrated in Table 9.1. As can be seen from this table, there is a fair amount of overlap in characteristics between the two major internalizing domains. Other researchers have described the domain of internalizing problems in a somewhat different light (e.g., Achenbach, 1982b), but Quay's description serves to illustrate the overlapping characteristics within types of internalizing problems.

To identify and define more clearly the major subcomponents of internalizing problems, this section includes brief discussions of symptomology based on a breakdown into three separate areas: depression, anxiety, and related problems. In examining this three-part breakdown of internalizing problems, keep in mind that there is more confusion over terminology and classification subtypes for internalizing problems than for externalizing problems (Kauffman, 1989). Thus any categorical breakdown in the internalizing domain is bound to have some level of imprecision. This discussion of general characteristics of internalizing disorders only addresses etiology at a superficial level; a thorough treatment is beyond the scope of this book. An excellent source for a comprehensive treatment of various internalizing problems, including etiologic information, is the *Handbook of Developmental Psychopathology,* edited by Lewis and Miller (1990).

TABLE 9.1 Major behavioral characteristics of two dimensions of internalizing problems identified through multivariate statistical techniques

Anxiety-Withdrawal-Dysphoria	Schizoid-Unresponsive
Anxious, fearful, tense	Won't talk
Shy, timid, bashful	Withdrawn
Depressed, sad, disturbed	Shy, timid, bashful
Hypersensitive, easily hurt	Cold and unresponsive
Feels inferior, worthless	Lack of interest
Self-conscious, easily embarrassed	Sad
Lacks self-confidence	Stares blankly
Easily flustered and confused	Confused
Cries frequently	Secretive
Aloof	Likes to be alone
Worries	

SOURCE: Adapted from H. C. Quay, "Classification," in H. C. Quay and J. S. Werry (eds.), *Psychopathological Disorders of Childhood,* 3rd ed. (New York: Wiley, 1986).

Depression

To better understand what the target is when assessing depression, some definitions and distinctions are in order. The term *depression* can be construed to mean a broad range of behaviors, characteristics, and symptoms. This broad and imprecise use of the term has been a problem in the research literature, resulting in many studies using the same basic terminology to describe different facets of behavioral and emotional functioning. Three common uses of the term *depression* have been noted by Cantwell (1990): depression as a symptom, depression as a syndrome, and depression within the context of a depressive disorder.

Depression as a Symptom.   As a symptom, depression involves a dysphoric mood state—feeling unhappy or sad, being "down in the dumps," feeling miserable, or feeling melancholic or "blue." These subjective states are only a small part of the syndrome of depression or depression as a disorder. It is important to recognize that depressive symptoms are typical across the life span of most persons and that they are typically transient and usually not part of a depressive disorder or serious problem. It is also possible that depressive symptoms may exist as part of other disorders. Thus symptoms of depression alone usually will not provide the impetus for conducting an assessment of depression.

Depression as a Syndrome.   The term *syndrome* is used to describe something that is more than a dysphoric mood state. This term is usually understood to describe the coexistence of behavioral and emotional symptoms that often occur together are thus are not simply associated by chance. Cantwell (1990) notes that a depressive syndrome commonly involves not only mood changes but additional changes in psychomotor functioning, cognitive performance, and motivation. These additional changes usually occur in a negative direction, reducing the functional capacity of the person who experiences them. Depression as a syndrome is less common than depression as a symptom. It may be brought on by certain types of life stress, may exist concurrently with various medical problems, or may occur in conjunction with psychological and psychiatric disorders such as disruptive behavior disorders, schizophrenia, and anxiety disorders. Depression as a syndrome may also occur as the primary problem with no preexisting or comorbid syndromes. Of course, depressive syndrome may also be a part of depressive disorders.

Depression as a Disorder.   The distinction between depressive syndromes and depressive disorders is not quite as clear as the distinction between depressive symptoms and depressive disorders. While depressive syndromes are typically part of depressive disorders, more is usually implied by the latter term. By saying that a depressive disorder exists, there is an implication that a depressive syndrome exists, but that the syndrome has occurred for a specified amount of time, has caused a given degree of functional incapacity, and has a characteristic outcome such as duration and responsiveness to treatment (Cantwell, 1990). The most common way of referring to depression as a disorder is within the context of the DSM classification system. DSM-III-R includes 12 different general categories for the diagnosis of mood disorders, and three general categories for the diagnosis of depressive disorders. In order for the diagnosis of a major depressive episode to occur, at least five out of nine possible specified symptoms (ranging from a depressed mood to recurrent thoughts about death) must have occurred within a two-week period, in addition to certain exclusionary criteria being met (American Psychiatric Association, 1987). One of the major challenges of using standard criteria like the DSM system for diagnosing depressive disorders is that these systems may not be equally effective or useful across different age ranges (Carlson & Garber, 1986). Thus assessment of depression as a disorder in children and adolescents requires particular care, skill, and caution.

Causal Factors.   Given that entire volumes have been devoted to the etiology of childhood depression, treating these topics in such a short space is highly presumptuous, to say the least. The purpose of this discussion is simply to provide a brief description of some of the recent key findings on causal factors. Miller, Birnbaum, and Durbin (1990) reviewed the literature on parental influences, life events, and family interaction patterns associated with depression in children and proposed some general findings. A relationship has been found to exist between what is commonly referred to as "loss" and childhood depression, with this relationship most readily verified by studies of mother or father loss due to death or family separation. Children of parents who are themselves depressed have been shown to be at heightened risk for developing depression, as well as other psychological disorders. High rates of parental stress and family conflict have been found to be associated with childhood depression as well. Additionally there is some evidence that negative events outside the family context, such as school and friendship problems, may be associated with childhood depression.

Within the social learning perspective of this book, it is also useful to consider some other models of how depression develops. The *learned helplessness* model (Seligman, 1974) suggests that some forms of depression may occur under learning conditions where children do not recognize a relationship between their actions and the consequences of these actions. Lewinsohn (1974) proposed a highly influential model suggesting that the disruption of pleasurable and otherwise reinforcing events may predispose a person to depression, an idea definitely worth considering when conducting a comprehensive child assessment wherein environments as well as behavioral characteristics are evaluated. Additionally strong evidence is emerging in the psychobiology literature suggesting that some forms of childhood depression are related to personal variables, namely the interrelated areas of family genetics and brain chemistry.

Anxiety

Anxiety is a class of internalizing responses that may involve subjective feelings (e.g., discomfort, fear, dread), overt behaviors (e.g., avoidance, withdrawal), and physiological responses (e.g., sweating, nausea, general arousal). Anxiety is closely related to two other areas, *fears* and *phobias*. While anxiety, fears, and phobias have a great deal of overlap, there have been some distinctions historically drawn among the three categories. Fears have been described as "reactions to perceived threats that involve avoidance of the threatening stimuli, subjective feelings of discomfort, and physiological changes" (Barrios & Hartmann, 1988, p. 197). Fears are usually distinguished from anxiety in that the former involves distinct reactions to very specific stimuli (such as darkness or noise), while the latter tends to involve a more diffuse type of reaction (apprehension) to stimuli that are not as specific in nature. Phobias are similar to fears in that they involve intense reactions to specific stimuli but are differentiated from fears in that they are more persistent, maladaptive, and debilitating (Barrios & Hartmann, 1988; Morris & Kratochwill, 1983). Given that the focus of this section is a general treatment of the subject, anxiety will be the topic of this overview rather than the more specific categories of fears and phobias.

It is interesting that the topic of anxiety in children has often been overlooked. The topic deserves attention particularly in light of evidence that a significant portion of child clients at mental health clinics are treated for anxiety disorders (Miller, Boyer, & Rodoletz, 1990) and that childhood anxiety may be predictive of adult psychopathology (Bowlby, 1973). One of the reasons that anxiety in children may be overlooked is that it is believed to be both common and transient (Wolfson, Fields, & Rose, 1987). Given that the DSM-III-R lists three different childhood disorders in which anxiety is the major feature (separation anxiety disorder, avoidance disorder of childhood and adolescence, and overanxious disorder), the remainder of our discussion of childhood anxiety follows this topical breakdown into three categories.

Separation Anxiety. Separation anxiety traditionally has been thought of and defined as anxiety reactions over the possibility of or actual separation from persons to whom the child is attached. These persons are typically, but not necessarily, the mother or father of the child. As infants grow into toddlers, their cognitive and social maturation allows for greater recognition and discrimination between persons, and this maturation is usually accompanied by some indications of "stranger anxiety" as a normal part of development. This normal response is different from separation anxiety as a disorder, which is characterized by more intense and persistent responses. Based on the DSM-III-R criteria, separation anxiety disorder involves, in addition to other possible features, unrealistic and persistent worry about attachment figures being the victims of major harm or death, refusal to go to school or day care in order to remain with the attachment figure, persistent avoidance of being out of sight of the attachment figure (i.e., "clinging" and "shadowing"), and persistent nightmares.

An interesting sidelight to this general description is that recent research has produced some evidence that separation anxiety may be strongly correlated with the quality of attachment to caregivers. In other words, children who are less securely attached to their parents or other caregivers are more likely to experience separation anxiety to the point where it becomes a serious problem. Building on the initial pioneering work of developmental psychologist Mary Ainsworth (e.g., Ainsworth, 1979; Ainsworth, Blehar, Waters, & Walls, 1978), recent investigations have further suggested that the quality of attachment is improved when maternal responses during infancy are consistent, accurate, and predictable (Isabella, Belsky, & von Eye, 1989) and that father-infant interactions can be highly predictive of infant sociability with strangers (Bridges, Connell, & Belsky, 1988).

Avoidant Anxiety.   Avoidant anxiety is a condition in which the child shrinks from contact with unfamiliar persons to such a degree that the child's social relations with peers are severely impaired. The DSM-III-R criteria for avoidant disorder of childhood or adolescence excludes children under the age of two and a half, requiring that the problem persist at a significant level for at least six months in order for a diagnosis to be made. Since very little has been empirically tested about this form of anxiety (Miller, Boyer, & Rodoletz, 1990), little is known about the validity of the classification, the etiology, or the key behavioral correlates.

Overanxious Anxiety.   The DSM-III-R diagnostic category of overanxious disorder is characterized by excessive and unrealistic levels of anxiety for a period of at least six months, related to phenomena such as future events, past behavior, and personal competence in a variety of areas. The disorder may also include a variety of somatic complaints, extreme levels of self-consciousness, subjective and measurable levels of tension, and the constant need for reassurance. While less is known about this form of anxiety than about separation anxiety, several studies have shown this category to have convergent and discriminant validity (Miller, Boyer, & Rodoletz, 1990). Obviously children who exhibit these types of anxiety symptoms to a significant degree will experience a great deal of discomfort and distress, and they may experience serious problems in their social adjustment. Thus they may be prime candidates for assessment and subsequent interventions.

Causal Factors.   Although a fair amount of effort has been devoted to exploring causal factor associated with the development of depression, comparatively little has been done on the development of anxiety, particularly in relation to children. One of the problems in making a few general statements about the causes of anxiety in children is that the causes have been viewed very differently by professionals with different theoretical orientations, such as psychoanalytic, behavioral, and cognitive perspectives (Miller, Boyer, & Rodoletz, 1990). Given that so little empirical work has been devoted to the causes of anxiety in children, perhaps the most appropriate statement about causation and one that is compatible with the social learning perspective of this book is that "the child's temperamental characteristics, in combination with early socialization experiences and the nature of the current . . . environment, probably account for the development (of anxiety-related problems)" (Kauffman, 1989, p. 334).

Related Problems

In addition to the characteristics of depression and anxiety, the broader category of internalizing disorders includes a number of other behavioral, social, and emotional problems. One of the major correlates of depression and anxiety is social withdrawal or isolation. As Kauffman (1989) notes, social isolation can result from either behavioral excesses (e.g., aggression or hyperactivity) or behavioral deficits. It is the category of behavioral deficits that is most closely linked with internalizing disorders. Children who are socially isolated or withdrawn due to behavioral deficits tend to lack responsiveness to the social initiations of others—in other words, they lack the specific social skills to make and keep friends. Often, a severe lack of social skills is accompanied by immature or socially inadequate behavior that further compounds the problem by making the child an easy target of ridicule (Kauffman, 1989). Internalizing social withdrawal and isolation seem to be related not only to incompetent adult social models but to a temperamental characteristic referred to by Kagan, Reznik, and Snidman (1990) as *behavioral inhibition to the unfamiliar.* When present, this characteristic appears to emerge in infants at about eight months, and it leads to a tendency to become inhibited or withdrawn when presented with unfamiliar stimuli. There may be biological contributions to this temperamental characteristic, but it probably interacts with behavior and environment in a complex manner that results in characteristic social withdrawal.

Another common correlate of internalizing disorders is a broad range of physical symptoms and problems collectively referred to as *somatic complaints.* There is a strong probability that persons who experience significant depression or anxiety will have concurrent physical symptoms. These somatic symptoms associated with internalizing characteristics are presumably psychological in origin, although physical infections or injuries may cause similar symptoms. One of the subscales of the Child Behavior Checklist that turns up primarily along the internalizing dimension is labeled somatic complaints, and it includes rating items such as "feels dizzy," "overtired," and "physical problems without known medical cause." The last item has seven possible specifications, including aches and pains, headaches, nausea, problems with eyes, rashes or other skin problems, stomachaches or cramps, and vomiting. Any or all of these physical symptoms may be reported by children who are experiencing depressive, anxious, or withdrawn symptoms. Interestingly the congruence of somatic complaints and anxious-depressed-withdrawn characteristics in psychological assessment even predates the use of factor analytic assessment techniques. The first three of the MMPI clinical scales (hypochondriasis, depression, and hysteria), sometimes referred to as the "neurotic triad," all contain items relating to physical complaints as well as statements about depressive, anxious, and withdrawn symptomology. First developed in the 1940s using empirical criterion keying procedures, these three scales have been shown to reliably differentiate among different psychiatric groups in numerous studies.

Fears and phobias, a more specific group of characteristics that relate to anxiety, were touched upon very briefly earlier in this chapter. However what is usually referred to as *school phobia* deserves some additional discussion because it is a set of problems commonly encountered by mental health professionals who work with children and adolescents. The DSM-III-R does not have a separate diagnostic classification for school phobia but considers it one of the nine key features of separation anxiety disorder. Thus traditional thinking considers fear of and subsequent refusal to attend school as an internalizing problem that relates to a child's inner state of anxiety. More recently, this traditional anxiety-based view of school phobia has come under criticism, and the problem has been reconceptualized as *school refusal,* a broader term indicating a possible heterogeneity of symptoms. Pilkington and Piersel (1991) conducted a comprehensive review of the literature on school phobia and criticized the separation-anxiety-based theory on three grounds: (*a*) methodological problems of the research, (*b*) lack of generalizability concerning pathological mother-child relationships, and (*c*) lack of emphasis on possible external or ecological variables. With respect to this third criticism, an alternative conceptualization of school phobia has been presented, in which many cases of refusal to attend school can be explained as "a normal avoidance reaction to a hostile environment" (Pilkington & Piersel, p. 290). Realistically avoidance of or refusal to attend school probably includes a more heterogeneous group of conditions than was once thought, and anxiety problems as well as avoidant behavioral reactions are both likely culpable explanations. The implication of this new conceptualization of school phobia is that clinicians should consider assessing the school environment as well as child characteristics when refusal to attend school is a presenting problem. This implication is compatible with the transational-interactional model within social learning theory, which suggests that refusal to attend school may be explained by an interaction of parent and child characteristics, coupled with the environmental and behavioral conditions at school.

Finally there are a few additional characteristic conditions that are often part of the larger internalizing syndrome. Obsessive thought processes and compulsive behavioral rituals are thought to be closely related to the anxiety disorders, although in DSM terms they constitute separate classification paradigms. Various forms of eating disorders, including anorexia nervosa, bulimia, pica, and rumination disorders, have all been shown to be related to the broad internalizing syndrome (Kauffman, 1989). Some stereotypical movement disorders, such as motor tics, may also be a part of the internalizing picture. Finally elimination disorders (enuresis and encopresis) may occur with other internalizing problems, although there are also a number of physiologic causes for these problems.

IMPLICATIONS OF INTERNALIZING PROBLEMS

There has been disagreement in the developmental psychopathology literature as to the potential long-term consequences of internalizing disorders, and more research in this area is needed. At the present time, there seems to be general agreement in the field that serious internalizing symptoms of childhood may persist for long periods of time, perhaps as long as two years (Quay & Werry, 1986). In terms of the persistence of these "neurotic" characteristics into adulthood, there is much less agreement. Quay and Werry stated that symptoms of anxiety-withdrawal "do not have the rather foreboding prognosis that is associated with undersocialized conduct disorders" (1986, p. 101) and cited Robins's long-term follow-up research of neurotic children (1966) as an example that internalizing symptoms during childhood may not accurately predict the presence of internalizing problems during adulthood. However, other researchers have found evidence for a less optimistic prognosis for children with internalizing disorders. Social withdrawal and inadequate levels of social competence have been found to be associated with a number of later negative outcomes, but the evidence to date suggests that the prognosis is worse for aggressive than nonaggressive socially withdrawn children (Kauffman, 1989; Putallaz & Dunn, 1990). When childhood depression is the internalizing disorder of interest, there seems to be stronger evidence for persistence across the life span, particularly in the case of adolescent depression (Cantwell, 1990). Thus there may be some hope that the existence of internalizing disorders during childhood does not hold as poor a prognosis as does externalizing disorders; nevertheless there is evidence to suggest the potential for negative outcomes later in life.

INTERNALIZING PROBLEMS AND THE SELF-CONCEPT

Since internalizing problems have sometimes been thought of as being self-related or directed, a psychological construct that is particularly relevant to our discussion of internalizing problems is the *self-concept*. Kazdin (1988) has connected the constructs of depression and self-concept, noting that diminished self-esteem is often a prominent feature of depression. Given the overlap among depression, anxiety, and other internalizing symptoms, it is logical to assume that self-concept and internalizing symptoms in general may be negatively associated.

Harter (1990) notes that self-concept can have a number of different definitions, depending upon the theoretical framework adopted. The definition of self-concept utilized in this book is that of *multidimensional* self-concept. When defined from a multidimensional viewpoint, self-concept includes not only a person's overall self-evaluation and level of self-esteem but also self-evaluation of particular aspects of functioning, such as physical appearance and skills, academic competence, and social-emotional functioning. In a multidimensional framework, a person's overall self-concept is not merely a summation of how he or she feels about or evaluates any of the different aspects of life. Instead a person's evaluation of a particular aspect of self-functioning may contribute somewhat to the person's overall view of the self, with each dimension of self operating somewhat independently. For example, a person might have a very negative evaluation of a particular dimension of the self (e.g., physical appearance or athletic competence) but still have a relatively high global self-concept, or overall view of the self.

Earlier work in the area of self-concept, as typified by research and theoretical writing prior to the 1970s, tended to regard self-concept in a unidimensional fashion. The unidimensional view suggests that self-concept is assessed best by presenting the subject with a number of different items that tap various aspects of self-functioning, giving each different aspect of the self-concept equal weight and then providing a global estimate of self-concept by simply summing the item responses. The assessment of self-concept from this unidimensional viewpoint is typified by two instruments originally developed during the 1960s, the Coopersmith Self-Esteem Inventory (Coopersmith, 1981), and the Piers-Harris Children's Self-Concept Scale (Piers & Harris, 1969).

During the 1970s and 1980s, a number of researchers began to explore self-concept in a manner that identified specific domains of self-evaluation, which were thought to operate somewhat independently while at the same time correlating moderately with one another. This multidimensional approach to self-concept is typified by the work of Harter (1985a, 1986) and Marsh (1987). This view contends that overall self-concept is affected by individual areas of self-evaluation, but the contribution from each individual area is not necessarily the same. From a practical standpoint, viewing self-concept from a multidimensional perspective has important implications for a clinician conducting an assessment. For example, a child or adolescent client might have a very negative view of his or her academic competence but not consider this area to be very important and thus feel okay about himself or herself in a general sense. On the other hand, a client may see himself or herself as very competent and successful in most areas of functioning but assign great or undue weight to an unfavorable self-concept in the area of physical appearance, thus having a poor global self-concept.

The best evidence to date suggests that self-concept does indeed have a strong functional role that may impact such diverse aspects of human development as affect, motivation, and energy level, all of which have strong implications when it comes to internalizing problems. Commenting on this functional role of the self-concept, Harter (1990) stated the following:

> We have also been concerned with the mediational role that self-worth may play in impacting both affective state, along a dimension of depressed to cheerful, and motivation, along a dimension of low to high energy. Our studies provide strong support for the impact that self-worth has on affect, which in turn influences the child's energy level. The implications of these findings for childhood depression as well as adolescent suicide have also been explored within this context. (p. 319)

The construct of self-concept not only has significant implications in relation to internalizing problems but in relation to a number of other aspects of living as well. Since the 1970s, there have been strong nationwide efforts to provide affective education in public schools with the goal of enhancing students' self-concept. Bloom (1976) suggested that academic self-concept is the single most powerful affective predictor of academic success, accounting for about 25 percent of the variance in academic achievement after the elementary school period. More recently, many school-based intervention programs designed to prevent substance abuse and gang membership have focused on enhancing children's self-esteem as one preventative measure. Although there has been some disagreement regarding how to best enhance the self-concept, there is no question that the construct holds a place of prominence in the goals of most educators. Thus clinicians working with children and adolescents should have a basic understanding of the issues involved in assessing self-concept. Some multidimensional self-concept assessment instruments for children and adolescents will be discussed later in this chapter.

METHODS OF ASSESSING
INTERNALIZING PROBLEMS

The assessment of internalizing problems presents a peculiar problem for clinicians and researchers. By definition and practice, internalizing problems tend to involve internal states and subjective perceptions. Not surprisingly then, assessing characteristics such as depression and anxiety using external methods (e.g. direct observation, sociometrics, and to some extent, rating scales) can be quite problematic (Links, Boyle, & Oxford, 1988). Partially as a result of this problem, the research base on internalizing problems has historically lagged behind that of externalizing problems (Cicchetti & Toth, 1991). In terms of clinical practice with internalizing problems, this state of affairs has created similar problems. Because they are for the most part assessing internal and subjective states when evaluating internalizing problems, clinicians have tended to rely on various forms of self-reporting. With child and adolescent clients (particularly very young children) however, there is often a reluctance to relinquish the use of external methods of assessment, due to the supposedly questionable accuracy of information obtained with self-report methods.

Thus while this chapter covers assessment of internalizing problems using each of our five methods of direct and objective assessment, the larger focus will be on the use of objective self-report tests and interview methods.

Direct Behavioral Observation

Although assessment of internalizing problems through methods other than self-report (interviewing and objective tests) presents a number of problems, several characteristic internalizing behaviors can be directly observed, and there has been some experimentation with the use of behavioral observation codes for assessment. Unlike self-report methods, which assess client perceptions of internalizing symptoms, or rating scales, which assess internalizing symptoms retrospectively, the aim of direct behavioral observation is to assess these symptoms as they actually occur. Kazdin (1988) listed several symptoms of depression that are measurable through direct behavioral observation. Some of these include diminished motor and social activity, reduced eye contact with others, and slowed speech. Additional anxiety-related internalizing symptoms that might be assessed through direct observation include avoidance of feared or anxiety-provoking stimuli, facial expressions, and stance (Miller, Boyer, & Rodoletz, 1990). Using these characteristics as examples, it becomes very clear how important it is to observe some of the basic rules for conducting effective observations, such as defining the observation domain and selecting an appropriate recording system, as discussed in chapter 3.

An interesting observational technique used in the assessment of anxiety and related symptoms since the 1930s (Jersild & Holmes, 1935) is the Behavioral Avoidance Test (BAT). The BAT can be implemented in a variety of ways, and it is quite simple to use. The original BAT technique involved having the client or subject enter a room where the anxiety- or fear-provoking stimulus is present (e.g., animal, insect, separation from parent, darkness) and then approach the feared stimuli. The observational measures that can be taken include latency of approach, duration of time in the presence of the stimulus, and the number of approaches completed (Miller, Boyer, & Rodoletz, 1990). A variation of the BAT involves having the subject imagine the feared stimuli or situation and then recording the overt responses to the task. This variation may be particularly useful for assessing overt responses to anxiety-provoking situations that cannot be contrived in a clinical setting, such as fear of imagined "monsters," injury or death of a caregiver, or clouds.

Kazdin (1990) listed three general classes of behavioral codes that could be used for direct observational assessment of childhood depression. These general codes are listed as follows with specific target codes under each class:

1. *Social Activity:* Talking, playing a game, participating in a group activity
2. *Solitary Behavior:* Playing a game alone, working on an academic task, listening and watching, straightening one's room, grooming
3. *Affect-Related Expression:* Smiling, frowning, arguing, complaining

These types of observational target codes have been successfully used in the measurement of depression and related internalizing problems in several studies. For example, Williams, Barlow, and Agras (1972) found significant negative correlations with self-reports of depression and observations of verbal activity, smiling, and motor activity in depressed patients. Kazdin, Esveldt-Dawson, Unis, and Rancurello (1983) used behavioral codes from these three general categories to observe in-patient children (ages 8–13) over a one-week period, and they found that those children who were high in depression engaged in significantly less social behavior and exhibited significantly less affect-related expression than other children. From these two studies, we can see that internalizing problems can be effectively assessed through direct observation. However, it is important to keep in mind that the overt or easily observable characteristics of internalizing problems are only a part of the picture; the subjective emotional state and cognitive processes of the subject are also extremely important, and these must be assessed primarily through client self-report. Since so many aspects of internalizing problems are subtle or covert, it is very important to carefully design the observation, using procedures such as those outlined in chapter 3.

Self-monitoring, a specific facet of direct behavioral observation, has not been widely researched as an assessment method for internalizing problems, but it appears to hold some promise in this regard. Given that there is considerable evidence that children and adolescents can be trained to accurately monitor and record their own behavior (Gettinger & Kratochwill, 1987), there is no a priori reason why they could not also be trained to accurately monitor and record internal or private events. For example, a clinician working with a depressed adolescent might train the client to periodically record the number of positive and negative internal self-statements he or she makes, and use this data to chart both baseline rates and treatment progress. Likewise, children and adolescents could be trained to record their own perceptions of various somatic complaints, their pulse rate, engagement in pleasurable activities, or positive self-affirming thought processes. Of course, there may be some important limitations of self-monitoring observation with internalizing problems. Self-monitoring may be *reactive*, in that it may produce change in the subject (Kratochwill, 1982). Thus self-monitoring may be more useful in assessment during a follow-up or intervention period than during baseline data gathering. An obvious concern with self-monitoring of internalizing problems may surface when working with children or adolescents who exhibit obsessive-compulsive behaviors. Logically and intuitively, obsessive thought or compulsive behavior potentially could be strengthened by the increased focus placed upon it. In spite of these potential problems, self-monitoring of internalizing problems appears to be a plausible alternative to direct observation by an independent observer, although its use has not been widely reported for this purpose in the professional literature.

Interviewing Techniques

Whether structured, traditional, or behavioral in nature, the clinical interview is perhaps the most widely used method for the assessment of internalizing problems (Miller, Boyer, & Rodoletz, 1990). Virtually any of the interview techniques discussed in chapter 5 can be useful in the assessment of depression, anxiety, social withdrawal, and related internalizing symptoms. In terms of structured or semistructured interview schedules, each of the four discussed in chapter 5 (K-SADS, DICA-R, CAS, and ISC) are directly relevant for assessing internalizing symptomology, and they include a number of areas of questioning that are very specific to this domain. As such, any of these interview schedules are worthy of consideration for assessing internalizing problems.

The Children's Depression Rating Scale (CDRS) is an interview schedule developed specifically for use in assessing depression (Poznanski, Cook, & Carroll, 1979). This instrument was developed as a downward extension and adaptation of the Hamilton Rating Scale for Depression (Hamilton, 1967), an instrument used in assessing depression in adults. Although the CDRS is not as widely used as the interview schedules reviewed in chapter 5, it is of interest because of its ease of use and specificity of design. The CDRS includes 17 interview items, covering a range of depressive symptoms, such as inability to have fun and the appearance of sad affect. The interviewing clinician questions the child regarding each item but may also consult other informants such as parents or teachers. Each interview time is ultimately rated for symptom severity by the clinician, using an eight-point scale (0 = unable to rate; 7 = severe symptoms). Although the research base on the CDRS is relatively sparse, there have been some encouraging findings (Poznanski, Cook, Carroll, & Corzo, 1983; Poznanski, Grossman, Buchsbaum,

Benegas, Freeman, & Gibbons, 1984). For example, the CDRS has been found to have relatively high inter-rater agreement (.75 and higher), high correlations with global clinical ratings of depression (.85 and higher), and high test-retest reliability at up to six-week intervals (.81).

Behavior Rating Scales

Each of the three general-purpose behavior rating scales or rating-scale systems discussed in chapter 4 (the Child Behavior Checklist System, the Revised Behavior Problem Checklist, and the Conners rating scales) include rating items and subscales specifically directed at measuring internalizing problems, and all of these instruments have been validated to a significant extent for this purpose. Additionally the Personality Inventory for Children (the combination rating scale/objective inventory discussed in chapter 7) includes a large number of statements and subscales aimed at the internalizing dimension, and it has also been the subject of a number of investigations that have validated the PIC in this regard. Thus there are several widely used general-purpose rating instruments very pertinent to the assessment of such varied internalizing symptom areas as anxiety, depression, social withdrawal, and schizotype behaviors. Although a few behavior rating scales that are aimed at specific types of internalizing symptomology have been reported in the literature, for the most part, these instruments have not been validated or are not in wide enough use to justify their inclusion in this chapter. Therefore these four general purpose instruments are recommended as the instruments of choice when objective behavior ratings of internalizing problems are needed. Additionally it may be useful to consider any of the three social competence rating scales or systems discussed in chapter 10 (the Social Skills Rating System, School Social Behavior Scales, and Walker-McConnell Scale of Social Competence and School Adjustment) when there are concerns about assessing internalizing problems. Given that social withdrawal often accompanies depression and anxiety and that deficits in social competence may be correlated with internalizing problems, such an assessment strategy may be very useful.

Sociometric Approaches

Like direct behavioral observation, sociometric approaches can be used to assess internalizing problems, but they pose some challenges in the process. As is true in behavioral observation, a major difficulty with the use of sociometric assessment for measuring internalizing problems is that subjective internal states, thought patterns, and other covert characteristics may not be easily observed and perceived by peers. An additional difficulty surfaces when young children are being assessed. Given their experiential limitations due to their age, very young informants may lack the maturity to make differentiations among subtle emotional characteristics. While it may be relatively easy for a child to name three classmates who are likely to fight on the playground, the identification of peers who are sad, lonely, or nervous may become confounded with a number of other personality characteristics. With adults, sociometric assessment of internalizing characteristics is perhaps more effective. Kane and Lawler (1978) reviewed 19 peer assessment studies where the subjects were adults and concluded that several of the investigations were reasonably valid in measuring various internalizing characteristics.

Although sociometric approaches will seldom be the first method for assessing internalizing problems, they nevertheless can and have been useful for this purpose. As an assessment component for internalizing problems, sociometric approaches are probably used best as a screening device for identifying potentially at-risk children who then may be administered further assessments. Virtually all of the general sociometric assessment methods presented in chapter 6 are flexible enough to be implemented appropriately in this manner. The teacher ranking procedure for internalizing problems from the Systematic Screening for Behavior Disorders (Walker & Severson, 1992) shown in Figure 6.4 is an example of a sociometric-type method targeted specifically at internalizing characteristics. Typical peer nomination, rating, or ranking methods could all be used to target specific internalizing characteristics. As is true with behavioral observation, it will be necessary for a valid assessment to define carefully the target characteristic. For example, a nomination procedure used to screen for social withdrawal with a statement worded something like "Write down the names of three students who always seem to be alone" might also screen in children who are socially isolated due to their aggressive behavior.

A number of studies have shown that sociometric assessment approaches can effectively screen for internalizing problems in children. McConnell and Odom (1986) reviewed 46 different investigations that utilized sociometric methods with children for various research purposes, and several of these studies directly assessed at least some internalizing characteristic, such as withdrawal or depression. It is interesting that several of the studies reviewed by McConnell and Odom found that targeted subjects were likely to exhibit both internalizing and externalizing symptoms. Thus the distinction between these two domains of problems found through Behavioral Dimensions research does not always exist in individual cases.

An additional sociometric assessment procedure used on a fairly wide basis in the measurement of depression is the Peer Nomination Inventory for Depression (Lefkowitz & Tesiny, 1980). The PNID consists of 20 statements that comprise 3 subscales (depression, 14 times; happiness, 4 items; and popularity, 2 times). Individuals within a group (usually a classroom) are asked to identify peer(s) to whom the statements apply. Examples of some of the statements on the depression subscale include "often plays alone," "often sleeps in class," "worries a lot," and "often looks sad." Kazdin (1988) notes that the PNID has solid internal consistency (.85 or higher), acceptable test-retest reliability at two- to six-month intervals, and adequate inter-rater agreement, and normative data on the PNID have been gathered for over 3,000 children in grades 3–5. Validation studies of the PNID (e.g., Lefkowitz, Tesiny, & Gordon, 1980; Lefkowitz & Tesiny, 1985; Tesiny & Lefkowitz, 1982) have shown that it has only weak correlations with self-report and teacher ratings of depression but strong correlations with measures of school performance, self-concept, teacher ratings of social behavior, and other peer ratings of happiness and popularity. The PNID is an innovative assessment method in that it is one of the few sociometric measures designed specifically or solely for assessing internalizing problems. However at the present time, it is probably best used as a research or broad screening tool.

Assessment with Self-Reports

Because the primary method for assessing internalizing problems is through the use of self-report data, there are many more objective self-report tests available than can be adequately addressed in this chapter. Five different self-report instruments have been selected for further discussion: three instruments designed to assess symptoms of depression and two instruments designed to assess symptoms of anxiety. These five instruments were selected for inclusion over other potential measures due to their commercial availability, psychometric properties, ease of use, and the amount and/or sophistication of available research data. Table 9.2 (see p. 205) presents information summarizing some of the major characteristics of each of the tests.

Children's Depression Inventory (CDI).   The Children's Depression Inventory (Kovacs, 1980–1981, 1991) is a 27-item self-report measure of depressive symptomology for use with school-age children and adolescents (6–17 years). Without question, this instrument was the most widely used and researched child self-report/depression instrument during the 1980s. The number of published studies using the CDI has been remarkable—a review of the research literature from 1987 through 1991 alone found 142 studies that used the CDI as a primary measure. The CDI was developed as a downward extension of the Beck Depression Inventory and was first reported in the research literature in the early 1980s. For several years, the instrument and an accompanying unpublished manuscript were available in various versions from the author, but it was only recently (1991) that the CDI was commercially published and thus became more easily available.

Each of the 27 items of the CDI has three statements about a particular depressive symptom, and the respondent chooses the statement that best describes his or her feelings during the past two weeks. Each item is scored 0, 1, or 2, with statements reflecting the greater severity of symptoms receiving the higher value. The following is an item from the CDI, which illustrates the structure of the items and how they are scored:

____ I hate myself (scored 2)
____ I do not like myself (scored 1)
____ I like myself (scored 0)

The CDI is easy to administer and score, usually taking no more than 20 minutes for the entire process. The CDI manual suggests that a cutoff score of 11 be used if the purpose of the administration is to screen for depression with few false-negative errors. If the purpose of the administration is to assess the presence of depression in children with behavioral and emotional problems, 13 is suggested as the appropriate cutoff score.

Normative data from the recently published version of the CDI manual are based on a study by Finch, Saylor, and Edwards (1985), wherein CDI score norms for 1,463 Florida public school children in grades 2–8 were reported. These normative data are broken down by gender and grade level. Previous versions of the unpublished CDI manual manuscript provided score norms based on a sample of 860 Canadian school children aged 8–13. Although the CDI total score is the measure of interest, various factor analyses of the CDI have been reported in the literature, wherein five to seven factors typically have been extracted. The current version of the CDI manual advocates a five-factor solution.

The psychometric properties of the CDI have been documented in a large number of published research reports. Most studies have found the internal consistency of the CDI to be in the mid to upper .80s. With some exceptions where lower correlations were obtained, test-retest reliability of the CDI typically has been found to be in the .70 to .85 range at short (1 week to 2 month) intervals and in the same general range at several month intervals. The relative stability of the CDI over time is an interesting trend, considering that the author of the instrument has recommended it as a measure of state depression rather than trait depression. Perhaps the CDI measures trait depression as well.

The most common method of determining the validity of the CDI has been through obtaining correlations of concurrent scores from other internalizing measures. In this regard, a plethora of studies has found the CDI to have significant relationships to instruments such as the Revised Children's Manifest Anxiety Scale, Reynolds Child Depression Scale, State-Trait Anxiety Inventory for Children, and Personality Inventory for Children. Other types of validity studies have included finding negative correlations between the CDI and measures of self-esteem (Kovacs, 1983) and social competence (Helsel & Matson, 1984), using CDI scores as a predictive measure of psychiatric diagnoses (Hodges, 1990; Cantwell & Carlson, 1981), and using CDI scores to predict future emotional and behavioral adjustment problems (Mattison, Handford, Allen, Kales, & Goodman, 1990).

There have been numerous criticisms of the CDI, particularly that the cutoff-score criteria may be problematic and that the instrument lacks a nationally standardized normative group (e.g., Kavan, 1990; Knoff, 1990). However the CDI has the distinct advantage of being one of the most widely researched child self-report instruments in existence, and its psychometric properties and discriminant abilities are generally quite good. The commercial publication of the CDI with the concurrent development of a standard test manual incorporating the vast research on the instrument is a positive and major development. The CDI should continue to have wide use in research. For clinical applications, a conservative approach to the use of cutoff scores is recommended, given the lack of nationwide norms and some previous criticisms of the predictive value of the cutoff scores.

Reynolds Child Depression Scale (RCDS).   The Reynolds Child Depression Scale (Reynolds, 1989) is a self-report measure of depressive symptomology for children in grades 3–6 (ages 8–12). It contains 30 items that are responded to in a four-point format ("almost never" to "all the time"). The 30 items were primarily based on depressive symptomology from the DSM-III. Some of these items are phrased to represent the presence of depressive symptoms (e.g., "I feel I am no good"), while others are phrased to reflect the absence of such symptoms (e.g., "I feel like playing with other kids"). The items are written at about a second-grade reading level and are administered orally to children in grades 3 and 4 and to older children who have reading problems. The self-report protocol is scored by means of an easy-to-use key, which assigns values from 1 to 4 for each item with higher scores reflecting item endorsement in the direction of depressive symptoms. A mail-in scoring service is also available through the publisher.

The RCDS was standardized on a group of over 1,600 children from the midwestern and western United States. Technical information provided in the test manual indicates that the instrument has acceptable to excellent psychometric properties. Internal consistency of the total sample is .90 with similar levels reported by grade, gender, and ethnic group breakdowns. Test-retest reliability estimates are reported at .82 at two-week intervals and from .81 to .92 at four-week intervals. A variety of information on the validity of the RCDS is presented in the test manual, including six different correlational studies of the RCDS and CDI (with correlations ranging from .68 to .79) and four different studies correlating the RCDS with self-report measures of anxiety (.60 to .67) and self-esteem ($-.46$ to $-.71$). Factor analytic research indicates the presence of a reasonably strong five-factor structure, although separate factor scores are not obtained in normal scoring of the RCDS. Interpretation of RCDS total scores is based on raw score to percentile score conversions and critical raw score values. The raw score value of 74 is the critical value for "clinical" level scores, and evidence presented in the test manual suggests that scores at this level have a high "hit rate" for identifying children who meet other criteria for depressive symptomology.

The manual for the RCDS is exceptionally well written and documented, the research data presented are impressive, and the instrument has a great deal of face validity and usability. It appears to be an excellent addition to the self-report instrumentation for assessing internalizing problems and should be very useful for both research and clinical purposes.

Reynolds Adolescent Depression Scale (RADS).   The Reynolds Adolescent Depression Scale (Reynolds, 1986) is a self-report measure of depressive symptomology for adolescents aged 13–18. It is a "sister" instrument to the RCDS (the RADS was actually developed first), and it is very similar in structure and format to the RCDS. Like the RCDS, the RADS contains 30 times that are responded to in a four-point format ("almost never" to "all the time"), developed to coincide with depressive symptomology from the DSM-III. The majority of items on the RADS are the same as RCDS items, although some are written to reflect adolescent concerns and adolescent-appropriate language, and a handful of items are specific to each scale. The RADS can be administered either individually or with groups, and the items are written at a low enough reading level so that even adolescents with reading problems should be able to understand them. Three forms of the RADS are available: a hand-scored version, an optical scanning version, and a mail-in version for scoring large-group administrations.

The RCDS was standardized on a group of over 2,400 adolescents from a variety of U.S. geographical regions, and descriptive statistics are reported in the test manual for over 7,000 adolescents in addition to the standardization population. Technical information provided in the test manual indicates that the instrument has acceptable to excellent psychometric properties. Internal consistency for the total sample is reported at .92 with similarly high levels reported by grade, gender, and additional sample breakdowns. Test-retest reliability estimates are reported at .80 at six-week intervals, .79 at three-month intervals, and .63 at one year. Adequate validity information is presented in the RADS test manual with the greatest amount of external validation evidence coming from studies correlating the RADS with three other self-report measures of internalizing problems completed by adolescents (Beck Depression Inventory, Zung Self-Rating Depression Scale, and CDI). The correlations between the RADS and these three criterion measures ranged from .68 to .76 across 11 different studies. Correlational studies are also reported in which the RADS was compared with various adolescent self-esteem measures, with the resulting correlations reported at − .56 to − .71 and .50 to .80 across 11 different studies. Additional concurrent and convergent validity studies of the RADS and other self-report and rating measures are also reported. Like the RCDS, factor analytic research on the RADS indicates the presence of a five-factor structure, although separate factor scores are not obtained in normal scoring of the RCDS. The author of the RADS suggests that interpretation of factor scores should be done in terms of the first four factors, as the fifth factor only contains two items and these items load sufficiently on factor 1. Interpretation of RCDS total scores is based on raw score to percentile score conversions and critical raw score values. The raw score value of 77 is the critical value for "clinical" level scores, and evidence presented in the test manual suggests that scores at this level have a high "hit rate" for identifying adolescents who meet other criteria for depressive symptomology. For example, one study reported in the manual found that RADS scores at the cutoff level of 77 correctly classified 82 percent of adolescent subjects who had been formally diagnosed as being depressed.

Like the RCDS, the manual for the RADS is exceptionally well written and documented, the research data presented are impressive, and the instrument has a great deal of face validity and usability. It is recommended that the RADS be used in lieu of the Beck Depression Inventory (an adult measure often used with adolescents) as a self-report screening measure for adolescent clients. The RADS items are more specifically and logically related to adolescent concerns, the size of the adolescent standardization group is impressive, and the documentation of research evidence specific to adolescent populations is greater than what is available for the Beck Inventory. The RADS represents an excellent and much needed addition to the adolescent self-report instruments, and it too should gain wide clinical and research acceptance.

Revised Children's Manifest Anxiety Scale (RCMAS).   The Revised Children's Manifest Anxiety Scale (Reynolds & Richmond, 1985) is a self-report instrument for 6- to 17-year-old children. It consists of 37 statements that are responded to in a yes/no fashion and is designed as a measure of trait anxiety (the tendency to be anxious over settings and time). Scoring the RCMAS involves simply summing the number of "yes" responses for each of the three subscales (physiological anxiety, worry and oversensitivity, concentration anxiety) and a lie scale, then calculating a total score. The three RCMAS subscales were developed through factor analytic research (Reynolds & Paget, 1981), while the lie scale consists of nine items that are socially desirable but almost never true (e.g., "I never say things I shouldn't," and "I am always nice to everyone").

Normative data for the RCMAS are from nearly 5,000 cases obtained in each geographical region of the United States. These data were first reported in a study by Reynolds and Paget (1983), and they include separate norms based on age, gender, and black/white racial breakdowns.

Psychometric properties of the RCMAS, as reported in the test manual and in other published research, indicate that the instrument has for the most part adequate levels of reliability and validity. Internal consistency reliability of the total RCMAS score has been reported at .79 for males and .85 for females in a study with kindergarten children (Reynolds, Bradley, & Steele, 1980). Internal consistency coefficients for the RCMAS subscales are at a somewhat troubling lower level than for the total score, ranging from .50 to .70 across groups for physiological anxiety and .70 to .90 for the lie scale. One test-retest reliability study of the RCMAS found short-term reliability coefficients of .88 for 1 week and .77 for 5 weeks (Wisniewski, Mulick, Genshaft, & Coury, 1987), while another study found a coefficient of .68 at a nine-month interval (Reynolds, 1981). Evidence for the concurrent validity of the RCMAS comes from a large number of studies correlating the RCMAS with other self-report instruments, including the State-Trait Anxiety Inventory for Children (.85 correlation between the RCMAS total score and the trait anxiety scale of the STAIC) and the Children's Anxiety Scale (.29 to .69 correlations). Evidence for discriminant validity of the RCMAS comes from studies that found the scores of gifted children to be lower than the scores of average children (Reynolds & Bradley, 1983), and scores of learning disabled children to be higher than those of average children (Paget & Reynolds, 1982). A number of other studies have found RCMAS score elevations in children with various internalizing disorders.

Although the reported psychometric data for the RCMAS are relatively sparse for the amount of research that has gone into it and the internal stability of the RCMAS subscales is questionable, this instrument can be recommended on several grounds. The norm group(s) are very large (including a large norm group for black children), and there are a large number of published studies (40 between 1987 and 1991 alone) that attest to various properties and uses of the scale. The RCMAS is easy to use, has strong face validity, and can be recommended as part of a battery for assessing internalizing problems with children. However given the questionable stability of the three RCMAS subscales, it is recommended that the total score be used rather than the subscales scores for most purposes.

State-Trait Anxiety Inventory for Children (STAIC). The State-Trait Anxiety Inventory for Children (Speilberger, 1973) is a self-report assessment of trait anxiety and state anxiety for children ages 9–12. It was developed as a downward extension of the State-Trait Anxiety Inventory (Speilberger, Gorsuch, & Lushene, 1970), a self-report measure for adolescents and adults. The STAIC consists of two separate scales with 20 items each: one to assess state anxiety (which asks the child how anxious she or he feels at the time the inventory is being completed) and one to assess trait anxiety (which asks the child how anxious she or he feels in general). The two scales can be administered separately or together. The STAIC may be administered individually or in groups and typically requires about 10 minutes for each scale. Like the CDI, each item of the STAIC requires the subject to choose the one of three statements that best describes how he or she feels. The items are scored 1, 2, or 3 points, with the higher score reflecting the statement indicating stronger symptoms of anxiety. Some of the STAIC items are reverse worded and keyed in order to control for acquiescent response sets.

The differentiation between state and trait anxiety is based on theoretical underpinnings previously postulated by Speilberger (1966, 1972). Children who are trait anxious tend to respond to a variety of situations as if they are threatening, while children who score high on the state-anxiety scale but low on the trait-anxiety scale are thought to feel anxious due to a specific situation or event. Previous reviews of the STAIC (e.g., Martin, 1988) have considered the theoretical orientation of the instrument to be a definite advantage.

Normative data for both scales of the STAIC are from 1,554 subjects in the fourth, fifth, and sixth grades in the state of Florida. The norm sample includes a large percentage (approximately 35 percent) of African-American subjects. The test manual includes normative data for the total sample and for gender and grade level breakdowns. STAIC raw scores may be converted to T-scores and percentiles using tables provided in the manual.

Psychometric properties of the STAIC, as reported in the test manual and subsequent research literature, have generally been adequate to good. Internal consistency coefficients for both scales have generally been reported in the .80s range. Consistent with the theoretical underpinnings of the STAIC, test-retest reliability coefficients reported in the manual are higher for the trait-anxiety scale (.65 to .71) than for the state-anxiety scale (.31 to .41) at six-week intervals. A number of studies have assessed the concurrent validity of the STAIC by obtaining significant correlations with other internalizing self-report instruments (e.g., Hodges, 1990; Rhone, 1986). Interestingly some of the validation studies reported in the test manual found significant negative relationships between trait anxiety and measures of academic achievement, such as the California Achievement Test. More recent studies have found the STAIC to have discriminant validity in identifying child psychiatric patients (Hodges, 1990) and in differentiating anxiety

TABLE 9.2 Self-report instruments for assessing internalizing problems and related characteristics: summary of characteristics of instruments reviewed in chapter 9

Instrument	Focus	Age Range	Items and Format	Technical Properties	Available Research
Children's Depression Inventory	Depressive Symptomology	6–17	27 items, forced choice among three statements	good	extensive
Reynolds Child Depression Scale	Depressive Symptomology	8–12	30 statements responded to on a 4-point scale	good	adequate
Reynolds Adolescent Depression Scale	Depressive Symptomology	13–18	30 statements responded to on a 4-point scale	good	adequate
Revised Children's Manifest Anxiety Scale	General Anxiety	6–17	37 yes/no statements	fair to good	extensive
State-Trait Anxiety Inventory for Children	State Anxiety and Trait Anxiety	9–12	2 scales with 20 items each; forced choice among 3 statements	good	extensive
Multidimensional Self-Concept Scale	Dimensions of Self-Concept	9–19	150 items rated using a Likert-type scale	good	adequate
Self-Perception Profile for Children	Dimensions of Self-Concept	9–14	36 statement pairs with 2 score options each	fair to good	more needed
Self-Perception Profile for Adolescents	Dimensions of Self-Concept	13–18	45 statement pairs with 2 score options each	fair to good	more needed

levels among public school students with varying degrees of academic achievement problems (Rhone, 1986).

Overall the STAIC has many qualities to recommend its use. The division of state and trait types of anxiety scales is interesting and useful from a theoretical standpoint, and a number of studies validated the differential measurement properties of the two scales. Previous reviews of the STAIC (e.g., Martin, 1988) noted that the two major weaknesses of the instrument were a shortage of psychometric validation studies and a geographically limited normative population. The first weakness is now less of a problem, as over 40 studies were published between 1987 and 1992 alone using the STAIC as a primary measure. The second weakness continues to be a problem. Not only is the norm sample limited to one state, but the norms are now approximately 20 years old. A current and nationally representative standardization of the STAIC would be of great use in increasing the confidence in obtained test scores and in ensuring the continued use of the test.

Instruments for Assessing Multidimensional Self-Concept

In our earlier discussion of self-concept, it was made clear that the definitional focus for self-concept in this chapter would be on a multidimensional, as opposed to a unidimensional, model. Thus the following overview of self-concept assessment will preclude any of the several instruments designed to assess the latter view of the construct. The nature of the self-concept construct necessarily precludes any assessment methods that rely on observations or perceptions of persons other than the subject. Within the realm of self-report, the preferred assessment method is objective self-report tests rather than interviews, since no structured or standardized interview methods have yet been developed to systematically assess self-concept. Three self-report instruments are presented in this section as examples of multidimensional self-concept evaluation tools. These include Bracken's Multidimensional Self-Concept Scale (1992), and Harter's two Self-Perception Profiles (1985, 1988). Note also that a pictorial self-concept test has been developed by Harter (Harter & Pike, 1984) for use with very young children, but it is not reviewed in this chapter.

Multidimensional Self-Concept Scale (MSCS).   The Multidimensional Self-Concept Scale (Bracken, 1992) is the most recent addition to the growing body of self-report instruments for assessing self-concept in a multidimensional fashion. The MSCS was developed for use by children and adolescents in grades 5–12, and it includes 150 items. These items are rated by examinees on a Likert-type response scale, with a four-point range from "strongly agree" to "strongly disagree." The construction of MSCS items and the overall scale structure were theoretically driven, based on a view of the self-concept as "a behavioral construct, not a part of a larger cognitive self-system" (Bracken & Howell, 1991, p. 323). The items are divided into 6 subscales of 25 times each, based on Bracken's multidimensional factors and global self-concept theory. These subscales include affect, social, physical, competence, academic, and family, with a score for global self-concept that subsumes the six factors in Bracken's theory. For each of the seven possible score areas, raw scores are converted to standard scores with a mean of 100 and standard deviation of 15. Tables for *T*-score conversions, percentile scores, and self-concept classifications are provided in the MSCS manual.

The MSCS was normed on a group of 2,501 students in grades 5–12 in the United States, with adequate representation given to each geographical region. Strong internal consistency reliabilities are reported for the six subscales (.85 to .90) and the total score (.98). The MSCS has also been found to have strong stability over time with subscale reliability coefficients ranging from .73 to .81 and a total score coefficient of .90 at four-week retest intervals. At the time this chapter was being written, the MSCS was newly introduced, and thus a wide body of external research has not yet been accumulated. However two published investigations (Bracken & Howell, 1991; Delugach, Bracken, Bracken, & Schicke, 1992) and several unpublished master's theses have found moderate to strong relationships between the MSCS and other multidimensional and unidimensional self-construct instruments, and these have provided convergent and discriminant support for the construct of multidimensional self-concept as measured by the MSCS. The MSCS manual is very well written and documented, and the instrument itself is easy to use and appears to be a useful and well-designed self-report.

Self-Perception Profile for Children (SPPC).   Susan Harter's Self-Perception Profile for Children (Harter, 1985) is a self-report instrument designed to assess multidimensional self-concept with children ages 8 to 15. The SPPC includes 36 pairs of statements that reflect opposing views of particular aspects of self-concept (e.g., "Some kids wish their body was different, BUT Other kids like their body the way it is"). Examinees are asked to first choose which statement in the pair is most like them, and after they have made this initial choice, they are then asked to determine whether the statement they have chosen is *really true* or *sort of true* for them. Each test item is scored using a four-point scale, with 1 point reflecting the lowest and 4 the highest self-concept rating.

The 36 SPPC items are divided into six dimensions: scholastic competence, social acceptance, athletic competence, physical appearance, behavioral conduct, and global self-worth. Unlike the MSCS, the global self-worth scale is not a summation of the other subscales but is comprised of six statements that reflect how the subject feels about himself or herself in an overall sense. Scoring the SPPC is done by determining the raw score mean value for each of the six dimensions and then comparing these scores with means and standard deviations of grade and gender specific score breakdowns from the normative group, as well as plotting the mean scores on a pupil profile form where score levels are seen to be in either the low, medium, or high range. Higher mean scores for each scale indicate higher perceptions of self-worth.

The SPPC also includes two corollary instruments: a rating scale for teachers and an *importance* rating scale for subjects. The teacher rating scale provides a basis for comparing a child's responses against an objective rating, while the importance rating allows the examiner to determine if any discrepancies exist between the child's self-perception ratings and the importance of those ratings to their overall self-esteem. For example, a low score on athletic competence may or may not be cause for concern, depending on how important athletic competence is for the child.

The SPPC was normed on four samples of children ($N = 1,543$) from Colorado in grades 3–8. Tables of mean scores and standard deviations from the norm group are presented in the test manual based on gender and grade-level breakdowns. Internal consistency reliabilities on the SPPC range from .80 to .90 across a number of samples, and test-retest correlations across subscales have been found to range from .40 to .65 at one-month to one-year intervals (Harter, 1990). The factor structure of the SPPC appears to be quite strong with items loading strongly into their respective factors and the six scales having only moderate inter-correlations. Significant gender effects in self-concept are reported in the SPPC manual with the most systematic effects indicating that boys see themselves as significantly more athletically competent than girls and girls see themselves as significantly better behaved than boys. Some additional significant gender effects were found in the areas of global self-worth and physical appearance, but these effects were not consistent across grade levels. An interesting and disturbing finding in this regard is that at the elementary level, there are no significant differences between boys' and girls' scores on these two dimensions, but at the middle school level, boys' scores in both areas are significantly higher than girls' scores.

The SPPC is a unique and innovative instrument, and it can be recommended on several grounds. However there are a number of weaknesses that warrant using it with caution. Unfortunately the SPPC norm group was taken from only one state, thus reducing the confidence with which score interpretations can be generalized. Additional empirical evidence of validity of the SPPC would be useful, as would raw score to standard score and percentile conversion tables. The SPPC is not commercially published at the present time but can be obtained from Dr. Susan Harter at the University of Denver, Department of Psychology.

Self-Perception Profile for Adolescents (SPPA).   Harter's Self-Perception Profile for Adolescents (1988) is a 45-item self-report instrument very similar in design to the SPPC. The items and scales use the same type of rating and scoring format as the SPPC. Only the SPPA characteristics that differ from those of the SPPC will be discussed in this section.

Some items in the SPPA are worded specifically for use by teenage subjects (e.g., "Some teenagers wish their physical appearance was different, BUT Other teenagers like their physical appearance the way it is"). In addition to the rewording of items from the SPPC, more times were added to the SPPA in order to reflect specific concerns of teenagers, such as job competence, close friendship, and romantic appeal. These three areas of concern appear as additional subscales on the SPPA, and thus the SPPA has nine subscales instead of six as in the SPPC. Like the SPPC, the SPPA includes an importance rating scale for examinees, and a teacher rating scale for assessing actual student behavior (e.g., "This individual is good looking OR This individual is not that good looking").

The SPPA was normed on a group of 651 students in grades 8–11 from four samples in the state of Colorado. For each of the three grade levels, separate norms are provided for males and females. Internal consistency reliability of the SPPA is reported to range from .74 to .91. The factor structure of the SPPA appears adequate, and the generally moderate intercorrelations among the nine subscales suggest a basis for a multidimensional construction of self-concept. Like the SPPC, the SPPA has tremendous face validity and offers an innovative and comprehensive method of assessing adolescent self-concept. Unfortunately, the SPPA also suffers from the same limitations as the SPPC (lack of a national norm sample and limited external validation research), so it should be used with a good deal of caution.

LINKING ASSESSMENT TO INTERVENTION

Of the three specific types of behavioral, social, and emotional constructs covered in this text (externalizing problems, internalizing problems, and social competence), the area of internalizing problems is perhaps the most difficult in establishing a solid link between assessment and intervention. One of the major reasons that this link has been so tenuous has to do with the nature of internalizing problems. Commenting on this issue in regard to children's fears and anxiety, Barrios and Hartmann (1988) stated, "at this time, the utility of assessment is not easy to evaluate" (p. 254). Likewise, Kazdin (1990) noted that "relatively little controlled outcome research is available on the treatment of childhood depression" (p. 188). Given that internalizing problems often involve subjective individual perceptions and states, there are not likely to be many tangible and directly observable behaviors to consider for intervention. That is not to say that effective treatment for internalizing disorders is impossible. On the contrary, a number of interventions have been demonstrated for a variety of internalizing problems of childhood (e.g., Mash & Barkley, 1989), encompassing a broad range of approaches. The treatment approaches likely to be utilized by a given clinician may guide the choice of assessment methods, but at the present time, the state of the art for assessing internalizing problems appears to be linked mostly to the processes of description and classification. Making intervention decisions should not be done in isolation from the assessment data, but most assessment data for internalizing problems will describe rather than prescribe. It will be a great challenge for the current generation of professionals to develop strongly linked methods of assessment and intervention for internalizing problems.

CASE STUDY

Background Information
J.H. is a 15-year-old girl who is a tenth-grade student at a small high school in a rural/small town area. She lives with her mother, a community college instructor, and an 11-year-old brother. J.'s parents are divorced and her father lives in a distant city, rarely seeing her more than two times per year. J. participated in an intake interview and initial screening assessment at a community psychology clinic. The referral was made by J.'s mother, Mrs. H., and while J. was initially reluctant to participate in the intake

interview/assessment, she became very cooperative, and good rapport was established between her and the intake interviewer. J. agreed to go the clinic at the urging of her mother, who was concerned that her daughter was "very depressed and doesn't understand her feelings."

Basic information for the intake forms was obtained from both Mrs. H. and J. Mrs. H. noted that J. often cries for no apparent reason, has low self-esteem, and feels as though she has to be perfect, but on the other hand, J. goes through occasional periods of time where she has plenty of energy and sleeps very little. Mrs. H. noted that J. has sometimes made statements such as "it would be easier if I were dead" but has made no suicidal attempts or definitive threats. She is concerned that her daughter "is too thin and has a unhealthy eating habits." J. reported on the intake forms that she gets "real down" at times and occasionally "gets hyper." She noted that "sometimes I sleep too much and sometimes I don't sleep at all." J. reported being worried about a wide variety of things, such as her school grades, whether her friends are "on my side or not," and her looks (she reports feeling "ugly"). She also said that she has frequent headaches and stomachaches, and that "I get dizzy and feel like fainting sometimes." At school, J. receives good to excellent grades (3.8 G.P.A. for the past two years), is in some advanced courses, and is active in student government and a dance team. Mrs. H. reports that J. is popular and well liked by other students but "is always anxious about keeping her friends."

Assessment Data
The intake/initial assessment on J. included a behavior rating scale completed by Mrs. H., three self-report tests completed by J., and interviews with J. and Mrs. H., both together and individually.

Behavior Rating Scales. Before the initial intake interview in the community clinic, J.H.'s mother completed the Child Behavior Checklist. This was the only external rating scale completed for this assessment, but J.H. did complete the CBCL Youth Self-Report. Both sets of scores are listed in the following table:

CBCL scores

Cross-Informant Syndromes and Broad-Band Areas	J.H.'s Self-Report	J.H.'s Mother
Aggressive Behavior	50	51
Anxious/Depressed	68	79
Attention Problems	65	57
Delinquent Behavior	50	50
Social Problems	58	50
Somatic Complaints	78	70
Thought Problems	68	63
Withdrawn	59	57
INTERNALIZING PROBLEMS	72	73
EXTERNALIZING PROBLEMS	49	49
TOTAL PROBLEMS	66	64

Self-Report Data. In addition to the Youth Self-Report, J. completed the Revised Children's Manifest Anxiety Scale (RCMAS) and the Reynolds Adolescent Depression Scale (RADS).

RADS: Raw score = 85; percentile rank for girls = 93rd; "critical items" endorsed: (20) "I feel I am no good," (26) "I feel worried."

RCMAS: Total Anxiety: raw score = 19, 92nd percentile; T-score = 64; Physiological Anxiety: raw score = 6, 91st percentile; Worry/Oversensitivity: raw score = 8, 77th percentile; Social Concerns/Concentration: raw score = 5, 90th percentile; Lie Scale: raw score = 0, 13th percentile.

Interview Data. Interviews were conducted by the clinic intake worker with both J. and Mrs. H., together and individually. The interview format was slightly structured, following a standardized intake clinic form. A variety of developmental and background information was obtained during the interviews, but the major perceived or presenting problems from both J.'s and Mrs. H.'s viewpoints are listed in the following table:

J.'s Perspective	Mrs. H.'s Perspective
J. gets "too hyper"	J. doesn't understand her feelings
J.'s friends let her down	J. is too hard on herself
J. might not get into a good college	J. is too thin
J. is unattractive	J. has poor eating habits
J. has a harder time doing things than most kids her age	J. is depressed
J. does "bad things"	J. thinks she has to be perfect
J. has "bad headaches and stomachaches"	J. doesn't want to talk about things with Mrs. H.
Something is wrong with J.'s body	J. tries to do too much
Other kids are out to get J.	Mrs. H. expects too much from J.
Mrs. H.'s rules are unfair	Mrs. H. doesn't spend enough time with J.
Mrs. H. worries too much about J.	
Mrs. H. doesn't trust J.	

Questions to Consider

1. The assessment data presented for this case are from an intake process and should be considered preliminary screening data. What other information regarding J. would be useful, and what assessment tools or methods would best provide this information?

2. An important concept noted in this chapter is that of *comorbidity* of internalizing problems, that is, different types of internalizing problems often occur in combination. The self-report screening of J. focused for the most part on possible depression and anxiety. Which, if any, of the following

characteristics often related to internalizing problems should be pursued in greater detail: somatic problems, social isolation, specific fears or phobias, self-concept problems, eating disorders?

3. Assume that J. has only one of the following two types of disorders: a depressive disorder or an anxiety disorder. Using only the information obtained from J.'s intake assessment, attempt to make a differential classification of the major problem. What additional information would be needed to make a formal differential diagnosis?

4. Compare the information obtained from J. and the information obtained from Mrs. H. What are the major points of convergence and the major points of disagreement?

5. Based on the information provided in this scenario, make a general statement about the severity of J's internalizing problems.

CHAPTER 10

Social Competence: Assessment of Social Skills and Peer Relations

INTRODUCTION

In recent years, there has been a tremendous amount of interest and activity related to assessing aspects of children's social competence and using these assessment data in designing appropriate interventions. School and clinical psychologists, as well as professionals from related fields who work with children and adolescents, will certainly encounter numerous assessment and intervention questions that require a sound knowledge of the overall construct of social competence and of effective methods of assessing it.

This chapter is designed to provide these professionals with the background knowledge needed to conceptualize the different aspects of social competence in childhood and adolescence appropriately, conduct effective assessments, and use the obtained information in developing sound intervention recommendations. The chapter begins with an overview of the three major areas of social competence and the reasons they are important to child and adolescent development. Next specific methods of assessing aspects of social competence are presented, relating to the five assessment modalities of interest in this book. The chapter ends with a discussion of "best practices" in linking social competence assessment data to effective interventions.

AN OVERVIEW OF THE CONSTRUCT
OF SOCIAL COMPETENCE

Social competence is a complex, multidimensional construct, consisting of a variety of behavioral and cognitive variables, as well as aspects of emotional adjustment useful and necessary to developing adequate social relations and obtaining desirable social outcomes. Social competence transcends the divisions of internalizing and externalizing behaviors, discussed at length in chapters 8 and 9. Interestingly peer relationship problems and deficits in specific social skills have been shown to be a component of both the internalizing and externalizing domains (Merrell, 1993b). Gresham (1986) conceptualized the broad domain of social competence as comprising the following three subdomains: (*a*) *adaptive behavior,* (*b*) *social skills,* and (*c*) *peer acceptance.* This dimensional breakdown of social competence is diagrammed in Figure 10.1. Gresham's model is a very suitable way of envisioning the overall construct of social competence, and it is utilized in the format of this chapter. Each of these three areas of social competence will now be overviewed individually.

FIGURE 10.1   Three subdomains of social competence

souRCE: Adapted from F. M. Gresham, "Conceptual Issues in the Assessment of Social Competence in Children," in P. Strain, M. Guralnick, and H. Walker (eds.), *Children's Social Behavior: Development, Assessment, and Modification* (New York: Academic Press, 1986).

Adaptive Behavior

Perhaps the most widely cited definition of adaptive behavior is ". . . the effectiveness or degree with which the individual meets the standards of personal independence and social responsibility . . ." (Grossman, 1983, p. 1). Adaptive behavior is a developmental construct in that expectations for independent and responsible behavior vary based upon age (Reschly, 1990). It is also important to view adaptive behaviors within cultural and environmental contexts, as expectations and demands for independence and responsibility also vary based upon the specific culture or subculture in which the individual develops (Reschly, 1990).

The assessment of adaptive behavior is a critical aspect of the classification of developmental delays and mental retardation, and the current definition of mental retardation by the American Association on Mental Deficiency (AAMD) includes the construct of adaptive behavior (Grossman, 1983). In practice, the measurement of adaptive behavior includes assessing functional living skills. Such assessment tends to require a qualitatively different evaluation approach and is essential for individuals with pervasive intellectual deficits and developmental disorders. As the populations of interest and the assessment methods differ somewhat from those focused on elsewhere in this book, this chapter will not cover adaptive behavior assessment but will focus on the other two areas of social competence, namely social skills and peer relations.

Social Skills

Social skills have been explained in a number of ways, including cognitive, behavioral, and ecological definitions (Merrell, Merz, Johnson, & Ring, 1992). For the purposes of this chapter, a good working definition of social skills is that they are specific behaviors that lead to desirable social outcomes for the person initiating them. From a behavioral standpoint, initiation of social skills increases the probability of reinforcement and decreases the probability of punishment or extinction based upon one's social behavior (Gresham & Reschly, 1987a). For children and adolescents, examples of behavioral classes representing social skills include academic and task-related competence, cooperation with peers, reinforcement of peers' behavior, and social initiation behaviors.

Peer Relations

Although peer acceptance (which is referred to hereafter by the more generic label *peer relations*) is considered the third overall component or domain of social competence, it is often thought of as a result or product of one's social skills. This view of peer relations is reasonable in that social reputation and the quality of one's social relations are in great measure a result of how effectively one interacts socially with peers (Landau & Milich, 1990; Oden & Asher, 1977). Positive peer relations are associated with peer acceptance while negative peer relations are linked with peer rejection.

IMPORTANCE OF SOCIAL COMPETENCE

A growing body of literature in the fields of child development, education, and psychology collectively points to the conclusion that the development of adequate social skills and peer relationships during childhood has important and far-reaching ramifications. It has been established that development of appropriate social skills is an important foundation for adequate peer relationships (Asher & Taylor, 1981). There is also evidence that childhood social skills and consequent peer relationships have a significant impact on academic success during the school years (Walker & Hops, 1976). In reviewing the literature on peer relations, Hartup (1983) demonstrated that the ability to relate effectively to others provides an essential contribution to the progress and development of the child.

Given that adequate social skills and peer relations are an important foundation for various types of success in life, it stands to reason that inadequate development in these areas is related to a variety of negative outcomes. A classic and frequently cited investigation by Cowen, Pederson, Babigan, and Trost (1983) involving an 11-to-13-year follow-up study of third-grade students provides convincing evidence that early peer relationship problems are strong predictors of mental health problems later in life. These researchers found that "peer judgment (using a negative peer nomination procedure) was, by far, the most sensitive predictor of later psychiatric difficulty" (p. 438). Other frequently cited studies have suggested that inadequate social skills and poor peer relations during childhood may lead to a variety of other problems later in life, such as juvenile delinquency, dropping out of school, conduct-related discharges from military service, chronic unemployment and underemployment, and psychiatric hospitalizations (Loeber, 1985; Parker & Asher, 1987; Roff, 1963; Roff & Sells, 1968; Roff, Sells, & Golden, 1972).

As the literature on the social, emotional, and behavioral characteristics of children with disabilities continues to grow, it has become increasingly clear that these children are at significantly heightened risk for developing social skills deficits and experiencing peer rejection. Students identified as learning disabled have been found to experience high rates of social rejection by other children (Bryan, 1974; Cartledge, Frew, & Zacharias, 1985; Sater & French, 1989), poor ratings of interpersonal behavior by teachers (Gresham & Reschly, 1986), and maladaptive social behaviors in instructional settings (Epstein, Cullinan, & Lloyd, 1986; McKinney & Feagans, 1984; McKinney, McClure, & Feagans, 1982). Students identified as mentally retarded have been found to exhibit deficits in adaptive-social competencies (Gresham & Reschly, 1987b), to experience high rates of peer rejection (Gresham, 1982), and to receive inadequate amounts of social support (Park, Tappe, Carmeto, & Gaylord-Ross, 1990). Likewise students identified as having behavior disorders have been found to be discriminated readily from nonhandicapped students by their maladaptive social-emotional behaviors (Merrell, et al., 1992; Stumme, Gresham, & Scott, 1982; Vaughn, 1987), and they experience significant rates of social rejection by other children (Hollinger, 1987). Therefore, clinicians who work with disabled and other at-risk children should be especially aware of the social problems these children face, and they should keep up-to-date on appropriate methods of assessment.

METHODS OF ASSESSING SOCIAL COMPETENCE

Each of the five general assessment methods covered within this book can be used in assessing social skills and peer relations. Direct behavioral observation and behavior rating scales have been used more frequently for this purpose in educational and clinical practice. Sociometric approaches have been frequently employed in research on social skills and peer relations but are more limited in terms of day-to-day use. Interview methods hold some promise as a method of social competence assessment but are most commonly used for other purposes. The use of self-reports in assessing social competence is a relatively new endeavor, but it does show some promise, based on what has been accomplished with the self-report component of the Social Skills Rating System. The use of each of the five assessment methods in evaluating social competence is discussed in this section.

Direct Behavioral Observation

Many of the general behavioral observation techniques overviewed in chapter 3 are highly relevant for assessing social skills and peer relations. In discussing behavioral observation as a method of assessing social skills, Elliott and Gresham (1987) stated that "analyzing children's behavior in natural settings . . . is the most ecologically valid method of assessing children's social skills" (p. 96). For the clinician or investigator who is serious about conducting valid assessments of child and adolescent social behaviors, mastering the basic methods of observational measurement overviewed in chapter 3 is a must.

Several other sources provide reviews of methods for assessing child and adolescent social behavior through direct behavioral observation (e.g., Asher & Hymel, 1981; Gresham, 1981; Hops & Greenwood, 1981), but this chapter will look at two examples of recently published investigations of how behavioral observation techniques have been used for assessing social behavior.

Target/Peer Interaction Code (TPIC).   Four related studies of the development of antisocial behavior in boys (Shinn, Ramsey, Walker, Steiber, & O'Neil, 1987; Walker, Shinn, O'Neil, & Ramsey, 1987; Walker, Steiber, Ramsey, & O'Neil, in press; Walker, Steiber, & O'Neil, in press) used a variety of assessment methods, including direct observation, to assess both positive and negative social behaviors. Of specific interest for this chapter is the use of an observational code for recording the social behavior of children in playground settings, the Target/Peer Interaction Code.

The TPIC requires coding of both the target subject and interacting peers' social behaviors during continuous 10-second intervals. While a complete description of the TPIC codes is beyond the scope of this chapter, certain aspects of the coding structure are of unique interest for assessing social skills and peer relations. One of the observational areas is *target subject interactive behavior,* which includes the behavioral classes of verbal behavior and physical contact. Within these response classes, behaviors are recorded as positive or negative and initiated or noninitiated. Another observational category of interest is *peer interactive behavior,* which includes verbal and physical interactive behavior directed at the target child by peers. It is coded in much the same way as target subject interactive behavior. Additionally under the peer interactive behavior category, target subjects' responses to peer behaviors are coded according to whether or not the subjects ignored, complied with, or appropriately resisted negative requests from peers.

While each of the four studies varied somewhat in overall methodology and findings, there were some generalized results: Direct observations conducted using the TPIC were effective at discriminating antisocial and at-risk subjects from normal control subjects, and certain components of the observational data were found to correlate significantly with teacher ratings of social skills. Interestingly classroom observations during academically engaged time were also found to correlate significantly with teacher ratings of social competence, in some cases to a higher degree than playground social-behavioral observations.

Behavioral Assertiveness Test (BAT).   Originally developed by Eisler, Hersen, and Miller (1973), the Behavioral Assertiveness Test was revised by Bornstein, Bellack, and Herson (1977) for use in assessing children's social skills. This observation system has been successfully used in intervention studies where social skills training interventions were implemented with both aggressive and withdrawn children. The BAT utilizes an analogue situation that requires children to role-play in as many as 48 situations, eliciting both assertive and nonassertive responses. The analogue situations are videotaped for later coding by observers. The BAT coding system includes 10 targeted behavioral categories plus an overall social skills rating. Several clinical outcomes studies (e.g., Bornstein, et al., 1977; Bornstein, Bellack, & Herson, 1980) have demonstrated that the BAT has strong construct validity and robust psychometric properties. Although the BAT was originally designed for use in either inpatient or outpatient clinical settings, it can also be used in school-based assessment, although it does not lend itself to naturalistic observation in the classroom.

The use of the TPIC and BAT observation systems in these methodologically sound investigations illustrates how direct behavioral observation can be used effectively to assess the social skills and peer relations of children and adolescents in both naturalistic and analogue settings. Obviously many variations on what social behaviors to observe and what observational methods to employ are possible. In using behavioral observation techniques to assess social skills and peer relations, two specific observational validity issues are particularly important: defining the observation domain and obtaining social comparison data (Merrell, 1989a). In defining which social behaviors to observe and how to code them, clinicians and investigators would do well to base their targeted behaviors and codes on what is known about the domains of social skills and peer relations and to define each class of behavior within the domains somewhat narrowly, thereby increasing the specificity of the observation. Obtaining social comparison data is especially important for observations within these domains because it allows the observer to make inferences about the effectiveness or deficiency of the observed child's social skills and peer relations.

Interviewing Techniques

By their very nature, social skills and peer relations are difficult to assess through interviewing techniques. The essence of these constructs is the behavioral skills a child or adolescent uses to initiate and maintain social communication and the quality and nature of the subject's resulting relationships with peers. Thus in attempting to obtain high-quality information about a client's social skills or peer relations within the context of an interview, the clinician is in the position of having to rely on subjective and difficult-to-verify reports from the child or adolescent client or on interview information obtained from parents or other informants. Elliott and Gresham (1987) noted that although behavioral interviews may be the most frequently used assessment method in the initial stages of intervention, they have not been investigated systematically as a social skills assessment technique.

At the present time, there are no widely available structured or semistructured interview schedules that have been developed primarily for the assessment of social skills and peer relations. Accordingly the use of less structured, open-ended techniques is the only alternative for those wishing to assess social skills and peer relations through the medium of an interview. Although this method may not be as desirable or direct as behavior rating scales or sociometric approaches, a good clinician may still find it useful in obtaining information on a client's social skills and peer relations.

Within the context of interviewing a child or adolescent client, there are several points and techniques that will facilitate obtaining good data on the client's social skills or peer relationships. One point to keep in mind is that the report of a child experiencing strained peer relationships or rejection may be colored by lack of insight, defensiveness, or hurt feelings. The younger the subject is the more likely the interview information will be influenced by these factors. As Boggs and Eyberg (1990) noted, children may not accurately or completely describe the events in their environment due to limited verbal skills or compliance with self-censoring rules they have learned. Clinicians with experience interviewing children known to be suffering severe rejection by peers often find that when subjects are asked to report on the amount and quality of their peer relations, most will report having several friends and getting along well with them. When asked to "name names," these children will even provide a detailed list of their "best friends." Clinicians conducting interviews of this type need to corroborate the client's report with more objective data, and they are advised to conduct the interview in a structured, detailed manner in order to increase the objectivity of the results.

The use of role-playing within a child or adolescent interview, when combined with a careful observation of the client's behavior, can provide some potentially useful information on the client's level of social skills. Given a carefully structured analogue situation, the clinician may be able to obtain a direct observation within the interview session of such important social skills as eye contact, entering into a conversation, dealing with peer pressure or harassment, requesting help, and giving or receiving a compliment. The process of social skills observation during role-playing is relatively easy: The interviewer simply needs to set up the format and expectations and then observe the client functioning within the designated role. For example, the clinician might say something like the following:

> Let's pretend that I am a kid at your school who you might want to become friends with. I am going to act like I am sitting down in the cafeteria eating my lunch, and I want you to come up to me and start talking with me about anything you want. Okay? Let's give it a try now.

Engaging in a role-play situation such as this one can alert the interviewer to any social skills deficits that may be negatively affecting the child or adolescent's peer relations. The type of information obtained through this process not only can provide good assessment data but also can be helpful in establishing appropriate interventions following the assessment.

When conducting an interview with a parent of a child or adolescent client, useful social skills and peer relations information may be obtained by carefully structuring the interview questions and by providing the parent with specific guidelines on how to respond to questions. Keep in mind that the behavior of the interviewer may have a significant impact on the responses of the client during the interview (Gross, 1984). Since the goal of the interview in this instance is to obtain specific information on the social skills and peer relations of the child, it will be helpful for the interviewer to provide specific prompts to the parent in order to increase the quality of the interview data. The following scenario illustrates how an interviewer can maximize the quality of the information obtained by carefully structuring questions and prompts:

INTERVIEWER: Tell me about how Jamie gets along with other children.

PARENT: Not very well.

INTERVIEWER: Can you tell me some more about that?

PARENT: Jamie doesn't have many friends . . . when she does have other children over to the house to play, they usually don't want to come back again because they get mad at her.

INTERVIEWER: Could you tell me specifically what kinds of things the other kids seem to get mad at Jamie about?

PARENT: Usually, when they are playing with toys or a book or something, Jamie won't share with them . . . she wants to dominate everything and gets upset when they have something that belongs to her. She wants to take toys and things that they bring over and use them the whole time.

INTERVIEWER: So Jamie has a difficult time sharing with others and doing what they want to do . . . this seems to be a real problem for her in making friends.

PARENT: Yeah, it's a real problem all right . . . if she could see the other kids' point of view, give in a little bit, and not be so jealous of her things, I think she could have a lot more friends to play with.

This interchange shows how the interviewer, by moving from the general to the specific and providing the parent with specific prompts, is able to pinpoint specific types of social skills and peer interaction problems. The parent interview can vary from being very open-ended to highly structured, but the specific level of structure ought to depend on the purpose of the interview. Therefore if the goal is to obtain useful information on the social skills and peer relations of the child, a higher degree of structure and prompting seems most useful.

Behavior Rating Scales

Until the mid-1980s, the vast majority of behavior rating scales were developed as omnibus measures of problem behavior or for assessment of specific dimensions of problem behavior, such as hyperactivity. No rating scales specifically designed for assessing general social competence or social skills were widely available. Within the past decade, there has been a strong surge of interest in school-based assessment of social skills and in providing training to children with social skills deficits. This increased interest stimulated the development of several commercially available behavior rating scales with good standardization and psychometric properties. Three of these rating scales or systems are overviewed in this section. All three instruments meet the criteria of having large standardization samples, good psychometric properties, and wide availability (i.e., commercially produced and marketed).

The Walker-McConnell Scales of Social Competence and School Adjustment (SSCSA). The Walker McConnell Scales of Social Competence and School Adjustment (Walker & McConnell, 1988; Walker, Steiber, & Eisert, 1991) are social skills rating scales for teachers and other school-based professionals. Two versions of the scale are available: an elementary version for use with students in grades K–6 and an adolescent version for use with students in grades 7–12. The elementary version contains 43 positively worded items that reflect adaptive social-behavioral competencies within the school environment. The items are rated using a 5-point scale, ranging from 1 = never occurs to 5 = frequently occurs. The scale yields standard scores on three subscales ($M = 10$, $SD = 3$) as well as a total score ($M = 100$, $SD = 15$), which is a composite of the three subscales. Subscale 1 (teacher-preferred social behavior) includes 16 items measuring peer-related social behaviors highly valued by teachers and reflective of their concerns for empathy, sensitivity, self-restraint, and cooperative, socially mature peer relationships (e.g., "Is considerate of the feelings of others" and "Is sensitive to the needs of others"). Subscale 2 (peer-preferred social behavior) includes 17 items measuring peer-related social behaviors highly valued by other children and reflective of peer values involving social relationships, dynamics, and skills in free-play settings (e.g., "Spends recess and free time interacting with peers" and "Invites peers to play or share activities"). Subscale 3 (school adjustment behavior) includes 10 items reflecting social-behavior competencies especially important in academic instructional settings, such as having good work and study habits, following academic instructions, and behaving in ways conducive to classroom management (e.g., "Attends to assigned tasks" and "Displays independent study skills").

The adolescent version of the scale is very similar to the elementary version, of which it is an upward extension. The adolescent version includes the 43 items from the elementary version (with nine revised scale items that better reflect adolescent behavioral content) plus an additional 10 items designed to measure *self-related* social adjustment, based on content from an adolescent social skills training curriculum (Walker, Todis, Holmes, & Horton, 1988). The factor structure of the adolescent version includes the same three factors found on the elementary version plus a fourth subscale containing six items labeled as the empathy subscale. This fourth factor includes items designed to measure sensitivity and awareness in peer relationships such as "Listens while others are speaking" and "Is considerate of the feelings of others." The adolescent version of the scale uses the same rating format and scoring system as the elementary version, and the four subscale scores are summed into a total score.

Extensive information on the standardization data and psychometric properties of the two versions of the SSCSA are reported in the scale manual. The scales were standardized on groups of approximately 2,000 students representing all four U.S. geographical regions. Studies undertaken during the development of the scales cited in the scale manual indicate adequate to excellent psychometric properties.

Reliability of the scales was established using test-retest (e.g., .88 to .92 correlations over a 3-week period with 323 subjects), internal consistency (e.g., alpha coefficients ranging from .95 to .97) and inter-rater (e.g., a .53 correlation between teacher and aide ratings on the total score in a day treatment facility) procedures. Validity of the scales was assessed using a variety of procedures. Discriminant validity was established in studies finding the SSCSA to differentiate effectively among groups of students expected to differ behaviorally (e.g., behavior disordered and normal, antisocial and normal, behaviorally at risk and normal, and those with and without learning problems). Criterion-related validity was demonstrated by finding significant correlations between the SSCSA and a number of criterion variables, including other rating scales, sociometric ratings, academic achievement measures, and systematic behavioral screening procedures. Construct validity of the scales was demonstrated by finding strong correlations between evaluative comments on subjects by their peers and teacher ratings on the scales and by finding low social skills ratings to be strongly associated with the emergence of antisocial behavior in a longitudinal study of elementary-age boys. A number of other psychometric validation studies are reported in the test manual that substantiate the reliability and validity of the scale. Subsequent investigations have found the SSCSA to correlate highly with other behavioral rating scales (Merrell, 1989b) and to accurately discriminate groups of students referred for learning problems from average students (Merrell et al., 1992; Merrell & Shinn, 1990). The six-item empathy subscale from the adolescent version of the SSCSA has been found to discriminate between a group of antisocial subjects with a record of arrests and an at-risk control group (Walker, Steiber, & Eisert, 1991). The factor structure of the SSCSA scales has been shown to be very strong.

Both versions of the SSCSA are brief and easy to use and contain items highly relevant for assessing social skills in educational settings. The research base behind the scales is truly exemplary, particularly considering that the scales have only been recently published. Since neither version of the SSCSA was designed to measure problem behaviors, these instruments should be supplemented with an appropriate problem-behavior assessment if the referral issues warrant it.

The School Social Behavior Scales (SSBS).   The School Social Behavior Scales (Merrell, 1993a) are school-based social behavior rating scales for use by teachers and other school personnel in assessing both social competence and antisocial problem behaviors of students in grades K–12. Included are two separate scales with a total of 65 items, describing both positive and negative social behaviors which commonly occur in educational settings. Items are rated using a 5-point scale ranging from 1 = never to 5 = frequently. Each of the two scales of the SSBS yields a total score, using a raw to standard score conversion with a mean of 100 and standard deviation of 15. The two scales each have three subscales with scores reported as four different *social functioning levels,* including "high functioning," "average," "moderate problem," and "significant problem."

Scale A (social competence) includes 32 items describing adaptive, prosocial behavioral competencies as they commonly occur in educational settings. Subscale A1 (interpersonal skills) includes 14 items measuring social skills important in establishing positive relationships and gaining social acceptance from peers (e.g., "Offers help to other students when needed" and "Interacts with a wide variety of peers"). Subscale A2 (self-management skills) includes 10 items measuring social skills relating to self-restraint, cooperation, and compliance with the demands of school rules and expectations (e.g., "Responds appropriately when corrected by teacher" and "Shows self-restraint"). Subscale A3 (academic skills) consists of eight items relating to competent performance and engagement in academic tasks (e.g., "Completes individual seatwork without being prompted" and "Completes assigned activities on time").

Scale B (antisocial behavior) includes 33 negatively worded items describing problematic behaviors that are either other-directed in nature or likely to lead to negative social consequences, such as peer rejection or strained relationships with the teacher. Subscale B1 (hostile-irritable) consists of 14 items describing behaviors considered self-centered, annoying, and likely to lead to peer rejection (e.g., "Will not share with other students" and "Argues and quarrels with other students"). Subscale B2 (antisocial-aggressive) consists of 10 behavioral descriptors relating to overt violation of school rules and intimidation or harm to others (e.g., "Gets into fights" and "Takes things that are not his/hers"). Subscale B3 (disruptive-demanding) includes 9 items reflecting behaviors likely to disrupt ongoing school activities and place excessive and inappropriate demands on others (e.g., "Is overly demanding of teacher's attention" and "Is difficult to control").

A number of studies and procedures are reported in the SSBS manual concerning the psychometric properties and validity of the instrument. The scales were standardized on a group of 1,856 K–12 students from the United States, with each of the four U.S. geographical regions represented in the standardization process. The percentage of special education students in various classification categories in the standardization group very closely approximates the national percentages of these figures. Various reliability procedures reported in the SSBS manual indicate the scales have good to excellent stability and consistency. Internal consistency and split-half reliability coefficients range from .91 to .98. Test-retest reliability at three-week intervals is reported at .76 to .83 for the social competence scores and .60 to .73 for the antisocial behavior scores. Inter-rater reliability between resource room teachers and paraprofessional aides ranges from .72 to .83 for the social competence scores and .53 to .71 for the antisocial behavior scores.

Validity of the scales has been demonstrated in several ways. Moderate to high correlations between the SSBS and three other behavior rating scales (including the 39-item version of the Conners Teacher Rating Scale, the Waksman Social Skills Rating Scale, and the adolescent version of the Walker-McConnell Scale of Social Competence and School Adjustment) suggest that the scale has good criterion-related validity. Other findings indicate that the scales can adequately discriminate between gifted and nongifted children (Merrell & Gill, in press), between students with disabilities and regular education students (Merrell, 1993b), and between behavior disordered and other special education students (Merrell, 1991). The factor structure of the two scales is strong, with all items having a factor loading into their respective subscale of .50 or greater and no item duplicated across subscales.

The SSBS shows promise as a school-based rating scale that provides norm-referenced data on both positive and social skills and antisocial problem behavior. It has satisfactory to good psychometric properties and is easy to use, and its items and structure are highly relevant to the types of behavioral issues encountered by school-based professionals. The antisocial behavior scale is designed specifically to measure behavior problems that are directly social in nature or that would have an immediate impact on strained relations with peers and teachers. The scale was not designed to measure overcontrolled or internalizing behavior problems such as those associated with depression and anxiety, nor was it designed to measure behavior problems associated with attention-deficit hyperactivity disorder. If these types of problem behaviors are a significant issue in an assessment case, the assessment should be bolstered by the addition of an appropriate measure designed specifically for these behaviors.

The Social Skills Rating System (SSRS)-Parent and Teacher Forms.   The Social Skills Rating System (Gresham & Elliott, 1990) is a multicomponent social skills rating system focusing on behaviors that affect parent-child relations, teacher-student relations, and peer acceptance. The system includes separate rating scales for teachers and parents as well as a self-report form for students, which will be described later in this chapter. Each component of the system can be used alone or in conjunction with the other forms. Separate instruments and norms are provided for three developmental groups: preschool level (ages 3–5), elementary level (grades K–6), and secondary level (grades 7–12). Since a detailed description and review of each of the SSRS forms are beyond the scope of this chapter and since there is considerable conceptual overlap between the different forms, an overview of only the elementary-level teacher rating form will be provided here. The preschool and secondary forms differ from the elementary forms mainly in the description and type of items since each form was developed so that the items would represent age-appropriate clusters of behaviors.

The elementary-level teacher rating form of the SSRS consists of 57 items divided over three scales: social skills, problem behaviors, and academic competence. For social skills and problem-behavior items, teachers respond to descriptions using a 3-point response format based on how often a given behavior occurs (0 = never, 1 = sometimes, and 2 = very often). On the social skills items, teachers are also asked to rate (on a 3-point scale) how important a skill is to success in the classroom. The importance rating is not used to calculate scores for each scale but for planning interventions. On the academic competence scale, teachers compare students to other students on a 5-point scale. Scale raw scores are converted to standard scores (M = 100, SD = 15) and percentile ranks. Subscale raw scores are converted to estimates of functional ability called *behavior levels.*

The social skills scale consists of 30 items rating social skills in the areas of teacher and peer relations. This scale contains three subscales, cooperation, assertion, and self-control. The cooperation subscale identifies compliance behaviors important for success in classrooms (e.g., "Finishes class assignments on time" and "Uses time appropriately while waiting for help"). The assertion subscale includes initiating behaviors that help make and maintain friendships and that respond to actions of others (e.g., "Invites others to join in activities" and "Appropriately questions rules that may be unfair"). The self-control subscale includes responses occurring in conflict situations such as turn-taking and peer criticism (e.g., "Cooperates with peers without prompting" and "Responds appropriately to teasing by peers").

The problem-behaviors scale consists of 18 items reflecting behaviors that might interfere with social skills performance. The items are divided into three subscales, including externalizing problems, internalizing problems, and hyperactivity. The externalizing problems subscale items reflect inappropriate behaviors indicating verbal and physical aggression toward others and a lack of temper control (e.g., "Threatens or bullies others" and "Has temper tantrums"). The subscale for internalizing problems includes behaviors indicating anxiety, sadness, and poor self-esteem (e.g., "Shows anxiety about being with a group of children" and "Likes to be alone"). The hyperactivity subscale includes activities involving excessive movement and impulsive actions (e.g., "Disturbs ongoing activities" and "Acts impulsively").

The third scale, academic competence, includes nine items reflecting academic functioning, such as performance in specific academic areas, student's motivation level, general cognitive functioning, and parental support (e.g., "In terms of grade-level expectations, this child's skills in reading are:" and "The child's overall motivation to succeed academically is:"). Behavior is rated on a 5-point scale that corresponds to percentages ranging from 1 = lowest 10 percent to 5 = highest 10 percent.

The SSRS was standardized on a national sample of more than 4,000 children representing all four U.S. geographical regions. The demographic information is difficult to interpret because the manual does not provide a detailed normative breakdown based on the different test forms. However, given the large number of subjects overall who were rated in the SSRS national standardization, it can be assumed that the norms for each rating form in the system were developed using a sufficient number of cases.

The overall psychometric properties obtained during scale development ranged from adequate to excellent. For the teacher scale, reliability was measured using internal consistency (i.e., alpha coefficients ranged from .74 to .95), inter-rater, and test-retest (i.e., .75 to .93 correlations across the three scales) procedures. Criterion-related and construct validity were established by finding significant correlations between the SSRS and other rating scales. Subscale dimensions were determined through factor analyses of each scale. Items that met a criterion of a .30 or greater factor loading were considered to load on a given factor.

The SSRS has the distinct strength of an integrated system of instruments for use by teachers, parents, and students. It is the only rating scale system of the three reviewed in this chapter that not only provides a school-based assessment but also a parent rating form for assessing social skills. The manual is very well written, and the rating instruments are easy to use and understand. The sections of the instruments that measure social skills are comprehensive and useful, but the sections measuring problem behaviors and academic competence are quite brief. The latter should be considered as short screening sections to be used in conjunction with more appropriate measures of behavioral/emotional problems, when indicated.

Sociometric Approaches

Sociometric approaches constitute a potentially useful method for assessing social skills and peer relations, particularly when used for screening or research purposes. Virtually any of the sociometric approaches covered in chapter 6 can be easily adapted to assess directly aspects of peer relations, which is their main purpose and use. Actual social skills tend be assessed less directly with sociometric approaches than do peer relations, but as peer relations are closely linked with social skills (Hartup, 1978), sociometric assessment should hold a great deal of heuristic interest for conducting social skills assessments as well. Since the general methods, techniques, and properties of sociometric approaches were mapped out in chapter 6, this section will focus on a few issues and applications of sociometric assessment for measuring social skills and peer relations, rather than duplicating the general information presented in chapter 6.

Some discussion on the nature of the relationship between the two constructs of interest for this chapter—social skills and peer relations—may be useful at this point. Perhaps the best way of conceptualizing this relationship is to look at it as *reciprocal* in nature. On one hand, peer relations are seen as being an *outcome* of social skills in that the greater degree of adaptive social competency a person possesses, the greater will be his or her ability to develop positive and fulfilling relationships with other persons (Gresham & Reschly, 1987a). On the other hand, it has also been demonstrated that peer relations to some extent are a *determinant* of social skills in that the social learning process involved in peer relationships contributes significantly to the development of social skills (Hartup, 1978, 1983). Thus the relationship between these two subdomains of social competence is complex and best described as mutually influential or reciprocal.

In preparing to conduct an assessment of social skills or peer relations using any of the sociometric approaches covered in chapter 6, the clinician or investigator must consider two aspects of the assessment in order to make it as useful as possible. The first area to be considered is which *general* technique to use. Based on Connolly's review (1983), the choice of sociometric approaches at the general level is between using a peer nomination procedure or a peer rating procedure. You might remember from chapter 6 that peer nomination procedures have been the traditional method of choice in sociometrics, but peer rating procedures may also be a useful alternative. The main difference between the two general types of procedures is that peer nominations tend to produce a measure of popularity, whereas peer ratings tend to produce a measure of average "likability" (Connolly, 1983). Although these two procedures seem to tap similar constructs, there is an important difference, illustrated by the example of a child who in peer ratings receives an average rating but is not positively or negatively nominated by any other children in the peer nomination procedure. Is this a typical child or a socially neglected child? It depends on which procedure you use and how you interpret it. Of course, a good compromise would be to use both types of sociometric approaches in the assessment if possible, which should strengthen the generalizability of your results. When practical considerations keep you from using both types of procedures in an assessment, it is important to carefully define what your intended goal or outcome for the assessment is and to select accordingly the general type of procedure you will use.

The second aspect to be considered is what specific procedure to use within your selected general method. Two needs will guide this decision. The first need is the capability level of your subjects. When assessing younger or lower-performing subjects, it is necessary to select a procedure that will not require any extensive reading or writing. In such a case, McAndless and Marshall's picture board adaptation of the peer nomination procedure (1957) would be a good choice, as would the simplified pictorial rating scale procedure for peer ratings (Asher, Singleton, Tinsley, & Hymel, 1979). The other need that will guide your decision as to which specific procedure to use is the specific aspect of peer relations or social skills you want to measure. In this regard, you should carefully evaluate the face validity of the procedures you are considering (as well as the formal validity properties) against the specific assessment needs you have and choose accordingly.

In sum, the use of sociometric approaches is a time-honored and empirically validated method of assessing peer relations that also will have indirect validity in assessing social skills. Virtually any of the general methods and specific procedures covered in chapter 6 (with proper selection and modification) can be of great use to the clinician or investigator in assessing these specific aspects of behavioral, social, and emotional problems.

Assessment with Self-Reports

At the present time, very little has been done in the area of developing a self-report assessment instrument for measuring social competence with children or adolescents. The only widely available self-report form for this purpose that meets the psychometric, standardization, and availability criteria for inclusion in this book are the two student forms of the Social Skills Rating System. These forms are overviewed as follows.

The Social Skills Rating System (SSRS)-Student Forms.   As part of the larger, integrated Social Skills Rating System described earlier in this chapter, there are two different self-report forms for children or adolescents to use in assessing their social skills. The Student Form-Elementary Level is designed to be used by children in grades 3–6, and it includes 34 items rated on a 3-point scale (0 = never, 1 = sometimes, 2 = very often). The elementary form includes four subscales (cooperation, assertion, self-control, and empathy) in which the raw scores are converted to behavior levels, and a total score is converted to a standard score (based on a mean of 100 and standard deviation of 15) and a percentile ranking based on same gender norms. Three examples of items on the elementary form include "I make friends easily," "I do my homework on time," and "I ask classmates to join in an activity or game."

The Student Form-Secondary Level is designed to be completed by students in grades 7–12. It includes 39 items that are rated by the student according to two rating sets. The first set of ratings is a "how often" rating, in which the student rates how often each item is true for him or her. Like the elementary-student version, the "how often" rating on the secondary-student form is done according to the criteria of 0 = never, 1 = sometimes, and 2 = very often. The second set of ratings is a "how important" rating, in which the student rates how important a specific behavior is in his or her relationship with others. This second set of ratings is also on a 0 to 2 scale, where 0 = not important, 1 = important, and 2 = critical. The inclusion of the importance ratings allows for a comparison on specific rating items for any discrepancies between the way a behavioral item was rated and how important it is to that student. For example, if a student rates "never" on item 1, "I make friends easily," yet the importance rating is "critical," this discrepancy suggests that the student's perceived difficulty in making friends is particularly painful for him or her. The secondary-student form includes the same four-subscale breakdown, and the same raw score converted to standard score system. The items on the secondary-student form are in some cases different from those on the elementary form, allowing for a rating of social skills particularly important to adolescents. Examples of some of the unique types of items on the secondary-student form include "I am confident on dates," "I end fights with my parents calmly," and "I give compliments to members of the opposite sex."

The psychometric properties of the two student forms reported in the SSRS manual do not appear to be as strong as those for the parent and teacher rating forms but are still generally in the adequate to acceptable range, particularly when considering that the student forms are designed to be used as part of a multirating system rather than by themselves. Internal consistency alpha coefficients for the student scales range from .51 to .77 for the subscale scores and are at .83 for the total scores. Test-retest reliability coefficients for the students forms (at four-week intervals) range from .52 to .68 on the elementary form but are not reported for the secondary form. Concurrent validity of the elementary-student form was assessed through correlations with the Piers-Harris Children's Self-Concept Scale, and the obtained coefficients ranged from − .02 to .43. These modest concurrent validity coefficients probably have a great deal to do with the fact that self-concept and self-ratings of social skills are two different constructs—there was no other self-rating of social skills instrument to compare the SSRS to.

Like the other components of the SSRS, the two student forms have the distinct advantage of being part of an integrated social skills assessment structure and of having been developed on a large, nationwide sample of subjects. They should be a useful adjunct to the teacher and parent rating forms in assessing social skills, and they will provide a good deal of social validity to the process of assessing social skills and peer relations by obtaining the student's own perspective.

LINKING ASSESSMENT TO INTERVENTION

In this chapter, the construct of social competence has been defined, its importance illustrated, and various methods and instruments for assessing social skills and peer relations have been overviewed. While each of the five assessment areas has some relevance for measuring social competence, behavioral observation, behavior rating scales, and sociometric approaches are particularly useful, and they have been widely reported in the research literature. Some summary information on the standardized assessment instruments that have been covered in this chapter is presented in Table 10.1.

It is obvious that assessing social competence has a great deal of importance for making classification and intervention decisions, but the specific link between social competence assessment data and effective social competence interventions is sometimes vague. This chapter concludes with two suggestions for increasing the treatment validity of social competence assessment.

The first suggestion is that *recommended treatments should match identified problems.* Over the course of several years as a school psychologist, program administrator, university trainer of school psychologists, and clinical supervisor, I have read assessment reports in which certain social skills deficits and peer relations problems were identified, and the resulting recommendation from the clinician was that "social skills training should be provided." This generic type of treatment recommendation is somewhat akin to a physician diagnosing bronchial pneumonia in a patient and then recommending that the client needs

TABLE 10.1 Summary of the reviewed standardized assessment instruments for measuring social skills and peer relations

Name of Instrument	Type	Used by	Number of Items	Grade Range
Walker-McConnell Scale of Social Competence and School Adjustment	Behavior Rating Scale	School personnel	43 on elementary, 53 on secondary	K–6 and 7–12
Social Skills Rating System-Parent and Teacher Forms	Behavior Rating Scale	School personnel and parents	Range of 38 through 42 at different levels	Pre-K to 12
School Social Behavior Scales	Behavior Rating Scale	School personnel	65; 32 social competence, 33 antisocial behavior	K–12
Social Skills Rating System-Student Forms	Self-Report	Students	34 for elementary, 39 for secondary	3–6 and 7–12

"medical care"; neither recommendation is particularly helpful in developing an effective treatment. One of the consistent findings over several years of research on effective interventions for children and adolescents with behavioral and emotional problems is that the more closely the treatment matches the problem, the greater the chance the intervention has of being successful (Peacock Hill Working Group, 1991). Presumably an effective assessment of social skills and peer relations should result in identifying some very specific aspects of the child's or adolescent's behavior that need attention. A best practice is to identify the specific skills deficits or behavioral excesses that exist and recommend interventions for those areas, rather than provide a generic treatment regimen that may or may not address the problems that have been identified.

The second suggestion, which is aimed specifically at school-based practitioners, is that *Individual Education Plan goals can be developed by modifying rating-scale items.* One of the advantages of using rating scales is that the descriptions they contain are usually concise, well thought out, and specific in nature. As such, social skills rating-scale items are often amenable to being developed into good intervention goal statements with a minimum amount of modification. For example, if a boy named Steven consistently received "never" ratings on item 4 ("Offers help to other students when needed") and item 19 ("Interacts with a wide variety of peers") on the interpersonal skills subscale of the School Social Behavior Scales, these items could be reworded into general goal statements as follows:

1. Steven will increase his level of providing help to other students when it is appropriately needed.
2. Steven will increase the number of his interactions with other students in the classroom and on the playground.

Of course, specific behavioral objectives would need to be developed following the statement of the general goals.

These two examples illustrate how clinicians can develop intervention recommendations using the actual data obtained during the assessment. At this point, the effectiveness of social skills and peer relations interventions do not have the long history of efficacy research which certain other behavioral problem interventions do. Consequently, any steps taken to make the assessment ecologically valid and to base intervention recommendations on specific assessment findings are especially important.

CASE STUDY

Background Information

This case study involves a concurrent analysis and comparison of two different children (J.T. and J.B.) who were referred for assessment due to social skills deficits and peer relationship problems. As you will see, although these two cases share the commonality of having social skills deficits and poor peer relations, they are considerably different from each other and serve to illustrate how diverse this type of social-behavioral problem can be. Both of the children illustrated in this case study are eight-year-old boys, and they are from the same second-grade classroom. Their second-grade teacher requested assistance from the multidisciplinary team at the school in the form of more in-depth study of the two boys and possible participation in a social skills training group, which the school counselor was planning to begin in one month.

J.T. is reported to be doing adequately on his academic work, but he has no friends, is very shy, and often withdraws from classmates. J.T. seldom tries to initiate friendships, and when he does, he seems to lack awareness of how to go about it. He does not seem to be disliked by his classmates but is pretty well ignored by them. He is very sensitive and will easily burst into tears when upset. J.T. lives with both parents, who are professionals, and a two-year-old sister.

J.B. is reported to be doing poorly on his academic work and is said to be not working up to his potential. He receives remedial help in reading and math. He is reported to be very assertive and aggressive, both verbally and physically. J.B. appears to want to build friendships, often initiating conversations or activities with other children, but these attempts often result in problems when he loses his temper or tries to coerce the other children into doing what he wants. He is frequently in trouble for fighting or otherwise violating school rules. J.B. lives with both parents, who run a small business, and three older brothers.

Assessment Data

The assessment was conducted by various members of the multidisciplinary child-study team at the school and was done strictly for purposes of problem identification and intervention planning; no classification or eligibility decisions were sought at this time. The special education teacher at the school completed classroom and playground observations of the two boys, the school counselor asked the teacher and parents of the boys to complete social skills rating scales on them, and the teacher conducted a sociometric assessment within the classroom.

Behavioral Observations. The special education teacher who conducted the classroom and playground observations conducted the classroom observation for a total of 30 minutes during an academic task in the classroom (alternating each one-minute interval so that each boy was observed for 15 minutes), and for a total of 20 minutes during lunch recess (alternating each one-minute interval so that each boy was observed for 10 minutes). No social comparison data was obtained. The observational coding system utilized was a simple narrative/event recording system, with frequency counts also taken for a list of problem behaviors on the observation form. The following table summarizes the main findings from the observation.

Behavior Rating Scales. J.T. and J.B.'s second-grade teacher, Mrs. C., rated both of them using the School Social Behavior Scales. The obtained raw and standard scores, percentile ranks, and social functioning levels from the SSBS are presented in the second table. Remember that on this test, higher scores

Classroom Observation of J.T.	Classroom Observation of J.B.
Engaged in the academic task most of the time	Was frequently off-task (no formal count taken)
Did not raise his hand to respond to any of the teacher's questions	Raised hand 2 times to respond to teacher's questions
Did not interact with any classmates during the seatwork portion of the activity	Was out of seat 6 times
	Asked for teacher's help 7 times
	Hit neighboring classmate in the back of the head
	Threatened another classmate
	Teased a classmate who responded incorrectly to the teacher's question

Playground Observation of J.T.	Playground Observation of J.B.
Interacted with only 1 peer during the observation, and only for a brief period of time	Interacted with 6 different peers
	Engaged in physically aggressive behavior 7 times
Spent the entire recess playing alone on the toys or walking around the playground	Engaged in verbally aggressive/threatening behavior 10 times
	On 2 occasions, peers actively tried to get away from J.B.
	Was reported to playground monitor by peers 2 times

School Social Behavior Scales teacher ratings for J.T. and J.B.	Raw Score		Standard Score		Percent Rank		Social Function Level	
SSBS Scores	*JT*	*JB*	*JT*	*JB*	*JT*	*JB*	*JT*	*JB*
A1 Interpersonal skills	16	28					SD	MD
A2 Self-management skills	25	19					MD	SD
A3 Academic skills	19	14					MD	SD
AT Social competence total	60	61	72	73	3	4	SD	SD
B1 Hostile-irritable	16	58					AV	SP
B2 Antisocial-aggressive	12	47					AV	SP
B3 Demanding-disruptive	18	32					AV	MP
BT Antisocial behavior total	46	*137*	95	146	55	99	AV	SP

on the social competence scale indicate greater levels of social-behavioral adjustment, while higher scores on the antisocial behavior scale indicate greater levels of social behavior problems. The abbreviations for the social functioning levels are as follows: for social competence scores, HF (high functioning), AV (average), MD (moderate deficit), and SD (significant deficit); for antisocial behavior scores, AV (average), MP (moderate problem), SP (significant problem).

In addition to the School Social Behavior Scales ratings from Mrs. C., both J.T. and J.B. were rated by their parents using the Social Skills Rating System. Both boys are from two-parent families, and in both cases, the mother and father completed the ratings jointly. The obtained raw and standard scores, percentile ranks, and behavior levels are presented in the table below. Remember that on the SSRS, like the SSBS, higher social skills scores indicate greater social-behavioral functioning, while higher problem-behavior scores indicate greater social-behavioral problems. The behavior-level abbreviations for the SSRS are as follows: FW (fewer), AV (average), MR (more).

Social Skills Rating System parent ratings for J.T. and J.B.	Raw Score		Standard Score		Percent Rank		Behavior Level	
SSRS Scores	*JT*	*JB*	*JT*	*JB*	*JT*	*JB*	*JT*	*JB*
Cooperation	9	8					AV	FW
Assertion	6	12					FW	FW
Responsibility	6	10					FW	FW
Self-Control	11	4					AV	FW
Social Skills Total	32	24	70	73	2	4	FW	FW
Externalizing Problems	3	11					AV	MR
Internalizing Problems	11	6					MR	AV
Hyperactivity	4	7					AV	AV
Problem Behaviors Total	18	24	112	127	79	96	AV	MR

Sociometric Assessment. Mrs. C. conducted a sociometric procedure within her classroom, using a nomination procedure that included five each of both positive and negative items. The nomination items were as follows:

Positive Nomination Items	*Negative Nomination Items*
1. Who is your best friend?	1. Who is in trouble a lot?
2. With whom would you most like to play?	2. Who fights with other kids?
3. With whom would you most like to work?	3. Who doesn't follow the rules?
4. Who is a good leader?	4. Who has few friends?
5. Who helps other kids?	5. Who is angry a lot?

Neither J.T. nor J.B. received any positive nominations. J.T. received nominations from three different classmates on negative item 4. J.B. was nominated by classmates on each of the negative items; by four classmates on item 1, by three classmates on item 2, by five classmates on item 3, by three classmates on item 4, and by two classmates on item 5.

Questions to Consider

1. It is obvious that although both J.T. and J.B. have some social skills deficits, their behavior patterns are different in many regards. Analyze the SSBS and SSRS social skills ratings (not problem behavior) by looking at both their subscale and total scores. Why is it important to look at individual items and subscale scores rather than making a simple general judgment from a single (total) score?
2. Looking at all of the rating-scale scores for the two boys, analyze the general level of agreement between raters and instruments. How much rater, setting, and instrument variance is evident?
3. Using all of the available data, attempt to classify both boys according to Coie and colleagues' various dimensions of social status discussed in Chapter 6.
4. Using the internalizing/externalizing dichotomy of behavior problems discussed at length in this book, is it possible to classify differentially the behavior-problem patterns of either boy?
5. One of the motives the classroom teacher had for gathering social assessment data on J.T. and J.B. was that she wanted both of them to participate in a social skills training group the school counselor was going to start. What are the potential effects or consequences of having both J.T. and J.B. in the same training group?
6. Based on the available assessment data, make a list of the specific social skills that each boy appears to lack, as if you were targeting behaviors for a social skills training group. Be as specific as possible, behaviorally defining the target skills.

CHAPTER 11

Severe Behavioral, Social, and Emotional Problems: Assessment of Autism, Schizophrenia, and Related Disorders

INTRODUCTION

Unlike externalizing disorders, internalizing disorders, and social competence deficits, which are commonly observed in children and adolescents, the categories of childhood and adolescent disorders covered in this chapter are quite rare. Psychologists, counselors, and social workers employed in general community setting such as regular schools, child guidance clinics, and private practices will probably not encounter child and adolescent clients with autism, psychotic disorders, or related personality disorders on a regular basis. Professionals who frequently confront these types of child and adolescent disorders are more likely to work in specialized settings such as self-contained special education schools or classrooms and psychiatric hospitals, and they are also likely to work in conjunction with other professionals who have special interest and training in the low-incidence disabilities. While the generalist child and adolescent mental health professional will probably not deal with these disorders with much frequency, there are still two compelling reasons for developing a basic understanding of this class of problems and how to assess them: (*a*) the generalist mental health professional will undoubtedly face these types of problems several times over the course of a career and will be expected to have some helpful expertise, and (*b*) these disorders can be so striking and disabling that they might totally disarm the practitioner who is not aware of and prepared to deal with them. Thus this chapter provides a basic overview of the more serious and pervasive behavioral, social, and emotional problems, geared to the needs of the general practitioner. Professionals who work in highly specialized settings obviously will need more detailed information and preparation than this basic chapter can provide, but there are numerous books, journals, and other resources available that specifically address autism and psychotic disorders in great depth.

This chapter begins with a discussion of classification and taxonomy issues involving the most serious behavioral, social, and emotional problems, addressing them from the standpoint of both the DSM system and multivariate Behavioral Dimensions classification schemes. Following this overview of classification, the characteristics of these disorders are discussed in some detail. The disorders are divided into three general areas: autism, psychotic disorders, and a related class of problems referred to as the *schizoid disorders*. As in chapters 8, 9, and 10, the nuts and bolts of assessment using our five general methods of interest will be explored next. The chapter concludes with some guidelines for linking the assessment of severe behavioral, social, and emotional problems to specific intervention strategies.

CLASSIFICATION AND TAXONOMY ISSUES

From the very beginnings of psychology as a scientific discipline in the late 1800s, definition and classification of the most severe behavioral, social, and emotional problems has been a very difficult problem. Because these disorders are relatively rare and because the three classes utilized in this chapter have a fair amount of overlapping characteristics, the research base for classification and taxonomy has lagged behind other types of child and adolescent disorders. Until the 1960s, it was common for the generic term *childhood psychosis* to be used in the classification of all these severe disorders, although a number of other labels were used earlier with some regularity, including *dementia precocissma, dementia infantilis, childhood schizophrenia, infantile autism, autistic psychopathy, symbiotic psychosis,* and *atypical child* (Howlin & Yule, 1990). Since the term childhood psychosis has no precise meaning, it is seldom used today, and most current classification paradigms are connected to the DSM system.

The DSM Approach to Classification

The evolving versions of the DSM have likewise shared this generally confusing and ever-changing approach to classification of the severe behavioral and emotional disorders. The DSM III-R classification system for severe behavioral disorders of childhood represents an improvement over previous versions, but even the most ardent supporters of this multiaxial system admit there are a number of problems still to be worked out, owing to the lack of a strong empirical base and the overlapping characteristics of disorders. The DSM-III-R has several axis I and axis II diagnostic categories that broadly fit what this author refers to as severe behavioral, social, and emotional problems. Under axis II, the class of disorders called Pervasive Developmental Disorders is of specific interest, and it includes the diagnostic categories Autistic Disorder and Pervasive Developmental Disorder Not Otherwise Specified. Under axis I, a group of three classes of disorders, which can loosely be referred to as psychotic disorders, is also important: Schizophrenia, Delusional (Paranoid) Disorder, and Psychotic Disorders Not Elsewhere Classified. Finally cluster A of the personality disorders (axis II) is of direct interest for this chapter, particularly the Schizoid and Schizotypal personality disorders. This varied grouping of DSM-III-R disorders is listed, with code numbers, in Table 11.1. It is worth mentioning that the classification of mental retardation often includes symptoms of severe behavioral and social maladjustment, especially in its most severe and profound forms. However since the major defining feature of mental retardation is severe deficits in intellectual functioning, it is not exclusively a cluster of behavioral problems and is not covered in any detail this book.

Behavioral Dimensions
Approaches to Classification

As was mentioned earlier, empirical efforts at establishing a reliable taxonomy of severe behavioral disorders have been plagued by problems stemming from very small sample sizes and overlapping behavioral and emotional characteristics. One of the earlier efforts at developing a statistical taxonomy of the broad category of "childhood psychoses" was a study by Prior, Boulton, Gajzago, and Perry (1975), who used an analysis of 162 cases, ultimately leading to a division into two categories: one subgroup with early onset and autismlike features and another subgroup with later onset of symptoms and less debilitating impairment in social relationships. Although this interesting study has not been replicated, the general idea of these two divisions has caught on to some extent in the professional literature, and such a division has been suggested as a general rule of thumb by some prominent scholars in child psychopathology (e.g., Cantor, 1987; Howlin & Yule, 1990).

TABLE 11.1 DSM-III-R diagnostic categories relevant to the assessment of severe behavioral, social, and emotional problems

Axis I Disorders

Schizophrenic Disorders

295.2x	Schizophrenia, catatonic
295.1x	Schizophrenia, disorganized
295.3x	Schizophrenia, paranoid
295.9x	Schizophrenia, undifferentiated
295.6x	Schizophrenia, residual

Delusional (Paranoid Disorder)

297.10	Delusional (Paranoid) disorder (6 subtypes)

Psychotic Disorders Not Elsewhere Classified

298.80	Brief reactive psychosis
295.40	Schizophreniform disorder
295.70	Schizoaffective disorder
297.30	Induced psychotic disorder
298.90	Psychotic disorder, not otherwise specified

Axis II Disorders

Pervasive Developmental Disorders

299.00	Autistic disorder
299.80	Pervasive developmental disorder, not otherwise specified

Personality Disorders (cluster A)

301.00	Paranoid personality disorder
301.20	Schizoid personality disorder
301.22	Schizotypal personality disorder

SOURCE: American Psychiatric Association, *Diagnostic and Statistical Manual of Mental Disorders,* revised 3rd ed. (Washington, D.C., 1987).

An interesting and promising effort at establishing a Behavioral Dimensions taxonomy for severe behavioral disorders was conducted by Quay (1986a), through his analysis of 61 multivariate statistical studies describing facets of child psychopathology. Although Quay noted that "the problems associated with describing childhood psychosis have not readily yielded to clarification by multivariate statistical analysis" (p. 16), his effort resulted in an interesting organization into two types of syndromes that are relevant for this chapter. One of these syndromes was labeled *Schizoid-unresponsive,* with the most frequently identified behaviors being refusal to talk, social withdrawal, extreme timidity, a cold and unresponsive disposition, and an aloof behavioral picture referred to as "cold and unresponsive." The second of these two syndromes was labeled *Psychotic Disorder,* with the few key behavioral features identified including incoherent and

TABLE 11.2 Major behavioral characteristics of two types of severe behavioral syndromes identified through multivariate statistical techniques

Schizoid-unresponsive	Psychotic Disorder
Refusal to talk	Incoherent speech
Socially withdrawn	Repetitive speech
Shy, timid, bashful	Acts bizarre, odd, peculiar
Cold and unresponsive	Visual hallucinations
Lack of interest	Auditory hallucinations
Sad affect	Has strange ideas, behavior
Stares blankly	
Confused	
Secretive behavior	
Prefers to be alone	

SOURCE: Adapted from H. C. Quay, "Classification," in H. C. Quay and J. S. Werry (eds.), *Psychopathological Disorders of Childhood*, 3rd ed. (New York: Wiley: 1986).

repetitive speech, bizarre behavior, auditory and visual hallucinations, and a group of odd characteristics referred to as "strange ideas, behaviors" (p. 16). These two syndromes are listed with their characteristic behavioral symptoms in Table 11.2. Again, it is important to recognize that this taxonomy effort was fraught with methodological difficulties and should be considered a preliminary or experimental effort, but it is a promising type of what future efforts at multivariate analysis might reveal.

AN OVERVIEW OF SEVERE BEHAVIORAL, SOCIAL, AND EMOTIONAL PROBLEMS

Before getting into assessment of the more severe and pervasive disorders, it is useful to explore these details about each: description, prevalence, etiology, onset, and long-term implications. For purposes of this chapter, the severe disorders have been divided into three general categories: autism and other pervasive developmental disorders, psychotic disorders, and the schizoid disorders, a set of related personality disorders described in the DSM-III-R.

Autism and Pervasive Developmental Disorders

Description. Leo Kanner, a pioneer in the study of autism, first described a group of children who fit the general diagnostic picture in 1943. Kanner noted that their fundamental disorder was the "inability to relate themselves in the ordinary way to people and situations from the beginning of life" and that a characteristic of this disorder is an aloneness that "disregards, ignores, shuts out anything that comes to the child from the outside" (Kanner, 1943, p. 43). This syndrome was labeled by Kanner as "early infantile autism," because the tendency to display these characteristics seemed inborn and present from birth. Howlin and Rutter (1987) have noted that although there have been a number of changes since 1943 in the way that this disorder is conceptualized, Kanner's general description of autism is still fundamentally accurate.

Based on the DSM-III-R definition and a consensus of the current thinking about the disorder (see page 259), the major characteristics of autism include severe impairment in reciprocal social interaction and in verbal and nonverbal communication as well as in imaginative activity, with a severely restricted repertoire of activities and interests. Specific characteristics commonly seen in autistic children are somewhat varied, but a general pattern is often observed. In terms of severely impaired social relationships, individuals with autism usually appear to be socially aloof and detached; they may fail to make eye contact, have a noticeably flat affect, shrink from physical contact, and often seem to relate to other persons as objects or conglomerations of parts rather than as people (Ornitz, 1989). In terms of the specific disorders of communication, individuals with autism may not engage in speech, or they may speak in a peculiar manner, such as using a robotic monotone voice, displaying an odd vocal rhythm and meter, or repeating words and phrases in a stereotypical manner (Howlin & Yule, 1990). Additionally, individuals with autism often lack or fail to grasp the pragmatics of interpersonal communication, possibly due to an inability to interpret the facial expressions, intonation, and gestures of others (Prior & Werry, 1986). The severely restricted repertoire of activities and interests of the autistic individual is characterized by stereotyped body movements (spinning, twisting, head banging, flipping the hands), a peculiar preoccupation with parts of objects (e.g., doorknobs, on-off switches), and exhibition of great distress when routines or insignificant parts of the environment are changed (Harris, 1987). Behaviors that are part of this third characteristic often take the form of obsession with routine and objects, such as a child repetitively dumping a pile of sticks on the floor and then lining them up in a particular manner.

Aside from the three major features of autism, there are some other interesting correlates to consider. IQ scores of individuals with autism are sometimes in the normal range or higher, but this is not the norm; the majority of individuals with autism consistently test out in the moderate to severely mentally retarded range (Prior & Werry, 1986). Autism may often bring with it problems of sensory integration and perception (Wing, 1969) and poor psychomotor development (Fulkerson & Freeman, 1980). Since the combination of social impairment and low intellectual ability are usually part of the picture, persons with autism almost always have difficulty learning new materials or tasks.

In DSM-III-R terms, autism is the only recognized subtype of the category pervasive developmental disorder and it is the most severe and prototypical form of it. However there are occasional situations where a child will exhibit severe developmental problems with several features of autism but not to the extent that a diagnosis of autism is appropriate and without the specific characteristics of other developmental disorders such as mental retardation. In such cases, the

DSM-III-R provides another diagnostic category, namely, Pervasive Developmental Disorder Not Otherwise Specified (PDDNOS). (See Table 11.1 on page 238.) Again PDDNOS is not considered a separate condition but probably is a less severe manifestation of the same pervasive developmental problem. DSM-III-R contends that PDDNOS should be utilized for diagnosis when there is marked impairment in social and communication skills but not enough impairment for a diagnosis of autism and when the restricted repertoire of activities and interests may not be present.

Prevalence, Onset, and Etiology.   The best current estimates suggest that between 2 and 5 of every 10,000 children (.0002 to .0005 percent) in the United States and England meet the DSM-III-R criteria for autism. For PDDNOS, the prevalence is slightly higher; it is estimated at 10 to 15 of every 10,000 children (.001 to .0015 percent). Autism has been found to occur at least three times more frequently in males than in females with most studies showing a 3:1 or 4:1 ratio.

In the vast majority of cases, the pervasive developmental disorders have an onset before three years of age. The DSM-III-R notes that very few cases are reported with an onset after age five or six. In making a formal diagnosis, it is assumed that the onset is before age three, and if in an unusual circumstance it is later than this, the term "childhood onset" is used for specification.

Kanner's early writings on autism (1943) posited a strong probability that the disorder has a constitutional or biological origin. However during this same seminal period of discovery, Kanner and others noted that parents of children with autism often showed a tendency toward emotional insulation, aloofness, or detachment toward the child. Thus the notion was born and perpetuated by prominent writers (e.g., Bettelheim, 1967; O'Gorman, 1970) that autism may be due to abnormal family functioning. The problem with these theories was that they usually failed to take into account the reciprocal effect of parent-child interactions and placed too much weight on parent behaviors. The social learning approach would suggest that although parents of children with autism might respond at times in a manner that could be interpreted as emotionally detached, the characteristics of the child may have a great deal of influence on eliciting these behaviors. In spite of this line of thinking, popular until the 1970s, research efforts have failed to support the notion that autism is caused by abnormal parenting or family functioning (Howlin & Yule, 1990).

Although there is no conclusive evidence on the specific causes of autism at the present time, current thinking suggests that genetic and other biochemical influences are probably the most direct etiologic factors. Howlin and Yule (1990) reviewed a number of studies addressing concordance rates for autistic symptoms and concluded that "all these findings indicate the presence of importance genetic influences" (p. 375).

Long-Term Implications.   The best evidence from follow-up studies of children with autism suggests that although some improvements may occur over time (particularly with intense early intervention efforts), many if not most individuals with the disorder will continue to exhibit characteristic problem symptoms over the course of their lives. Howlin and Yule (1990) have noted that individuals with autism who have the greatest chance of achieving social independence and making satisfactory adjustments are those few with high IQ scores and reasonably good language skills and that "total social independence is gained by only a very small minority of autistic individuals" (p. 376). Thus although a select few children with autism may completely overcome their disability, the long-term implications of the disorder are severe, and most individuals with autism will require a high degree of personal, social, and occupational support throughout life.

Psychotic Disorders of Childhood and Adolescence

Description.   As Table 11.1 indicates, there are three groups of axis I disorders from the DSM-III-R that roughly fall under the category of psychotic disorders: schizophrenia, delusional (paranoid) disorder, and a collection of very specific types of disorders referred to as Psychotic Disorders Not Elsewhere Classified. Because delusional disorder typically is associated with middle age or older and because little is known about the prevalence and onset of the omnibus third category, our discussion of psychotic disorders will be confined for the most part to schizophrenia as it relates to children and especially to adolescents. Furthermore, because an empirically sound Behavioral Dimensions approach to the classification of psychotic behavior in children has not yet evolved (Quay & Werry, 1986), the DSM-III-R will be our main point of reference from a diagnostic standpoint.

The term *psychosis* does not have an exact or universal meaning, but it is generally used to indicate a break with reality or a severe impairment of one's sense of reality and ability to perceive and function as most other persons do. The terms *childhood psychosis* and *childhood schizophrenia* were used earlier in this century to indicate autistic disorder also, but the modern understanding of these terms generally preclude autism. An essential feature of schizophrenia and the related psychotic disorders is that the advent of the disorder causes a lowering or impairment of functioning from a previous level. Autism is now considered to be a developmental disorder, involving severe limitations in the normal course of development, while schizophrenia normally occurs after the early childhood developmental period and brings with it a loss of functioning.

The DSM-III-R does not contain a separate category of schizophrenic or other psychotic disorders exclusively for children, but it provides general axis I diagnostic categories under which children and adolescents may be classified when they exhibit the necessary features. The major diagnostic picture of schizophrenia includes the following symptoms: delusions of thought, prominent and lasting hallucinations, incoherence or a marked loosening of associations, catatonic behavior (severe restriction of motor activity that sometimes alternates with wild hyperactivity), and flat or grossly inappropriate affect. The delusions of thought in schizophrenia are typically bizarre and implausible, and hallucinations are characteristically pronounced, such as hearing voices for long periods of time. Along with these severe disturbances of perception, thought, and affect, a severe decline in personal and social functioning typically occurs, which might include significantly poor personal hygiene, inability to function effectively at school or work, and a severe impairment in social relationships. Using the DSM system, these characteristic symptoms must be present on a continuous basis for a period of at least six months in order to make a diagnosis.

Voluminous materials on the nature and characteristics of schizophrenia are available, and it is not possible to consider all of these sources within this chapter. However some additional important associated features of schizophrenia should be considered. Individuals suffering from schizophrenia tend to display markedly peculiar behavior, such as talking to themselves in public, collecting garbage, and hoarding food or items that appear to be of little value. Schizophrenia is often accompanied by very strange beliefs or magical thinking not in line with the cultural milieu; the afflicted person might believe that her or his behavior is being controlled by another person or force or that he or she has the power of clairvoyance. Some of the characteristics of schizophrenia can be brought on by other conditions, such as severe affective disorders or the use of psychoactive substances. However a true diagnosis of schizophrenia implies that the symptoms are pervasive and long lasting and not brought on by a temporary biochemical or affective change. Although the DSM-III-R criteria are the best working criteria for schizophrenia currently available, it is important to consider that they may not always best describe the development of the disorder during childhood. In fact, Cantor (1987, 1989) noted that the DSM symptoms may not always be the most prominent features of schizophrenia developed during childhood and that the childhood diagnostic picture is often complicated and clouded.

Prevalence, Onset, and Etiology.   The DSM-III-R notes that schizophrenia is diagnosed with less frequency in Europe and Asia (where prevalence estimates have been as low as 0.2 percent) than it is in the United States, where broader criteria and heavily urban survey populations have been utilized, generally resulting in estimates of about 1 percent. However the 1 percent figure does not hold true for children, as schizophrenia usually develops either during mid to late adolescence or in early adulthood, and "classic" DSM symptoms of schizophrenia are rare before puberty. Though few large epidemiological studies have been conducted with children, a frequently quoted prevalence figure is 4 or 5 cases per 10,000 (Cantor, 1989). With adults and older adolescents, schizophrenia tends to occur in similar numbers with males and females. However with the preadolescent population, the equal gender balance does not hold true. Cantor (1989) noted that the general agreement for a sex ratio for childhood psychosis is 4 or 5 males per 1 female.

The cause of schizophrenia has been a controversial topic for centuries, where explanations of etiology have run the gamut from demon possession to a weak constitution to poor parenting. In recent years, a plethora of research has strongly suggested that schizophrenia has a biochemical basis. The neurotransmitter dopamine has been implicated as a critical variable, since drugs that block dopamine receptor sites tend to be highly effective in controlling the more severe symptoms of schizophrenia, such as delusions and hallucinations. Family and adoption studies conducted in the United States and Europe over the past several decades have provided additional evidence for a genetic explanation of schizophrenia, since the degree of genetic relatedness to an individual with schizophrenia is a strong factor in predicting the occurrence of the disorder (Gottesman, 1991). For example, in cases where one individual in a set of twins develops schizophrenia, the probability is almost four times greater that the other twin will develop the disorder when the twins are identical rather than fraternal. While biochemical-genetic factors are certainly prominent in explaining etiology, behavioral and environmental factors are likely to interact with the personal variables to increase or decrease the likelihood of schizophrenia. Thus if two individuals have an equal biochemical/genetic predisposition for developing the disorder, the individual with a dramatically higher level of psychosocial distress may be more likely to ultimately exhibit the symptoms.

Long-Term Implications. For children and adolescents who develop schizophrenia, the prognosis is not good, but it is much more promising than it was several decades ago. This increased optimism is due to the availability of powerful "antipsychotic" drugs (i.e., the neuroleptics) that help control the major symptoms (though perhaps not as well in children as in adults—see Cantor, 1987) and the refinement of methods of psychological treatment to help individuals cope with the distressing psychosocial effects.

Eggers (1978) found that children who develop schizophrenic symptoms between the ages of 10 and 14 are likely to have more persistent delusions than children who develop the disorder at a younger age, but it is important to consider that very few children develop schizophrenic symptoms before age 10. However, other prominent researchers in the field of childhood schizophrenia have contended that prognosis is more related to severity of symptoms than to age of onset (Cantor, 1987, 1989).

There seems to be wide variability in how schizophrenia affects individuals over the long haul, and the availability of social support, medical care, and mental health services may be critical factors in how debilitating the disorder becomes. Part of the clinical lore in psychology and psychiatry is the so-called "rule of thirds," which contends that of all individuals who develop schizophrenic symptoms, one-third will eventually get much better, one-third will remain the same, and one-third will get progressively worse. However, this "rule" has not been empirically validated. In general, the long-term prognosis for individuals with schizophrenia varies depending on many factors, and under optimum conditions, many of the symptoms can be controlled and, in some cases, will go into remission.

The Schizoid Disorders

Description. As we have already seen, Quay's exploratory attempt (1986a) at developing a multivariate Behavioral Dimensions taxonomy for severe behavior disorders resulted in two classes of symptoms: psychotic disorder and schizoid-unresponsive. This second category is of particular interest here. The exact meaning of the term "schizoid" is not precise, but it is generally thought of as indicating "schizophrenia-like" (but not quite schizophrenic) symptoms. The term "unresponsive" was used by Quay to indicate not only detached and aloof peer relations but a general pattern of alienation and withdrawal as well. These terms describe a cluster of behavioral, social, and emotional problems that have commonalities with autism and schizophrenia but that are for the most part more subtle and less blatant than the most severe symptoms of the latter two conditions (see Table 11.2). Wolf (1989) noted that a perplexing number of terms have been used to describe the so-called schizoid disorders since they were first discussed by Hans Asperger in the 1940s, a fact which has not helped to clarify the confusion that generally exists regarding them.

Children and adolescents who exhibit the characteristics found in the schizoid-unresponsive category may not clearly meet the diagnostic criteria for autism or schizophrenia but are likely to exhibit the following core characteristics: (*a*) solitariness, (*b*) impaired empathy and emotional detachment, (*c*) increased sensitivity (to external stimuli), (*d*) a rigid mental set, and (*e*) an odd or unusual way of communicating (Wolf, 1989). Children and adolescents who exhibit these characteristics present a considerable challenge to the clinician for appropriate assessment, classification, and intervention.

Quay (1986a) suggested that the schizoid-unresponsive dimension may be the extreme of the personality style commonly referred to as *introversion* and may also be a counterpart of the DSM-III category of Schizoid Disorder. The revised third edition of the DSM is somewhat different from the third edition with respect to these characteristics. Under the axis II class of personality disorders, two of the "A" cluster personality disorders in DSM-III-R are highly relevant to Quay's schizoid-unresponsive dimension: Schizoid Personality Disorder and Schizotypal Personality Disorder. These two personality disorders are typified by various degrees and manifestations of social withdrawal, unresponsiveness, and peculiar or odd thought and behavior patterns.

DSM-III-R states that the essential feature of Schizoid Personality Disorder "is a pervasive pattern of indifference to social relationships and a restricted range of emotional experience and expression" (p. 339). Individuals who fit this diagnostic picture do not desire or enjoy close social relationships, including familial relationships. They exhibit a highly restricted range of emotional behavior and come across to others as being cold and aloof. Schizotypal Personality Disorder is described in the DSM-III-R as being typified by "a pervasive pattern of peculiarities of ideation, appearance, and behavior and deficits in interpersonal relatedness" (p. 340). Both of these personality disorders share some common characteristics with autism and more particularly with schizophrenia, but the symptoms are not as severe. Although there are some common symptoms of these two personality disorders, there is a clear line of demarcation for differential diagnosis: Schizoid Personality Disorder does not include peculiarities of thought, behavior, and speech, while Schizotypal Personality Disorder is not characterized as much by the extreme voluntary social detachment of the former disorder. A differential diagnosis might normally be possible when considering the two disorders, but their symptoms may occur concomitantly in some cases. DSM-III-R indicates that "some people may have both disorders" (p. 340), which probably indicates that they exhibit the entire range of symptoms identified in Quay's schizoid-unresponsive dimension (1986a).

Prevalence, Onset, and Etiology.   Very little is known about the prevalence of these disorders in the general population. The DSM-III-R states that the prevalence of both conditions is low but provides no objective data in this regard. Sula Wolf, one of only a few experts on the schizoid disorders in children and adolescents, stated that "nothing is yet known about the prevalence (of the disorder)" (1989, p. 224). Thus while we can assume that these disorders will be rare in the child and adolescent population, there is no benchmark to go by for determining how often they can be expected. Part of the problem in conducting an epidemiological study in this area is the difficulty in defining the boundaries between normal variations of personality and psychopathology (Wolf, 1989). Because so little is known about prevalence, the gender distribution of these disorders is quite speculative at this time. One of the few clinical studies of the schizoid disorders (Wolf & Chick, 1980) found a gender ratio of 3.3 males for every 1 female, but the investigators warned that this ratio to some extent may have been a referral artifact.

The essential features of these disorders most likely will be present during early childhood, but differential diagnosis at this stage is difficult, given the overlapping symptoms existing between them and several of the developmental disorders. Thus onset of the schizoid disorders tends to be most clear and well defined in middle childhood (Wolf, 1989).

There is no clear evidence at the present time as to the etiology of the schizoid disorders, but some interesting speculations have been offered. One prominent etiological theory contends that a genetic link between the schizoid disorders and schizophrenia should be considered, as about half of the individuals with schizophrenia displayed schizoid characteristics prior to the onset of psychosis, children of schizophrenics often exhibit schizoidlike characteristics, and parents of children with the schizoid disorders often exhibit similar behaviors (Bleuler, 1978; Erlenmeyer-Kimling, Kestenbaum, Bird, & Hildoff, 1984; Wolf, 1989). This theory makes some sense, and it will undoubtedly be the subject of future research. However when utilizing comparisons between individuals with schizophrenia and their family members, it is important to recognize that social learning and reciprocal deterministic effects between parents and children may also play an important role in the development of schizoid-type characteristics.

Long-Term Implications.   Based on Wolf and Chick's 10-year follow-up study of schizoid children (1980), there is evidence that the essential features of the schizoid disorders carry on into adult life. Further evidence from Wolf's ongoing follow-up research with this cohort (1989) suggests that the intellectual ability of individuals with the disorder may be a critical variable in the quality of their social adaptation over time. "Our tentative impression is that the more gifted people are now less solitary, some having married, but their basic personality characteristics remain distinct. On the other hand, some of the less able and withdrawn people, while often working satisfactorily, remain single and excessively dependent on their families'' (p. 223). Aside from this information, very little is known about the long-term implications of the schizoid disorders. It is probably prudent to assume that children and adolescents who exhibit these characteristics to the extent that their social and personal judgment is severely impaired will continue these struggles to some extent during the adult life.

METHODS OF ASSESSMENT

An interesting aspect of the severe behavioral and emotional disorders covered in this chapter is that their characteristics are diverse and do not fit neatly within the internalizing/externalizing dichotomy discussed at length in this book. For example, individuals with schizophrenia may experience characteristic private or internal events (such as various disorders of thought and sensation) while at the same time exhibiting characteristically overt and easily observed behaviors (such as psychomotor agitation or retardation, highly unusual verbal behavior, and wildly inappropriate social behavior). Combinations of internal and external behaviors are also prevalent to some extent in autism (though the internal behaviors are very difficult to assess with this disorder) and in the schizoid disorders. Thus of our five general assessment methods, there is no ''best'' choice for use in evaluating these severe disorders. The skilled clinician will likely use a carefully selected combination of the five methods, depending on the nature and severity of the specific problems in question. Thus each of the five assessment methods may potentially be a unique and valuable avenue for gathering information.

Direct Behavioral Observation

Virtually any of the direct behavioral observation methods discussed in chapter 3 may be useful in assessment of the severe disorders so long as appropriate design and methodology are employed in the development of the observation system and the selected target behaviors are relatively overt. Regarding this second prerequisite to effective observation, there is a potential problem: Particularly with schizophrenia and the schizoid disorders, many of the characteristic problem behaviors are not overt or blatant and thus may be difficult to adequately assess using direct behavioral observation alone. For example, hallucinations, delusions, odd thought processes, and a desire to avoid other persons may be extremely difficult to observe unless they are also accompanied by overt behavioral signals such as language, psychomotor agitation with explanatory language signs, or obvious social withdrawal. Thus to design an effective observational system for assessing the characteristics of schizophrenia or the schizoid disorders, the clinician must necessarily focus on the more overt aspects of these disorders, operationally define them so they can be observed and coded without question, and defer the assessment of the more internal or covert characteristics of the disorders to other methods (i.e., interviews, self-report, or rating scales completed by individuals who have observed the child over a long period of time).

Given the potential difficulties in assessing schizophrenia and the schizoid disorders through direct observation, it is not surprising that this method of assessment has been more successful and better documented in measuring the characteristics of autism and other pervasive developmental disorders. O'Leary and Johnson (1986) have noted that the target behavior approach to direct behavioral observation (i.e., concentrating on specific problem behaviors to be changed) has proven to be a reliable and useful methodology in assessing the pervasive developmental disorders in children and adolescents. The same general rules for effective observation that have already been discussed apply to measuring autism through direct behavioral observation (i.e., carefully selecting the target behaviors and an appropriate coding system). Fortunately, many of the characteristics associated with autism are overt enough to make direct behavioral observation an excellent choice as an assessment method, and there is a relatively large body of literature that has documented the reliability and validity of direct behavioral observation not only in assessing the characteristics of autism but in measuring changes occurring with intervention. Two of the standardized observation systems that have proven to be quite effective in assessing the characteristics of autism, the Autism Diagnostic Observation Schedule and the Behavior Observation Schedule, are particularly noteworthy and will be briefly discussed here.

Autism Diagnostic Observation Schedule (ADOS).   The Autism Diagnostic Observation Schedule (Lord, Rutter, Goode, Heemsbergen, Jordan, Mawhood, & Schopler, 1989) is a standardized protocol for observation of the social and communicative behavior typically associated with autism in children. The ADOS differs from most other standardized observation schedules in that it is *interactive,* requiring the observer to engage with the target child as an experimenter/participant on several standardized tasks designed to yield a better qualitative analysis of autistic behaviors than would be possible through simple observation and coding. The ADOS does not focus as much on specific autistic-type behaviors as some other observation schedules but was designed to "facilitate observation of social and communicative features specific to autism rather than those accounted for or exacerbated by severe mental retardation" (Lord et al., 1989, p. 187). Thus through its interactive nature, emphasis on examiner behavior, and qualitative focus, the ADOS allows for assessment of some of the crucial features of autism that may distinguish the disorder from other severe developmental disorders.

The ADOS consists of eight tasks that are presented to the subject by the observer within a 20–30-minute time frame. Two sets of materials are required for most tasks (a puzzle or pegboard and a set of familiar and unusual miniature figures), and the content and specific demands of these tasks can vary according to the age and developmental level of the subject. The eight tasks include construction, unstructured presentation of toys, drawing, demonstration, a poster task, a book task, conversation, and socioemotional questions. Within these tasks, 11 strands of target behaviors are coded, and general ratings are made following the interaction/observation according to a 3-point qualitative severity scale, in four different areas: reciprocal social interaction, communication/language, stereotyped/restricted behaviors, and mood and nonspecific abnormal behaviors. Reliability and validity data presented by the authors of the ADOS are encouraging and have demonstrated that the observation has adequate inter-rater and test-retest reliability, as well as discriminant validity between autistic subjects and subjects with and without other types of developmental disabilities. Although the ADOS is still new and experimental, it appears to be an observational method that may provide a rich array of information on the qualitative aspects of autism.

Behavior Observation Scale (BOS). The Behavior Observation Scale (Freeman, Ritvo, Guthrie, Schroth, & Ball, 1978; Freeman & Schroth, 1984) is a standardized observation procedure designed to provide an objective basis for measuring the behavioral characteristics of autism in children. It is currently considered to be an experimental system and is designed to be used under specific conditions. The most current version of the BOS includes a checklist of 35 behaviors intended to differentiate autistic from mentally retarded and normal children. The observation procedure occurs by observing the target child for 27 minutes (9 intervals of 3 minutes each) behind a two-way mirror. The first and last intervals serve as data baselines, while the child is presented with various stimuli during the first part of the remaining seven intervals. Each of the BOS checklist items are scored from 0 to 3 based on the frequency of the observed behaviors. The ultimate goal for the advancement of the BOS is to establish behavioral norms for normal, retarded, and autistic children and for different stages of development. Although it is still in the research-and-development phase, there is some evidence that the BOS is able to discriminate the three conditions based on objective observational criteria (Freeman & Schroth, 1984; Freeman et al., 1981; Freeman, Schroth, Ritvo, Guthrie, & Wake, 1980).

Although additional research will need to emerge before either the BOS or ADOS are developed to the point of gaining widespread use, they represent a promising and innovative methodology in the objective assessment of children with autism. Researchers desiring to utilize standardized observation schedules for use with autistic populations should consider one of these, while clinicians will probably find either of these observation systems to be interesting and informative additions to their battery of assessment methods for measuring the characteristics of autism.

Interviewing Techniques

In order to appropriately assess severe disorders of behavior and emotion, a carefully conducted interview is virtually essential. In some cases (i.e., with autistic or severely agitated psychotic subjects) the interview of necessity will have to be conducted with the parent or primary caregiver of the referred child, due to the difficulty in obtaining accurate self-report data. Harris (1987) noted that some research on clinical interviews with parents of psychotic children has shown strong convergence between the information obtained from parents and other objective sources of behavioral data. In other cases (i.e., the schizoid disorders and less aggravated cases of schizophrenia), an interview directly with the child or adolescent client may be quite useful.

Most of the interview methods mentioned in chapter 5 can be utilized at least to some extent in the assessment of autism, schizophrenia, and the schizoid disorders. The specific choice of technique will vary depending on the presenting problems exhibited by the referred child/adolescent client, his or her age level, language capability, and social maturity, as well as the availability and cooperation of a parent or primary caregiver. The parent/caregiver behavioral interview will be critically important if the child or adolescent client is not capable of engaging in a traditional interview or if the referral necessitates the immediate development of a behavioral intervention plan. Traditional unstructured types of interviews with the child or adolescent client will be of little use in these cases but may provide some additional insights in cases where psychotic features are emerging or the schizoid disorders are suspected.

Virtually any of the four structured interview schedules reviewed elsewhere in this book (K-SADS, DICA-R, CAS, and DISC) are potentially useful in assessing schizophrenia or the schizoid disorders with children and adolescent clients, particularly when a corollary parent version of the interview is available. Each of these four interview schedules consists of at least some items relevant to the severe behavioral and emotional disorders and include scoring algorithms designed to generate hypotheses about the existence of axis I and axis II disorders from the DSM. An example of the utility of one of these structured interviews in assessing and diagnosing psychotic behaviors comes from research conducted by Haley, Fine, and Marriage (1988), who compared DISC interview data from both psychotic and nonpsychotic depressed adolescent inpatients. In this case, several strands of the DISC interview data were found to discriminate between the two groups, as the psychotic group subjects were more likely to have a history of sexual abuse, more serious depression, and more symptoms of hypomanic behavior than the nonpsychotic group subjects. Other research lending support to the use of structured interviews for assessing the severe disorders comes from an epidemiological study conducted by Cohen, O'Connor, Lewis, Velez, and Noemi (1987), who found that the DISC and K-SADS both provided moderate to moderately high accuracy estimates of the prevalence of various DSM disorders.

A potential caution in conducting interviews for the assessment of severe disorders concerns making inquiries about low-frequency and bizarre symptoms such as delusions, hallucinations, thought problems, and obsessive-compulsive behaviors. Clinicians must word their questions about these areas most carefully and gauge the responses of both children and their parents with caution. Research by Breslau (1988) has helped to verify the notion that both referred children and their parents may misunderstand structured interview questions about psychotic behavior and related characteristics and may thus provide answers that lead to high false-positive errors. Her research found that subjects often misunderstand the intent of these types of questions, and when appropriate follow-up questioning is introduced, many of the positive responses to such questions are recoded as negative responses. For example, a child might respond positively to a question such as "do you ever see things that no one else can see," when he or she is thinking about seeing unique shapes in cloud formations or wallpaper designs rather than any visual hallucinations. Thus when questioning about "the bizarre," it is extremely important to follow-up on affirmative responses and to obtain specific examples.

Autism Diagnostic Interview (ADI).   In addition to the general types of interview formats already discussed, an additional standardized interview schedule is noteworthy within the context of this chapter. The Autism Diagnostic Interview (Le Couteur, Rutter, Lord, Rios, Robertson, Holdgrafer, & McLennan, 1989) is a standardized interview schedule designed to assess the critical characteristics of autism and to differentiate autism and pervasive developmental disorders from other developmental disorders such as mental retardation. The ADI was developed for use by highly trained clinicians in conducting interviews with the principal caregiver(s) of individuals who are at least five years old with a mental age of at least two years. The ADI is considered to be an *investigator-based* rather than a *respondent-based* interview, as it requires the interviewer to be familiar with the conceptual distinctions of pervasive developmental disorders and to actively structure the interview probes by providing examples and getting the interviewees to provide highly detailed qualitative information rather than simple yes/no responses.

The basic interviewing task is to obtain detailed descriptions of the actual behavior of the target subject in three general areas: reciprocal social interaction, communication and language, and repetitive, restricted, and stereotyped behaviors. The caregiver descriptions are scored according to a scale ranging from 0 to 3, where a score of 0 indicates the specified behavior is not present and 3 indicates that the behavior is present to a severe degree. Individual item scores are converted into three area scores and a total score, based on a scoring algorithm devised using the World Health Organization ICD-10 diagnostic criteria for autism. The actual length of time required for the interview will vary according to the skill of the examiner and the amount of information provided by the caregiver, but the developers of the ADI note that test interviews conducted during initial research tended to last two to three hours.

Reliability and validity research reported by the authors of the ADI are indicative of strong psychometric properties. The ADI item, area, and total scores have been shown to have good reliability (generally in the .70 range), based on agreement between raters from an experiment with 32 videotaped interviews scored by four independent raters. The ADI area scores, total scores, and most individual item scores have been shown to differentiate between autistic and mentally retarded target subjects to a significant degree, indicating that the instrument is sensitive to qualitative differences in developmental problem patterns. The ADI item scores and many of the individual items were also found to have high sensitivity and specificity properties in differentially diagnosing autism and mental retardation. Thus it can be assumed that the ADI is able to differentiate between autism and the milder developmental disorders (such as developmental delays and routine learning disabilities) quite easily.

In sum, although there are very few standardized interviews for autism, the ADI represents a very strong though preliminary step in this area. It should be seriously considered by researchers conducting epidemiological studies and by clinicians who desire a structured method of obtaining information on pervasive developmental problems from caregivers. Proper use of the ADI requires both intensive training of interviewers and a considerable amount of time to actually administer the interview, so potential users should keep these constraints in mind.

Behavior Rating Scales

Two of the general-purpose problem-behavior rating scales reviewed in chapter 4, the Child Behavior Checklist system (CBCL) and the Revised Behavior Problem Checklist (RBPCL), are both potentially very useful in screening for severe behavioral and emotional problems. Even though both of these rating scales are broad-use instruments not designed specifically for assessing autism, schizophrenia, or related problems, they contain a number of items and subscales that appear to have good utility for the assessment of the severe disorders.

The CBCL includes two cross-informant scales containing some potentially useful items in this regard. For example, the thought problems scale includes such behavioral items as "Hears sounds or voices that aren't there," "Sees things that aren't there," "Stares blankly," and "Strange behavior," which appear to be relevant to the conditions of schizophrenia and schizotypal personality disorder. The withdrawn scale includes several items that appear to be relevant to the conditions of autism and schizoid personality disorder such as "Refuses to talk," "Secretive, keeps things to self," "Withdrawn, doesn't get involved with others," and "Likes to be alone." In addition to these two scales, the social problems scale includes some items reflecting poor peer relationships, which may be an important area for assessment. Although subscale configurations of CBCL scores may have some heuristic value in decision making, caution should be used to ensure that multiple sources of data are utilized in the assessment, as these scales do not necessarily discriminate between different types of problem syndromes.

The RBPCL contains a subscale labeled psychotic behavior (PB) which includes the following items: "Expresses beliefs that are clearly untrue (delusions)," "Tells imaginary things as though true; unable to tell real from imagined," "Repeats what is said to him or her; parrots others' speech," "Expresses strange, farfetched ideas," "Incoherent speech, says same thing over and over," and "Incoherent speech; what is said doesn't make sense." The RBPCL manual suggests that some of the principal correlates of this scale include DSM-III-R psychotic diagnoses and schizoid characteristics. Data reported in the test manual also indicate that mean scores on the PB scale are significantly higher for adolescents with psychotic psychiatric diagnoses than adolescents with diagnoses of internalizing or externalizing disorders. The same cautions suggested for using the CBCL in assessing the severe disorders are warranted with the RBPCL: Individual scale scores may not always have diagnostic validity across problem conditions, and multiple data sources are always necessary.

In addition to these two general-purpose problem-behavior rating instruments, a few rating scales have been developed for use in assessing specific severe disorders. The symptom scale is one of the very few rating instruments developed specifically for use in diagnosing schizophrenia in children and adolescents. A few more rating scales have been developed specifically for use in diagnosing autism, and the Child Autism Rating Scale is representative of the best efforts to date for this purpose. These two instruments will be briefly reviewed as follows.

The Symptom Scale.   The late Sheila Cantor developed the Symptom Scale, one of the very few research-based rating instruments designed specifically for use in assessing the symptoms of schizophrenia in children and early adolescents (Cantor, 1987, 1989; Cantor, Pearce, Pezzot-Pearce, & Evans, 1981). This instrument is technically closer to being a checklist than a rating scale (see chapter 4 for a discussion on the difference between the two), as it provides a means of indicating whether or not specific symptoms are present but was not constructed to allow severity or frequency ratings of symptoms. The Symptom Checklist consists of 18 descriptors found through a review of the literature to be associated with schizophrenia in children and youth. Examples of these descriptors include "constricted affect," "perserveration," "inappropriate affect," "anxiety," "loose associations," "grimacing," and "incoherence." Each of 54 schizophrenic children and youth in a study were rated by two clinical psychologists for the presence or absence of the 18 symptoms. The population was broken into three age groups: preschool ($N = 25$), latency ($N = 15$), and adolescent ($N = 14$). Most of the symptoms were found to be present in more than 50 percent of the subjects in each group, and a few of the symptoms were found to be present in more than 50 percent of the subjects in one or two groups, but three symptoms (clang associations, echolalia, and neologisms) were found to be present in less than 50 percent of the subjects in all three groups, indicating that they had relatively poor diagnostic validity. Although the Symptom Scale was not designed to be a norm-referenced diagnostic test, it may be useful in research or in validating behavioral characteristics of schizophrenia obtained from multiple assessment data.

Childhood Autism Rating Scale (CARS).   The Childhood Autism Rating Scale (Schopler, Reichler, & Renner, 1988) is a 15-item rating scale designed to identify children with autism and to distinguish them from individuals with other types of developmental disorders. It was designed to be completed by a variety of professionals who work with children in educational, medical, or mental health settings, and it can be used with children ages two and up. The items of the CARS are rated according to a 7-point scale with a continuum of anchor points ranging from *within normal limits* to *severely abnormal.* The item content of the CARS is based on a broad view of autism from multiple diagnostic systems, including the DSM. The ratings may be based on a direct observation of child behavior within a given setting, a review of other relevant assessment data, or impressions of observations over time. After the child has been rated on each item, a total score is obtained, and these scores are classified according to the categories of nonautistic, mild to moderate autism, or severe autism. Although the CARS is not a norm-referenced test in the traditional sense, the total score classifications are based on over 1,500 cases over a several-year period.

Data reported in the CARS manual and in the professional literature (e.g., Dawson, Hill, Spencer, Galpert, & Watson, 1990; Lord & Schopler, 1989; Ozonoff, Pennington, & Rogers, 1990) indicate that the CARS has strong reliability and is valid for several purposes. Internal consistency reliability has been reported at .94, median inter-rater reliability has been found to be in the .70 range, and one-year test-retest reliability is reported to be .88. Strong correlations have been found in comparing CARS scores to subjective clinical ratings of autistic behavior, and the scale has been shown to produce similar results when completed by professionals from different disciplines evaluating the same child.

Although there are several other good rating scales for use in assessing the characteristics of autism, the CARS was selected for description in this chapter because of its long tradition, sound technical properties, ease of use, and wide availability. If the CARS is not the best rating scale for assessing autism currently available, then it is surely one of the best. Clinicians who are faced with the task of assessing a child who exhibits some or many of the characteristics of autism will find the CARS to be a useful addition to their assessment design.

Sociometric Approaches

Although sociometric approaches to assessment of the severe behavioral, social, and emotional problems have not been reported in the literature to the extent that some other uses of sociometrics have been, there is some evidence that they can be effectively used for research and screening purposes. In their excellent chapter on sociometrics, McConnell and Odom (1986) cited 20 different studies, many of them considered to be classic, which provided evidence for the predictive validity of sociometrics. Of the 20 studies, 3 were specifically designed to test sociometric assessment with schizophrenic or similar severity populations. Bower, Shelhamer, and Daily (1960) used a retrospective analysis of the social behavior of 88 adult males hospitalized for schizophrenic symptoms and found that as adolescents the subjects were rated as being less interested in girls and less liked by peers and teachers than were control subjects. Kohn and Clausen (1955) also used a retrospective sociometric assessment method with a population primarily diagnosed as having schizophrenia, but in this case, the data did not support the hypothesis that social isolation during adolescence was associated with adult schizophrenia. Pritchard and Graham (1966) used a prospective approach to analyzing sociometric data from the hospital records of 75 inpatient children in psychiatric hospitals and found that their childhood diagnoses and social behavior problems were related to later diagnoses as adults. Thus not only is there evidence that sociometric assessment can be effective with the more severe disorders, but it stands to reason that virtually any form of sociometric assessment could be useful for this purpose if the questions or activities are specifically well designed.

Perhaps the central issue in regard to sociometrics is not so much whether these procedures are effective for assessing children and adolescents with severe disorders but when they should be used. The use of sociometrics for research on severe behavioral, social, and emotional problems is an excellent avenue for adding new knowledge to the field, but perhaps clinical applications should be more circumspect in this regard. Since many of the characteristics of autism, schizophrenia, and even the schizoid disorders are quite conspicuous, these types of problems are perhaps best and more simply assessed through rating scales, direct observations, and interviews. Therefore sociometrics may be best utilized as an early screening tool for helping identify children who may be starting to develop symptoms of schizophrenia or the schizoid disorders. Since children with autism are typically identified by age three and since the characteristics of autism are normally quite blatant by the elementary school years, sociometric assessment approaches appear to have little use for this disorder.

Assessment with Self-Reports

Depending on the type of problems present, self-report tests will range in usefulness from not useful at all to somewhat useful in assessing the severe disorders of behavior and emotion. In most cases, it would be a futile effort to attempt to assess individuals with pervasive developmental disorders or severe active psychotic behavior, as the most severe manifestations of these problems will usually make the type of self-reflective contact and tasks involved in a self-report test insurmountable. For the schizoid disorders and for emerging, less active, or residual cases of schizophrenia, self-report tests may be of some use. Since there are no self-report tests that can be recommended which have been developed specifically for schizophrenia or the schizoid disorders in children and adolescents, this section will discuss the potential of the three general self-report tests reviewed in chapter 7 for these purposes.

Some of the items and cross-informant scales of the Youth Self-Report (YSR) appear to have some utility in the assessment of the schizoid-unresponsive and psychotic disorder behavioral dimensions (see Table 11.2). The thought problems and withdrawn scales appear to be of particular use in this regard. These three scales contain some items that are highly congruent with some of the characteristics of psychotic behavior and the schizoid disorders, such as "I have thoughts that other people would think are strange," "I store up things I don't need," "I see things that nobody else seems to be able to see," "I refuse to talk," "I hear things that nobody else seems to be able to hear," "I feel that others are out to get me," and "I like to be alone." As discussed in chapter 7, the YSR should be used cautiously, as it contains no controls to detect manipulation or faking, and some research has suggested that it may not effectively discriminate groups of children and adolescents with severe psychopathology (e.g., Bird et al., 1991; Thurber & Snow, 1990). Another important consideration in using the YSR is that unusual responses on some of the items on the thought problems and withdrawn scales should be followed-up with additional questioning since they are not always indicative of psychopathology. For example, it is not uncommon for adolescent respondents to endorse the item "I hear things that nobody else seems to be able to hear" when they are simply thinking of something as benign as a favorite song continually repeating in their mind, or to endorse the item "I store up things I don't need" to indicate a normal activity like collecting stickers or baseball cards.

The Millon Adolescent Personality Inventory (MAPI) may also have some potential utility in assessing the characteristics of the schizoid disorders but is probably of much less use in assessing psychotic behavior. The item content in two of the scales in the MAPI Personality Style dimension (introversive and inhibited) is somewhat congruent with some of the characteristics of schizoid personality disorder from the DSM-III-R, but there is no specific evidence as to the discriminant validity of the MAPI for this purpose. The lack of discriminant validity evidence is the major problem in general for using the MAPI in assessing the severe disorders of behavior and emotion; though it has some clinical face validity in this regard, a leap of faith is required to correlate test results with specific disorders.

The MMPI (and presumably the MMPI-A) is probably the best documented and validated self-report instrument for use in assessing the symptoms of psychotic behavior and the schizoid disorders in adolescents. As chapter 7 indicates, use of the original MMPI with adolescents has been known to produce high false-positive error rates in screening for severe psychopathology. However the use of special norms and interpretive techniques with the MMPI may greatly increase the predictive validity of test scores, and the introduction of the MMPI-A is a major positive step in self-report technology for use with adolescents.

The best guidebooks for using the MMPI and MMPI-A in assessing adolescent psychopathology are Archer's two books (1987, 1992), which go beyond a simple "cookbook" approach to test interpretation and address the critical issues of adolescent development and psychopathology vis-a-vis their performance on self-report tests. Archer has noted that although some MMPI/MMPI-A scales (most notably scale 8, schizophrenia) will produce high false-positive rates for detecting severe psychopathology with adolescents when used in isolation, screening and classification accuracy for the severe disorders can be greatly improved through carefully interpreting code types and understanding the meaning of absolute score levels on individual scales. For example, extremely high T-scores (higher than on scale 8, schizophrenia) usually are *not* indicative of psychotic behavior but commonly are reflective of intense, acute situational distress. However, extreme elevations (T-scores of 75 or higher) on scale 6, paranoia, "typically identify persons with a psychotic degree of paranoid symptomology such as paranoid schizophrenics and individuals manifesting paranoid states." Certain two-point code types may also be indicative of the types of serious psychopathology associated with psychotic behavior, most notably 6-8/8-6 (paranoia-schizophrenia), 8-9/9-8 (schizophrenia-hypomania), and 4-8/8-4 (psychopathic deviate-schizophrenia). It is interesting to note that the MMPI-A manual contains correlates of the various scales for both the normative and clinical samples and that some interesting differences between the two groups are found on items from several scales, including 4, 6, and 8. The MMPI/MMPI-A may also be very useful in assessing the schizoid disorders, although much less is known about the predictive validity of specific scores or code types for this purpose. The new MMPI-A content scales appear to hold great promise for diagnosis and classification of specific disorders in adolescents, but future research will be needed to verify this hope.

LINKING ASSESSMENT TO INTERVENTION

Virtually all of the types of information obtained in assessing autism, schizophrenia, and the schizoid disorders discussed in this chapter will have direct utility for diagnostic purposes. However whether or not assessment data are useful in intervention planning and implementation for these problems depends to a great extent on the specifics of the assessment data, the problem, and the type of intervention that is needed.

The most widely utilized and documented interventions for autism at the present time are behavioral in nature, and they tend to focus on altering either behavioral deficits (i.e., lack of communication and poor eye contact) or behavioral excesses (i.e., stereotypical behaviors such as echolalia and spinning) that tend to compound the social consequences of the disorder. Kauffman (1989) has noted that early and intensive behavioral interventions are especially critical for successful treatment of autism and that the prognosis for this disorder is not as bleak as was once thought when early interventions are successfully employed. Most of the assessment methods for gauging the characteristics of autism that have been described in this chapter are quite useful in pinpointing specific behavioral excesses and deficits that are cause for concern. Beyond that, whether or not the assessment data will be of additional use in determining specific targets for intervention will depend on how *functional* they are. By definition, functional assessment data are those pieces of information that help to identify the antecedents, consequences, and frequency or intensity of occurrence of specific target behaviors. Assessment data obtained from behavioral observation and behavioral interviews with parents or caretakers are particularly likely to be of functional use.

Linking assessment data to intervention planning in cases of schizophrenic or other psychotic disorders can be a complex challenge. Kauffman (1989) has stated that behavioral interventions have been highly successful with psychotic children in a number of research situations, but the results of these projects have not always provided direct and practical treatment implications for classroom teachers. Thus functional assessment data from observations or behavioral interviews might provide a basis for modifying the child's immediate environment to remediate specific behavioral excesses or deficits, but implementing these interventions outside of a highly controlled environment may be challenging. Smith and Belcher (1985) have noted that individuals with autism and schizophrenia often require considerable training in basic life skills such as grooming, hygiene, and community living. For identifying specific areas for these life skills interventions, the use of behavior rating scales may also prove to be useful. In many cases, effective management of schizophrenia in children and adolescents will involve medical referral and the possible use of neuroleptic (antipsychotic) medications. Medical referral and intervention are especially critical in cases where child or adolescent clients are experiencing full-blown psychotic symptoms such as hallucinations and delusions or when there is an increased probability of their doing harm to themselves or others. Rating scales, interviews, observations, and in some cases, self-report tests may all be useful for identifying the overt symptoms of schizophrenia that warrant intervention.

The schizoid disorders, like other specific disorders in the general DSM category of personality disorders, are notoriously difficult to effectively treat (Butcher, 1990). Part of the problem in linking assessment data to interventions in an effective manner in these cases in that the individuals involved are often very resistant to treatment, particularly when the treatment involves establishing a trusting relationship with a therapist in a one-on-one intervention setting. Self-report data from structured interviews and self-report tests may be useful in diagnosis but are difficult to convert to an intervention plan with the schizoid disorders. Behavioral assessment data from observations, rating scales, and behavioral interviews with parents or caregivers are potentially useful in pinpointing target behaviors for intervention and in some cases, for determining potential sources of reinforcement available within the immediate environment. Part of the clinical picture usually seen with the schizoid disorders is extremely poor social skills and peer rejection. In this regard, there is some hope that structured social skills training conducted in group settings might be an effective approach, although generalizing social skills training effects across settings and time is often difficult (Kauffman, 1989). If a child or adolescent client exhibits schizoidlike characteristics with severe social deficits and poor relationships, the assessment design could benefit from the inclusion of a specific social skills appraisal (see chapter 10), which might help in identifying distinctive clusters of social skills deficits.

CASE STUDY

This case involves the difficult problem of ruling in or ruling out a diagnosis of autism with a young child with severe developmental delays. To use this particular case study most effectively, it is recommended that you review the section on autism in this chapter and consult the complete diagnostic criteria for autistic disorder from the DSM. The major characteristics of the diagnostic criteria for autistic disorder and pervasive developmental disorder not otherwise specified from the DSM-III-R are presented below:

Background Information
C.F., a three-year-old boy (44 months) lives with his parents, fraternal twin brother, and a 17-year-old sister in a large city. C.'s father works as a computer programmer, and C.'s mother is a homemaker. Information from C.'s file indicates that with the exception of C. and his twin brother being delivered by cesarean section and C. having the umbilical chord wrapped around his

Major components of DSM-III-R diagnostic criteria for autistic disorder (Refer to the DSM-III-R for specific examples of types of impairment)

At least eight of the following sixteen items are present, these to include at least two items from A, one from B, and one from C. Criteria are considered to be met *only* if the behavior is abnormal for the person's developmental level.

A. Qualitative impairment in reciprocal social interaction manifested by the following:
   (1) marked lack of awareness of the existence or feelings of others
   (2) no or abnormal seeking of comfort at times of distress
   (3) no or impaired imitation
   (4) no or abnormal social play
   (5) gross impairment in ability to make peer friendships

B. Qualitative impairment in verbal and nonverbal communication, and in imaginative activity, as manifested by the following:
   (1) no mode of communication
   (2) markedly abnormal nonverbal communication
   (3) absence of imaginative activity
   (4) marked abnormalities in the production of speech
   (5) marked abnormalities in the form or content of speech
   (6) marked impairment in the ability to initiate or sustain a conversation with others, despite adequate speech

C. Markedly restricted repertoire of activities and interests, as manifested by the following:
   (1) stereotyped body movements
   (2) persistent preoccupation with parts of objects
   (3) marked distress over changes in trivial aspects of environment
   (4) unreasonable insistence on following routines in precise detail
   (5) markedly restricted range of interests and a preoccupation with one narrow interest

D. Onset during infancy or childhood

SOURCE: American Psychiatric Association, *Diagnostic and Statistical Manual of Mental Disorders,* revised 3rd ed. (Washington, D.C., 1987).

DSM-III-R description for diagnostic category of Pervasive Developmental Disorder Not Otherwise Specified

This category should be used when there is a qualitative impairment in the development of reciprocal social interaction and of verbal and nonverbal communication skills, but the criteria are not met for Autistic Disorder, Schizophrenia, or Schizotypal or Schizoid Personality Disorder. Some people with this diagnosis will exhibit a markedly restricted repertoire of activities and interests, but others will not.

SOURCE: American Psychiatric Association, *Diagnostic and Statistical Manual of Mental Disorders,* revised 3rd ed. (Washington, D.C., 1987), p. 39.

neck, there were no prenatal or birth abnormalities. However developmental problems were noted early on with C., and he was placed in a special education preschool at age two. The I.E.P. goals from C.'s first preschool were extremely basic, with such goal statements as "will respond to sounds," and "will make eye contact." Copies of several evaluations of C. by medical specialists were found in his file with no specific medical pathology identified. At the time of the assessment, C. was placed in a special education preschool four afternoons per week, while also receiving direct related services at home from a communication disorders specialist because of speech and language delays. His current I.E.P. goals involve increasing attending, social, and toileting skills (C. is partially toilet-trained), implementing a total communication program with three basic signs (head nods and shakes for eat, drink, and move), following one-concept commands, and improving his vocal imitation. The reason for the assessment referral was to conduct a screening to evaluate the possibility of C. having autistic disorder. The special education preschool staff members were doubtful that autism was an appropriate diagnosis for C., but they indicated he had many "autistic-like behaviors." C.'s mother was thoroughly convinced that her son was autistic, after reading volumes of literature on autism from the local public library.

Assessment Data

Previous Assessment Data. C.'s file contains results of three assessment procedures conducted by various professionals within two months prior to the current assessment. Scores from the Vineland Adaptive Behavior Scales, Classroom Edition (completed by C.'s preschool teacher) indicate that C. has significant deficits in adaptive behavior, as evident by domain standard scores on the Vineland scales (based on a mean of 100 and standard deviation of 15) as follows: communication, 52; daily living skills, 62; socialization, 53; motor skills, 63; adaptive behavior composite, 53, all of which are in the "low" adaptive level. A psychologist attempted to conduct an intellectual assessment of C. using the Stanford-Binet Intelligence Scale, Fourth Edition, but was unable to get C. to comply with the test tasks enough to render a valid score. However using an informal observation and interaction procedure with various objects aimed at eliciting specific developmental skills, the psychologist provided a "very rough estimate" of C.'s current intellectual functioning as being somewhere between 12 to 24 months, or at about 30 percent to 50 percent of his chronological age level at 44 months. An assessment report by a speech-language pathologist, who evaluated C. using the Developmental Communication Curriculum Inventory one month prior to the current evaluation, indicated that C. was functioning at the 0–12-month level in overall communication abilities, with no skills observed at the 18–36- and 30 + month levels. It was also noted that C.'s receptive skills appear to be greater than his expression communication skills.

Behavior Rating Scales. The examiner rated C. using the Child Autism Rating Scale (CARS). The ratings on this 15-point scale were made at the end of the assessment session, after the examiner had observed in C.'s preschool classroom for over two hours and had taken the opportunity to interview C.'s teacher and C.'s mother in detail. The obtained score from the CARS was in a borderline region between the nonautistic level and the mild/moderate autism level. The total score was actually in the nonautistic range but was within two points of being at the mild/moderate autism level.

Interview Data. C.'s mother and C.'s teacher were interviewed at length regarding C.'s developmental skills and behavior problems, using a combination of unstructured problem-behavior identification and developmental

Interview with C.'s Mother	Interview with C.'s Teacher
Positive Behavioral Skills	*Positive Behavioral Skills*
Seems very aware of what is going on in the home	Seems very attached to his mother
	Responds positively to two children
Has "good" receptive language skills (up to 40 words)	Can match same-color blocks
	Is "mostly" toilet trained
Seeks comfort when he is upset	Gets a drink by himself
Understands feelings of other family members	Can feed himself
	Has improved in the last five months
Developmental-Behavioral Problems	*Developmental-Behavioral Problems*
Does not play appropriately with other children	Seldom makes eye contact
	Extremely noncompliant
Constantly engages in imitation	Bangs head on floor when frustrated
Very noncompliant	Occasionally bites when frustrated
Becomes upset when daily routine changes	Uses almost no verbal language
Very little expressive language	Engages in repetitive and stereotypic play with various objects
Engages in severe tantrum behavior when upset	

history interviews. Extensive information on C. was obtained during these interviews: the key points from each interview are summarized as follows, with a breakdown of positive behavioral skills and developmental-behavioral problems:

Behavioral Observations. C. was observed for a period of approximately two hours in the preschool setting during a variety of different activities. Both interval recording and event recording observation methods were utilized. C. was observed to isolate himself socially and not seek out activities with peers, although he did smile at two different peers who approached him and talked to him, and he smiled at the observer several times during the observation period. C. did appear to relate to other people as more than objects and demonstrated a strong attachment to his mother when she arrived to pick him up at the end of the school day, by smiling and running toward her. C. produced various incomprehensible vocalizations throughout the observation period (whining, babbling, etc.) but occasionally produced a totally articulate word at an appropriate time (e.g., "please"). He engaged in occasional self-stimulatory behavior, such as banging his head on the floor, pulling his pants down, and spitting water from the drinking fountain. It was noted that C. became very stimulated by certain objects that he selected and obviously preferred, such as a can of wooden sticks, which he constantly poured out and put back in the can. He was also observed engaging in some maladaptive behaviors such as trying to eat glue, shred paper, and put scissors in his mouth. During a 30-minute observation period using partial interval recording with 20-second intervals, C. was on task during 14 percent of the intervals, while social comparison peers were on task during 72 percent of the intervals.

Questions to Consider

1. Is the information from this screening sufficient to determine whether or not C. has autistic disorder? If it is not sufficient, list other types and specific kinds of assessment data that would help provide more definitive information.

2. In terms of conducting a differential diagnosis (autistic disorder or Pervasive Developmental Disorder Not Otherwise Specified), which condition seems to be most appropriate, based only on the information provided in this case study and on the diagnostic criteria indicated in the tables on page 259?

3. Are there other dimensions or specific classification categories of disorders that should be considered as possibilities in C.'s case? If so, list them and indicate what type of additional information would be needed to rule them in or out.

4. Develop some basic intervention goals for C., linking the assessment data provided in this case study to the intervention goals as directly as possible.

5. Is there any additional developmental history or medical information on C. that would be useful in answering questions 1–3? If so, what specific kinds of developmental history or medical information would be useful?

Sources for Assessment Instruments and Systems

This appendix was prepared in order to facilitate the location of sources for assessment instruments and systems presented in the book. Within this appendix, the names of all of the assessment instruments or systems reviewed are listed, according to the breakdown between types of assessment procedures followed in the book. The instruments are listed alphabetically within each of the five divisions of assessment methods.

Two methods are utilized in listing sources. In the case of commercially marketed instruments, the names, addresses, and in some cases the phone numbers of the publishers are listed. These listings were current at the time this book was prepared, but there is no guarantee that they will remain current since publishers occasionally merge or choose to discontinue certain products. In the case of assessment instruments not commercially marketed but reported on in the professional literature, the first or prototype reference for the instrument is listed in APA reference style.

Most of the instruments discussed within the book are referenced in several or, in some cases, many places in the professional literature. To obtain information for a given instrument, note the citations in the section of the text where the instrument is introduced, and then look them up in the reference section.

BEHAVIORAL OBSERVATION CODING SYSTEMS

Autism Diagnostic Observation Schedule

Lord, C., Rutter, M., Goode, S., Heemsbergen, J., Jordan, H., Mawhood, L., & Schopler, E. (1989). Autism Diagnostic Observation Schedule: A standardized observation of communicative and social behavior. *Journal of Autism and Developmental Disorders, 19,* 185–213.

Behavioral Assertiveness Test

Eisler, R. M., Miller, P. M., & Herson, M. (1973). Components of assertive behavior. *Journal of Clinical Psychology, 29,* 295–299.

Behavioral Avoidance Test

Jersild, A. T., & Holmes, F. B. (1935). Children's fears. *Child Development Monograph, 20.*

Behavior Coding System

Harris, A. M., & Reid, J. B. (1981). The consistency of a class of coercive child behaviors across school settings for individual subjects. *Journal of Abnormal Child Psychology, 9,* 219–227.

Behavioral Observation System

Freeman, B. J., & Schroth, P. C. (1984). The development of the Behavioral Observation System (BOS) for autism. *Behavioral Assessment, 6,* 177–187.

Child Behavior Checklist-Direct Observation Form

University Associates in Psychiatry
1 South Prospect Street
Burlington, VT 05401-3456
802-656-8313

Dyadic Parent-Child Interaction Coding System

Robinson, E. A., & Eyberg, S. (1981). The dyadic parent-child interaction coding system: Standardization and validation. *Journal of Consulting and Clinical Psychology, 49,* 245–250.

Family Interaction Code

Weinrott, M. R., & Jones, R. R. (1984). Overt versus covert assessment of observer reliability. *Child Development, 55,* 1125–1137.

Social Interaction Coding System

Weinrott, M. R., & Jones, R. R. (1984). Overt versus covert assessment of observer reliability. *Child Development, 55,* 1125–1137.

Systematic Screening for Behavior Disorders Observation Procedures

Sopris West
1140 Boston Avenue
Longmont, CO 80501

Target/Peer Interaction Code

Shinn, M. R., Ramsey, E., Walker, H. M., Steiber, S., & O'Neil, R. E. (1987). Antisocial behavior in school settings: Initial difference in an at-risk and normal population. *Journal of Special Education, 21,* 69–84.

Teacher Behavior Code

Weitz, S. E. (1981). A code for assessing teaching skills of parents of developmentally disabled children. *Journal of Autism and Developmental Disorders, 12,* 13–24.

BEHAVIOR RATING SCALES

Attention Deficit Disorders Evaluation Scales

Hawthorne Educational Services
800 Gray Oak Drive
Columbia, MO 65201
314-874-1710

Child Autism Rating Scale

Western Psychological Services
12031 Wilshire Boulevard
Los Angeles, CA 90025-1251

Child Behavior Checklist and Teacher's Report Form (CBCL & TRF)

University Associates in Psychiatry
1 South Prospect Street
Burlington, VT 05401-3456
802-656-8313

Conners Rating Scales (CTRS & CPRS)

Multi-Health Systems, Inc.
908 Niagara Falls Boulevard
North Tonowanda, NY 14120-2060
800-456-3003

Eyberg Child Behavior Inventory

Boggs, S. R., Eyberg, S., & Reynolds, L. A. (1990). Concurrent validity of the Eyberg Child Behavior Inventory. *Journal of Clinical Child Psychology, 19,* 75–78.

Home Situations Questionnaire/ School Situations Questionnaire

Barkley, R. A., & Edelbrock, C. S. (1987). Assessing situational variation in children's behavior problems: The Home and School Situations Questionnaires. In R. Prinz (ed.), *Advances in behavioral assessment of children and families* (vol. 3, pp. 157–176). Greenwich, CT: JAI.

Personality Inventory for Children

Western Psychological Services
12031 Wilshire Boulevard
Los Angeles, CA 90025-1251

Revised Behavior Problem Checklist (RBPCL)

Herbert C. Quay, Ph.D.
P.O. Box 248074
Coral Gables, FL 33124

School Social Behavior Scales (SSBS)

Clinical Psychology Publishing Company
4 Conant Square
Brandon, VT 05733
800-433-8234

Social Skills Rating System (SSRS)

American Guidance Service
Publishers Building
Circle Pines, MN 55014-1796
800-328-2560

The Symptom Scale

Cantor, S. (1989). Schizophrenia. In C. G. Last & M. Herson (eds.), *Handbook of Childhood Psychiatric Diagnosis* (pp. 279–298). New York: Wiley.

Cantor, S., Pearce, J., Pezzot-Pearce, T., & Evans, J. (1981). The group of hypotonic schizophrenics. *Schizophrenia Bulletin, 7,* 1–11.

Walker-McConnell Scale of Social Competence and School Adjustment (SSCSA)

Pro-Ed
5341 Industrial Oaks Boulevard
Austin, TX 78735

INTERVIEW SCHEDULES

Autism Diagnostic Interview

Le Couteur, A., Rutter, M., Lord, C., Rios, P., Robertson, S. Holdgrafer, M., & McClenna, J. (1989). Autism Diagnostic Interview: A standardized investigator-based instrument. *Journal of Autism and Developmental Disorders, 19,* 363–387.

Child Assessment Schedule (CAS)

Hodges, K., McKnew, D., Cytryn, L., & McKnew, D. (1982). The Child Assessment Schedule (CAS) diagnostic interview: A report on reliability and validity. *Journal of the American Academy of Child Psychiatry, 10,* 173–189.

Children's Depression Rating Scale

Poznanski, E. O., Cook, S. C., & Carroll, B. J. (1979). A depression rating scale for children. *Pediatrics, 64,* 442–450.

Diagnostic Interview for Children and Adolescents-Revised (DICA-R)

Reich, W., & Welner, Z. (1989). *Diagnostic Interview for Children and Adolescents-Revised.* St. Louis: Washington University Division of Child Psychiatry.

Diagnostic Interview Schedule for Children (DISC), Version 2.3

Division of Child and Adolescent Psychiatry
New York State Psychiatric Institute
722 West 168th Street
New York, NY 10032

Schedule for Affective Disorders and Schizophrenia for School-Age Children

Puig-Antich, J., & Chambers, W. (1978). *The Schedule for Affective Disorders and Schizophrenia for School-Age Children.* New York: New York State Psychiatric Association.

Structured Clinical Interview for Children

University Associates in Psychiatry
1 South Prospect Street
Burlington, VT 05401-3456
802-656-8313

SOCIOMETRIC ASSESSMENT PROCEDURES

The Class Play

Bower, E. (1969). *Early identification of emotionally handicapped children in school* (2nd ed.). Springfield, IL: Charles C. Thomas.

Peer Nomination Inventory for Depression

Lefkowitz, M. M., & Tesiny, E. P. (1980). Assessment of childhood depression. *Journal of Consulting and Clinical Psychology, 48,* 43–50.

Picture Sociometric Technique

McAndless, B., & Marshall, H. (1957). A picture sociometric technique for preschool children and its relation to teacher judgments of friendship. *Child Development, 28,* 139–148.

Revised PRIME Guess Who Measure

Kauffman, J. M., Semmell, M. I., & Agard, J. A. (1974). PRIME: An overview. *Education and Training for the Mentally Retarded, 9,* 107–112.

Systematic Screening for Behavior Disorders

(Stage One: Teacher Ranking)
Sopris West
1140 Boston Avenue
Longmont, CO 80501

SELF-REPORT INSTRUMENTS

Bracken Multidimensional Self-Concept Scale

Pro-Ed
5431 Industrial Oaks Boulevard
Austin, TX 78735

Children's Depression Inventory (CDI)

Multi-Health Systems, Inc.
908 Niagara Falls Boulevard
North Tonowanda, NY 14120-2060
800-456-3003

Harter Self-Perception Profiles for Children and Adolescents

Susan Harter, Ph.D.
Department of Psychology
University of Denver
Denver, CO 80208

Jesness Inventory of Adolescent Personality (JIAP)

Multi-Health Systems, Inc.
908 Niagara Falls Boulevard
North Tonowanda, NY 14120-2060
800-456-3003

Millon Multiaxal Adolescent Personality Inventory (MAPI)

National Computer Systems
Professional Assessment Services
P.O. Box 1416
Minneapolis, MN 55440
800-627-7271

Minnesota Multiphasic Personality Inventory, Adolescent Version (MMPI-A)

National Computer Systems
Professional Assessment Services
P.O. Box 1416
Minneapolis, MN 55440
800-627-7271

Revised Children's Manifest Anxiety Scale (RCMAS)

Western Psychological Services
12031 Wilshire Boulevard
Los Angeles, CA 90025

Reynolds Adolescent Depression Scale (RADS)

Psychological Assessment Resources
P.O. Box 998
Odessa, FL 33556
800-331-8378

Reynolds Child Depression Scale (RCDS)

Psychological Assessment Resources
P.O. Box 998
Odessa, FL 33556
800-331-8378

Social Skills Rating System

American Guidance Service
Publishers Building
Circle Pines, MN 55014-1796
800-328-2560

State-Trait Anxiety Inventory for Children (STAIC)

Consulting Psychologists Press
P.O. Box 10096
Palo Alto, CA 94303
800-624-1765

Youth Self-Report (YSR)

University Associates in Psychiatry
1 South Prospect Street
Burlington, VT 05401-3456
802-656-8313

References

Achenbach, T. M. (1966). The classification of children's psychiatric symptoms: A factor analytic study. *Psychological Monographs, 80* (Whole no. 615).

Achenbach, T. M. (1978). The child behavior profile I: Boys aged 6–11. *Journal of Consulting and Clinical Psychology, 46,* 478–488.

Achenbach, T. M. (1982a). Assessment and taxonomy of children's behavior disorders. In B. B. Lahey & A. E. Kazdin (eds.), *Advances in Child Clinical Psychology* (vol. 5). New York: Plenum.

Achenbach, T. M. (1982b). *Developmental Psychopathology* (2nd ed.). New York: Wiley.

Achenbach, T. M. (1985). *Assessment and Taxonomy of Child and Adolescent Psychopathology.* Newbury Park, CA: Sage.

Achenbach, T. M. (1986). *Child Behavior Checklist-Direct Observation Form* (rev. ed.). Burlington, VT: University-Associates in Psychiatry.

Achenbach, T. M. (1991a). *Manual for the Child Behavior Checklist and 1991 Profile.* Burlington, VT: University of Vermont Department of Psychiatry.

Achenbach, T. M. (1991b). *Manual for the Teacher's Report Form and 1991 Profile.* Burlington, VT: University of Vermont Department of Psychiatry.

Achenbach, T. M. (1991c). *Manual for the Youth Self-Report and 1991 Profile.* Burlington, VT: University of Vermont Department of Psychiatry.

Achenbach, T. M., & Edelbrock, C. S. (1979). The child behavior profile II: Boys aged 6–12 and girls aged 6–11 and 12–16. *Journal of Consulting and Clinical Psychology, 47,* 223–233.

Achenbach, T. M., & Edelbrock, C. S. (1981). Behavior problems and competencies reported by parents of normal and disturbed children aged 14–16. *Monographs of the Society for Research in Child Development, 46,* (1, Serial No. 188).

Achenbach, T. M., & Edelbrock, C. S. (1983). Taxonomic issues in child psychopathology. In T. H. Ollendick & M. Herson (eds.), *Handbook of Child Psychopathology.* New York: Plenum.

Achenbach, T. M., & Edelbrock, C. S. (1984). Psychopathology of childhood. *Annual Review of Psychology, 35,* 227–256.

Achenbach, T. M., McConaughy, S. H., & Howell, C. T. (1987). Child/adolescent behavioral and emotional problems: Implications of cross-informant correlations for situational specificity. *Psychological Bulletin, 101,* 213–232.

Ackerson, F. (1942). *Children's Behavior Problems.* Chicago: University of Chicago Press.

Ainsworth, M. D. S. (1979). Attachment as related to mother-infant interaction. In J. S. Rosenblatt, G. A. Hinde, C. Beer, & M. Busnel (eds.), *Advances in the Study of Behavior* (vol. 9). New York: Academic Press.

Ainsworth, M. D. S., Blehar, S., Waters, E., & Walls, S. (1978). *Patterns of Attachment.* Hillsdale, NJ: Lawrence Erlbaum.

Alberto, P. A., & Troutman, A. C. (1990). *Applied Behavior Analysis for Teachers* (3rd ed.). Columbus, OH: Merrill Publishing.

Alessi, G. J. (1988). Direct observation methods for emotional/behavior problems. In E. S. Shapiro & T. R. Kratochwill (eds.), *Behavioral Assessment in Schools: Conceptual Foundations and Practical Applications* (pp. 14–75). New York: Guilford Press.

Alessi, G. J., & Kaye, J. H. (1983). *Behavior Assessment for School Psychologists.* Kent, OH: National Association of School Psychologists.

Altepeter, T. S., & Breen, M. J. (1989). The Home Situations Questionnaire (HSQ) and the School Situations Questionnaire (SSQ): Normative data and an evaluation of psychometric properties. *Journal of Psychoeducational Assessment, 7,* 312–322.

Aman, M. G. & Werry, J. S. (1984). The Revised Behavior Problem Checklist in clinic attenders and nonattenders: Age and sex differences. *Journal of Clinical Child Psychology, 13,* 237–242.

American Psychiatric Association (1987). *Diagnostic and Statistical Manual of Mental Disorders* (revised 3rd ed.). Washington, DC.

American Psychological Association (1982). *Ethical Principles of Psychologists and Code of Conduct.* Washington, DC.

Anastasi, A. (1988). *Psychological Testing* (6th ed.). New York: Macmillan.

Aragona, J. A., & Eyberg, S. M. (1981). Neglected children: Mother's report of child behavior problems and observed verbal behavior. *Child Development, 52,* 596–602.

Archer, R. P. (1987). *Using the MMPI with Adolescents.* Hillsdale, NJ: Lawrence Erlbaum.

Archer, R. P. (1988, August). *Interpreting the Adolescent MMPI.* Presented at the meeting of the American Psychological Association, Atlanta, Georgia.

Archer, R. P. (1992). *MMPI-A: Assessing Adolescent Psychopathology.* Hillsdale, NJ: Lawrence Erlbaum.

Archer, R. P., & Gordon, R. A. (1988). MMPI and Rorschach indices of schizophrenic and depressive diagnoses among adolescent inpatients. *Journal of Personality Assessment, 52,* 707–721.

Arkes, H. R. (1981). Impediments to accurate clinical judgment and possible ways to minimize their impact. *Journal of Consulting and Clinical Psychology, 49,* 323–330.

Asher, S. R. (1990). Recent advances in the study of peer rejection. In S. R. Asher & J. D. Coie (eds.), *Peer Rejection in Childhood* (pp. 3–14). New York: Cambridge University Press.

Asher, S. R., & Hymel, S. (1981). Children's social competence in peer relations: Sociometric and behavioral assessment. In J. D. Wine & M. D. Smye (eds.), *Social Competence* (pp. 125–157). New York: Guilford Press.

Asher, S. R., & Parker, J. G. (1989). Significance of peer relationship problems in childhood. In B. H. Schneider, G. Attili, J. Nadel, & R. P. Weissberg (eds.), *Social Competence in Developmental Perspective* (pp. 5–23). Boston: Kluwer Academic Publishers.

Asher, S. R., & Renshaw, P. D. (1981). Children without friends: Social knowledge and skill training. In S. R. Asher & J. M. Gottman (eds.), *The Development of Children's Friendships* (pp. 273–296). New York: Cambridge University Press.

Asher, S. R., Singleton, L. C., Tinsley, B. R., & Hymel, S. (1979). The reliability of a sociometric rating method with preschool children. *Developmental Psychology, 15,* 443–444.

Asher, S. R., & Taylor, A. R. (1981). The social outcomes of mainstreaming: Sociometric assessment and beyond. *Exceptional Children Quarterly, 1,* 13–30.

Baer, D. M. (1982). Applied behavior analysis. In G. T. Wilson & C. M. Franks (eds.), *Contemporary Behavior Therapy: Conceptual and Empirical Foundations* (pp. 277–309). New York: Guilford Press.

Baer, D. M., Wolf, M. M., & Risley, T. R. (1968). Some current dimensions of applied behavior analysis. *Journal of Applied Behavior Analysis, 1,* 91–97.

Ball, J. C. (1962). *Social Deviancy and Adolescent Personality.* Lexington: University of Kentucky Press.

Bandura, A. (1977). *Social Learning Theory.* Englewood Cliffs, NJ: Prentice-Hall.

Bandura, A. (1978). The self system in reciprocal determinism. *American Psychologist, 33,* 344–358.

Bandura, A. (1986). *Social Foundations of Thought and Action.* Englewood Cliffs, NJ: Prentice-Hall.

Barkley, R.A. (1981). *Hyperactive Children: A Handbook for Diagnosis and Treatment.* New York: Guilford Press.

Barkley, R. A. (1990). Attention deficit disorders. In M. L. Lewis & S. M. Miller (eds.), *Handbook of Developmental Psychopathology* (pp. 65–75). New York: Plenum Press.

Barkley, R. A., & Edelbrock, C. S. (1987). Assessing situational variation in children's behavior problems: The home and school situations questionnaires. In R. Prinz (ed.), *Advances in Behavioral Assessment of Children and Families* (vol. 3, pp. 157–176). Greenwich, CT: JAI.

Barkley, R. A., Karlsson, J., & Pollard, S. (1985). Effects of age on the mother-child interactions of ADD-H and normal boys. *Journal of Abnormal Child Psychology, 13,* 631–638.

Barnett, D. W., & Zucker, K. B. (1990). *The Personal and Social Assessment of Children.* Boston: Allyn and Bacon.

Barrios, B. A., & Hartmann, D. P. (1988). Fears and anxieties. In E. J. Mash & L. G. Terdal (eds.), *Behavioral Assessment of Childhood Disorders* (2nd ed., pp. 196–262). New York: Guilford Press.

Barton, E. J., & Ascione, F. R. (1984). Direct observation. In T. H. Ollendick & M. Herson (eds.), *Child Behavioral Assessment: Principles and Procedures* (pp. 166–194). New York: Pergammon Press.

Baughman, E. E., & Dahlstrom, W. G. (1968). *A Psychological Study in the Rural South.* New York: Academic Press.

Befera, M., & Barkley, R. A. (1985). Hyperactive and normal girls and boys: Mother-child interactions, parent psychiatric status, and child psychopathology. *Journal of Child Psychology and Psychiatry, 26,* 439–452.

Ben-Porath, Y. S., & Butcher, J. N. (1989). Psychometric stability of rewritten MMPI items. *Journal of Personality Assessment, 53,* 645–653.

Berg, I. A. (1967). The deviation hypothesis: A broad statement of its assumptions and postulates. In I. A. Berg (ed.), *Response Set in Personality Assessment* (pp. 146–190). Chicago: Aldine.

Berg, L., Butler, A., Hullin, R., Smith, R., & Tyrer, S. (1978). Features of children taken to juvenile court for failure to attend school. *Psychological Medicine, 9,* 477–453.

Bersoff, D. N. (1982a). The legal regulation of school psychology. In C. Reynolds & T. Gutkin (eds.), *The Handbook of School Psychology* (pp. 1043–1074). New York: Wiley.

Bersoff, D. N. (1982b). *Larry P.* and *PASE:* Judicial report cards on the validity of individual intelligence testing. In T. Kratochwill (ed.), *Advances in School Psychology* (vol. 2, pp. 61–95). Hillsdale, NJ: Lawrence Erlbaum.

Bettelheim, B. (1967). *The Empty Fortress: Infantile Autism and the Birth of the Self.* New York: Free Press.

Bierman, K. L. (1983). Cognitive development and clinical interviews with children. In B. Lahey & A. E. Kazdin (eds.), *Advances in Clinical Child Psychology* (vol. 6, pp. 217–250). New York: Plenum Press.

Bird, H. R., Gould, M. S., Rubio-Stipec, M., & Staghezza, B. M. (1991). Screening for childhood psychopathology in the community using the Child Behavior Checklist. *Journal of the American Academy of Child and Adolescent Psychiatry, 30,* 116–123.

Bloom, B. S. (1976). *Human Characteristics and School Learning.* New York: McGraw-Hill.

Blueler, M. (1978). *The Schizophrenic Disorders.* New Haven: Yale University Press.

Boggs, S. R., & Eyberg, S. (1990). Interview techniques and establishing rapport. In L. M. LaGreca (ed.), *Through the Eyes of the Child* (pp. 85–108). Boston: Allyn and Bacon.

Boggs, S. R., Eyberg, S., & Reynolds, L. A. (1990). Concurrent validity of the Eyberg Child Behavior Inventory. *Journal of Clinical Child Psychology, 19,* 75–78.

Bonney, M. E. (1943). The relative stability of social, intellectual, and academic status in grades II to IV, and the inter-relationships between these various forms of growth. *Journal of Educational Psychology, 34,* 88–102.

Bornstein, M. R., Bellack, A. S., & Herson, M. (1977). Social skills training for unassertive children: A multiple-baseline analysis. *Journal of Applied Behavior Analysis, 10,* 183–195.

Bornstein, M. R., Bellack, A. S., & Herson, M. (1980). Social skills training for highly aggressive children in an inpatient psychiatric setting. *Behavior Modification, 4,* 173–186.

Bower, E. (1969). *Early Identification of Emotionally Handicapped Children in School* (2nd ed.). Springfield, IL: Charles C. Thomas.

Bower, E. (1981). *Early Identification of Emotionally Handicapped Children in School* (3rd ed.). Springfield, IL: Charles C. Thomas.

Bower, E. M. (1982). Defining emotional disturbance. Public policy and research. *Psychology in the Schools, 19,* 55–60.

Bower, E. M., Shalhamer, T. A., & Daily, J. M. (1960). School characteristics of male adolescents who later become schizophrenics. *American Journal of Orthopsychiatry, 30,* 712–729.

Bowlby, J. (1973). *Attachment and Loss: Vol. 2: Separation.* New York: Basic Books.

Bracken, B. A. (1992). *The Multidimensional Self-Concept Scale.* Austin, TX: Pro-Ed.

Bracken, B. A., & Howell, K. K. (1991). Multidimensional self concept validation: A three instrument investigation. *Journal of Psychoeducational Assessment, 9,* 319–328.

Breen, M. J., & Altepeter, T. S. (1991). Factor structures of the Home Situations Questionnaire and the School Situations Questionnaire. *Journal of Pediatric Psychology, 16,* 59–67.

Breslau, N. (1987). Inquiring about the bizzare: False positives in Diagnostic Interview Schedule for Children (DISC) ascertainment of obsessions, compulsions, and psychotic symptoms. *Journal of the American Academy of Child and Adolescent Psychiatry, 26,* 639–644.

Bridges, L. J., Connell, J. P., & Belsky, J. (1988). Similarities and differences in infant-mother and infant-father interaction in the strange situation: A component-process analysis. *Developmental Psychology, 24,* 92–100.

Brown, F. G. (1983). *Principles of Educational and Psychological Testing* (3rd ed.). Fort Worth, TX: Holt, Rinehart, and Winston.

Bryan, T. (1974). Peer popularity of learning disabled children. *Journal of Learning Disabilities, 7,* 261–268.

Burisch, M. (1984). Approaches to personality inventory construction: A comparison of merits. *American Psychologist, 38,* 214–227.

Burke, P. & Puig-Antich, J. (1990). Psychobiology of childhood depression. In M. Lewis & S. M. Miller (eds.), *Handbook of Developmental Psychopathology* (pp. 327–339). New York: Plenum Press.

Burns, G. L., & Patterson, D. R. (1991). Factor structure of the Eyberg Child Behavior Inventory: Unidimensional or multidimensional measure of disruptive behavior? *Journal of Clinical Child Psychology, 20,* 439–444.

Burns, G. L., & Patterson, D. R., & Nussbaum, B. R. (1991). Disruptive behaviors in an outpatient pediatric population: Additional standardization data on the Eyberg Child Behavior Inventory. *Psychological Assessment, 3,* 202–207.

Butcher, J. N. (1979). *New Developments in the Use of the MMPI.* Minneapolis: University of Minnesota Press.

Butcher, J. N. (1990). *The MMPI-2 in Psychological Treatment.* New York: Oxford University Press.

Butcher, J. N., Williams, C. L., Graham, J. R., Archer, R. P., Tellegen, A., Ben-Porath, Y. S., & Kaemmer, B. (1992). *Minnesota Multiphasic Personality Inventory-Adolescent.* Minneapolis: National Computer Systems.

Campbell, S. B. (1991). Active and aggressive preschoolers. In D. Cicchetti & S. L. Toth (eds.), *Internalizing and Externalizing of Dysfunction* (pp. 57–89). Hillsdale, NJ: Lawrence Erlbaum.

Campbell, S. B., & Steinert, Y. (1978). Comparison of rating scale of child psychopathology in clinic and nonclinic samples. *Journal of Consulting and Clinical Psychology, 46,* 358–359.

Campbell, S. B., & Werry, J. S. (1986). Attention-deficit disorder (hyperactivity). In H. C. Quay & J. S. Werry (eds.), *Psychopathological Disorders of Childhood* (3rd ed., pp. 111–144). New York: Wiley.

Cantor, S. (1987). *Childhood Schizophrenia.* New York: Guilford Press.

Cantor, S. (1989). Schizophrenia. In C. G. Last & M. Herson (eds.), *Handbook of Childhood Psychiatric Diagnosis* (pp. 279–298). New York: Wiley.

Cantor, S., Pearce, J., Pezzot-Pearce, T., & Evans, J. (1981). The group of hypotonic schizophrenics. *Schizophrenia Bulletin, 7,* 1–11.

Cantwell, D. P. (1990). Depression across the early life span. In M. Lewis & S. M. Miller (eds.), *Handbook of Developmental Psychopathology* (pp. 293–309). New York: Plenum Press.

Cantwell, D. P., & Carlson, G. A. (1981, October). *Factor analysis of a self rating depressive inventory for children: Factor structure and nosological utility.* Paper presented at the annual meeting of the American Academy of Child Psychiatry, Dallas, TX.

Carlson, G. A., & Garber, J. (1986). Developmental issues in the classification of depression in children. In M. Rutter, C. E. Izard, & P. B. Read (eds.), *Depression in Young People* (pp. 399–434). New York: Guilford Press.

Cartledge, G., Frew, T., & Zacharias, J. (1985). Social skills needs of mainstreamed students: Peer and teacher perceptions. *Learning Disability Quarterly, 8,* 132–140.

Cattell, R. B., Eber, W. H., & Tatsuoka, M. M. (1970). *Handbook for the Sixteen Personality Factor Questionnaire.* Champaign, IL: Institute for Personality and Ability Testing.

Chambers, W., Puig-Antich, J. Hersche, M., Paey, P., Ambrosini, P. J., Tabrizi, M. A., & Davies, M. (1985). The assessment of affective disorders in children and adolescents by semistructured interview: Test-retest reliability of the K-SADS-P. *Archives of General Psychiatry, 42,* 696–702.

Christenson, S. L. (1990). Review of the Child Behavior Checklist. In J. J. Kramer & J. C. Conoley (eds.), *The Supplement to the Tenth Mental Measurement Yearbook* (pp. 40–41). Lincoln, NE: Buros Institute of Mental Measurements.

Cicchetti, D., & Toth, S. L. (1991). A developmental perspective on internalizing and externalizing disorders. In D. Cicchetti & S. L. Toth (eds.), *Internalizing and Externalizing Expressions of Dysfunction* (pp. 1–19). Hillsdale, NJ: Lawrence Erlbaum Associates.

Cohen, M. (1988). The revised Conners Parent Rating Scale: Factor structures with a diversified clinical sample. *Journal of Abnormal Child Psychology, 2,* 187–196.

Cohen, M., & Hynd, G. W. (1986). The Conners Teacher Rating Scale: A different factor structure with special education students. *Psychology in the Schools, 23,* 13–23.

Cohen, P., O'Connor, P., Lewis, S., Velez, C., & Noemi, S. (1987). Comparison of DISC and K-SADS-P interviews of an epidemiological sample of children. *Journal of the American Academy of Child and Adolescent Psychiatry, 26,* 662–667.

Coie, J. D., Belding, M. & Underwood, M. (1988). Aggression and peer rejection in childhood. In B. B. Lahey & A. Kazdin (eds.), *Advances in Clinical Child Psychology* (vol. 2, pp. 125–158). New York: Plenum Press.

Coie, J. D., Dodge, K. A., & Coppotelli, H. (1982). Dimensions and types of social status: A cross-age perspective. *Developmental Psychology, 18,* 557–570.

Cone, J. D. (1978). The behavioral assessment grid (BAG): A conceptual framework and taxonomy. *Behavior Therapy, 9,* 882–888.

Cone, J. D. (1981). Psychometric considerations. In M. Herson & A. S. Bellack (eds.), *Behavioral Assessment: A Practical Handbook* (pp. 36–68). New York: Pergammon.

Cone, J. E., & Hawkins, R. P. (1977). *Behavioral Assessment: New Directions in Clinical Psychology.* New York: Bruner/Mazel.

Conners, C. K. (1969). A teacher rating scale for use in drug studies with children. *American Journal of Psychiatry, 126,* 884–888.

Conners, C. K. (1990). *Conners Rating Scales Manual.* North Tonawanda, NY: Multi-Health Systems.

Conners, C. K., & Werry, J. S. (1979). Pharmacotherapy. In H. C. Quay & J. S. Werry (eds.), *Psychopathological Disorders of Childhood* (2nd ed.). New York: Wiley.

Connolly, J. (1983). A review of sociometric procedures in the assessment of social competencies in children. *Applied Research in Mental Retardation, 4,* 315–327.

Connolly, J., & Doyle, A. B. (1981). Assessment of social competence in preschoolers: Teachers versus peers. *Developmental Psychology, 17,* 451–456.

Cooper, J. (1981). *Measurement and Analysis of Behavioral Techniques* (2nd ed.). Columbus, OH: Merrill.

Coopersmith, S. (1981). *Self-Esteem Inventories.* Palo Alto, CA: Consulting Psychologists Press.

Corey, G., Corey, M. S., & Callanan, P. (1988). *Issues and Ethics in the Helping Professions* (3rd ed.). Pacific Grove, CA: Brooks-Cole.

Cormier, W. H., & Cormier, L. S. (1985). *Interviewing Strategies for Helpers* (2nd ed.). Pacific Grove, CA: Brooks-Cole.

Costello, A. J., Edelbrock, C. S., Dulcan, M. K., & Kalas, R. (1984). *Testing of the NIMH Diagnostic Interview Schedule for Children (DISC) in a clinical population* (Contract No. DB-81-0027, final report to the Center for Epidemiological Studies, National Institute of Mental Health). Pittsburgh: University of Pittsburgh Department of Psychiatry.

Costello, A. J., Edelbrock, C., Kalas, R., Kessler, M. D., & Klaric, S. H. (1982). *The NIMH Diagnostic Interview Schedule for Children.* Unpublished interview schedule, Department of Psychiatry, University of Pittsburgh.

Council for Children with Behavioral Disorders (1991). New definition of EBD proposed. *Council for Children with Behavioral Disorders Newsletter, February.* Reston, VA: Council for Exceptional Children.

Cowen, E. L., Pederson, A., Babigan, H., Izzo, L. D., & Trost, M. A. (1973). Long-term follow-up of early detected vulnerable children. *Journal of Consulting and Clinical Psychology, 41,* 438–446.

Cronbach, L. J. (1949). *Essentials of Psychological Testing.* New York: Harper and Row.

Cronbach, L. J., & Gleser, G. C. (1965). *Psychological Tests and Personnel Decisions.* Urbana: University of Illinois Press.

Cunningham, R. (1951). *Understanding Group Behavior of Boys and Girls.* New York: Bureau of Publications, Teachers College of Columbia University.

Darlington, R. B., & Bishop, C. H. (1966). Increasing test validity by considering interitem correlations. *Journal of Applied Psychology, 50,* 322–350.

Dawson, G., Hill, D., Spencer, A., Galpert, L., & Watson, L. (1990). Affective exchanges between young autistic children and their mothers. *Journal of Abnormal Child Psychology, 18,* 335–345.

Delugach, R. R., Bracken, B. A., Bracken, M. J., & Schicke, M. C. (1992). Self concept: Multidimensional construct exploration. *Psychology in the Schools, 29,* 213–223.

DeMers, S. T. (1986). Legal and ethical issues in child and adolescent personality assessment. In H. Knoff (ed.), *The Assessment of Child and Adolescent Personality* (pp. 35–55). New York: Guilford Press.

Deutsch, C. K., & Kinsbourne, M. (1990). Genetics and biochemistry in attention deficit disorder. In M. Lewis & S. M. Miller (eds.), *Handbook of Developmental Psychopathology* (pp. 93–107). New York: Plenum Press.

Dodge, K. Coie, J., & Brakke, N., (1982). Behavior patterns of socially rejected and neglected adolescents: The roles of social approach and aggression. *Journal of Abnormal Child Psychology, 10,* 389–410.

DuPaul, G. J. (1992). How to assess attention-deficit hyperactivity disorder within school settings. *School Psychology Quarterly, 7,* 61–74.

Edelbrock, C. S., & Costello, A. J. (1988). Structured psychiatric interview for children. In M. Rutter, A. H. Tuma, & I. S. Lann (eds.), *Assessment and Diagnosis in Child Psychopathology* (pp. 87–112). New York: Guilford Press.

Edelbrock, C. S., Greenbaum, R., & Conover, N. C. (1985). Reliability and concurrent relations between the teacher version of the Child Behavior Profile and the Conners Revised Teacher Rating Scale. *Journal of Abnormal Child Psychology, 13,* 295–303.

Eggers, C. (1978). Course and prognosis of childhood schizophrenia. *Journal of Autism and Childhood Schizophrenia, 8,* 21–36.

Ehrenworth, N. V., & Archer, R. P. (1985). A comparison of clinical accuracy ratings of interpretive approaches for adolescent MMPI responses. *Journal of Personality Assessment, 49,* 412–421.

Eisler, R. M., Miller, P. M., & Herson, M. (1973). Components of assertive behavior. *Journal of Clinical Psychology, 29,* 295–299.

Elliott, S. N., & Buse, R. T. (1990). Review of the Child Behavior Checklist. In J. J. Kramer & J. C. Conoley (eds.), *The Supplement to the Tenth Mental Measurements Yearbook* (pp. 41–45). Lincoln, NE: Buros Institute of Mental Measurements.

Elliott, S. N., & Gresham, F. M. (1987). Children's social skills: Assessment and classification practices. *Journal of Counseling and Development, 66,* 96–99.

Endicott, J., & Spitzer, R. L. (1978). A diagnostic interview: The Schedule for Affective Disorders and Schizophrenia. *Archives of General Psychiatry, 35,* 837–844.

Epps, S. (1985). Best practices in behavioral observation. In A. Thomas & J. Grimes (eds.), *Best Practices in School Psychology* (pp. 95–111). Washington, DC: National Association of School Psychologists.

Epstein, M. H., Cullinan, D., & Lloyd, J. W. (1986). Behavior problem patterns among the learning disabled: Ill-replication across age and sex. *Learning Disability Quarterly, 9,* 43–54.

Erikson, E. (1963). *Childhood and Society.* New York: Norton.

Erlenmeyer-Kimling, L., Kestenbaum, C., Bird, H., & Hildoff, U. (1984). Assessment of the New York High Risk Project subjects in sample A who are now clinically deviant. In N. F. Watt, E. J. Anthony, L. C. Wynne, & J. E. Rolf (eds.), *Children at High Risk of Schizophrenia.* Cambridge: Cambridge University Press.

Eyberg, S. M. (1980). Eyberg Child Behavior Inventory. *Journal of Clinical Child Psychology, 9,* 29.

Eyberg, S. M., & Matarazzo, R. G. (1980). Training parents as therapists: A comparison between individual parent-child interaction training and parent group didactic training. *Journal of Clinical Psychology, 36,* 492–499.

Eyberg, S. M., & Robinson, E. A. (1982). Conduct problem behavior: Standardization of a behavior rating scale with adolescents. *Journal of Clinical Child Psychology, 12,* 347–357.

Eyberg, S. M., & Robinson, E. A. (1983). Dyadic Parent-Child Interaction Coding System: A manual. *Psychological Documents, 13.* (Ms. No. 2582)

Farrington, D. (1978). The family backgrounds of aggressive youths. In L. A. Hersov, A. L. Berger, & D. Shaffer (eds.), *Aggression and Antisocial Behavior in Childhood and Adolescence* (pp. 73–93). London: Pergammon Press.

Federal Register, February 20, 1993, p. 7938. Invitation to comment on the regulatory definition of "serious emotional disturbance" and the use of this term in the Individuals with Disabilities Education Act.

Feldman, D., Kinnison, L., Jay, R., & Harth, R. (1983). The effects of differential labeling on professional concepts and attitudes towards the emotionally disturbed/behavioral disordered. *Behavioral Disorders, 8,* 191–198.

Finch, A. J., Saylor, C. F., & Edwards, G. L. (1985). Children's Depression Inventory: Sex and grade norms for normal children. *Journal of Consulting and Clinical Psychology, 53,* 424–425.

Fine, G. A. (1981). Friends, impression management and preadolescent behavior. In S. R. Asher & J. M. Gottman (eds.), *The Development of Children's Friendships* (pp. 29–52). New York: Cambridge University Press.

Fish, B., & Shapiro, T. (1964). A descriptive topology of children's psychiatric disorders: II: A behavioral classification. In R. L. Jenkins & J. O. Cole (eds.), *American Psychiatric Association Psychiatric Research Reports #18.* Washington, DC: American Psychiatric Association.

Fisher, P., Wicks, J., Shaffer, D., Piacentini, J., & Lapkin, J. (1992). *National Institute of Mental Health Diagnostic Interview Schedule for Children Users' Manual.* New York State Psychiatric Institute, Division of Child and Adolescent Psychiatry.

Forehand, R., & McMahon, R. J. (1981). *Helping the Noncompliant Child: A Clinician's Guide to Parent Training.* New York: Guilford Press.

Forehand, R., & Peed, S. (1979). Training parents to modify noncompliant behavior of their children. In A. J. Finch & P. C. Kendall (eds.), *Treatment and Research in Child Psychopathology* (pp. 159–184). New York: Spectrum.

Forehand, R., Peed, S., Roberts, M., McMahon, R., Griest, D., & Humphreys, L. (1978). *Coding manual for scoring mother-child interactions.* Unpublished manuscript, University of Georgia, Department of Psychology.

Forness, S. R., & Knitzer, J. (1992). A new proposed definition and terminology to replace "serious emotional disturbance" in the Individuals with Disabilities Education Act. *School Psychology Review, 21,* 12–20.

Freeman, B. J., Ritvo, E. R., Guthrie, D., Schroth, P., & Ball, J. (1978). The Behavior Observation Scale for Autism. *Journal of the American Academy of Child Psychiatry, 24,* 290–311.

Freeman, B. J., & Schroth, P. C. (1984). The development of the Behavioral Observation System (BOS) for autism. *Behavioral Assessment, 6,* 177–187.

Freeman, B. J., Schroth, P., Ritvo, E., Guthrie, D., & Wake, L. (1980). The Behavior Observation Scale for Autism (BOS): Initial results of factor analyses. *Journal of Autism and Developmental Disorders, 10,* 343–346.

Fuchs, D., & Fuchs, L. S. (1986). Test procedure bias: A meta-analysis of examiner familiarity effects. *Review of Educational Research, 56,* 243–262.

Fulkerson, S. C., & Freeman, W. M. (1980). Perceptual-motor deficiency in autistic children. *Perceptual and Motor Skills, 50,* 331–336.

Gelman, R., & Baillageon, R. (1983). A review of some Piagetian concepts. In P. H. Mussen (ed.), *Armichael's Manual of Child Psychology* (pp. 167–230). New York: Wiley.

Gettinger, M., & Kratochwill, T. R. (1987). Behavioral assessment. In C. L. Frame & J. L. Matson (eds.), *Handbook of Assessment in Childhood Psychopathology* (pp. 131–161). New York: Plenum.

Gillberg, I. C., & Gillberg, I. C. (1983). Three-year follow-up at age 10 of children with minor neurodevelopmental disorders: I Behavioural Problems. *Developmental Medicine and Child Neurology, 25,* 438–449.

Glow, R. A., Glow, P. A., & Rump, E. E. (1982). The stability of child behavior disorders: A one year test-retest study of adelaide versions of the Conners Teacher and Parent Rating Scales. *Journal of Abnormal Child Psychology, 10,* 33–60.

Goh, D. S., & Fuller, G. B. (1983). Current practices in the assessment of personality and behavior by school psychologists. *School Psychology Review, 12,* 240–243.

Goldberg, L. R. (1974). Objective diagnostic tests and measures. *Annual Review of Psychology, 25,* 343–366.

Gottesman, I. I. (1991). *Schizophrenia and Genesis: The Origins of Madness.* New York: Freeman.

Goyette, C. H., Conners, C. K., & Ulrich, R. F. (1978). Normal data on revised Conners Parent and Teachers Rating Scales. *Journal of Abnormal Child Psychology, 6,* 221–236.

Graham, J. R. (1987). *The MMPI: A Practical Guide* (2nd ed.). New York: Oxford Press.

Graham, J. R. (1990). *MMPI-2: Assessing Personality and Psychopathology.* New York: Oxford Press.

Greene, R. L. (1980). *The MMPI: An Interpretive Manual.* New York: Grune & Stratton.

Greene, R. L. (1991). *The MMPI-2/MMPI: An Interpretive Manual.* New York: Grune & Stratton.

Greenwood, C. R., Walker, H. M., Todis, N. M., & Hops, H. (1979). Selecting a cost-effective screening measure for the assessment of preschool social withdrawal. *Journal of Applied Behavior Analysis, 12,* 639–652.

Gregory, R. J. (1987). *Adult Intellectual Assessment.* Boston: Allyn and Bacon.

Gresham, F. M. (1981). Assessment of children's social skills. *Journal of School Psychology, 17,* 120–133.

Gresham, F. M. (1986). Conceptual issues in the assessment of social competence in children. In P. Strain, M. Guralnick, & H. Walker (eds.), *Children's Social Behavior; Development, Assessment, and Modification* (pp. 143–179). New York: Academic Press.

Gresham, F. M., & Davis, C. J. (1988). Behavioral interviews with parents and teachers. In E. S. Shapiro & T. R. Kratochwill (eds.), *Behavioral Assessment in Schools: Conceptual Foundations and Practical Applications* (pp. 455–493). New York: Guilford Press.

Gresham, F. M., & Elliott, S. N. (1990). *The Social Skills Rating System.* Circle Pines, MN: American Guidance.

Gresham, F. M., & Gansle, K. A. (1992). Misguided assumptions of the DSM-III-R: Implications for school psychological practice. *School Psychology Quarterly, 7,* 79–95.

Gresham, F. M., & Reschly, D. J. (1986). Social skills deficits and low peer acceptance of mainstreamed learning disabled children. *Learning Disability Quarterly, 9,* 23–32.

Gresham, F. M., & Reschly, D. J. (1987a). Dimensions of social competence: Method factors in the assessment of adaptive behavior, social skills, and peer acceptance. *Journal of School Psychology, 25,* 367–381.

Gresham, F. M., & Reschly, D. J. (1987b). Issues in the conceptualization, classification, and assessment of social skills in the mildly handicapped. In T. Kratochwill (ed.), *Advances in School Psychology* (pp. 203–264). Hillsdale, NJ: Lawrence Erlbaum.

Griest, D. L., Forehand, R., Wells, K. C., & McMahon, R. J. (1980). An examination of differences between nonclinic and behavior-problem clinic-referred children and their mothers. *Journal of Abnormal Psychology, 89,* 497–500.

Gronlund, N. E., & Linn, R. L. (1990). *Measurement and Evaluation in Teaching* (6th ed.). New York: Macmillan.

Gross, A. M. (1984). Behavioral interviewing. In T. H. Ollendick & M. Herson (eds.), *Child Behavior Assessment: Principles and Practices* (pp. 61–79). New York: Pergammon Press.

Grossman, H. J. (Ed.). (1983). *Classification in Mental Retardation.* Washington DC: American Association on Mental Deficiency.

Hagborg, W. J. (1990). The Revised Behavior Problem Checklist and severely emotionally disturbed adolescents: Relationship to intelligence, achievement, and sociometric ratings. *Journal of Abnormal Child Psychology, 18,* 47–53.

Haley, G. M., Fine, S., & Marriage, K. (1988). Psychotic features in adolescents with major depression. *Journal of the American Academy of Child and Adolescent Psychiatry, 27,* 498–493.

Harris, A. M., & Reid, J. B. (1981). The consistency of a class of coercive child behaviors across school settings for individual subjects. *Journal of Abnormal Child Psychology, 9,* 219–227.

Harris, S. L. (1987). Infantile disorders and childhood schizophrenia. In C. L. Frame & J. L. Matson (eds.), *Handbook of Assessment in Childhood Psychopathology* (pp. 323–340). New York: Plenum Press.

Harter, S. (1985a). Competence as a dimension of self-evaluation: Toward a comprehensive model of self-worth. In R. Leahy (ed.), *The Development of the Self.* New York: Academic Press.

Harter, S. (1985b). *Self-Perception Profile for Children.* Denver, CO: University of Denver, Department of Psychology.

Harter, S. (1986). Processes underlying the construct, maintenance, and enhancement of the self-concept in children. In J. Suls & A. Greenwald (eds.), *Psychological Perspectives on the Self,* (vol. 3, pp. 137–181). Hillsdale, NJ: Lawrence Erlbaum.

Harter, S. (1988). *Self-Perception Profile for Adolescents.* Denver, CO: University of Denver, Department of Psychology.

Harter, S. (1990). Issues in the assessment of the self-concept of children and adolescents. In A. M. LaGreca (ed.), *Through the Eyes of the Child* (pp. 292–325). Boston: Allyn and Bacon.

Harter, S., & Pike, R. (1984). The pictorial perceived competence scale for young children. *Child Development, 55,* 657–692.

Hartup, W. W. (1978). Peer relations and the growth of social competence. In. M. Kent & J. Rolf (eds.), *Social Competence in Children.* Hanover, NH: University Press of New England.

Hartup, W. W. (1983). Peer relations. In E. M. Hetherington (ed.), *Handbook of Child Psychology (Vol. 4): Socialization, Personality, and Social Development* (pp. 103–198). New York: Wiley.

Hase, H. D., & Goldberg, L. R. (1967). Comparative validity of differing strategies of constructing personality inventory scales. *Psychological Bulletin, 67,* 231–248.

Hathaway, S. R., & Monachesi, E. D. (1963). *Adolescent Personality and Behavior.* Minneapolis: University of Minnesota Press.

Haynes, S. N., & Wilson, C. C. (1979). *Behavioral Assessment.* San Francisco: Jossey-Bass.

Helsel, W. J., & Matson, J. L. (1984). The assessment of depression in children: The internal structure of the Child Depression Inventory. *Behavior Research and Therapy, 22,* 289–298.

Hepperlin, C. M., Stewart, G. W., & Rey, J. M. (1990). Extraction of depression scores in adolescents from a general-purpose behaviour checklist. *Journal of Affective Disorders, 18,* 105–112.

Herjanic, B., & Campbell, W. (1977). Differentiating psychiatrically disturbed children on the basis of a structured interview. *Journal of Abnormal Child Psychology, 5,* 127–134.

Herjanic, B., Herjanic, M., Brown, F., & Wheatt, T. (1975). Are children reliable reporters? *Journal of Abnormal Child Psychology, 3,* 41–48.

Herjanic, B., & Reich, W. (1982). Development of a structured psychiatric interview for children: Agreement between child and parent on individual symptoms. *Journal of Abnormal Child Psychology, 10,* 307–324.

Hetherington, E. M., & Martin, B. (1986). Family factors and psychopathology in children. In H. C. Quay & J. S. Werry (eds.), *Psychopathological Disorders of Childhood* (3rd ed., pp. 332–390). New York: Wiley.

Hinshaw, S. P. (1987). On the distinction between attentional deficits/hyperactivity and conduct problems/aggression in child psychology. *Psychological Bulletin, 101,* 443–463.

Hodges, K. (1987). Assessing children with a clinical research interview: The child assessment schedule. In R. J. Prinz (ed.), *Advances in Behavioral Assessment of Children and Families* (vol. 3, pp. 203–223). Greenwich, CT: JAI Press.

Hodges, K. (1990). Depression and anxiety in children: A comparison of self-report questionnaires to clinical interview. *Psychological Assessment, 2,* 376–381.

Hodges, K., Cools, J., & McKnew, D. (1989). Test-retest reliability of a clinical research interview for children: The Child Assessment Schedule. *Psychological Assessment: A Journal of Consulting and Clinical Psychology, 1,* 317–322.

Hodges, K., Kline, J., Barbero, G., & Flanery, R. (1985) Depressive symptoms in children with recurrent abdominal pain and in their families. *Journal of Pediatrics, 107,* 622–626.

Hodges, K., Kline, J., Barbero, G., & Woodruff, C. (1985). Anxiety in children with recurrent abdominal pain and in their parents. *Psychosomatics, 26,* 859–866.

Hodges, K., McKnew, D., Burbach, D. J., & Roebuck, L. (1987). Diagnostic concordance between the Child Assessment Schedule (CAS) and the Schedule for Affective Disorders and Schizophrenia for school-age children (K-SAD) in an outpatient sample using lay interviewers. *Journal of the American Academy of Child and Adolescent Psychiatry, 26,* 654–661.

Hodges, K., McKnew, D., Cytryn, L., & McKnew, D. (1982). The Child Assessment Schedule (CAS) diagnostic interview: A report on reliability and validity. *Journal of the American Academy of Child Psychiatry, 10,* 173–189.

Hollinger, J. D. (1987). Social skills for behaviorially disordered children as preparation for mainstreaming: Theory, practice, and new directions. *Remedial and Special Education, 11,* 139–149.

Hops, H., & Greenwood, C. R. (1981). Social skills deficits. In E. J. Mash & L. G. Terdal (eds.), *Behavioral Assessment of Childhood Disorders* (pp. 347–394). New York: Guilford Press.

Hops, H., & Lewin, L. (1984). Peer sociometric forms. In T. H. Ollendick & M. Herson (eds.), *Child Behavioral Assessment* (pp. 124–147). New York: Pergammon Press.

Howlin, P., & Rutter, M. (1987). With Berger, M., Hemsley, P., Hersov, L., & Yule, W. *Treatment of Autistic Children.* Chichester, England: Wiley.

Howlin, P., & Yule, W. (1990). Taxonomy of major disorders in childhood. In M. Lewis & S. M. Miller (eds.), *Handbook of Developmental Psychopathology* (pp. 371–383). New York: Plenum Press.

Hughes, H. M., & Haynes, S. N. (1978). Structured laboratory observation in the behavioral assessment of parent-child interactions: A methodological critique. *Behavior Therapy, 9,* 428–477.

Hughes, J. N., & Baker, D. B. (1990). *The Clinical Child Interview.* New York: Guilford Press.

Hutton, J. B., Dubes, R., & Muir, S. (1992). Assessment practices of school psychologists: Ten years later. *School Psychology Review, 21,* 271–284.

Hymel, S. & Asher, S. R. (1977, April). *Assessment and training of isolated children's social skills.* Paper presented at the biennial meeting of the Society for Research in Child Development, New Orleans (ERIC Document Reproduction Service No. ED 136 930).

Isabella, R. A., Belsky, J., & von Eyre, A. (1989). Origins of infant-mother attachment: An examination of interactional synchrony during the infant's first year. *Developmental Psychology, 25,* 12–21.

Jacob, S., & Hartshorne, T. (1991). *Ethics and Law for School Psychologists.* Brandon, VT: Clinical Psychology Publishing.

Jersild, A. T., & Homes, F. B. (1935). Children's fears. *Child Development Monograph, 20.*

Jesness, C. F. (1962). *The Jesness Inventory: Development and Validation* (Research report no. 29). Sacramento: California Youth Authority.

Jesness, C. F. (1963). *Redevelopment and Validation of the Jesness Inventory* (Research report no. 35). Sacramento: California Youth Authority.

Jesness, C. F. (1965). *The Fricot Ranch study: Outcomes with large vs. small living units in the rehabilitation of delinquents* (Research report no. 47). Sacramento: California Youth Authority.

Jesness, C. F. (1988). *Jesness Inventory of Adolescent Personality.* North Tonawanda, NY: Multi-Health Systems.

Jones, R. R., Reid, J. B., & Patterson, G. R. (1979). Naturalistic observation in clinical assessment. In P. McReynolds (ed.), *Advances in Psychological Assessment* (vol. 3, pp. 42–95). San Francisco: Jossey-Bass.

Kagan, J., Reznick, J. S., & Snidman, N. (1990). The temperamental qualities of inhibition and lack of inhibition. In M. Lewis & S. M. Miller (eds.), *Handbook of Developmental Psychopathology* (pp. 219–226). New York: Pergammon Press.

Kahn, M. W., & McFarland, J. (1973). A demographic and treatment evaluation study of institutionalized juvenile offenders. *Journal of Community Psychology, 1,* 282–284.

Kane, J. S., & Lawler, E. E. (1978). Methods of peer assessment. *Psychological Bulletin, 85,* 555–586.

Kanner, L. (1943). Autistic disturbances of severe contact. *Nervous Child, 2,* 217–250.

Kauffman, J. M. (1989). *Characteristics of Behavior Disorders of Children and Youth* (4th ed.). Columbus, OH: Merrill Publishing.

Kauffman, J. M., Semmell, M. I., & Agard, J. A. (1974). PRIME: An overview. *Education and Training for the Mentally Retarded, 9,* 107–112.

Kavan, M. G. (1990). Review of the Children's Depression Inventory. In J. J. Kramer & J. C. Conoley (eds.), *The Supplement to the Tenth Mental Measurements Yearbook* (pp. 46–48). Lincoln, NE: Buros Institute of Mental Measurements.

Kazdin, A. E. (1979). Situational specificity: The two-edged sword of behavioral assessment. *Behavioral Assessment, 1,* 57–75.

Kazdin, A. E. (1981). Behavioral observation. In M. Herson & A. S. Bellack (eds.), *Behavioral Assessment: A Practical Handbook* (pp. 101–124). New York: Pergammon Press.

Kazdin, A. E. (1982). *Single-Case Research Designs: Methods for Clinical and Applied Settings.* New York: Oxford University Press.

Kazdin, A. E. (1988). Childhood depression. In E. J. Mash & L. G. Terdal (eds.), *Behavioral Assessment of Childhood Disorders* (2nd ed., pp. 157–195). New York: Guilford Press.

Kazdin, A. E., Esveldt-Dawson, K., Unis, A. S., & Rancurello, M. D. (1983). Child and parent evaluations of depression and aggression in psychiatric inpatient children. *Journal of Abnormal Child Psychology, 11,* 401–413.

Keller, H. R. (1986). Behavioral observation approaches to assessment. In H. Knoff (ed.), *The Assessment of Child and Adolescent Personality* (pp. 353–397). New York: Guilford Press.

Kelly, E. (1986). *The differential problem sorter: Rationales, procedures, and statistical/clinical values.* Unpublished manuscript. University of Nevada at Las Vegas, Department of Educational Psychology.

Kelly, E. J. (1989). Clarifications of federal eligibility criteria for students identified as "seriously emotionally disturbed" versus exclusion for the "social maladjustment" from C.F.R. part 300.5 (i) (A–E) and (ii). *Nevada Clarifications.* Las Vegas: University of Nevada at Las Vegas, Department of Special Education.

Kendell, R. E. (1991). Relationship between the DSM-IV and the ICD 10. *Journal of Abnormal Psychology, 100,* 297–301.

Kent, R. N., & Foster, L. F. (1977). Direct observational procedures: Methodological issues in naturalistic settings. In A. R. Ciminero, K. S. Calhoun, & H. E. Adams (eds.), *Handbook of Behavioral Assessment* (pp. 279–328). New York: Wiley.

Kent, R. N., O'Leary, K. D., Diament, C., & Deitz, A. (1974). Expectation biases in observational utility of therapeutic change. *Journal of Consulting and Clinical Psychology, 42,* 774–780.

Kerr, M. M., & Nelson, C. M. (1989). *Strategies for Managing Behavior Problems in the Classroom* (2nd ed.). Columbus, OH: Merrill Publishing.

Kestenbaum, C. J., & Bird, H. R. (1978). A reliability study of the Mental Health Assessment Form for school-aged children. *Journal of the American Academy of Child Psychiatry, 7,* 338–347.

King, C., & Yount, R. D. (1982). Attentional deficits with and without hyperactivity: Peer and teacher perceptions. *Journal of Abnormal Child Psychology, 10,* 483–495.

Knoff, H. M. (1986). Identifying and classifying children and adolescents referred for personality assessment: Theories, systems, and issues. In H. M. Knoff (ed.), *The Assessment of Child and Adolescent Personality* (pp. 3–33). New York: Guilford Press.

Knoff, H. M. (1989). Review of the Personality Inventory for Children, Revised Format. In J. C. Connolly and J. C. Kramer (eds.), *The Tenth Mental Measurements Yearbook* (pp. 624–630). Lincoln, NE: Buros Institute of Mental Measurements.

Knoff, H. M. (1990). Review of the Children's Depression Inventory. In J. J. Kramer & J. C. Conoley (eds.), *The Supplement to the Tenth Mental Measurements Yearbook* (pp. 48–50). Lincoln, NE: Buros Institute of Mental Measurements.

Kohlberg, L. (1969). Stage and sequence: The cognitive-developmental approach to socialization. In D. A. Goslin (ed.), *Handbook of Socialization Theory and Research.* Chicago: Rand-McNally.

Kohn, M. L., & Clausen, J. A. (1955). Social isolation and schizophrenia. *American Sociological Review, 20,* 265–273.

Kovacs, M. (1980–81). Rating scales to assess depression in school-aged children. *Acta Paedapsychiatrica, 46,* 305–315.

Kovacs, M. (1982). *The Interview Schedule for Children (ISC).* Unpublished interview schedule, Department of Psychiatry, University of Pittsburgh.

Kovacs, M. (1983). *The Children's Depression Inventory: A self-rated depression scale for school-aged youngsters.* Unpublished test manual.

Kovacs, M. (1991). *The Children's Depression Inventory (CDI).* North Tonawanda, NY: Multi-Health Systems.

Kratochwill, T. R. (1982). Advances in behavioral assessment. In C. R. Reynolds & T. B. Gutkin (eds.), *The Handbook of School Psychology* (pp. 314–350). New York: Wiley.

Lachar, D. (1990). *Multidimensional description of child personality: A manual for the Personality Inventory for Children.* Los Angeles: Western Psychological Services.

Landau, S., & Milich, R. (1990). Assessment of children's social status and peer relations. In A. M. LaGreca (ed.), *Through the Eyes of the Child* (pp. 259–291). Boston: Allyn and Bacon.

Lanyon, R. (1984). Personality assessment. *Annual Review of Psychology, 35,* 667–701.

Lanyon, R. I., & Goldstein, L. D. (1984). *Personality Assessment* (2nd ed.). New York: Wiley.

Laughlin, F. (1954). *The Peer Status of Sixth and Seventh Grade Children.* New York: Bureau of Publications, Teachers College of Columbia University.

Le Couteur, A., Rutter, M., Lord, C., Rios, P., Robertson, S. Holdgrafer, M., & McClenna, J. (1989). Autism Diagnostic Interview: A standardized investigator-based instrument. *Journal of Autism and Developmental Disorders, 19,* 363–387.

Lefkowitz, M. M., & Tesiny, E. P. (1980). Assessment of childhood depression. *Journal of Consulting and Clinical Psychology, 48,* 43–50.

Lefkowitz, M. M., & Tesiny, E. P. (1985). Depression in children: Prevalence and correlates. *Journal of Consulting and Clinical Psychology, 53,* 647–656.

Lefkowitz, M. M., Tesiny, E. P., & Gordon, N. H. (1980). Childhood depression, family income, and locus of control. *Journal of Nervous and Mental Disease, 168,* 732–735.

Lewinsohn, P. (1974). A behavioral approach to depression. In R. Friedman & M. Katz (eds.), *The Psychology of Depression: Contemporary Theory and Research.* Washington, DC: U.S. Government Printing Office.

Lewis, M., & Miller, S. M. (1990). *Handbook of Developmental Psychopathology.* New York: Plenum Press.

Links, P. S., Boyle, M. H., & Offord, D. R. (1983). The prevalence of emotional disorders in children. *The Journal of Nervous and Mental Disease, 77*(2), 85–91.

Loeber, R. (1985a). Patterns of development of antisocial child behavior. *Annals of Child Development, 2,* 77–116.

Loeber, R. (1985b, November). The selection of target behaviors for modification in the treatment of conduct disordered children: Caretaker's preferences, key-stone behaviors, and stepping stones. In B. B. Lahey (chair), *Selection of targets for intervention for children with conduct disorder and ADD/hyperactivity.* Symposium conducted at the meeting of the Association for Advancement of Behavior Therapy, Houston.

Loeber, R., & Dishion, T. J. (1983). Early predictors of male delinquency: A review. *Psychological Bulletin, 94,* 68–99.

Loeber, R., Dishion, T. J., & Patterson, G. R. (1984). Multiple gating: A multistage assessment procedure for identifying youths at risk for delinquency. *Journal of Research in Crime and Delinquency, 21,* 7–32.

Loeber, R., & Schmaling, K. B. (1985). Empirical evidence and covert patterns of antisocial conduct problems. *Journal of Abnormal Child Psychology, 12,* 337–352.

Loney, J., & Milich, R. (1982). Hyperactivity, inattention, and aggression in clinical practice. In M. Wolrach & D. Routh (eds.), *Advances in Behavioral Pediatrics* (vol. 2, pp. 113–147). Greenwich, CT: JAI.

Lord, C., Rutter, M., Goode, S., Heemsbergen, J., Jordan, H., Mawhood, L., & Schopler, E. (1989). Autism Diagnostic Observation Schedule: A standardized observation of communicative and social behavior. *Journal of Autism and Developmental Disorders, 19,* 185–213.

Lord, C., & Shopler, E. (1989). Stability of assessment results of autistic and non-autistic language-impaired children from preschool years to early school age. *Journal of Child Psychology and Psychiatry and Allied Disciplines, 30,* 575–590.

Mack, J. (1985). An analysis of state definitions of severely emotionally disturbed children. *Policy Options Report.* Reston, VA: Council for Exceptional Children.

Margalit, M. (1983). Diagnostic application of the Conners Abbreviated Symptom Questionnaire. *Journal of Clinical Child Psychology, 12,* 355–357.

Marks, P. A., Seeman, W., & Haller, D. L. (1974). *The Actuarial Use of the MMPI with Adolescents and Adults.* Baltimore, MD: Williams & Wilkins.

Marsh, H. W. (1987). The hierarchical structure of self-concept: An application of hierarchical confirmatory factor analysis. *Journal of Educational Measurement, 24,* 17–39.

Martin, B., & Hoffman, J. A. (1990). Conduct disorders. In M. Lewis & S. M. Miller (eds.), *Handbook of Developmental Psychopathology* (pp. 109–118). New York: Plenum Press.

Martin, R. P. (1988). *Assessment of Personality and Behavior Problems.* New York: Guilford Press.

Martin, R. P., Hooper, S., & Snow, J. (1986). Behavior rating scale approaches to personality assessment in children and adolescents. In H. Knoff (ed.), *The Assessment of Child and Adolescent Personality* (pp. 309–351). New York: Guilford Press.

Maser, J. D., & Cloninger, C. R. (1990). *Comorbidity of Mood and Anxiety Disorders.* Washington, DC: American Psychiatric Press.

Mash, E. J., & Barkley, R. A. (1989). *Treatment of Childhood Disorders* (2nd ed.). New York: Guilford Press.

Masten, A. S., Morrison, P., & Pelligrini, D. S. (1985). A revised class play method of peer assessment. *Developmental Psychology, 21,* 523–533.

Mattison, R. E., Handford, H. A., Kales, H. C., & Goodman, A. L. (1990). Four-year predictive value of the Children's Depression Inventory. *Psychological Assessment, 2,* 169–174.

McAndless, B., & Marshall, H. (1957). A picture sociometric technique for preschool children and its relation to teacher judgments of friendship. *Child Development, 28,* 139–148.

McCarney, S. B. (1989a). *Attention Deficit Disorders Evaluation Scale-Home Version.* Columbia, MO: Hawthorne Educational Services.

McCarney, S. B. (1989b). *Attention Deficit Disorders Evaluation Scale-School Version.* Columbia, MO: Hawthorne Educational Services.

McConaughy, S. H., & Achenbach, T. M. (1990). *Guide for the Semistructured Clinical Interview for Children Aged 6–11.* Burlington, VT: University of Vermont, Department of Psychiatry.

McConaughy, S. H., Achenbach, T. M., & Gent, C. L. (1988). Multiaxal empirically based assessment: Parent, teacher, observational, cognitive, and personality correlates of child behavior profile types for 6- to 11-year-old boys. *Journal of Abnormal Child Psychology, 16,* 485–509.

McConnell, S. R., and Odom, S. L. (1986). Sociometrics: Peer-referenced measures and the assessment of social competence. In P. Strain, M. J. Guralnick, & H. M. Walker (eds.), *Children's Social Behavior: Development, Assessment, and Modification* (pp. 215–284). New York: Academic Press.

McKinney, J. D., & Feagans, L. (1984). Academic and behavioral characteristics of learning disabled children and average achievers: Longitudinal studies. *Learning Disability Quarterly, 7,* 251–264.

McKinney, J. D., McClure, S., & Feagans, L. (1982). Classroom behavior of learning disabled children. *Learning Disability Quarterly, 5,* 45–52.

McMahon, R. J. (1984). Behavioral checklists and rating scales. In T. H. Ollendick & M. Herson (eds.), *Child Behavioral Assessment: Principles and Practices* (pp. 80–105).

McMahon, R. J., & Forehand, R. (1984). Parent training for the noncompliant child: Treatment outcome, generalization, and adjunctive therapy procedures. In R. F. Dangel & R. A. Polster (eds.), *Parent Training: Foundations of Research and Practice* (pp. 298–328). New York: Guilford Press.

McMahon, R. J., & Forehand, R. (1988). Conduct disorders. In E. J. Mash & L. G. Terdal (eds.), *Behavioral Assessment of Childhood Disorders* (2nd ed., pp. 105–153). New York: Guilford Press.

McNamee, G. D. (1989). Language development. In J. Garbarino, F. M. Stott, & Faculty of the Erikson Institute (eds.), *What Children Can Tell Us* (pp. 67–391). San Francisco: Jossey-Bass.

McReynolds, P. (1986). History of assessment in clinical and educational settings. In R. O. Nelson & S. C. Hayes (eds.), *Conceptual Foundations of Behavioral Assessment* (pp. 42–80). New York: Guilford Press.

Meichenbaum, D., & Cameron, R. (1982). Cognitive-behavior therapy. In G. T. Wilson & C. M. Franks (eds.), *Contemporary Behavior Therapy: Conceptual and Empirical Foundations* (pp. 310–338). New York: Guilford Press.

Merrell, K. W. (1989a). Validity issues in direct behavioral observation: Applications for behavioral assessment in the classroom. *Canadian Journal of School Psychology, 5,* 57–62.

Merrell, K. W. (1989b). Concurrent relationships between two behavioral rating scales for teachers: An examination of self-control, social competence, and school behavioral adjustment. *Psychology in the Schools, 26,* 267–271.

Merrell, K. W. (1990). Teacher ratings of hyperactivity and self-control in learning disabled boys: A comparison with low achieving and average peers. *Psychology in the Schools, 27,* 289–296.

Merrell, K. W. (1991, November). *The utility of the School Social Behavior Scales in differentiating behavior disordered students from other handicapped students.* Paper presented at the TECBD Conference on Severe Behavior Disorders of Children and Youth, Tempe, AZ.

Merrell, K. W. (1993a). *The School Social Behavior Scales*. Brandon, VT: Clinical Psychology Publishing Company.

Merrell, K. W. (1993b). Using behavior rating scales to assess social skills and antisocial behavior in school settings: Development of the School Social Behavior scales. *School Psychology Review, 22,* 115–133.

Merrell, K. W., & Gill, S. J. (in press). Social and behavioral characteristics of gifted students: A comparative study. *Roeper Review.*

Merrell, K. W., Merz, J. N., Johnson, E. R., & Ring, E. N. (1992). Social competence of mildly handicapped and low-achieving students: A comparative study. *School Psychology Review, 21,* 125–137.

Merrell, K. W., & Shinn, M. R. (1990). Critical variables in the learning disabilities identification process. *School Psychology Review, 19,* 74–82.

Messick, S. (1965). Personality measurement and the ethics of assessment. *American Psychologist, 35,* 1012–1027.

Milich, R., & Landau, S. (1984). A comparison of the social status and social behavior of aggressive and aggressive/withdrawn boys. *Journal of Abnormal Child Psychology, 12,* 277–278.

Miller, S. M., Birnbaum, A. & Durbin, D. (1990). Etiologic perspectives on depression in childhood. In M. Lewis & S. M. Miller (eds.), *Handbook of Developmental Psychopathology* (pp. 311–325). New York: Plenum Press.

Miller, S. M., Boyer, B. A., & Rodoletz, M. (1990). Anxiety in children. In M. Lewis & S. M. Miler (eds.), *Handbook of Developmental Psychopathology* (pp. 191–207). New York: Plenum Press.

Millon, R. (1969). *Modern Psychopathology: A Biosocial Approach to Maladaptive Learning and Functioning.* Philadelphia: W. B. Saunders.

Millon, T. (1981). *Disorders of Personality: DSM-III, Axis II.* New York: Wiley.

Millon, T., Green, C. J., & Meagher, R. B. Jr. (1982). *Millon Multiaxal Personality Inventory.* Minneapolis: National Computer Systems.

Mooney, K. C. (1984). The Jesness Inventory. In D. J. Keyser & R. C. Sweetland (eds.), *Test Critiques* (vol. 1, pp. 381–393). Kansas City, MO: Test Corporation of America.

Moreno, J. L. (1934). *Who Shall Survive?* Washington, DC: Nervous and Mental Disease Publishing.

Morris, R. J., & Kratochwill, T. R. (1983). *Treating Children's Fears and Phobias: A Behavioral Approach.* New York: Pergammon Press.

National Association of School Psychologists (1984). *Standards for the Provision of School Psychological Services.* Washington, DC: Author.

Nelson, C. M., Rutherford, R. B., Center, D. B., & Walker, H. M. (1991). Do public schools have an obligation to serve troubled children and youth? *Exceptional Children, 57,* 406–415.

Nuttall, E. V., DeLeon, B., & Valle, M. (1990). Best practices in considering cultural factors. In A. Thomas & J. Grimes (eds.) *Best Practices in School psychology-II* (pp. 219–234). Washington DC: National Association of School Psychologists.

Oden, S. L., & Asher, S. R. (1977). Coaching children in social skills for friendship making. *Child Development, 48,* 496–506.

O'Gorman, G. (1970). *The Nature of Childhood Autism* (2nd ed.). London: Butterworths.

O'Leary, K. D., & Johnson, S. B. (1986). Assessment and assessment of change. In H. C. Quay & J. S. Werry (eds.), *Psychopathological Disorders of Childhood* (3rd ed., pp. 423–454). New York: Wiley.

Olweus, D. (1979). Stability of aggressive reaction patterns in males: A review. *Psychological Bulletin, 86,* 852–875.

Ornitz, E. M. (1989). Autism. In C. G. Last & M. Hersen (eds.), *Handbook of Child Psychiatric Diagnosis* (pp. 233–278). New York: Wiley.

Overaschel, H., Puig-Antich, J., Chambers, W., Tabrizi, M. A., & Johnson, R., (1982). Retrospective assessment of prepubertal major depression with the Kiddie-SADS-E. *Journal of the American Academy of Child Psychiatry, 21,* 392–397.

Ozonoff, S., Penington, B. F., & Rogers, J. (1990). Are there emotion perception deficits in young autistic children? *Journal of Child Psychology and Psychiatry, 31,* 341–361.

Paget, K. D., & Reynolds, C. R. (1982, August). *Factorial invariance of the Revised Children's Manifest Anxiety Scale with learning disabled children.* Paper presented at the annual meeting of the American Psychological Association, Washington, DC.

Park, H. S., Tappe, P., Carmeto, R., & Gaylord-Ross, R. (1990). Social support and quality of life for learning disabled and mildly retarded youth in transition., In R. Gaylord-Ross, S. Siegel, H. S. Park, S. Sacks, & L. Goetz (eds.), *Readings in Ecosocial Development* (pp. 293–328). San Francisco: Department of Special Education, San Francisco State University.

Parker, J. G., & Asher, S. R. (1987). Peer relations and later personal development: Are low-accepted children "at-risk"? *Psychological Bulletin, 102,* 357–389.

Paternite, C., & Loney, J. (1980). Childhood hyperkinesis: Relationships between symptomatology and home environment. In C. K. Whalen & B. Henker (eds.), *Hyperactive children: The Social Ecology of Identification and Treatment* (pp. 105–141). New York: Academic Press.

Patterson, G. R. (1969). Behavioral techniques based upon social learning: An additional base for developing behavior modification technologies. In C. M. Franks (ed.), *Behavior Therapy: Appraisal and Status* (pp. 341–374). New York: McGraw-Hill.

Patterson, G. R. (1976). The aggressive child: Victim and architect of a coercive system. In E. Mash, L. Hammerlynck, & L. Handy (eds.), *Behavior Modification in Families: I Theory and Research* (pp. 267–316). New York: Bruner/Mazel.

Patterson, G. R. (1982). *Coercive Family Process.* Eugene, OR: Castalia.

Patterson, G. R. (1984). The contribution of siblings to training for fighting: A microsocial analysis. In J. Block, D. Olweus, & M. Radke-Yarrow (eds.), *Development of Antisocial and Prosocial Behavior.* New York: Academic Press.

Patterson, G. R., & Bank, L. (1986). Bootstrapping your way in the nomological thicket. *Behavioral Assessment, 8,* 49–73.

Patterson, G. R., & Dishion, T. J. (1985). Contributions of families and peers to delinquency. *Criminology, 23,* 63–79.

Patterson, G. R., Ray, R. S., Shaw, D. A., & Cobb, J. A. (1969). *Manual for Coding of Family Interactions.* New York: Microfiche Publications.

Peacock Hill Working Group (1991). Problems and promises in special education and related services for children and youth with emotional or behavioral disorders. *Behavioral Disorders, 16,* 299–313.

Peed, S., Roberts, M., & Forehand, R. (1977). Evaluation of the effectiveness of a standardized parent training program in altering the interaction of mothers and their noncompliant children. *Behavior Modification, 1,* 323–350.

Pekarik, E. Prinz, R., Liebert, D., Weintraub, S., & Neale, J. (1976). The pupil evaluation inventory: A sociometric technique for assessing children's social behavior. *Journal of Abnormal Child Psychology, 4,* 83–97.

Piaget, J. (1983). Piaget's theory. In P. H. Mussen (ed.), *Handbook of Child Psychology* (vol. 1). New York: Wiley.

Piers, E., & Harris, D. (1969). *The Piers-Harris Self-Concept Scale.* Nashville, TN: Counselor Recordings and Tests.

Pilkington, C. L., & Piersel, W. C. (1991). School phobia: A critical analysis of the separation anxiety theory and an alterative conceptualization. *Psychology in the Schools, 28,* 290–303.

Plomin, R., Nitz, K., & Rowe, D. C. (1990). Behavioral genetics and aggressive behavior in childhood. In M. Lewis & S. M. Miller (eds.), *Handbook of Developmental Psychopathology* (pp. 119–133). New York: Plenum Press.

Pollard, S., Ward, E. M., & Barkley, R. A. (1983). The effects of parent training and Ritalin on the parent-child interactions of hyperactive boys. *Child and Family Behavior Therapy, 5,* 51–69.

Poznanski, E. O., Cook, S. C., & Carroll, B. J. (1979). A depression rating scale for children. *Pediatrics, 64,* 442–450.

Poznanski, E. O., Cook, S. C., Carroll, B. J., & Corzo, H. (1983). Use of the Children's Depression Rating Scale in an inpatient psychiatric population. *Journal of Clinical Psychiatry, 44,* 200–203.

Poznanski, E. O., Grossman, J. A., Buchsbaum, Y., Benegas, M., Freeman, L., & Gibbons, R. (1984). Preliminary studies of the reliability and validity of the Children's Depression Rating Scale. *Journal of the American Academy of Child Psychiatry, 23,* 191–197.

Prior, M., Boulton, D., Gajzago, C., & Perry, D. (1975). The classification of childhood psychosis by numerical taxonomy. *Journal of Child Psychology and Psychiatry, 16,* 321–330.

Prior, M., & Werry, J. S. (1986). Autism, schizophrenia, and allied disorders. In H. C. Quay & J. S. Werry (eds.), *Psychopathological Disorders of Childhood* (3rd ed., pp. 156–210). New York: Wiley.

Pritchard, M., & Graham, P. (1966). An investigation of a group of patients who have attended both the child and adult departments of the same psychiatric hospital. *British Journal of Psychiatry, 112,* 603–612.

Puig-Antich, J., & Chambers, W. (1978). *The Schedule for Affective Disorders and Schizophrenia for School-age Children.* New York: New York State Psychiatric Association.

Pullatz, M., & Dunn, S. E. (1990). The importance of peer relations. In M. Lewis & S. M. Miller (eds.), *Handbook of Developmental Psychopathology* (pp. 227–236). New York: Pergammon Press.

Quay, H. C. (1975). Classification in the treatment of delinquency and antisocial behavior. In N. Hobbs (ed.), *Issues in the Classification of Children* (vol. 1). San Francisco: Jossey-Bass.

Quay, H. C. (1977). Measuring dimensions of deviant behavior: the Behavior Problem Checklist. *Journal of Abnormal Child Psychology, 5,* 277–289.

Quay, H. C. (1986a). Classification. In H. C. Quay & J. S. Werry (eds.), *Psychopathological Disorders of Childhood* (3rd ed., pp. 1–34). New York: Wiley.

Quay, H. C. (1986b). Conduct disorders. In H. C. Quay & J. S. Werry (eds.), *Psychopathological Disorders of Childhood* (3rd ed., pp. 35–72). New York: Wiley.

Quay, H. C., & Peterson, D. R. (1967). *Manual for the Behavior Problem Checklist.* Coral Gables, FL: Author.

Quay, H. C., & Peterson, D. R. (1987). *Manual for the Behavior Problem Checklist.* Coral Gables, FL: Author.

Quay, H. C., & Werry, J. S. (1986). *Psychopathological Disorders of Childhood* (3rd ed.). New York: Wiley.

Reich, W., & Welner, Z. (1989). *Diagnostic Interview for Children and Adolescents—Revised.* St. Louis: Washington University, Division of Child Psychiatry.

Reid, J. B. (1982). Observer training in naturalistic research. In D. P. Hartmann (ed.), *Using Observers to Study Behavior* (pp. 37–50). San Francisco: Jossey-Bass.

Reid, J. B., Baldwin, D. B., Patterson, G. R., & Dishion, T. J. (1988). Observations in the assessment of childhood disorders. In M. Rutter, A. H. Tuma, & I. S. Lann (eds.), *Assessment and Diagnosis of Child Psychopathology* (pp. 156–195). New York: Guilford Press.

Reilley, R. R. (1988). Using the Minnesota Multiphasic Personality Inventory (MMPI) with adolescents. In C. R. Reynolds & R. W. Kamphaus (eds.), *Handbook of Psychological and Educational Assessment of Children, Volume II* (pp. 324–342). New York: Guilford Press.

Reschly, D. J. (1990). Best practices in adaptive behavior. In A. Thomas & J. Grimes (eds.), *Best Practices in School Psychology-II* (pp. 29–42). Washington, DC: National Association of School Psychologists.

Reynolds, C. R. (1981). Long-term stability of scores on the Revised Children's Manifest Anxiety Scale. *Perceptual and Motor Skills, 53,* 702.

Reynolds, C. R., & Bradley, M. (1983). Emotional stability of intellectually superior children versus nongifted peers as estimated by chronic anxiety levels. *School Psychology Review, 12,* 190–193.

Reynolds, C. R., Bradley, M., & Steele, C. (1980). Preliminary norms and technical data for use of the Revised Children's Manifest Anxiety Scale with kindergarten children. *Psychology in the Schools, 17,* 163–167.

Reynolds, C. R., & Paget, K. D. (1981). Factor analysis of the Revised Children's Manifest Anxiety Scale for blacks, whites, males and females with a national normative sample. *Journal of Consulting and Clinical Psychology, 49,* 352–359.

Reynolds, C. R., & Paget, K. D. (1983). National normative and reliability data for the Children's Manifest Anxiety Scale. *School Psychology Review, 12,* 324–336.

Reynolds, C. R., & Richmond, B. O. (1985). *Revised Children's Manifest Anxiety Scale.* Los Angeles: Western Psychological Services.

Reynolds, W. M. (1986). *Reynolds Adolescent Depression Scale.* Odessa, FL: Psychological Assessment Resources.

Reynolds, W. M. (1989). *Reynolds Child Depression Scale.* Odessa, FL: Psychological Assessment Resources.

Reynolds, W. M. (1992). *Internalizing Disorders in Children and Adolescents.* New York: Wiley.

Rhone, L. M. (1986). Measurement of test anxiety among selected black adolescents: Appropriateness of four anxiety scales. *Journal of School Psychology, 24,* 313–319.

Roberts, G., Schmitz, K., Pinto, J., & Cain, S. (1990). The MMPI and Jesness Inventory as measures of effectiveness on an inpatient conduct disorders treatment unit. *Adolescence, 25,* 989–996.

Robins, L. N. (1966). *Deviant Children Grow Up.* Baltimore: Williams & Wilkins.

Robins, L. N. (1974). *The Vietnam Drug User Returns.* (Special Action Monograph, Series A, No. 2). Washington, DC: U.S. Government Printing Office.

Robins, L., Helzer, J. E., Croughan, J., & Radcliff, K. S., (1981). National Institute of Health Diagnostic Interview Schedule: Its history, characteristics, and validity. *Archives of General Psychiatry, 38,* 381–389.

Robinson, E. A., & Eyberg, S. (1981). The dyadic parent-child interaction coding system: Standardization and validation. *Journal of Consulting and Clinical Psychology, 49,* 245–250.

Robinson, E. A., Eyberg, S. M., & Ross, A. W. (1980). The standardization of an inventory of child conduct problem behaviors. *Journal of Clinical Child Psychology, 9,* 22–49.

Roff, M. (1961). Childhood social interactions and young adult bad conduct. *Journal of Abnormal Social Psychology, 63,* 333–337.

Roff, M. (1963). Childhood social interactions and young adult psychosis. *Journal of Clinical Psychology, 19,* 152–157.

Roff, M., & Sells, S. (1968). Juvenile delinquency in relation to peer acceptance-rejection and sociometric status. *Psychology in the Schools, 5,* 3–18.

Roff, M., Sells, B., & Golden, M. (1972). *Social Adjustment and Personality Development in Children.* Minneapolis: University of Minnesota Press.

Rogers, C. (1951). *Client-Centered therapy.* Boston: Houghton-Mifflin.

Rogers, C., Gendlin, E., Kiesler, D., & Truax, C. (1967). *The Therapeutic Relationship and Its Impact: A Study of Psychotherapy with Schizophrenics.* Madison: University of Wisconsin Press.

Rothstein, L. F. (1990). *Special Education Law.* New York: Longman.

Rutter, M., Graham, P., Chadwick, O. F. D., & Yule, W. (1976). Adolescent turmoil: Fact or fiction? *Journal of Child Psychology, 17,* 35–56.

Safer, D. J., & Allen, R. P. (1976). *Hyperactive Children: Diagnosis and Management.* Baltimore: University Park Press.

Salvia, J., & Hughes, C. (1990). *Curriculum-based Assessment: Testing What Is Taught.* New York: Macmillan.

Salvia, J., & Ysseldyke, J. E. (1991). *Assessment* (5th ed.). Boston: Houghton-Mifflin.

Sandoval, J. (1981). Format effects in two teacher rating scales of hyperactivity. *Journal of Abnormal Child Psychology, 9,* 203–218.

Sartorius, N. (1988). International perspectives of psychiatric classification. *British Journal of Psychiatry, 152* (suppl. 1), 9–14.

Sater, G. M., & French, D. C. (1989). A comparison of the social competencies of learning disabled and low-achieving elementary-age children. *The Journal of Special Education, 23,* 29–42.

Sattler, J. M. (1988). *Assessment of Children* (3rd ed.). San Diego: Jerome M. Sattler, Publisher.

Seligman, M. (1974). Learned helplessness and depression. In R. Friedman & M. Katz (eds.), *The Psychology of Depression: Contemporary Theory and Research.* Washington, DC: U.S. Government Printing House.

Serbin, L. A., Lyons, J. A., Marchessault, K., Schwartzman, A. E., & Ledingham, J. E. (1987). Observational validation of a peer nomination technique for identifying aggressive, withdrawn, and aggressive/withdrawn children. *Journal of Consulting and Clinical Psychology, 55,* 109–110.

Shapiro, E. S., & Skinner, C. H. (1990). Best practices in observation and ecological assessment. In A. Thomas & J. Grimes (eds.), *Best Practices in School Psychology-II* (pp. 507–518). Washington, DC: National Association of School Psychologists.

Shark, M. L., & Handel, P. J. (1977). Reliability and validity of the Jesness Inventory: A caution. *Journal of Consulting and Clinical Psychology, 45,* 692–695.

Shinn, M. R., Ramsey, E., Walker, H. M., Steiber, S., & O'Neil, R. E. (1987). Antisocial behavior in school settings: Initial differences in an at-risk and normal population. *Journal of Special Education, 21,* 69–84.

Shivrattan, J. L. (1988). Social interactional training and incarcerated juvenile delinquents. *Canadian Journal of Criminology, 30,* 145–163.

Shopler, E., Reichler, R. J., & Renner, R. R. (1988). *Child Autism Rating Scale.* Los Angeles: Western Psychological Services.

Slenkovitch, J. (1983). *P. L. 94-142 as applied to DSM-II diagnoses: An analysis of DSM-III diagnoses via-a-vis special education law.* Cupertino, CA: Kinghorn Press.

Smetana, J. G. (1990). Morality and conduct disorders. In M. Lewis & S. M. Miller (eds.), *Handbook of Developmental Psychopathology* (pp. 157–179). New York: Plenum Press.

Smith, M. D., & Belcher, R. (1985). Teaching life skills to adults disabled by autism. *Journal of Autism and Developmental Disorders, 15,* 163–175.

Speilberger, C. D. (1966). Theory and research on anxiety. In C. D. Speilberger (ed.), *Anxiety and Behavior* (pp. 3–22). New York: Academic Press.

Speilberger, C. D. (1972). Current trends in theory and research on anxiety. In C. D. Speilberger (ed.), *Anxiety: Current Trends in theory and Research* (vol. 1, pp. 3–19). New York: Academic Press.

Speilberger, C. D. (1973). *State-Trait Anxiety Inventory for Children.* Palo Alto, CA: Consulting Psychologists Press.

Speilberger, C. D., Gorsuch, R. L., & Luchene, R. E. (1970). *State-Trait Anxiety Inventory.* Palo Alto, CA: Consulting Psychologists Press.

Spitzer, R. E. (1991) An outsider-insider's view about revising the DSMs. *Journal of Abnormal Psychology, 100,* 294–296.

Sroufe, L. A., & Rutter, M. (1984). The domain of developmental psychopathology. *Child Development, 55,* 17–29.

Stokes, T. F., Baer, D. M., & Jackson, R. L. (1974). Programming among the generalization of a greeting response in four retarded children. *Journal of Applied Behavior Analysis, 7,* 599–610.

Stumme, V. S., Gresham, F. M., & Scott, N. A. (1982). Validity of social behavior assessment in discriminating emotionally disabled and nonhandicapped students. *Journal of Behavioral Assessment, 4,* 327–341.

Sue, D. W., & Sue, D. (1990). *Counseling the Culturally Different* (2nd ed.). New York: Wiley.

Taba, H., Brady, E. H., Robinson, J. T., & Vickery, W. E. (1951). *Diagnosing Human Relations Needs.* Washington, DC: American Council on Education.

Tesiny, E. P., & Lefkowitz, M. M. (1982). Childhood depression: A 6-month follow-up study. *Journal of Consulting and Clinical Psychology, 50,* 778–780.

Thurber, S., & Snow, M. (1990). Assessment of adolescent psychopathology: Comparison of mother and daughter perspectives. *Journal of Clinical Child Psychology, 19,* 249–253.

Todis, B., Severson, H., & Walker, H. M. (1990). The critical events scale: Behavioral profiles of students with externalizing and internalizing behavior disorders. *Behavioral Disorders, 15,* 75–86.

Trites, R. L., Blouin, A. G., & Laprade, K. (1982). Factor analysis of the Conners Teacher Rating Scale based on a large normative sample. *Journal of Consulting and Clinical Psychology, 50,* 615–623.

Ullman, C. A. (1957). Teachers, peers, and tests as predictors of adjustment. *Journal of Educational Psychology, 48,* 257–267.

Vaughn, S. (1987). TLC—Teaching, learning, and caring: Teaching interpersonal problem-solving skills to behaviorally disordered adolescents. *The Pointer, 31,* 25–30.

Veldman, D. J., & Sheffield, J. R., (1979). The scaling of sociometric nominations. *Educational and Psychological Measurement, 39,* 99–106.

Victor, J. B., & Halverson, C. F. (1976). Behavior problems in elementary school children: A follow-up study. *Journal of Abnormal Child Psychology, 4,* 17–29.

Wahler, R. G. (1975). Some structural aspects of deviant child behavior. *Journal of Applied Behavior Analysis, 8,* 27–42.

Wahler, R. G., & Cormier, W. H. (1970). The ecological interview: A first step in out-patient child behavior therapy. *Journal of Behavior Therapy and Experimental Psychiatry, 1,* 279–289.

Walker, H. M. (1982). Assessment of behavioral disorders in school settings: Outcomes, issues, and recommendations. In M. M. Noel & N. G. Haring (eds.), *Progress or Change:*

Issues in Educating the Emotionally Disturbed: Vol. 1. Identification and Program Planning (pp. 11–42). Seattle: University of Washington Press.

Walker, H. M. (1983). Assessment of behavior disorders in the school setting: Issues, problems, and strategies. In M. Noel & N. Haring (eds.), *Progress or Change? Issues in Educating the Mildly Emotionally Disturbed*. PDAS and USOSE Monograph Series.

Walker, H. M., & Hops, H. (1976). Increasing academic achievement by reinforcing direct academic performance and/or facilitating nonacademic responses. *Journal of Education Psychology, 68,* 218–225.

Walker, H. M., & McConnell, S. R. (1988). *The Walker-McConnell Scale of Social Competence and School Adjustment*. Austin, TX: Pro-Ed.

Walker, H. M., & Severson, H. (1992). *Systematic Screening for Behavior Disorders* (2nd ed.). Longmont, Co: Sopris West.

Walker, H. M., Severson, H., Stiller, B., Williams, G., Haring, N., Shinn, M., & Todis, B. (1988). Systematic screening of pupils in the elementary-age range at risk for behavior disorders: Development and trial testing of a multiple-gating model. *Remedial and Special Education, 9,* 8–14.

Walker, H. M., Severson, H., Todis, B., Block-Pedego, A. Williams, G., Haring, N., & Barckley, M. (1990). Systematic screening for behavior disorders (SSBD): Further validation, replication, and normative data. *Remedial and Special Education, 11,* 32–46.

Walker, H. M., Shinn, M. R., O'Neill, R. E., & Ramsey, E. (1987). A longitudinal assessment of the development of antisocial behavior in boys: Rationale, methodology, and first year results. *Remedial and Special Education, 8,* 7–16.

Walker, H. M., Steiber, S., & Eisert, D. (1991). Teacher ratings of adolescent social skills: Psychometric characteristics and factorial replicability. *School Psychology Review, 20,* 301–314.

Walker, H. M., Steiber, S., & O'Neil, R. E. (in press). Middle school behavioral profiles of antisocial and at-risk control boys: Descriptive and predictive outcomes. *Exceptionality.*

Walker, H. M., Steiber, S., Ramsey, E., & O'Neil, R. (in press). Arrest rate as predicted by measures of fifteen grade school adjustment: A longitudinal study of antisocial boys. *Exceptional Children.*

Walker, H. M., Todis, B., Holmes, D., & Horton, G. (1988). *The Walker Social Skills Curriculum: The ACCESS Program (Adolescent Curriculum for Communication and Effective Social Skills)*. Austin, TX: Pro-Ed.

Webster-Stratton, C. (1984). Randomized trial of two parent-training programs for families with conduct disordered children. *Journal of Consulting and Clinical Psychology, 52,* 666–678.

Weinrott, M. R., & Jones, R. R. (1984). Overt versus covert assessment of observer reliability. *Child Development, 55,* 1125–1137.

Weinstein, S. R., Noam, G. G., Grimes, K., & Stone, K. (1990). Convergence of DSM-III diagnoses and self-reported symptoms in child and adolescent inpatients. *Journal of the American Academy of Child and Adolescent Psychiatry, 29,* 627–634.

Weiss, G. (1983). Long-term outcome: Findings, concepts, and practical implications. *Developmental Neuropsychiatry*. New York: Guilford Press.

Weiss, G., Hechtman, L., Perlman, T., Hopkins, J., & Wener, A. (1979). Hyperactive children as young adults: A controlled prospective 10-year follow-up of the psychiatric status of 75 hyperactive children. *Archives of General Psychiatry, 36,* 675–681.

Weitz, S. E. (1981). A code for assessing teaching skills of parents of developmentally disabled children. *Journal of Autism and Developmental Disorders, 12,* 13–24.

Werry, J. S. (1986). Biological factors. In H. C. Quay & J. S. Werry (eds.), *Psychopathological Disorders of Childhood* (vol. 3, pp. 294–331). New York: Wiley.

West, D. J., & Farrington, D. P. (1973). *Who Becomes Delinquent?* London: Heineman Press.

Widiger, T. A. (1985). Review of Millon Adolescent Personality Inventory. In J. V. Mitchell, Jr. (ed.), *The Ninth Mental Measurements Yearbook* (pp. 979–981). Lincoln, NE: Buros Institute of Mental Measurement.

Widiger, T. A., Frances, A. J., Pincus, H. A., & Davis, W. W. (1991). DSM-IV literature reviews: Rationale, process, and limitations. *Journal of Psychopathology and Behavioral Assessment, 12,* 189–202.

Widiger, T. A., Frances, A. J., Pincus, H. A., Davis, W. W., & First, M. B. (1991). Toward an empirical classification for the DSM-IV. *Journal of Abnormal Psychology, 100,* 280–288.

Wiggins, J. S. (1981). Clinical and statistical prediction: Where are we and where do we go from here? *Clinical Psychology Review, 1,* 3–18.

Williams, C. L. (1985). Use of the MMPI with adolescents. In J. N. Butcher & J. R. Graham (eds.), *Clinical Applications of the MMPI* (pp. 37–39). Minneapolis: University of Minnesota, Department of Conferences.

Williams, C. L. & Butcher, J. N. (1989a). An MMPI study of adolescents: I. Empirical validity of the standard scales. *Psychological Assessment, 1,* 251–259.

Williams, C. L., & Butcher, J. N. (1989b). An MMPI study of adolescents: II. Verifications and limitations of codetype classifications. *Psychological Assessment, 1,* 260–265.

Williams, C. L., Butcher, J. N., Ben-Porath, Y. S., & Graham, J. R. (1992). *MMPI-A Content Scales: Assessing Psychopathology in Adolescents.* Minneapolis: University of Minnesota Press.

Williams, J. G., Barlow, D. H., & Agras, W. S. (1972). Behavioral assessment of severe depression. *Archives of General Psychiatry, 39,* 1283–1289.

Wing, L. (1969). The handicap of autistic children: A comparative study. *Journal of Child Psychology and Psychiatry, 10,* 1–40.

Wirt, R. D., Lachar, D., Klinedinst, J. K., & Seat, P. S. (1990). *Personality Inventory for Children-1990 Edition.* Los Angeles: Western Psychological Services.

Wisniewski, J. J., Mulick, J. A., Genshaft, J. L., & Coury, D. L. (1987). Test-retest reliability of the Revised Children's Manifest Anxiety Scale. *Perceptual and Motor Skills, 65,* 67–70.

Wolf, S. (1989). Schizoid disorders of childhood and adolescence. In C. G. Last & M. Hersen (eds.), *Handbook of Clinical Childhood Psychiatric Diagnosis* (pp. 209–232). New York: Wiley.

Wolf, S., & Chick, J. (1980). Schizoid personality disorder in childhood: A controlled follow-up study. *Psychological Medicine, 10,* 85–100.

Wolfson, J., Fields, J. H., & Rose, S. A. (1987). Symptoms, temperament, resiliency, and control in anxiety-disordered preschool children. *American Academy of Child and Adolescent Psychiatry, 26,* 16–22.

Worthen, B. R., Borg, W. R., & White, K. R. (1993). *Measurement and Evaluation in the Schools: A Practical Guide.* White Plains, NY: Longman.

Young, L. L., & Cooper, D. H. (1944). Some factors associated with popularity. *Journal of Educational Psychology, 35,* 513–535.

Zangwill, W. M., & Kniskern, J. R. (1982). Comparison of problem families in the clinic and at home. *Behavior Therapy, 13,* 145–152.

Index